ON FORESTRY ECONOMICS

林业经济论

第2版

祝列克
王爱民 著

中国林业出版社

图书在版编目（CIP）数据

林业经济论/祝列克，王爱民著．—2 版．—北京：中国林业出版社，2011.4
ISBN 978-7-5038-6147-5

Ⅰ. 林… Ⅱ. ①祝… ②王… Ⅲ. ①林业经济－经济发展－研究－中国
Ⅳ. ①F326.23

中国版本图书馆 CIP 数据核字（2011）第 063535 号

责任编辑 徐小英 何 鹏（第 2 版）
洪 蓉（第 1 版）
美术编辑 赵 芳

出 版 中国林业出版社（100009 北京西城区刘海胡同 7 号）
网 址 http://lycb.forestry.gov.cn
E-mail forestbook@163.com 电话 010－83222880
发 行 中国林业出版社
印 刷 北京北林印刷厂
版 次 2006 年 8 月第 1 版（共印 1 次）
2011 年 4 月第 2 版
印 次 2011 年 4 月第 2 次
开 本 185mm×245mm
印 张 19
字 数 290 千字
印 数 3001～6000 册
定 价 60.00 元

前 言

（第 2 版）

对于林业经济研究而言，国民经济发展水平与林业发展状况的对应关系已被研究者普遍发现，但目前对这种对应关系的解释多数还近似地停留在“因为经济发展水平不同，所以林业发展状况不同”这一较为粗略程度。显然，对其进行更加详细合理地解释是十分必要的，这不但是林业经济理论必须回答的问题，而且，对于像中国这样正在追求经济、社会和环境协调发展的发展中国家至少还具有以下现实意义：①正确判断林业政策制定的宏观经济约束条件；②从宏观经济发展的角度判断某一林业政策成功实施最佳时期。

正是基于以上原因，2006 年 8 月，本书第 1 版面世。如果说 5 年前的这本书更多体现在从整个国民经济发展对林业影响的角度来阐述林业发展的基本规律，那么修订后的这本书则力图对历史和现实资料进行更加充分的搜集和深入分析来证明已建立起来的理论，并试图用这种理论解释现实当中一些林业问题。

5 年来，包括中国在内的林业发展政策与环境均发生了很大的变化，我们研究的领域也力图与时俱进。较之第 1 版，本书增加了以下内容：一是回答了林业基本问题演进与林权政策演进的相互关系；二是证明了政府在林业生态环境产品供给和需求上的双重垄断特征；三是对林业碳汇问题进行了初步的经济学解释。

对于试图建立某种理论的人来说，其内心的期望不但在于建立理论本身，更期望的还在于建立的这种理论对现实问题的解释及解决能够起到“工具”性作用，这正是我们修订本书的动力。

在本书的修订过程中，国家林业局林业基金管理总站李冰副总站长、国家林业局亚太森林恢复管理网络中心王春峰副主任、河北农业大学戴芳博士均提出许多宝贵意见。另外，戴芳博士、河北农业大学外语学院陈雁青老师承担了修订后相关部分的英文翻译工作。本书得以面世，与他们付出的劳动是分不开的，在此一并深表谢意！

著　者

2011 年 4 月 18 日

Foreword

(2nd Edition)

Studies on forestry economy mostly remain no more than the theory that the relation between the forestry development and the national economy level, which most researchers have already found, is roughly defined as the forestry development depending on the latter. Obviously, it is necessary to provide more reasonable and detailed interpretation to answer the questions the study on forestry economic theory is faced with. Meanwhile, for developing countries like China trying hard to achieve the harmony among economic, social and environmental development, it is greatly practical to make a correct judgment about macroeconomic restrictions on forestry policy making and decide the bloom for a specific policy practice according to macroeconomics.

For those reasons, five years ago, in August, 2006, the first edition of the book was published, which mainly focused on illustrating the basic rule of forestry development in the view of the impact of national economic development on forestry. This revised edition, however, collected and made a further analysis about the historic and practical data to prove the present theory and use it to analyze some practical forestry issues.

In the last five years, there have been great changes both in policies of forestry development and in environment in China as well as in the world, and our study in this field tries to keep accordance with the changes. Compared with the first edition, this book has the addition to the content. First, it illustrates the relation between the evolutions of forestry basic issues and forestry rights. Second, it proves the government's double monopoly in the supply and demand of forestry ecological environmental products. Third, it makes an elementary economic interpretation about the forestry carbon exchanges.

For those who are trying hard to establish a certain theory, beyond longing for the establishment of their theory is that the theory can interpret some practical problems and act as a tool in resolving them, which is the motivation for us to revise the book.

In revising the book, Li Bing, Deputy chief of General Station of Forestry Fund Management, Wang Chunfeng, associate supervisor in Asia – Pacific Forest Restoration Network Center of State Forestry Bureau, Dai Fang, the doctor in Hebei Agricultural University have put forward many valuable comments. In addition, Dr. Dai Fang and Ms. Chen Yanqing, associate professor in Foreign Language College of Hebei Agricultural University undertook the translation work for the revised relevant English part. They all made great contribution to the publication of this book, many thanks to them.

Authors
April 18, 2011

前　言

（第 1 版）

随着人类社会的经济发展与文明进步，人们对森林的认识有了重大转变，社会对林业的需求也发生了很大的变化，森林维护与改善生态环境的功能在世界范围内得到了广泛的重视和关注。1992 年联合国召开的环境与发展大会上以“赋予林业以首要地位”作为最高级别的政治承诺，并特别强调“在世界最高级会议要解决的问题中，没有任何问题比林业更重要了”，将林业问题提到前所未有的高度，这是世界文明发展史上一个重要的里程碑。

联合国环境规划署的报告显示，世界林业的发展很不平衡。经济发达国家的森林资源在不断增长，而发展中国家的森林资源却在不断减少；经济发达国家的森林经营模式多表现为经济、社会和生态多效益可持续发展的综合模式，而绝大多数的发展中国家在这方面才刚刚起步，或是还停留在以木材为主的有形林产品利用阶段。这说明世界各国森林资源数量的消长、森林经营思想的演进和森林利用方式的改变，在经济发展水平不同的国家存在明显的差距。如何借鉴发达国家的经验，推进我国林业建设成为亟须解决的重要课题。

林业是国民经济和社会发展的重要组成部分，其发展进程既决定于其自身的特点和规律，也受外部环境的影响。如何从林业自身的特点和外部环境两方面探求林业发展的规律，这是我从事林业工作以来一直在思考的重大问题。多年来，我试图从世界各国的林业发展历史演进过程中，研究和发掘林业的内在规律，但由于社会发展阶段不同、经济发展水平不同、森林资源天然禀赋不同，林业所表现出的特点千差万别，因此这一研究非常艰难。我也试图通过发达国家和发展中国家的林业横向比较来说明林业发展存在的差距，再通过发达国家和发展中国家的经济社会条件的比较来说明这种现象产生的原因，但在研究思路上，却依然存在某种技术上的缺陷。几经反复，不懈探索，最终采取了将这两种研究路线有机结合的方法，即在侧重于发达国家和发展中国家横向比较的同时，兼顾纵向比较，并将林业置于世界经济和各国国民经济发展全局中进行研究分析，去揭示其内在的发展规律。

遵循上述思路研究可发现，世界林业的发展似乎存在着一个共同的轨迹，即无论是森林资源总量的非均衡变化，还是森林利用方式的阶段性差异以及森林经营思想的演进，都和林业的三个基本问题密切相关，这三个基本问题是：土地问题、资源问题和生态问题。而且，世界各国在这三个基本问题演进程度上的差异，又为各国的经济发展水平所制约。由此可见，经济发展水平不同的国家，在林业发展战略、经营思想、运行模式、政策调整等方面是有所不同的。

要对上述问题和观点进行科学合理的解释和论证无疑是十分艰巨的。这不仅是因为林业问题本身的复杂性，而且，就学术研究的继承而言，由于较为系统的林业经济研究始于第二次世界大战之后，迄今不过五十多年的历史，其完善程度远不能和经济学的其他学科相比，可供借鉴的成熟理论并不多。因此，不敢奢求有一个普遍适用的、自成一体的林业经济体系，仅就几个我本人感兴趣的问题，或者说仅从林业经济问题的几个层面，提出一家之言，期冀在学术界及林业政策研究领域抛砖引玉，希望能对我国的林业发展有所裨益。

祝列克

二〇〇六年六月六日

Foreword

(1st Edition)

With the development of both economy and civilization in human society, people have greatly improved their knowledge and understanding about forests. They therefore have also dramatically changed their social demands for forestry. As a result, more world attention has been widely paid to the function that forests play to maintain and improve environment. In 1992, UN Conference on Environment and Development bestowed priority on forestry and it became a political promise of the highest rank. In addition, it was particularly emphasized in the meeting that nothing has been more important than forestry among the problems that the world summit conferences will deal with. It is a distinct milestone in world civilization history to place forestry issues at such a high position.

It is reported by UN Environment Program Division that, however, forestry development in the world has not been balanced. Forest resources in economically advanced countries are increasing consistently but decreasing in developing countries. Furthermore, developed countries always administer their forests with economic, social and ecological multi – beneficial models for sustainable development, while most developing countries have just started their steps in this way or are even staying in the stage of utilization of tangible forest products mainly from wood. That show obvious differences between countries at various economic levels in their increased or decreased amount of forest resources, their evolution of forest administration ideologies, and their alteration of forest utilization types. So that it is crying obligation and vital theme to draw on the experiences of advanced countries for reference to give an impetus to China forestry development.

Forestry is an important component in the progress of national economy and society. The development of forestry relies on not only its own natural traits and inherent laws, but also the influence of exterior environment. How to study the forestry developing regulations from both its own characteristics and outside elements is a major issue which I have been pondering over since I began to devote myself to forestry. For many years I have been trying to study and seek the inherent law from the historical evolution courses of forestry in countries of the world. Nevertheless, the research is very hard due to the diverse characteristics of forest that were resulted from the differences between social developments and economic levels of various countries, and natural endowments of forest resources as well. I have also been trying synchronic comparison between the forestry of both developed and developing countries to explain the differences in forestry development. And then by comparison of social and economic conditions in both kinds of countries, I have been trying to indicate the reasons of the phenomena. In my research approach, however, there were still some technical defects. With unremitting and indefatigable efforts, I finally adopted the approach of organic combination of the two. That is, when the synchronic comparison between developed and developing countries is emphasized, diachronic comparison is also considered. Moreover, forestry is studied and analyzed in the overall world economy and national economic development of different countries, so that the inherent development law is explored. Following the research approach, it can be found that a common trail seems to exist in the forestry development in the world. The trail is that there are three essential problems which are closely connected with the imbalanced changes of total amount of forest resources, the periodical differences of forest utilization types, and the evolution of forestry administration ideologies. The three essential problems include the land problem, the resource problem, and the ecological problem. The evolutionary degrees involved in the three problems were limited by the economic development levels in various countries. As a result, it can be seen that forestry development strategies, administration ideologies, operation models, and policy adjustment differ from each other among countries with dissimilar economic development levels.

Obviously, it is arduous to scientifically and rationally explain and verify the above mentioned points. Complexity in forestry is one cause. In addition, as to the academic inheritance, the fairly systematic study of forestry economics started only after the Second World War. Since it has covered over 50 years, the research is much less perfect than other branches of economics and few mature theories can be provided for reference. Therefore, I dare not pursue a generally acceptable and independent forestry economic system. Instead, I submit my own academic conclusions, or points of forestry economics in some aspects, based on what I am interested in. As a Chinese saying, I only want to throw a brick in order to attract jade so as to benefit China forestry development.

Zhu Lieke

June 6, 2006

目　录

CONTENTS

绪　论

一、林业的发展历程及其基本问题

从林业本身来看，林业的发展历程至少可以从三个方面加以体现，即森林资源数量的消长、森林利用方式的改变和森林经营思想的演进。站在全球范围从同一时间截面上来看，处于不同经济发展水平的国家，上述三个方面的演变并不均衡。目前，美国、德国、法国、日本等发达国家已经历了森林资源从急剧减少到逐渐增长再到趋于稳定这一过程，其森林利用方式和经营方式也从单纯的资源开采，成功地过渡到经济、社会、生态多效益综合利用阶段。但中国、巴西、印度尼西亚等发展中国家从20世纪80年代开始，才着手开展大规模的森林保护活动，而非洲国家的林业仍处于原始利用阶段，其木材消耗中薪炭材的比例在20世纪90年代仍高达91%。发达国家林业走过的历程和当今世界林业的不均衡发展是否存在着客观必然性？对这一问题的回答将有助于揭示林业发展的内在规律，认识林业的发展趋势。

（一）森林资源的非均衡消长变化趋势

森林是以乔木为主体，乔、灌、草多种植物和动物、微生物群体共生，与相应的水、土、气资源共处于同一空间范围的自然资源综合体。森林是地球生物圈中最大的生产者，具有经济、生态和社会多重功能。然而，随着人类经济活动的扩大，森林资源大量减少。据估计，人类近1万年以来已使地球上的森林面积减少了1/3～1/2；1862～1958年的近100年时间里，全球森林面积从55亿hm^2下降到37亿hm^2，即从占陆地面积的1/3下降到1/4；1958～1978年的20年间，森林面积再次迅速减少，仅剩26亿hm^2，不到陆地面积的1/5。

如果从地区和国家的角度观察，森林资源的变化趋势并不一致，即发展中国家呈现减少的趋势，而发达国家却呈现增加的趋势。根据联合国粮农组织调查统计，1980～1995 年的 15 年时间里，发展中国家的森林面积减少了 9.1%。其中，非洲发展中国家减少得最多，达 10.5%，年均毁林率为 0.7%；其次是拉丁美洲和加勒比海地区，减少了 9.7%，年均毁林率为 0.65%；第三是亚太地区发展中国家，减少了 6.4%，年均毁林率为 0. 43%。而在同样的时间里，发达国家的森林面积却增加了 2.7%，年均增长率为 0.18%。其中，欧洲增长得最快，增加了 4.1%，年均增长 0.27%；其次是北美洲温带和寒带地区，增长了 2.6%，年均增长率为 0.17%；亚太地区发达国家相对增加得较为缓慢，只增长了 1.0%。

在世界森林资源总量呈现减少的情况下，欧洲和其他发达国家的森林资源却呈现明显增加的趋势，这其中是否隐藏着某种规律性的东西？正是这一疑问，使得世界各地区森林资源的不同变化趋势更加值得关注。

（二）森林利用方式改变的阶段性差异

对世界各区域森林资源的不同变化趋势关注的初步结果是，伴随着上述森林资源的消长变化趋势，人类从古到今的森林利用方式和森林经营思想也发生了相应的变化。这种变化不但表现为世界各国的森林利用方式和森林经营思想都有一个演进的过程，而且相同或相似的利用内容和经营思想在不同的区域和国家出现的历史阶段并不相同。尤其是处于不同经济发展水平的国家和地区，这种差异表现得更为明显。

从森林利用的角度来看，世界林业发展到底经历了哪些阶段？关于这一问题，现有的划分并不一致。有的学者认为，森林利用经历了依靠自然力开发利用森林、依靠工业化开发利用森林和多项利用开发森林三个阶段。并认为前两个阶段的共同特点是生产经营目标单一，即以木材生产作为获得利润的唯一目标。而有的学者则认为，森林利用经历了薪材阶段、工业用材阶段和木材综合利用阶段。显然，这两种划分的区别在于第一阶段和第三阶段。因为，如果森林利用的第一阶段是“薪材阶段”，其利用目的很大程度上将不是利润最大化，而森林的多项利用更是指森林的经济、社会、生态效益的综合开发，而木材综合利用的含义更多是指加工意义上的木材利用。

事实上，从人类利用森林的方式和内容上看，更应该将林业的发展历程划分为自然林业、农耕林业、工业资源林业和综合利用林业四个阶段。

所谓自然林业阶段，是指与后期各林业阶段相比，人类利用森林的活动更多出自其生存的本能，这一阶段发生在远古时期。这一时期人口密度低，生产力水平低下，人类依靠森林的天然恩惠维持生存。其主要特征表现为：低级的社会形态、狩猎与采集活动、游牧方式以及原始的农业与森林之间的有机结合，整个社会构成了以自然规律为基础的人类与森林之间的动态平衡。随着社会的发展，人类进入了农业社会，农牧业成为社会生产的主要方式，森林成为农业发展的主要障碍。此时的林业活动主要是毁林开荒，用于农业生产的需要。而农业的发展又促进了人口的迅速增长，反过来又引起了更大规模的森林开采。从农业社会到工业革命到来之前这一时期，采伐森林为农业生产创造条件成为这一时期林业活动的主要特征。因此，应将这一时期的林业称之为农耕林业。而工业资源林业阶段则发生在工业革命之后。与农耕林业阶段相比，这一时期林业活动的主要目的并不是获取农用土地，而是通过林木的采伐获取工业用原材料，木材开始作为资本进入到了工业生产领域。随着铁路、建筑、造纸等行业的发展，木材的需求数量越来越多，林业的工业资源功能也随之不断增强，并逐渐成为主要功能。人们共识的观点是，工业革命既促进了世界经济的巨大发展，同时也造成了资源的匮乏和生态状况的恶化，尤其是工业发展所造成的森林资源减少以及由于森林资源的减少而带来的水土流失等环境问题更为突出。在这一背景下，人类开始逐渐注意到林业与生态环境、社会发展的相互关系，在强调林业的经济效益的同时，开始注意林业的生态效益和社会效益，林业的综合利用阶段也随之到来。

从世界的角度来看，上述林业发展的各个阶段在时间上并不均衡。英国、荷兰等早期资本主义国家从 16 世纪开始，就以大量的木材制造商船、战舰和建造码头，并开始了海上木材贸易，应该说这些国家在 16 世纪就已进入了工业资源林业阶段。而在同一时期，世界上绝大多数国家工业文明尚未到来，林业仍处于农耕林业阶段。同样，到20世纪50年代，又是由联邦德国等经济发达国家率先提出了森林经济、社会和生态一体化、森林多效益主导利用、森林多效益综合利用等模式，并开始了相应的实践活动。而中国等发展中国家相近的林业活动到20世纪末期才真正开始。

（三）森林经营思想的演进

森林利用方式的改变必然带来森林经营思想的演进。在自然林业时期，森林不仅是人类进化的场所，更是人类的住所和食物的唯一来源。由于当时的人口密度低，科学技术不发达，并且有丰富的森林资源为依托。因此，相对森林的供应能力，这一时期人类对森林的影响是微弱的，更多地表现为森林对人类的单向呵护。随着农牧业的发展，森林被认为是妨碍农耕经济的自然障碍，因此，毁林开荒、毁林取薪就成为这一时期的重要特征。从本质上讲，在自然林业时期，“破坏森林的数量”成了人类展示其发展业绩的重要内容和征服自然能力的体现。应该说，这一时期人类的活动更多的是一种维持生存的本能活动，因此，不可能形成完整成熟的经营思想，至于中国的园圃制和德国10世纪所形成的地方性森林资源管理制度，只能是森林经营思想的萌芽。

真正的森林经营思想可上溯至17世纪末期。从那时起，随着新型产业的不断出现（如铁路、建筑、造纸、家具等），近代工业革命对森林的利用程度远大于数千年农业文明对森林的利用程度，森林的采伐速度开始大于森林植被的自然恢复速度，一些国家和地区不可避免地出现了“木材危机”。客观现实使人们认识到，为满足经济增长对木材的需求，应该采取多种有利于森林生长的人为干预措施，在这一背景下，系统的林业经营思想才开始出现。目前公认的观点是，德国是现代森林经营思想的发源地。当时，林业的主要任务是增加政府的财政收入，森林经营思想主要包含在财政学中。直到19世纪上半叶，以J·克里斯第安·洪德斯哈根（1783～1834）等为代表的林学家才创立了以森林永续收获为核心的法正林思想。1898年，盖耶等又提出了“近自然林业”理论，从此，开创了20世纪德国林业发展的新阶段。100多年来，以木材生产为核心的永续、均衡收获的理论体系和思想，对近代世界林业的发展产生了深刻的影响。这一时期森林经营理论的基本特点是：①以法正林思想为核心，不论是法正林还是完全调整林，不论是同龄林还是异龄林，均强调以木材生产为中心。②森林管理的目标是均衡地提供木材。③以调整森林蓄积量为准则来构建生产技术体系。显然，这一理论是欧洲中世纪自然经济向工业经济过渡的必然产物，是以森林单一的提供木材功能为前提而构建的理论体系。

进入到20世纪中期以后，随着社会经济的发展，人类对森林的需求开始发生变化。一方面，工业化程度的提高对木材的需求进一步扩大，与此同时，生活水平的上升使人类对森林生态环境安全的需求也与日俱增；另一方面，森林的供给能力和生态环境的质量却在进一步下降。这一社会、经济的现实情况，迫使林业必须寻求新的发展模式与途径。与此相对应，森林经营思想也必然做出相应的改变。从20世纪中期到20世纪80年代，先后出现了“林业政策效益论”、“船迹理论”、“和谐化理论”和“森林多功能理论”等。其中，“森林多功能理论”的影响最大，为许多国家所接受。以上述理论为基础，国际林联（IUFRO）于1960年在美国召开了以森林多元利用为中心议题的学术讨论会，会议明确提出了森林多目标多用途的经营思想和经营目标。也是在这一年，美国颁布了《森林多种用途永续收获法》，在此之后，相关研究在全球范围内正式展开。

应该说，20世纪中期的森林经营理论已经注意到了森林经营与生态环境、社会发展的关系，但理论界普遍认为，森林经营思想和理论的真正变革是1992年联合国环境与发展大会以后形成的“森林可持续经营”理论。20世纪90年代以来，许多国家和地区对森林可持续经营这一命题进行了卓有成效的研究和探讨，使森林可持续经营思想日益完善。例如，1992年3月，由加拿大联邦政府签订的第一个森林协议指出：“我们的目标是维持和加强森林生态系统的长期健康，以使国家和全球的所有生命受益，同时为当代和后代人的利益提供环境、经济、社会和文化的选择机会。”为实现这一目标，1992年，加拿大政府已在全国建立了10个不同类型的试验区，形成了“加拿大模式林网络”，为加拿大森林可持续经营提供了实践依据。美国林学会1993年1月发表了《保持长期森林健康和生产力》的专题报告，报告认为，生态系统经营是森林资源经营管理的生态过程，它试图长期维持森林生态系统复杂的自然过程、途径及生态系统之间的相互依赖，并保持完好的功能，使其具有短期压力下的弹性和长期的适应性。因此，生态系统经营是实现森林可持续经营的基本途径。

森林可持续经营理论与森林永续利用理论相比，其进步之处主要体现在以下几点：一是永续利用强调森林单一价值的生产，而可持续经营强调的是森林的全部价值；二是永续利用的经营单位是林分或林分集合体，而可持续经营的对象是景观和景观基础上的森林健康和生产力；三是永续经营与法正林经营模式相似，而可持续经营则反映了自然干扰的规律；四是永续经营注重森林的蓄积量和定期产量，而可持续经营首先注重的是林龄、结构、林木活力、动植物种类等森林状态，其次才是蓄积量和定期产量。

通过对上述森林经营思想的简要描述，可发现各个时期的森林经营思想总是首先产生于现今看来的经济发达国家，而发展中国家基本不存在自己独立和系统的森林经营思想，而且其对发达国家森林经营思想的借鉴，在时间上也存在明显的滞后性。例如，产生于19世纪前期，由德国人创立的法正林思想，到20世纪50年代才被中国的林业学者所关注，这一思想从产生到借鉴相隔100多年。而非洲等地区处于极度贫困阶段的发展中国家，在同期仍处于自然林业阶段，林业还没有作为一个产业部门出现，因此，还基本谈不上森林经营思想的借鉴。这种森林经营思想演进的非均衡性刚好与森林资源数量消长的非均衡性以及利用方式改变的非均衡性相对应。

（四）林业的三个基本问题

上述区域间森林资源总量消长的非均衡变化、森林利用方式改变的阶段性差异以及森林经营思想的演进，似乎都隐藏着某种规律性的东西。事实上，通过详细研究可发现，无论是森林总量的消长，还是森林利用方式的改变以及森林经营思想的演进，都是林业的三个问题所导致的结果。这三个问题分别是：土地问题、资源问题和生态问题。

依据古人类学家的研究成果，人类来自森林。因此，自诞生之日起人类的初始活动就是一个利用森林的活动。这种初始活动基本上是依靠自然力来完成的，是一种维持生存的本能活动，这种活动与现今意义上的生产经营活动有着本质的不同。因此，那一时期并不存在现今意义上的林业问题。此后，随着人类的定居和农业活动的开始，森林开始为人类提供薪材和必要的农业用地，而且随着农业技术的进步，人口数量急剧增加，人类社会越来越依靠占用林地来发展农业，林地和耕地开始出现此消彼长的趋势，林业的土地问题开始显现。18 世纪中期，随着工业革命的兴起，木材成为重要的工业原料。从这时开始，森林才成为经济学意义上的资源并进而成为生产要素，以获取利润为目的的森林开发利用活动才真正开始。也是从那时开始，人类利用森林的活动才具有了产业意义，即林业活动。应该说，从工业革命开始，为解决薪材和土地问题而进行的开发利用森林的活动一直没有停止，但我们同时发现，工业等非农产业的迅速发展使木材资源供应趋于紧张，资源问题开始显现，并逐渐上升为主要问题。在工业化初期，资源与环境问题并不突出，但随着世界经济进入一个又一个新的发展阶段，生态环境的退化日益加剧，环境问题越来越成为人类发展的严重制约因素，人类对生态环境安全的需求与日俱增。在这一背景下，森林利用的内容开始出现多样化倾向，即在注重经济功能的同时，也注重生态功能。而且随着经济发展水平的不断提高和生态问题的日趋严重，人类对环境改善的需求也在不断增强，这一趋势使得森林的经济功能正在让位于生态功能，进而使林业的主要问题逐渐转化为生态问题。

经济学认为，现实的需求必须满足两种基本条件，即购买欲望和购买能力。只有具备这两种条件才会有真正意义上的需求并从而带来相关产业的发展。而只有欲望或需要却没有满足欲望的能力并不能导致森林利用方式的真正改变。从这一角度来讲，由土地问题的出现，到资源问题的凸显，再到生态问题的产生以及相伴而生的森林利用方式的改变，既是人类欲望或需要不断演进的结果，也是随着社会经济的发展，其满足欲望或需要的能力不断增强的结果。这一论述的政策意义在于，如果一个政府单纯地以欲望或需要为依据而在某种程度上忽略其社会经济发展水平，就有可能在某一时期过早或过晚地解决某种林业问题，其结果都可能不会令人满意。因此，从社会经济发展的角度研究林业问题的演进过程就具有十分重大的意义。

二、林业经济研究的基本命题

（一）林业经济研究的进展

根据世界各国林业经济学的研究内容，可以将林业经济学的研究分成三大类：一是应用已有的理论和方法研究林业经济实践中的一些具体问题，即应用型林业经济研究。其内容包括林业的产权关系、林业与能源的关系、林产品贸易以及土地使用政策等。二是通过一些新的理论和方法的实际应用，验证、发展和完善这些理论和方法，即实证型林业经济研究。其内容包括各社会因素对林业的影响、林业生产与消费的动态市场模拟以及林业政策的数量化研究等。三是以一种积极的态度参与本学科的一些重大理论问题的研究，重点体现对本学科发展的新领域和新问题的超前性研究，即战略型林业经济研究。其内容包括林业与生态环境的协调、林业发展战略、林业的国际合作以及林业的结构调整等。

从近年来林业经济研究发展的现状来看，上述三个方面的研究有以下几个特点：一是理论的多样性。即现代经济学和社会学的一些新理论的不断引进，使林业经济学的研究领域、方法及实践正在发生着巨大的变化，林业经济研究正在成为世界上一个新的热点领域。同时，一些新理论的应用为林业经济研究开辟了更为广阔的空间，也为林业经济研究奠定了更为坚实的科学基础。二是方法和手段的先进性。在新理论引进的同时，也将与之相适应的新方法融入到林业经济学当中。林业经济研究方法的改进与发展，为林业经济研究提供了更多和更为有效的认识工具和手段，也使林业经济研究更具有科学性。三是研究的系统性。这种研究的系统性一方面表现在时间的连续上，如北美和欧洲的一些林业发达国家，很多林业经济研究项目是连续进行几年、几十年，甚至是跨世纪的；另一方面是研究的整体性加强，很多林业经济研究项目将政策、贸易、立法和国家宏观管理结合在一起，形成一个较为完整的研究领域。四是研究的国际性。随着当今世界对森林资源和生态环境的日益关注，国际性的协作日益广泛，使林业经济研究的国际化趋势不断加强。林业经济研究的国际化可以说是当今经济全球化的必然结果。

虽然林业经济研究具有以上特点，但总体来看，与农业经济等其他部门经济学科相比，其研究尚不成熟。例如从发达国家来看，自17世纪中叶以获取木材和经济效益为目的的森林永续利用理论到20世纪60年代强调生物、景观以及人文多样性的森林多功能理论，再到20世纪70年代强调集约经营的林业分工理论以及从林分和景观两个层次出发而构建的整体林业理论(有些学者又将其称为“新林业理论”)，被广泛认为是林业经济研究的重要成果。但是，这些理论能否归属于林业经济领域还有待于商榷。因为林业经济研究虽然不可避免多学科交叉，但其理论基础却应该是经济学，而且应该从经济的角度来研究林业的基本问题。而上述理论则更多的是从植物学、生物学、生态学和社会学的角度来探讨的，其内容更侧重于林业经营技术。至于近年来有关社会因素对林业的影响、林业生产与消费的动态市场模拟以及林业政策的数量化等方面的研究，虽然已经纳入了经济研究的轨道，但研究内容尚显分散，林业经济研究还没有形成一个完整的体系。从发展中国家来看，林业经济研究的不完善程度更高。虽然发展中国家的林业问题更为严重，但这些国家的科学发展和林业实践还没有为自己的林业经济学的发展奠定好基础，还远没有形成内容固定、结构合理和有系统理论支持的林业经济学。所以，在其林业实践中更多的是直接搬用发达国家的林业经济理论或研究成果，并在使用中进行改进，形成一些不系统、不成熟的林业经济理论。可以说，发展中国家的林业经济学还处在形成过程中的理论和实践准备阶段。

应该说明的是，中国和前苏联等国家在其计划经济时期，曾经形成了相对完整的与计划经济体制相适应的林业经济理论。但随着这些国家的市场化改革和经济的发展，以往的理论已不能对现今的林业问题进行很好的解释和实践指导，而对这些不同于以往的林业问题的相关研究正处在开始阶段。

（二）本书研究的方法及内容

以往林业经济的研究成果为新的研究打下了坚实的基础，同时其研究的不完善也给后续研究留下了广阔的研究空间。应该说，诸如林业产权、林业经营模式、林业产业结构、林业贸易、林业政策评价以及政府对林业的管理方式等当前林业经济有待研究的领域相当广泛。但从宏观的角度来看，上述具体林业问题都和林业发展的基本客观规律密切相关，只有在林业基本发展规律探讨清楚的基础上，才能对林业的具体问题进行有效的研究。因此，对林业基本发展规律的研究应该放在优先的位置，并将其作为林业经济学的基本内容。正是这一原因，我们将林业发展基本规律的探讨作为本书的核心研究内容。

在研究方法上，本书主要以发达国家为研究对象，通过对其林业问题历史演进过程的实证研究来说明林业发展的基本规律。在纵向比较的同时再通过发达国家和发展中国家林业的横向比较来说明林业发展存在的差距，通过发达国家和发展中国家的社会经济条件的比较来说明这种差距产生的原因。此外，林业作为整个国民经济中的一个部门，其自身的发展必然和国民经济的整体发展密切相关，孤立地从林业自身的发展来探讨林业问题，很难甚至无法对林业问题做出合理的解释。因此，必须站在宏观的角度，从整个国民经济发展对林业发展影响的角度来研究林业发展的基本规律。按照上述方法和思路所进行的研究使我们得出了以下结论。

对工业革命之前人类林业活动的研究使我们发现，为解决生存问题而进行的毁林开荒是那一时期林业活动的主要特征。这一特征导致了林业的恶性循环，即开垦林地使农作物的耕作面积得到扩大并从而促进了农业规模的粗放式扩张，而这种粗放式扩张又带来了人口的迅速增长，进而导致更加迅速和更大规模地砍伐森林来换取农耕用地，林地面积进一步缩小。我们把这一现象称之为工业化之前的林业土地问题。

随着经济的发展，世界各国先后加入了工业化进程当中。应该说，在工业化初期，世界各国尤其是发展中国家，为解决粮食供给不足而产生的林业土地问题依然存在，而且这一时期经济活动的复杂性导致林业土地问题产生的原因要比工业化之前复杂得多。在工业化发展的初期阶段，农业生产赶不上随人口和收入增长而增加的粮食需求，粮食价格面临向上的压力。而粮食价格上涨又会促使工资上涨，从而制约工业化和国民经济的发展，为此，发展中国家政府往往采取垄断收购等方式来压低农产品价格。这早在李嘉图研究英国产业革命问题时就已提出，后来舒尔茨把它称之为“粮食问题”(food problem)。压低农产品价格弱化了粮食供给的动机，从而使原本由农业生产赶不上随人口和收入增长而增加的粮食需求而造成的供需矛盾进一步增大，又由于进口农产品和技术开发解决粮食问题的路径受到限制，由此开垦林地来扩张农业用地就成了这一时期解决粮食问题的主要手段。我们把这一现象称之为发展中国家工业化初期的林业土地问题。

扩张农作物的耕作面积有两种途径：一是将林业用地转化为农业用地，即通过大面积的林木采伐来增加农作物的耕作面积；二是将林业用地以外的其他土地开垦为农业用地。为什么从现有的资料和现实情况来看，第一种途径似乎是主要的？为此，我们进行了以下解释：一是由于森林分布在广大的农村，农业活动依然和林业活动紧密交织在一起，林地和农用耕地接壤的现象极为普遍，而且由于森林所形成的富含腐殖质的土壤对农作物生长有利。因此，通过大面积的林木采伐来增加农作物耕作面积的做法就成了因惯性和自然环境而导致的顺理成章的事情。二是通过大面积的林木采伐来增加农作物耕作面积的做法还可以带来附加的好处，即通过采伐林木，可以解决农户薪材和房屋建材等问题。三是从发展中国家工业化的角度来看，通过林木的采伐来增加耕地可以收到一举两得的效果，即这种做法既可以扩张耕地面积，进而缓解粮食的供需紧张，又可以解决工业发展中的木材原料问题。这一解释使我们又有了一个新的发现，即工业化初期发展中国家的粮食问题和林业的土地问题是相互作用的，即在粮食问题导致了林业的土地问题的同时，林业也为农业生产提供了积累。而且，这种林业部门为农业部门提供的资本积累，事实上是在发展中国家实行工业化优先政策进而侵占农业利益的情况下，由林业部门对农业部门的经济补偿，这一补偿部分弥补了农业部门被工业侵占的利益，同时也对林地转化为耕地的行为起到了激励作用。

与粮食问题所导致的林业土地问题相比，在农村相对贫困阶段出现的林业土地问题有所不同。在农村相对贫困阶段产生的林业土地问题，是在推行非农产业优先政策和农业保护政策的双重背景下产生的林业土地问题。在这一阶段，林业开始为农业和非农产业同时提供资本积累，而且这种资本积累功能开始由以农业为主向以工业为主的非农产业转换。同时，在二元经济结构的发展过程中，由于工业用木材资源需求的上升和森林资源的迅速减少，木材的供需矛盾加大，政府对森林资源的管制会不断加强，在粮食问题阶段那种允许无偿或低价侵占林地的做法可能会有所改变，林地转化为耕地的制度成本会不断上升，因此这一阶段林地转化为耕地的数量和速度较之粮食问题阶段都将有所降低。

在相对贫困阶段，林地转化为耕地的数量和速度较之粮食问题阶段只是有所减缓，而真正林业土地问题的逆转是发生在农业调整阶段。在这一阶段，发达国家由于农业技术的高度发达，面临的是农产品过剩以及由此带来的与其他非农产业部门相比边际报酬率下降的问题。这一问题的出现，对林业至少产生了以下两个方面的影响：一方面，由于发达国家农产品的过剩并由此带来的农业生产边际报酬率下降，使农业生产要素投入的动力减弱，这其中包括耕地这一最基本的农业生产要素。因此，在农业调整阶段，不会再出现粮食问题和相对贫困问题阶段所出现的将林地转化为耕地这类林业土地问题。另一方面，在农业调整阶段，如果相应于农业生产率的提高，生产要素从需求已经饱和的粮食生产部门转移到需求还在扩大的其他部门，农产品的供给过剩以及与其他部门相比的边际报酬率下降问题就会解决。但我们研究发现，农业与各非农产业部门之间生产要素的移动的流畅程度并不均衡，而恰恰是这种生产要素移动流畅程度的不均衡，才导致了农业调整阶段新的林业问题出现，即和以往林地转化为农地的情况相反，在农业调整阶段，农地开始向林地转化。

上述林业问题的研究主要是从农业发展对林业影响的角度出发的。如果从工业化的角度来看，随着农业在整个国民经济中比重和地位的降低，林业的土地问题开始逐渐让位于林业的资源问题。

我们在这里所关注的问题是：工业化过程对林业到底产生了什么影响？尤其

从森林资源利用的角度来看，工业化过程对林业产生的影响有哪些？这种关注使我们发现，产生林业资源问题的原因主要来自于两个方面，即技术进步和资本的形成方式的演变。

在工业化的不同阶段，技术进步的类型有所不同，并从而构成了对森林资源的不同影响。工业化初期的技术进步，具有用资本替代劳动的取向，导致了机械的使用，这同时又和低收入水平阶段的产品同质性需求特征相适应。这对森林资源将产生两方面的影响：一方面，机械的使用带来生产能力的增强，导致了包括木材在内的原材料需求迅速上升，进而导致了林木等森林资源因大量消耗而锐减。另一方面，由于以原木为主的林产品具有很强的同质性，适用于节约劳动的机械化生产，而且这种生产同样具有在工资率被抑制的情况下增加资本收入份额的功效。因此，在机械化被其他部门采用的同时，也被林业部门采用。林业机械的使用，无疑提高了原木等林产品的供给能力，同时也加剧了森林资源的短缺。

但是，发达国家的实践证明，在工业化初期因节约劳动型技术的广泛采用而造成的森林资源问题并没有延续下去，这主要是由诱致性技术创新和社会需求的变化两个方面的原因造成的。一方面，由于诱致性技术创新，导致原木等林产品替代品的开发技术和林产品的节约使用技术出现，这些技术的应用，无疑可以减轻原木等林产品的供需矛盾，进而缓解森林资源问题。另一方面，社会需求的变化为森林资源问题的缓解提供了社会基础。其中森林的大量采伐造成了生态环境的急剧恶化，与此同时随着收入水平的不断提高，人们对生态环境改善和休闲娱乐的需求也不断增强。当这一需求已不是少数人的需求而成为民众的广泛需求，并且有能力支付这一需求时，森林资源问题缓解的社会基础就已形成。在这种情况下，如果国家的经济实力允许，就会对森林资源的开发采取较为严厉的限制性措施和出台有利于森林资源恢复的相关激励性政策。同时，森林资源保护也会在民间自发兴起。所有这些，都会对森林资源问题的缓解起到重要作用。

资本积累对森林资源的影响与技术进步的影响是相伴而生的。从森林资源的角度来看，资本积累对林业产生的影响源于两类资本积累形成方式，这两类资本积累方式分别是以政府行政手段为主导的资本积累和非政府手段主导的资本积累。

以政府行政手段为主导的资本积累方式对林业的影响，涵盖了林业生产剩余转移、运用财政政策进行政府融资以及出口木材换取外汇等多个方面。在林业生产剩余转移方面，发展中国家政府的主要做法包括：采取垄断收购、限制自由市场交易的方式压低木材价格等，其目的是降低工业部门的生产成本。前苏联和中国等国家在其计划经济时期这种做法较为普遍。在运用财政政策进行政府融资方面，发展中国家政府的主要做法包括：征收各种林业税费和林业企业利润上缴等。其目的是对工业企业进行资金支持，进而形成企业的资本积累。这实质上是通过财政渠道对林业生产剩余的一种转移。出口木材换取外汇是发展中国家政府进行工业化资本积累的另一种重要途径。由于技术水平的限制，发展中国家进行工业化的一些机械设备不能自行研制开发，必须从发达国家进口。同时，发达国家已经度过了通过掠夺资源来发展经济这一阶段，对森林资源开始进行全面和严格的保护，本国所需木材开始从国外进口。在这一背景下，很多发展中国家大量出口木材换取外汇，以此来购买国外的先进设备。

以政府行政手段为主导的资本积累方式一方面导致对森林资源进行大量开采，使森林资源迅速减少。另一方面对生产剩余的转移又使得林业部门无法获得充足的用于造林、森林管护等活动的资金，使森林资源难以恢复。这种双重影响必然导致森林资源危机的加剧。

相对于以政府行政手段为主导的资本积累方式对森林资源的影响，非政府手段主导的资本积累方式对森林资源危机起到了缓解的作用。在经济发达国家，无论是市场经济体制的成熟程度还是其经济发展水平，都已达到了相当的程度。因此，金融方式和企业本身的资本积累已成为资本形成的最主要方式。自 20 世纪 70 年代，包括中国在内的许多发展中国家先后开始了市场导向的经济体制改革和金融体制改革，随着改革的不断深入，以非政府手段为主导的资本积累方式正在逐渐替代以政府行政手段为主导的资本积累方式。这无疑缓解了资本积累对森林资源的压力。同时，随着经济的发展，政府对林业部门的税费征收程度开始减弱，而从其他部门获得的财政收入却大量增加，政府开始由过去的资金索取转向对林业进行资金支持，这也对缓解林业资源危机起到了重要作用。

林业的资源问题和生态问题是相伴而生的。森林的生态功能是天然的，但人类赋予林业以生态功能却是经济发展的结果。森林具有公共物品的特性，其效用的非竞争性和消费的非排他性导致了“搭便车”行为的产生，同时，人们对林业生态功能的需求愿望是根据收入水平和现有生态状况等级的不同反映在不同的无差异曲线上的。因此，将改善生态状况作为主要目的的林业经营行为只有在经济发展到一定水平时才会出现。发达国家的林业发展历程表明，随着经济的发展，人们对林业生态功能的认识经历了萌芽和凸显阶段，同时，森林的多效益一体化经营模式也是在经济发展到一定水平时才出现的。

与上述林业土地问题、资源问题、生态问题的演进相对应，林权政策也相应随之发生变迁。从现象上来，推动林权政策演进的主要影响因素包括森林资源的稀缺性和林产品市场化程度两个方面，同时，国家意志的转变也发挥着重要作用。但是，进一步的研究却会发现，上述因素的形成又取决于影响森林资源需求和供给的多种社会经济因素和这些因素的相互作用，这些因素包括：人口数量的增加、城市化进程的推进、伐木和造林技术的进步、环境保护意识的增强等诸多方面。在林业土地问题阶段，由于单纯的人口因素导致林地资源的稀缺性逐渐显现，林权政策呈现出依托于土地政策、以林地的归属权为核心内容、以非正式制度安排为主的特征；在林业资源问题阶段，森林资源的稀缺程度和市场化程度都有所增强，以林木资源为核心内容、以正式制度安排取代非正式制度安排成为这一时期林权政策的主要特征，并根据发展中国家体制的不同，形成了以国有林权为主和以私有林权为主两条不同的路径，但制定林权政策的主要目的均为强化林业提供原料、资金和外汇积累的功能；发展到林业生态问题阶段，虽然仍旧存在国有林权和私有林权两条路径，但从世界范围来看，一国经济和社会的发展程度以及市场化程度是影响两种林权政策实施范围与强度的主要因素。

当生态问题上升为林业的主要问题时，林业面临的主要也是难点问题是：运用何种机制配置林业资源才能提高生态改善的效率？主流经济学认为，生态环境环境产品不能被市场所覆盖，从而失去了运用市场机制治理生态环境的可能性，而政府应在环境治理中发挥基础作用。但是，现实中政府治理生态环境的效率却往往不尽如人意。针对这种情况，一部分“自由市场环境主义者”坚持否定政府在环境资源配置中的主体作用，认为通过生态私有化可以实现环境资源的有效配置。

与“自由市场环境主义者”的愿望和主张相反，在实践中，完全的生态私有化尚未发现，这究竟是人们没有发现这一方式，还是其缺乏必要的私有化条件？对于这一问题，需要在外部性和公共物品等理论以外，针对生态环境本身的特征给出理论上的回答。在这一背景下，本文从新的角度对生态环境产品的供需特征进行了理论分析。分析结果表明，在经济社会，面对公共物品或服务，免费搭车对任何人来说都是一种理性的选择。这样，即使在需求愿望很强时，公众也不会主动支付自己的收入来实现对环境产品的需求。既然环境产品不可或缺，免费搭车又不可避免，公众对环境产品的上述需求愿望就会通过政府对公众的强制性融资来实现。在这一过程中，公众和政府之间实质上形成了委托代理关系。与一般委托代理关系不同的是，公共管理者也是公众的一部分，他们同样也是环境产品的需求者，所以，在这一意义上，也可以将政府称之为环境产品需求者代表。这样，在购买环境产品这一事项中，政府就具有了需求者本身，需求者代表和需求者代理人的三重身份。面对环境产品的需求，有与公众在投票能力和投票动机上存在缺陷，这将导致多数投票规则发生异化，进而导致了环境产品的政府需求垄断。在需求垄断的情况下，私人部门在环境产品供给中的讨价还价的能力降低，再加之环境产品本身的不确定性和受益对象的不可替代性，私人部门供给环境产品的动机将被弱化。当这一动机弱化到一定程度的时，就将形成政府对环境产品供给的垄断。这样，就形成了政府在生态环境产品需求和供给上的双重垄断特征。

生态环境产品政府双重垄断这一论述的意义，不但是在理论上对林业生态私有化的障碍直接做出了回答，而且，也从理论上证明有人主张的“大户承包”、“产业化经营”、“股份化合作”等生态治理模式（这些治理模式曾在中国退耕还林工程中被某些地区采用和倡导）可能并不可取。此外，双重垄断理论还说明，在生态治理的过程中，私人治理主体(如农户)将丧失林木的经营自主权，并与政府的利益偏好产生偏差。因此，在私人利益驱动下，治理主体将利用信息优势增大政府监督成本，弱化政府监督效果。因此，政府应以激励相容为政策制定基点，这样才能有效地激励和约束私人治理主体，从而使其在追求私人利益的同时恰好实现政府生态治理的目标。

自20世纪80年代以来，全球气候变暖引起的一系列环境问题日益引起国际社会的广泛关注，并成为当前国际政治、经济、外交和国家安全领域的一个热点。由于森林具有固碳功能，因此，在上述背景下，林业活动受到的关注程度又进一步得到提高。但是，如果不能找到一种合理的激励相容机制，这种关注度的提高本身并不能改善林业在生态环境中的效率。“汇”机制的发明符合激励相容机制的内在机理，因此在解决气候变暖问题当中，人们对林业在碳汇领域的作用寄予了很高的期望。

正如人们对碳汇问题的理解，林业碳汇并不只是一个单纯的固碳过程，其更多是为促使森林固碳而从事的人类活动或机制。这种活动和机制依然是在资源的稀缺性和人类有限理性两个假设前提下被设计的，这一设计的主观动机或动力依然是如同企业活动一样的利益。因此，要想使林业在碳汇领域发挥其应有作用，必须首先要对诸如森林碳汇与林业碳汇的经济属性、林业碳汇交易的经济实质、林业碳汇市场化的内在机理与市场化障碍等问题进行理论上的解释。

Introduction

1 Forestry Developmental History and Essential Issues

Forestry developmental history can be seen from at least three aspects when forestry studied as an independent science: the growth and decline of the amount of forest resources, the changes of forest utilization types, and the gradual progress of forest management thought When the world is regarded as a whole and in a synchronic way, however, the development of these three aspects was not, and is not, balanced between countries at different economic levels As forest resources, many developed nations, such as the United States, Germany, France and Japan, have undergone a transition from sharp decrease, to gradual increase, tending towards stability. Their forest utilization and management have successfully evolved from sole and simple resources exploitation to comprehensive and integrated usage providing multi-benefits for the society, the economy, and the environment. While in developing countries, such as China, Brazil and Indonesia, large-scale forest protection was not introduced until 1980s. Furthermore, forestry management in Africa is still in a phase of primitive utilization, with the promotion of firewood to total wood consumption as high as 91%, even in the 1990s Therefore, a question is put forward: "Are there any actual regulations in forestry development that the developed countries have gone through, and in the unbalanced forestry development in the world as well?" The research required to reply to this question would be helpful in revealing any intrinsic regulations of forestry development, and to understand the developmental trend.

1.1 The Unbalanced Changing Tendency of Growth and Decline of Forest Resources

Forests are a synthesis of natural resources mainly consisting of arbor, but in the form of various kinds Of trees, bushes and grass living together with colonies of animals and microbes in a certain scope of space where corresponding resources of water, soil and air are also located. Forests are the greatest producer of raw materials in the ecosphere of the globe, playing many roles such as economical, ecological and social ones. Nevertheless, forest resources have been dramatically reduced as human economic activities have been steadily expanding. It is estimated that, during the past ten thousand years, human beings have caused a reduction of about 1/3 or 1/2 total forests on the earth. From 1862 to 1958, the global forest size decreased from 5500000000, hectares to 3700000000 hectares. In other words, it was a decrease from 1/3 of the total continental area to 1/4. In the 20 years between 1958 and 1978, the forest size was swiftly declined again to less than 1/5 of the continental area and only 2600000000 hectares were left.

If the changing trend of forest resources is observed in different regions and nations, it shows inconsistence in the way that the forest resources are reducing in developing countries but growing in developed nations. According to statistics published by the Food and Agriculture Organization of the United Nations, during the period between 1980 and 1995, there was a total reduction of 9.1% forest size in developing countries. Among that, the greatest reduction occurred in African developing countries with 10.5%, equal to an average of annual damage 0.7%. Latin America and the Caribbean regions showed a total of reduction of 9.7% and an annual damage 0.65%. The Asian -Pacific Region, being the third in the list, had a total 6.4% decrease and 0.43% annual damage. On the other hand, the total forest size in developed countries increased by 2.7% from 1980 to 1995, with an average annual increase of 0.18%. The greatest growth was found in Europe during the same period of time: a total of 4.1%,

0.27% each year. The temperate and frigid zones of North America we ranked second with a 2.6 % increase of forest size, and a 0.17% annual growth rate. The developed nations in Asian -Pacific region, increased their forest size at a comparatively slower rate of 1.0%.

Are there any regulations that we can find between the contrast of general decrease of total forest resources in the world and apparently increasing forest resources in Europe and other developed countries? It is because of the inquiry about the opposite changing tendencies in world forest resources that draws our more attentions.

1.2 The Periodical Differences in Forest Uses

The primary results have been obtained from the study of various changing tendencies of forest resources in different regions of the world. The approach of forest utilization and the idea of forest management have been changing correspondingly with the growth or decline of forest resources throughout human history, from ancient times until modern period. The changes show not only the evolution that approaches and ideas in different countries have to undertake, but also the different historical periods in which they occurred. Those differing periods can be illustrated more clearly between countries or regions with dissimilar levels of economic development.

So far there is no agreed classification in the world for certain periods of forest development in terms of how to use forests. Some scholars believe that forest utilization has undergone three periods: exploitation and utilization of forests in natural state, then by industrialization, and finally the exploitation and utilization of forests for multiple purposes. They also think that the former two kinds share the sole aim of production and management to obtain profits from timber production. But some other scholars maintain that forest utilization has covered the following three stages: firewood, wood for industrial purposes, and the integrated utilization of wood. Obviously, the distinction between those two classifications are laid on the first and the third categories, because, firstly, the utilization aim would not be maximizing benefits to a fairly great extent if the first period of forest utilization was grouped as "firewood stage". And secondly, the stage of "integrated utilization of wood, refers to the comprehensive exploitation of forests for economic, social and ecological profits, while the utilization of forests for multiple purposes mainly stresses wood utilization techniques in wood processing.

As a matter of fact, when approaches and purposes that human beings use forests are based on as criterion, it is better to classify forestry development into our historical periods of time: natural forestry, agro forestry, forestry for industrial resources, and integrated utilization forestry.

The period of natural forestry can be defined when it is compared to the later three periods. The period took place in an era o f remote antiquity, when the activities that human beings used forests were derived from basic survival instincts. In that epoch, people relied on the natural bounty of forests to sustain their lives, due to low population density and primitive production level. That period showed an organic combination of low grade social morphology, hunting and food collection, nomadic, and primitive agriculture linked with forests This meant that a dynamic balance between human beings and forests was constructed in the whole environment, based on natural regulations.

Man then entered into an agricultural society with social development. Since agriculture and animal husbandry were the main forms of social production, forests became an important obstacle of agricultural development of farming production. That development of agriculture, in turn promoted a rapid increase of human population. As a result, greater scaled forest exploitation occurred. Harvesting forests to prepare condition for agricultural production mainly symbolized the period from agricultural society, to the period before the industrial revolution. Thus the period was named Agro-forestry.

The period of forestry for industrial resources was found after the industrial revolution. Different from the period of agricultural forestry, in which the important forestry activities aimed at obtaining farming land, raw materials for industrial use supplied by harvesting forest timbers characterized the main aim in the new period. Wood began to go into industrial production as industrial capital for the first time. With the expansion railway construction, architecture, and the paper making industry amongst others, the demands of wood became increasingly great. Therefore, the function of resource supply became enhanced and gradually became the primary function.

It is commonly accepted that industrial revolution had brought not only huge development of world economy, but also a shortage of natural resources and deterioration of the environment. The vicious circle of the reduction of forest resources caused by industrial development, and the resulting environmental problems, such as water and soil erosion, became acute. Since then, human beings were gradually aware of the correlations between forestry, the ecosystem and general social development. When the economic benefits of forests are emphasized, the ecological and social effects are initially noticed. Thus the period of integrated forestry utilization starts.

Each of the periods mentioned above, however, did not take place simultaneously in various regions of the world. In the 16th century, some early capitalist countries, such as Britain and Holland, began to build merchant vessels and warships, as well as docks, requiring a great amount of wood. They also started marine timber trade. Therefore, it can be said that those countries entered the period of industrial resource forestry in the 16th century. In contrast, industrial civilization had not yet emerged in most other countries during the same period of time, and agro – forestry still predominating. Similarly, the economically advanced countries, like Germany, initiated in 1950s a series of models, such as forestry economics, social and ecological integration, leading utilization of forests for multi – benefits, and comprehensive multi – beneficial utilization of forests. Corresponding practice was carried out afterwards. While in China, and other developing countries, similar forestry activities were not actually started until the end of the 20th century.

1.3 The Progress of Forest Management Ideas

The changes of forest utilization types would inevitably result in the progress of forest management ideology. As early as the period of natural forestry, forests were not only a field for human beings to become civilized with, but also the only source of human shelter and food. Due to a low population density, and a very low level of science and technology, human beings enjoyed abundant forest resources. Compared to the provision power that forests gave human beings in that period, human beings could exert very weak influence on forests. So it displayed a one – way care that forests gave to human beings. However, with the growth of agriculture and animal husbandry, forests were regarded as a natural obstacle of agricultural farming economy, and therefore, forests being damaged for land reclamation and for fuel became the major features of that period. Substantially, the quantity of the destroyed forests showed the important human achievements of developments and capacity of conquering nature. So the human forestry activities in that period were based on the instinctive action of survival, and were unlikely to form perfect and mature management ideas. From that point of view, the gardening plot system in China, and the local forest resources management system formed in the 10th century in Germany, represented the beginnings of forest management ideas.

The most ingenious thoughts of forest management were conceived towards the end of the 17th century. From then on, with the continuous emergence of new type of industries, such as railway, architecture, paper making, and furniture construction, the degree of forest utilization during the industrial revolution was far greater than that of the agriculture civilization that that had existed for several thousand years. The speed of forest harvesting began to exceed that through natural recovery of the forest plantation. Even worse was the fact that a timber crisis inevitably took place in some countries and regions. Only because of that reality could people be led to realize that various measures beneficial to forest growth should be adopted in order to satisfy the timber demands resulting from economic growth. Under that background, systematic thoughts regarding forest management began to appear.

The generally accepted point is that Germany was at the forefront of modern forest management. Their main task of the forestry industry aimed at increasing government revenue at that time, and therefore the theory of forest management was mainly concerned with the study of finance. Then, in the first half of the 19th century, cilviculturists, represented by Hurdeshagen J. Chrian (1783 – 1834), established the theory of normal forest, which focuses on the sustained yield of forest. In 1898, Karl Gayer et al put forward the theory of close – to – nature forestry, which initiated a new era of German forestry development in the 20th century. For more than 100 years, the timber – production – centered theoretical system and thoughts for sustained and balanced harvesting have imposed profound impacts on modern forestry development. The basic features of forest management theory during that period included: 1) Normal forests or fully – regulated forests, even – aged forests or uneven – aged forests, all were managed under the theory of normal forest and focused on timber production. 2) Forest management was aimed to provide timber in a balanced way. 3) The Productive technology system was constructed by the criteria of adjusting forest stock quantity. The theory was obviously an inevitable result that the natural economy was transformed into an industrial economy across medieval Europe. Thus it was the theoretical system based on the premise of a single timber – producing function of forests.

The human need for forests began to change during the socio – economic development of the second half of the 20th century. On one hand, the rising degree of industrialization further increased the demands for wood. In addition, the elevation of people's living standard increasingly required the protection of forest ecological environment. On the other hand, the provision capacity and ecosystem quality of forests were declining to a more serious level. Because of this social and economic situation, new developmental models and approaches had to be researched for forestry, and the corresponding ideology of forest management had to be changed. So that between the 1950s and 1980s, theories of "the benefits of forestry policies, "ship's track", "harmonization" and "multi-functions of forests" were raised respectively. Among them, the last one was the most influential, and it was widely accepted by many states. Based on the above mentioned theories, in 1960, the IUFRO (International Union of Forest Research Organizations) held an academic seminar in the United States focusing on the issue of forest multi-utilization. The meeting explicitly advanced forest management thought and the management goals of multi-aims and multi-uses. It was also in the same year that the Unite States issued Multiple Use Sustained-Yield Act of June 1960. After those events, related researches were formally carried out globally.

It should be admitted that the relationship between forest management, ecological environment, and social development had been attached to the previously discussed theories of forest management in the middle of the 20th century. The theoretical circle, however, generally held the opinion that it was after the 1992 UN environment and development conference that the major revolution in forest management and theory began: the theory of sustainable forest management.

Since 90s, many countries and regions have undertaken efficient and fruitful studies and discussions on the proposition of sustainable forest management, and thus the theory of sustainable forest management has been gradually perfected. For example, in March 1992, the Canadian government signed the first forest agreement. It is pointed that their target is to maintain and enhance the long term health of the ecological system in forests, being able to benefit all the lives in the country, as well as in the world. It will also provide optional opportunities regarding the environment, economy, society and culture, for the benefits of the current and future generations. In order to realize that goal, the Canadian government established ten different experimental areas of different types all over the country, forming a Canadian model forest network, which provided practical ground for national sustainable forest management. The Society of American Foresters published a special report "The Task Force Report on Sustaining Long - term Forest Health and Productivity in January 1993. The report suggests that ecologically systematic management is an ecological process in forest resource management and administration. That type of management tries to maintain the complicated natural processes and channels of forest ecological systems, as well as the independence existing between different ecological systems. It also attempts to keep their functions in a good condition so that they will have flexibility under pressure in the short term and adaptability in the long term. Therefore, the management of an ecological system is the basic approach to the realization of sustainable forest management.

Compared to the theory of a sustained yield of forest, the progress of sustainable forest management theory can be seen by looking at four points: The sustained yield theory emphasizes the sole value of forest production; while the sustainable forest management theory stresses all the values of forest as a whole. Secondly, the management unit in sustained yield theory is a forest stand, or grouped forest stands; in contrast, in the sustainable forest management theory, the subject of the sustainable management is landscape, or forest health and productivity based on landscape. Thirdly, the sustained yield of forest management shares a similar management model with that of the normal forest; but the sustainable management reflects the regulations of natural intervention. Finally, the sustained yield theory attaches importance to the amounts of both stocking and periodical production, however, the sustainable forest management theory pays attention to the forest characteristics such as forest age, constructive elements, tree vitality, flora and fauna species, and then to the amounts of stocking and periodical production.

Using the brief description of forest management thoughts, it can be concluded that the theories of forest management established during different historical periods were always initiated in the countries that had a relatively high level of economic development. Developing countries, on the other hand, basically had no independent and systematic theories of forest management. Moreover, their employment of forest management theories from advanced countries was always delayed. For example, the thought of normal forest put forward by German in the early 19th century was not considered by Chinese cilviculturists until the 1950s. That constitutes a gap of more than 100 years since the establishment of the theory to its introduction to China. During the same stage when Chinese scientists found the theory, the countries in Africa and some other continents in extremely difficult situation, were still in a natural forest period on the whole. Since forestry has emerged as a production department, on the whole, it is impossible to talk about the reference to theories in developed countries. To sum up, the imbalance presented in the evolution of forest management corresponds directly to the imbalance in the growth and decline of forest resources quantity, and the imbalance in the utilization types of different historical periods.

1.4 Three Essential Problems in Forestry

Some regulations can be concluded from the imbalances. Our careful research shows that three problems caused all the imbalances: The problem of land, the problem of resources and the problem of ecology.

According to the evidence gathered by scholars of pale anthropologist, man came from forests. Therefore, initial human activity was the use of forests. That initial activity was basically fulfilled by natural power. Since it was an instinctive action meant for survival, it was very different from the activities of production and management in present era. Hence, during that epoch, there were no forestry problems similar to those in present times. when human settlement and agricultural activities began, forests started to provide human beings with firewood and necessary farming land. Afterwards, the increase and decrease between forest resources and agricultural land altered frequently. When agricultural technology became more advanced and human population expanded rapidly, the degree of agricultural development that relied on the use of forestland was continuously raised. As a result, the problem of forestland came into being.

In the middle of the 18th century, the industrial revolution began to thrive and timber thus became an important raw material for industry. Direct and indirect utilization of wood gradually replaced civil use, becoming the main content of forest utilization. From then on, forests became a significant resource of the global economy, and thus became an essential element in production. Consequently, forest exploitation and utilization for the purpose of obtaining profits gradually began. It was also from that time on that the performance that human beings made use of forests had an industrial purpose, and this is defined as forestry activity. It should be noted that the forest activities for firewood and farming land had not being stopped since the industrial revolution. It is simultaneously found that the swift development of non – agricultural industries led to the shortage of wood resource supply. Therefore the wood resource problem began to emerge and steadily rose to become a major one.

In the early stage of industrialization, the problems regarding the resource supply and ecological environment were not obvious. Later, when the world economy entered some new developmental stages, one after another, the deterioration of ecological environment became more serious. The environmental problem increasingly became a severe restrictive element to human development. Therefore, people have an even stronger demand for ecosystem conservation than ever before. Due to that background, a trend of diversity in forest utilization began to be displayed. The economic function was stressed, and the ecological function was equally emphasized. However, when economic development continuously rose to higher levels, the ecological environment was damaged to a more serious degree. On the other hand, human beings had a greater demand to improve the environment. Therefore the economic function of forest gradually gave place to ecological function, and the main problem of forestry became an ecological one.

According to economics, a practical requirement must satisfy two basic conditions: purchasing desire and purchasing capacity. Only when the two conditions are met, can a truly meaningful demand exist. This demand will further bring about the development of the relevant industry. If there is only desire, but no ability to realize this desire, then the true change of forest utilization type cannot take Place. From that point of view, the three problems regarding land, resources and ecosystem, as well as the resulting changes in forest utilization types, are not only the result of the continuous progress of human desire or demand, hut also the result of a continuously strengthened ability to satisfy the desire or demand due to socio – economic development. In the discussion, there is also significance for policy making: if a government purely relies on desire or demand, but ignores, to some degree, the socio – economic level, it will solve some forestry problems too early or too late in a certain period. And that will lead to unsatisfactory result. To conclude, it contains important interests to study the evolutionary process of forest problems in terms of socio – economic development.

2 Essential Propositions in the Study of Forestry Economics

2.1 Progress in the Study of forestry Economics

The study of forestry economics, in various countries can be classified into three categories according to what is emphasized: 1) Applied research of forestry economics. Some practical Problems in forestry economics are studied by applying the theories and methods that are already accepted. The main contents include: the relationship between forestry production and property rights of forests, the relationship between forest and energy, the trade of forest products, and policies to regulate land use. 2) Empirical research of forestry economics. Some new theories and methodologies are verified, developed and improved through practicing them in actual problems. The main themes consist of the impacts of various social elements on forestry, dynamic simulation in markets to see the relationship between forestry production and consumption, and quantified study on forestry policies. 3) Strategic study of forestry economics. Advanced research focuses on new fields and new problems that indicate the trend of research in forestry economics. That is, some vital theoretical issues in the specialty are studied in an active manner. The issues include the harmony between forestry and environment, strategies of forestry development, international cooperation in forestry, and adjustment of forestry structure.

The recent search in these three aspects shows the following characteristics: 1) Diversity in theories. Due to the steady introduction of new theories, from modern economics and modern sociology to forestry economics, its research fields, study methods and practice have been greatly changed. The study of forestry economics, therefore, has become a new hot specialty in the world. Furthermore, the application of some new theories has widened the space for the study of forestry economies. And ultimately, more solid scientific foundation has been laid for the research. 2) Advancements in methods and means. When new theories are introduced to forestry economics, the corresponding new methods are integrated into the research. Therefore, the improved and developed methods in the forestry economics provide more efficient tools and means for its study and make the research more scientific. 3) Systemic in research. One is shown in the time continuity in researches. For example, in some advanced forestry countries in North America and Europe, many of their research projects were, or are carried on for several years, several decades, or even across centuries. The other is displayed by its strengthened integrity. In many research programs, policies, trade, legislation, state macro – administration are integrated, so that forestry economics forms a well – organized and interrelated whole. 4) Internationalization in research. International cooperation has recently been expanded dramatically when forest resources and ecological environment draw increasingly more attention in the world. As a result, the internationalized searches in forestry economics have been gradually emphasized. It can be said that the internationalization in research of forestry economics is the inevitable outcome of economic globalization.

Although the study of forestry economics has shown those new features, it is generally at a less mature level compared to other branches of economics, such as agro – economics. Firstly, whether the following theories could be actually categorized in the field of forestry economics should be further discussed. The theories suggested by advanced countries included: the theory of "sustained yield of forest" established in the middle of 17th century aimed at timber harvest and economic profits; the theory of multi – functional forest management put forward in 1960s to emphasize biological, landscaping and humanistic diversities; ten years later, the theory of function – divided forestry focused on intensive management and the theory of integrated forestry constructed by the two parts: forest stand and landscape (some scholars call it "new forestry theory"). Although these theories were widely believed to be the most important achievements, they have been questioned if they are in the specialty of forestry economics. The reason is that, as an independent science, forestry economics must lay its theoretical ground on economics, although it's inevitably interrelated with other disciplines. Problems involved in forestry economics should also be economically studied. But the above mentioned theories always allocated the research in the fields of botany, biology, ecology and sociology. The theoretical contents tended to be involved in technology of forestry management. Secondly, although some researches have been contained in the science of economics, a complete study system of forestry has not been established, because of the dispersed and separated research contents. These research include: the impacts of social factor on forestry, dynamic marketing simulation between production and consumption, and the quantified forestry policies. On the other hand, in developing countries, the study on forestry economics remains at an even lower and less perfect level. Although there are more serious problems in forestry, these countries have not built up a solid foundation for the development of their own forestry economics due to their present level of scientific development and practice in forestry. So it is even far away to establish the discipline with fixed contents, rational structure and the framework of systematic theories. As a result, they always directly adapt theories of forestry economics or achievements in advanced countries for their own practice in forestry. In their application, some contents in the forestry economics are revised and improved but they are not systematic and mature. To sum up, therefore, the forestry economics in the developing countries has been staying in the preliminary stage of forming theories and practice.

It should be pointed out that a group of countries, such as China and former Soviet Union, during their planned economics dominated period, once had formed comparatively comprehensive and systematic forestry economics adaptable to their economic system. But after the reform towards market economics and economic development, their antiquated theories cannot provide reasonable explanations to present forestry problems as well as guidance for new forestry practice. Therefore, relevant researches for present forestry problems that are different from the past ones remain in an initial stage.

2.2 The Research Methods and Contents

The past research achievements in forestry economics have laid a solid foundation for the new studies. Meanwhile the imperfection in the researches also leaves a wide space for further work. There are extensively wide fields waiting for new research in present forestry economics, such as forestry property rights, forestry management models, forestry industry structure, forestry trade, evaluation and assessment of forestry policies, and the government style and manner. But from the macroscopic point of view, all those forestry problems are closely related to the basic regulations of forestry development. Only when these essential forestry development regulations are made clear, can the detailed and concrete forestry problems be efficiently studied. Therefore, the research on the underlying developmental regulations should have priority as elementary content of the forestry economics. It is because of that point we orient the research in this book towards the basic regulations of forestry development.

In this book the research was mainly focused on advanced countries. By studying their forestry problems in the historical evolution, essential regulations in forestry development were summarized. Besides the chronological analyses, a diachronic comparison between developed and developing countries was conducted to account for the differences existed in forest development. Then the causes of the differences were manifested through the contrast of the social and economic conditions between these countries.

Being a part of the overall national economy, forestry has to be closely related its own development to the whole development of the national economy? If the forestry problems are probed into only from forestry development itself, rational explanations will be difficult or even impossible. Therefore, it is necessary to study the basic regulations of forestry development from a macroscopic point of view. That is, the forestry development should be studied in terms of the impacts of total national economic development. Based on the approach, we have drawn the following conclusions from our research work.

It is found from human forestry activities before industry revolution that reclamation by damaging forests for survival purpose was the main feature of the forestry activities during that period of time. The action led to vicious circle in forestry: The reclamation of forestland resulted in the expansion of farming land and thus promoted extensive increase of agricultural scale. The expansion then caused rapid growth of human population. In return, even faster and wider disafforestation was attributed to the great number of people to obtain more agricultural land. Ultimately, forestland further shrank. We name that vicious circle "forestland problems during pre – industrialization period".

Different countries joined in the industrialization course early or late when the economy had developed in their countries. During the beginning period of the industrialization, forestland problems caused by insufficient food supply still existed in countries all over the world, especially in developing countries. Complexity of the economic activities during that period led to more complicated reasons that caused forestland problems than those during the pre – industrialization period. During the beginning period, agricultural production could not meet the increased food demand because of the population growth and their income improvement. As a result, grain was facing the pressure to raise its prices. The inflation of grain prices would force the increase of workers' wage. And that would then constrain industrialization and national economic development. Thus the governments of developing countries always adapted the means, such as monopolized purchase, to drive down the prices of agricultural products. The problem was put forward as early as David Ricard studied British industry revolution. Later Theodore W. Schultz called it "food problem". But when the prices of agricultural food were depressed, the farmers' motivation to provide food was weakened. And that further enlarged the supply -demand contradiction that originally caused by the gradually serious shortage of food due to the slower rate of, agricultural production than the rate of excessive population growth and income increase. Besides, the passages to import agricultural products and technology to solve the food problems were restricted, so that the main measure was the reclamation of forestland to expand farming land during that period of time. We call that phenomenon "forestland problems of developing countries during the initial period of industrialization".

Farm land was expanded in two ways to relieve the supply - demand inconsistency: One was to convert forestland into farming land by harvesting forest wood in large regions; the other was to reclaim other land. Both literature and reality showed that the first way seemed to be the main solution. That is because, first of all, forests were distributed in spacious rural areas and it was an extremely common phenomenon that forestland was adjacent to farmland. Therefore, agricultural activities were interrelated tightly with forestry activities. Besides, the soil with human formed by forests was beneficial to plant growth. Because of people's tradition to rely on natural environment, it became a logical way for them to cut down forest wood in tremendously large areas to increase farmland. Secondly, timber harvesting in great amount brought about additional benefits. That is to say, farmers obtained fuel wood and housing construction materials. Finally, farmland expansion by harvesting forest wood could win efforts in two ways in terms of industrialization in developing countries. It could both enlarge farming areas to further relieve the food supply – demand tension and to solve the problem of raw materials in industrial development.

Based on the above explanation, we further found out that the interrelationship between food problem and forestland problem was not a single direction one during the initial period of industrialization in developing countries. When food problem led to forestland problem forestry provided accumulation for agricultural production. Additionally, that kind of capital accumulation was in fact a kind of compensation provided by forests for agriculture when the policy of industrialization priority was carried out and agricultural interests were invaded in developing countries. The compensation partially covered the deficits that the agriculture was seized by industry and encouraged the action to transfer forestland to farmland.

Different form the forestland problems resulted from food problem, two policies led to a forestland problem in rural areas during the comparatively poor period: the policy of priority for non – agricultural industries and the policy of agriculture protection. During that period, forestry began to supply both agriculture and non – agricultural industry with capital accumulation simultaneously. And the function of the capital accumulation began to move from agriculture centered to non – agricultural industries centered fields. Moreover, during the developmental course with a structure of the binary economics, the wood supply – demand contradiction increased because of the growth of wood needs in industry and quick decline of forest resources. In that case, governments were likely to enhance continuously the control of forest resources. The permission of forest invasion without pay or with low pay during the period of food problems would be possibly changed. And the institutional cost to convert forestland to farmland would keep rising. As a result, the quantity and speed in transferring forestland into farmland during that period would be decreased compared to the period of food problem.

During the comparatively poor period, the amount of forestland converted into farmland was only reduced at a slower rate than that during the food problem period. However, this situation was completely reversed during the agricultural adjustment period. Due to the highly developed agricultural technology at the time, more advanced countries were experiencing a surplus of agricultural products. Because of this surplus, they were also facing the problem of marginal rate of return, which was not as serious as that in non – agricultural industries. Those two problems influenced forestry in at least two aspects. Firstly, the motivation to input the elements of agricultural production was weakened. Among the elements, the most important was farmland. Existed in both the food problem period and the comparatively poor period, but did not take place during the agricultural adjustment period. Secondly, during the agricultural adjustment period, the problems of food surplus marginal rate of return could have been solved if the production elements had been transferred from food production, where demand had already saturated, to other industries, where needs were expanding. Our research shows that there was no balanced and smooth transfer extent between agricultural and non – agricultural sectors. It was because of this imbalanced moving degree that new forestry problems emerged: agricultural land began to be used as forestland, but not the other way round as before.

So far the study focuses on the influence of agricultural development on forestry. However, when the study is focused on industrialization, it is found that the land problems in forestry were gradually being replaced by resource problems, with a steady decrease of both the agriculture proportion and the importance in the total national economy.

We attach importance to the impacts that the industrialization process had on forestry, particularly the effects on forest resource yield. Our attention has led us to find two reasons that caused the resource problems: technological progress, and the evolution of capital accumulation styles.

At different stages of industrialization, technology progressed in various ways, and thus they had different impacts on forest resources During the initial stages of technological progress, capital tended to replace laborers, which led to the increased use of machines. That property was similar to the demanding feature of product homogeneity in the low income period. Two consequences were therefore produced. The use of machines, first of all, brought about an increase in productivity, and thus the demands for raw materials, including timber, were swiftly increased. That ultimately resulted in rapid and tremendous consumption of timber and other forest resources. As for the second consequence, forestry products, mainly related to timber, shared obvious product homogeneity, and were thus suitable to labor - saving mechanical production. In addition, this kind of production had the same effects as increasing capital income proportion when the wage rate was restricted, so that mechanization was adapted in forestry production as it had been in other industries. The use of forestry machines definitely increased the supply capacity of forestry products, including timber. On the other hand, it also aggravated the shortage of forest resources.

The practical performance in advanced countries showed the fact that forest resource problems, caused by the wide spread adaptation of labor - saving technology during the initial period of industrialization did not last long. There were two reasons for this. One was the technological innovation of inducing - nature transition and the other was the change in social demands. Technological innovation eventually resulted in the emergence of new technologies that were aimed at exploiting forestry product substitutes, such as timber, as well as reducing production costs. The application of these technologies inevitably relieved the contradiction of supply - demand in forestry products, and further relieved the problems, regarding forest resources. Secondly, the changes in the requirements of society provided a social foundation for the relief of forest resource pressure. On the other hand, a large forest harvest deteriorated the ecological environment at a fairly high pace, and people's demand for improving the environment and leisure activity facilities was continually increasing as their income grew. Once those desires became widely accepted by the general public, with a realistic capacity to support these desires, the social, ground for relieving forest resource pressure was formed. Under the circumstances, any country, if economic power permitted, would take fairly strict restraining measures to limit forest resource exploitation, and introduce related policies beneficial to the recovery of forest resources. In the meantime, the action for protection of forest resources would be spontaneously brought up among ordinary people. All these would play a very important role in solving the forest resource problems.

The impact of capital accumulation on forest resources took place simultaneously with the impacts of technological progress. To see that point in terms of forest resources, the impact of capital accumulation on forestry contain two forms: capital accumulation dominated by governmental administrative means and by non – governmental administrative means.

The capital accumulation dominated by government influenced forestry in the aspects of transfer of forestry production surplus, governmental financing through financial policy, and timber export for foreign currency. The governments in developing countries dealt with the transfer of forestry production surplus mainly by means of monopolizing purchases and limiting free market business to depress timber prices, so as to decrease production cost in industry sector. Those measures were once commonly adapted in the countries such as the former Soviet Union and China during their plan economics period. As for governmental financing collected through financial policy, the governments in developing countries mainly levied various taxes and took the profits from forestry enterprises. The purpose was to supply other industrial enterprises with capital support, so that industrial capital accumulation was formed. It is in fact a form of transferring forestry production surplus through a financial channel. Timber export for foreign currency was another important method for the governments of developing countries to accumulate capital in their industrialization. Due to the limits of technology, these countries could not independently develop certain mechanical equipment to continue their industrialization. Instead, this equipment had to be imported from more developed countries. Meanwhile, developed countries had completed their period of economic development by taking resources from other countries, and began the comprehensive and careful protection of their forest resources. Thus they began importing the timber that they needed from other less developed countries. Based on this situation, many developing countries exported a large quantity of timber to obtain foreign currency and were thus able to purchase sophisticated equipment from more advanced countries.

The capital accumulation dominated by government led to great harvesting of forest resources, so that the resources were sharply reduced. On the other hand, however, the transfer of forestry production surplus rendered forestry enterprises unable to obtain sufficient investment for recovery of forest resources, such as afforestation, forest management, and protection. As a result, it was difficult for forests to rejuvenate. The dual impacts would consequentially cause a more serious forest resource crisis.

Different from the capital accumulation dominated by government, the capital accumulation dominated by non - governmental administrative means played a role to relieve the forest resource crisis. In economically advanced countries, either the maturity of their market economy system, or the level of their economic development, has reached a fairly good height. Therefore, the financing approach and enterprises ' own capital accumulation have become the most important methods of capital formation. Since 1970s, many developing countries, including China, have begun market - oriented economic reform and financial system reform. With the further deepening of these reforms, the capital accumulation dominated by non - governmental administrative means is gradually replacing that dominated by government. The situation has obviously relieved the pressure that capital accumulation exerts on forest resources. Additionally; governments have begun to reduce taxes on forestry enterprises as their national economies begin to flourish. If financial revenue is greatly increased from other sectors, governments can use this to provide financial support to the forestry industry, instead of levying taxes from is. That change also plays an important role in solving the forest resource crisis.

In forestry the problem relating resources always goes together with the ecological problem. The ecological functions in forests are natural, but these ecological functions nurtured by human beings are resulted from economic development. Forests at the same times show the nature of public property, so that they have non – competitiveness in their efficiency and non – exclusiveness in its consumption. This nature leads to the appearance of "free rider" behavior. In addition, the requirement that people have for ecological functions depends on different grades of income and present ecological situations, which are shown in various indifference curves drawn from investigations. Therefore, forest management behavior, mainly aimed at improving ecological conditions, cannot appear until the economy has developed to a certain level. The course of forestry development through history indicates that by two stages people learned the ecological functions of forests: the germinating stage at the beginning and the conspicuous stage now. Moreover, only when the economy reaches a certain level can the forest integration model of multi – benefits he seen.

Corresponding to the evolution of land problems, resource problems, ecological problems in forestry development, forest property rights policy had changed appropriately. On the surface, the main factors which influence the evolution of forest property rights policy include two aspects of the scarcity of forest resources and the market – oriented degree of forest products, while the change of state will also play an important role. However, through further research, it will find that the formation of the above factors depends on the so many socio – economic factors which influence the demand and supply of forest resources and the interaction of these factors. These factors include: the increase in population, the urbanization process, the technological progress of logging and plantation, the awareness of environmental protection, and so on. At the stage of land problems in forestry development, the scarcity of forestland resources was gradually emerging just because of demographic factors, forest property rights policy showing characteristics of relying on land policy, making the ownership of forestland as the core content, and mainly using informal institutional arrangements. At the stage of resource problems in forestry development, the scarcity of forest resources and market – oriented enhanced, and then making timber resource as the core content and the formal institutional arrangements replacing the informal institutional arrangements became the main characters of forest property rights policy in this stage, in addition, it formatted two different paths of state – owned forest property rights and private – owned forest property rights according to different national systems in different developing states, but the main object of making forest property rights was to enhance the function of forestry which providing raw materials, capital and foreign exchange accumulation. At the stage of ecological problems in forestry development, although there were still two paths of state – owned forest property rights and private – owned forest property rights, from a global perspective, the level of economic and social development and the degree of market – oriented are the main factors which influencing the implementation range and intensity of two types of forest property rights policy.

When the ecological problems increased into the main problem for forestry, the main and difficult problem is that what kind of configuration mechanism would be chosen in order to improve the efficiency of ecological improvements? Mainstream economists believed that eco – environment products can not be covered by the market, thus the possibility of governing ecological environment using market mechanisms was lost, and however, the government should play a fundamental role to environmental governance. But, in reality, the efficiency of governing ecological environment by the government was often unsatisfactory. For this situation, some "free market environmentalists" insisted on denying the main role of the government in the process of allocating environment resources, and consider that it should achieve the object of allocating environment resources effectively through ecological privatization.

In practice, it is contrary to the desire and ideas of "free market environmentalists" that complete ecological privatization has not yet found. Did people not find the way in the end, or is it lack of the necessary conditions for privatization? To solve this problem, we should apply the external theory and the theory of public goods. In addition, we should give the theoretical answer in connection with the characteristics of the ecological environment. In this context, we analyze the supply and demand characteristics of eco-environment products from a new perspective in this text. The results show that when consuming public goods in the economy and society, anyone should choose "free ride" rationally. Thus, even though the demand desire is strong, the public will not pay for the eco-environment products. Since eco-environment products are indispensable, and the "free ride" is inevitably, public's desire for the eco-environment products should be satisfied through the path of mandatory funding by the government. In this process, the relationship between the public and the government is agency relationship actually. Different from the common agency relationship, public managers are also part of the public, they also the demanders for the eco-environment products, so, in this sense, the government also could be called as the representatives of demanders for the eco-environment products. Thus, in the matter of purchase the eco-environment products, the government plays the roles of the demanders, the representatives of demanders and the agents of demanders. Because the public are defective at the aspects of vote ability and vote motivation, then the rule of majority voting changed, and then, the government monopolized the demand for the eco-environment products facing the demand for the eco-environment products. In the case of demand monopolistic, the bargaining power of the private sector in the supply of the eco-environment products reduce, and the uncertainty of the eco-environment product as well as the beneficiaries are irreplaceable, so the motives of the private sector for supplying the eco-environment products will be weakened. When the motives weakened to a certain degree, it should form the situation of the government monopolize the supply of the eco-environment products. Thus, it shows the characteristics of the government monopolized the demand and supply of the eco-environment products.

The sense of the dissertation that the government monopolizes the supply and demand of the eco-environment products is reflected in two aspects: on the one hand, it answered directly that it is difficult to achieve the object of forestry ecological privatization in theory; on the other hand, it proved that the ecological governance modes such as "contracted by the bigger household", "industrial management", "shares of cooperation" (these governance modes have been adopted and advocated in some areas in the implementation process of "Grain for Green Project" in China) may be undesirable in theory. In addition, the theory also proved that the private governance body (such as farmers) will lose the operational autonomy of timbers in the eco – governance process, and the private governance body's preference will become different from the Government's preference. Hence, driven by private interests, governance body will increase the cost of government oversight using the advantage of grasping more information and then weak the effects of government supervision. Therefore, the government should make incentive compatibility as the core work of policy formulation. It could incentive and restraint the private governance body effectively, and then promotes the private governance body to achieve the government's object of government eco – environment when they seek for private interests.

Since the 20th century 80 years, a series of environmental problems which caused by global warming had been concerned increasingly in the international community, and then became the hot issues in the field of international political, economic, diplomatic and national security in current. Because the forest has the function of carbon sequestration, therefore, in the above context, the concern degree of forestry activities are further improved. However, if we can not find a reasonable incentive mechanism, the increased attention is not useful for improving the efficiency of forestry in the process of governing ecological environment. The invention of "Sink" mechanism is consistent with the internal mechanism of incentive mechanism, and therefore, people pay more attention to the role of forestry in the field of carbon sequestration in the process of solving global warming problem.

As the same as the understanding of carbon sequestration, forestry carbon sequestration is not only a simple process of carbon sequestration, it is a human activities or mechanisms which people engage in order to promote forest carbon sequestration. The human activities or mechanism are remain designed under the two assumption of the scarcity of resources and human assumption of bounded rationality, and the subjective motive or motivation for the design remain is interests as the same as the interests of business activities. Therefore, in order to prompt forestry to play its role in the field of carbon sequestration, we should explain in theory some problems such as economic attributes of forest carbon sequestration and forestry carbon sequestration, the economic substance of forestry carbon sequestration trade, the internal mechanism of forestry carbon sequestration market, and the market barriers firstly.

第一章　林业发展中的土地问题理论

应该说，从人类定居和农业活动开始，林业问题就和农业问题紧密地联系在一起。因此，研究农业问题就成为研究林业问题的前提。从本书的绪论中可以发现，无论是森林资源的消长，还是森林利用方式的改变和经营思想的演进，处于不同经济发展水平的国家在趋势和时期上的变化并不均衡。发达国家森林资源的消长已经历了从减少到良好恢复的过程，同时其森林利用方式也进入了相对成熟的综合利用阶段，而大多数发展中国家，尤其是经济十分落后的发展中国家，森林资源仍呈现单方向减少趋势，其森林利用方式还停留在综合利用之前或刚刚进入这一阶段。因此，对这一问题的研究存在三种技术路线：一是以发达国家为研究对象，通过对其农业问题历史演进过程的实证研究来说明林业问题的产生。二是通过发达国家和发展中国家的横向比较来研究农业问题并进而说明林业问题。三是将前两种研究路线合理结合，通过纵向和横向的比较来说明林业问题。显然，采用第三种技术路线进行研究更为有效。由于资料获取方面的原因，本书采用了接近第三种技术路线的研究方法，即在侧重于发达国家和发展中国家横向比较的同时，兼顾纵向比较。

第一节　粮食问题阶段林业的土地问题

一、农业发展中的两种粮食问题

要说明农业发展中粮食问题阶段所存在的林业土地问题，首先必须回答什么是粮食问题。

（一）工业化之前的粮食问题

从人类更长的历史时期来看，自农业活动产生之日起，粮食问题就已存在。在工业化尚未到来的时期，整个人类所面临的最主要问题莫过于生存问题。在解决这一问题的过程中，人类不得不面临这样一种恶性循环：即依靠农业的发展来解决生存中的粮食问题，而农业的发展又带来人口的迅速增长，粮食的需求迅速扩大，粮食供给又变得更加严峻。这就是人类发展初期阶段所面临的粮食问题。这一粮食问题几乎所有国家都经历过。

（二）工业化初期发展中国家的粮食问题

与工业化之前的粮食问题相比，工业化初期发展中国家依然存在粮食问题，但这一阶段的粮食问题却相对复杂。在低收入的发展中国家，由于人口的迅速增长，粮食消费尚未得到满足，所以随着经济增长和收入水平的提高，粮食需求会迅速扩大。另一方面，受自然因素的制约，发达国家的农业技术难以转移到发展中国家，而且发展中国家自身通常实行的工业化优先战略又限制了对农业科研和农业基本建设等方面的投资，所以农业生产率提高缓慢，低收入国家粮食供给增长的速度比不上需求的增长。

按照市场均衡理论，我们可以假定农产品市场是一个完全竞争市场（农产品市场中的生产者、消费者以及产品的差异性基本和完全竞争市场的特征吻合）。这样，在粮食供给增长的速度慢于需求的增长时，粮食需求曲线右移的速度将快于其供给曲线的右移，结果农产品的价格将面临向上的压力。如果粮食的价格上涨，对于低收入的发展中国家将会产生什么样的影响呢？回答这一问题必须弄清发展中国家经济政策的主要目标。

发展中国家经济政策的主要目标基本上是引进现代技术，促进工业化建设，从而在经济上赶上先进国家。这样，在农产品价格上升的情况下，发展中国家将不能为工业等现代产业提供廉价的工资性商品（wage goods）。所谓工资性商品，是指那些占劳动者家庭消费比率很大，其价格对名义工资有决定性影响的商品。在恩格尔系数超过50%的发展中国家，粮食是最基本的工资性商品。这些国家工人的收入水平不高，粮食价格大幅度上升时将会直接导致生活困难，严重时可能危及社会稳定。为此，就必须按照粮食价格的上涨幅度相应地提高工人的工资水平。但提高工资又会使非农产业的工资成本上升，利润下降。这对主要依靠劳动密集型技术的发展中国家来说关系重大，因为利润率下降将使投资减少，而投资减少则可能使工业化本身遭受挫折。

在工业化发展的初期，农业生产赶不上随人口和收入增长而增加的粮食需求，粮食价格面临向上的压力。而粮食价格上涨又会促使工资上涨，从而制约工业化和国民经济的发展。这早在李嘉图研究英国产业革命问题时就已提出。后来舒尔茨把它称之为“粮食问题”(food problem)。

解决粮食问题的一种手段，就是像19世纪英国那样，从国外进口廉价的农产品。但问题是，许多发展中国家的工业处于进口替代型工业化政策的保护之下，工业本身没有那么大的出口竞争力，缺乏赚取足够的外汇以保证粮食进口的能力。剩下的方法就是只有在国内农业上做文章。为此，许多发展中国家的政府都采取了干预农产品市场、限制农产品价格上升的政策。

现今发展中国家所面临的粮食问题和工业化尚未到来时期整个人类所面临的粮食问题存在的区别除产生的历史阶段不同之外，还有以下两点：一是问题产生的动因不同，前者是为加速工业化进程而产生的粮食问题，而后者则是为解决人类的基本生存所产生的粮食问题；二是问题形成的路径不同，前者是发展中国家为加速工业化进程所制定的政策导致的结果，而后者更多地出自人类生存的本能。

二、两种粮食问题与林业的土地问题

(一)工业化之前林业的土地问题

当一个国家在工业化尚未到来时期面临粮食问题时，这一阶段的粮食问题本身究竟会对林业的发展产生什么样的影响？从现有的资料来看，将林地开垦为农业用地进而解决粮食问题是当时的主要做法。以美国为例，1785~1850年的65年时间里，美国人口增长了近7倍，由殖民时期的300万人达到2 330万人。在这种情况下，1800~1850年的50年中，其农田面积也从800万 hm^2 增加到3 040

万 hm^2。1850～1900 年的 50 年中，美国人口又增加了 2 倍多，从 2 330 万人增加到 7 600 万人。人口增长需要更多的土地。据统计，在当时美国每人大约需要 1.2hm^2的农地才能生存，因此，1850～1910 年全国农田面积增加了 3 倍多，即从 3 040万 hm^2 增加到 12 760 万 hm^2，而这些农田都是毁林得来的。1850～1910 年，太平洋沿岸约 32% 的林地（1 760 万 hm^2）被开垦为农业用地，在东部和南部约 76% 的林地（5 840 万 hm^2）转化为农业用地。除此之外，在其他地区另有 7 600 万 hm^2 的森林被开垦为农田和草场。1850～1910 年的 60 年时间里，美国的森林面积以每天 35km^2 的速度消失。仅仅 60 年的时间，北美大陆的森林覆盖率从 60% 下降到 25%，在西部的农业发达地区，许多地方的森林覆盖率仅为 4%。这 60 年间森林减少的数量，比过去 250 年间砍伐森林的面积总和还大。除美国外，世界上的其他国家也都经历过类似情况。

开垦林地使农作物的耕作面积得到扩大并从而促进了农业规模的粗放式扩张，而这种粗放式扩张又带来了人口的迅速增长，进而导致更加迅速和更大规模地砍伐森林来换取农耕用地，林地面积进一步缩小。我们把这一现象称之为工业化之前的林业土地问题。

（二）工业化初期发展中国家林业的土地问题

随着经济的发展，发达国家已经完成了其工业化进程，而经济水平相对落后的发展中国家尚处于工业化初期，这些国家所面临的粮食问题又会对林业发展产生什么样的影响？要想说明这一问题，必须搞清发展中国家解决粮食问题的基本路径。

处于工业化发展初期的发展中国家，政府为加速工业化进程，以限制农产品价格的方式来保证工业的资本积累，农产品的价格必然低于由供需关系调节的市场价格。政府限价的直接结果是粮食供给的动力弱化，这将使原本由农业生产赶不上随人口和收入增长而增加的粮食需求造成的供需矛盾进一步增大。这样，处于粮食问题阶段的发展中国家将面临一个必须解决的问题：如何解决国民的基本粮食需求？在前面的论述中已经阐述，由于许多发展中国家的工业处于进口替代型工业化政策的保护之下，工业本身没有那么大的出口竞争力，缺乏赚取足够的外汇以保证粮食进口的能力。因此，依靠从国外进口廉价的农产品来解决粮食供需矛盾的方法在发展中国家并不可行。另外一种解决粮食供需矛盾的方法是强化农业技术开发，降低农业生产成本，促使粮食等农产品供给曲线的移动。然而，许多发展中国家，并不重视这样的农业技术开发，在优先保证工业的政策框架下，政府预算的分配往往忽视农业，对农业技术的适应性研究以及水利灌溉等农业基本建设的投入资金不足。并且，进口替代型工业化政策在压低农产品价格的同时抬高了化肥、农药等农用物资的价格。后者又阻碍、挫伤了农民采用新技术、投入现代生产要素的积极性。而且由于受自然条件的限制，不同气候土壤条件下形成的农业技术很难在国际间转移。

由于进口农产品和技术开发解决粮食问题的路径受到限制，而粮食的供需矛盾又必须予以解决，采用扩张农作物耕作面积就成了发展中国家的主要做法。扩张农作物耕作面积有两种途径：一是将林业用地转化为农业用地，即通过大面积的林木采伐来增加农作物的耕作面积；二是将林业用地以外的其他土地开垦为农业用地。从现有的资料和现实情况来看，第一种途径似乎是主要的。这其中的原因主要有以下三点：一是自古以来，人类就以森林为伴，其最早的农耕活动就开始于原始森林，农业活动自其开始就和砍伐林木结合在了一起。当人类发展到今天，由于森林分布在广大的农村，农业活动和林业活动紧密交织在一起，林地和农用耕地接壤的现象极为普遍，因此，通过大面积的林木采伐来增加农作物耕作面积的做法就成了因惯性和自然环境而导致的顺理成章的事情。二是通过大面积的林木采伐来增加农作物耕作面积的做法还可以带来附加的好处，即通过采伐林木，可以解决农户薪材和房屋建材等问题。三是从发展中国家工业化的角度来看，通过林木的采伐来增加耕地可以获得一举两得的效果，即这种做法既可以扩张耕地面积进而缓解粮食的供需紧张，又可以解决工业发展中的木材原料问题。

压低农产品价格弱化了粮食供给的动机，从而使原本由农业生产赶不上随人口和收入增长而增加的粮食需求而造成的供需矛盾进一步增大，又由于进口农产品和技术开发解决粮食问题的路径受到限制，这样，开垦林地来扩张农业用地就成了这一时期解决粮食问题的主要手段。我们把这一现象称之为发展中国家工业化初期的林业土地问题。

如同工业化之前林业的土地问题一样，工业化初期林业的土地问题在发展中国家也较为普遍存在。关于这一问题，可以从发展中国家和发达国家森林面积增减趋势的对比中明显地看出(表1-1)。

表1-1　部分发展中国家和发达国家森林面积及耕地面积变化情

国家		时期(年)	森林面积变化(万 hm^2)	森林面积年均变化(万 hm^2)	耕地面积变化(万 hm^2)
发展中国家	印度尼西亚	1990～1995	-542.2	-108.4	-
	马来西亚	1990～1995	-200.1	-40.0	123.2
	菲律宾	1990～1995	-131.2	-26.2	-
	泰国	1990～1995	-164.7	-32.9	132.3
	坦桑尼亚	1990～1995	-161.3	-32.3	167.2
	南非	1990～1995	-7.5	-1.5	785.4
发达国家	英国	1990～1995	6.4	1.3	0
	法国	1990～1995	80.4	16.1	—
	美国	1990～1995	294.3	58.9	-158.2
	加拿大	1990～1995	87.3	17.5	-176
	德国	1990～1995	0	0	—

资料来源：1. 森林面积变化资料来自：施昆山．当代世界林业．中国林业出版社，2001

2. 耕地面积变化资料来自：聂振邦．世界主要国家粮食概况．中国物价出版社，2003

1990～1995年，发展中国家的森林面积呈现减少的趋势，而发达国家却呈现增加的趋势。根据联合国粮农组织调查统计，1990～1995年的5年时间里，发展中国家中的印度尼西亚、马来西亚、菲律宾、泰国等国家森林面积大量减少，其中印度尼西亚年均减少108.4万 hm^2，马来西亚年均减少40.0万 hm^2。1990～1995年，发达国家中的英国、法国、美国、加拿大等国家的森林面积却大量增加，其中美国年均增加58.9万 hm^2，加拿大和法国年均增加分别为17.5万 hm^2 和16.1万 hm^2。与年均增减趋势相对应，发展中国家在森林面积减少的同时耕地面积却在增加；与此相反，发达国家在森林面积增加的同时耕地面积却在减少。

森林采伐的主要目的是把林地转变为农业用地，全球的森林采伐量一直保持着惊人的比率，每年大约为 1 300 万 hm^2。同时，主要集中在北半球的植树造林、景观恢复和森林的自然扩展在很大程度上抵消了森林面积的净减少量。2000 ~ 2005 年全球的森林面积净减少量（森林采伐面积减去植树造林的面积）估计为每年 730 万 hm^2，大约相当于塞拉利昂或巴拿马的国土面积。2005 年全球森林覆盖面积估计占土地总面积的 30. 2%，比 2000 年的 30. 5% 和 1990 年的 31. 2% 略有下降。森林覆盖率减少的速度似乎略微有所减缓，有些地区呈现出持平甚至净增加的状况。

尽管拉丁美洲和加勒比海地区仍然占据全球最高的覆盖率，这一地区森林覆盖率的减少却十分显著：从 1990 年的 49. 2% 下降到 2005 年的 45. 8%。非洲的森林覆盖率同样也持续下降，2005 年的森林覆盖率为 21. 4%，低于 1990 年的 23. 6%。欧洲和北美洲的森林覆盖率在此期间持续适度增加，而亚太地区以及西亚地区的森林覆盖率基本没有什么变化（图 1-1）。

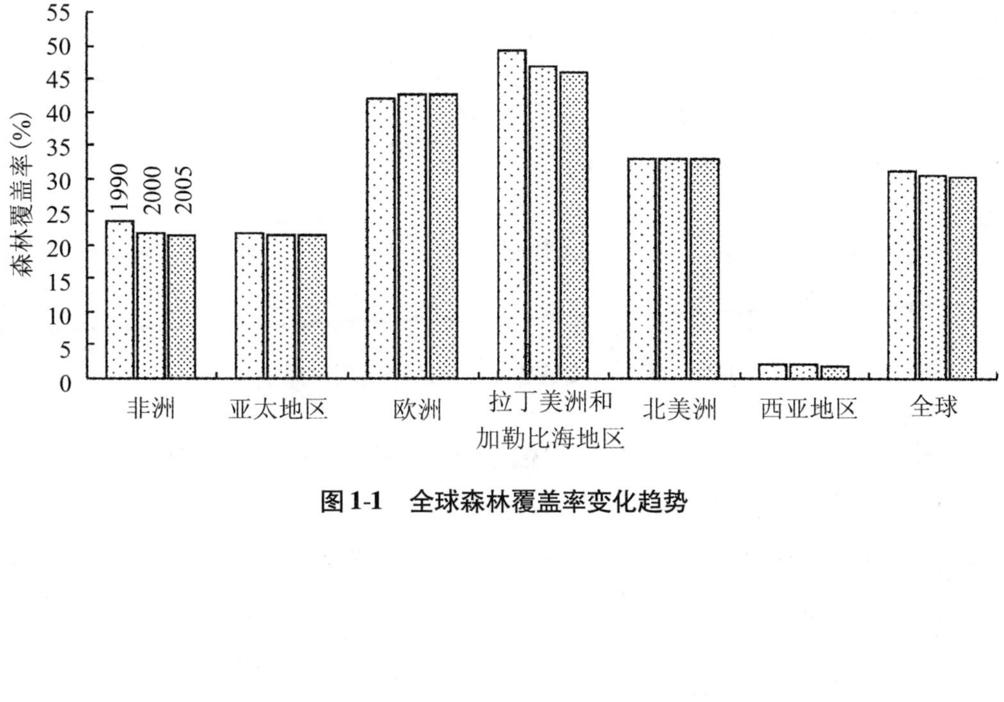

图 1-1　全球森林覆盖率变化趋势

三、林业土地问题的理论模型

（一）工业化之前林业土地问题的理论模型

工业化之前林业的土地问题，可以用图 1-2 来表示。在这里，出于模型表述技术的考虑，我们提出两个假设。第一个假设是：耕地的增加和林地的减少有着互为因果关系，且增减数量相等。这种假设虽然有可能与现实不完全相符，但并不影响结论的正确性。第二个假设是：单位面积耕地的粮食产量并不随时间的改变而改变。在工业化之前，农业技术的发展速度十分缓慢，所以这一假设与现实情况的相似性很强。

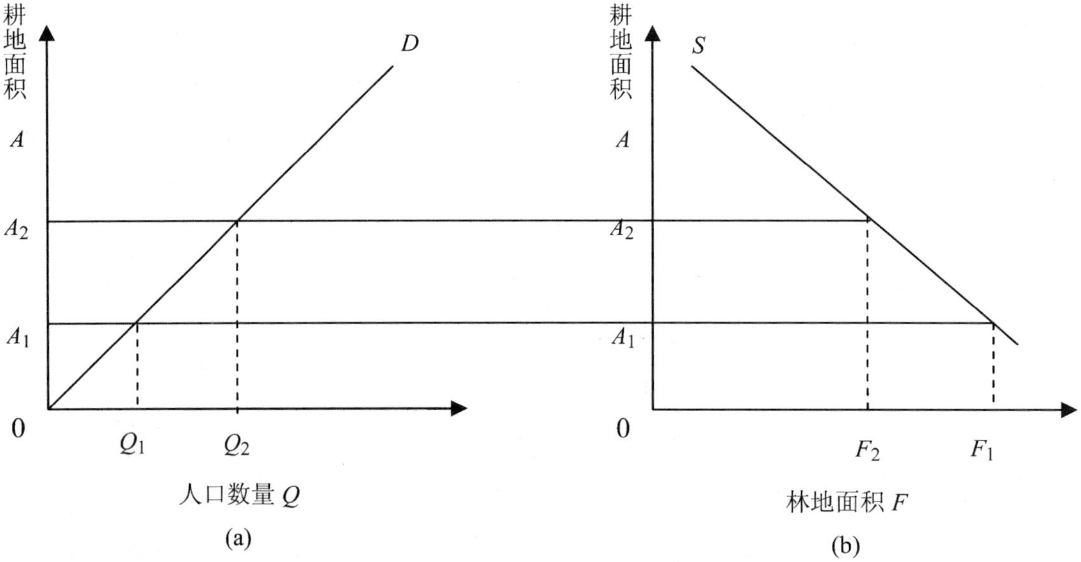

图 1-2　工业化之前林业土地问题的理论模型

在图 1-2（a）中，横坐标表示人口数量 Q，纵坐标表示耕地面积 A，曲线 D 表示人口数量和耕地面积的相互关系。在图 1-2 中，图(b)的纵坐标表示与图(a)相对应的耕地面积，横坐标表示林地面积，曲线 S 表示耕地面积和林地面积的相互关系。在图 1-2（a）中，由于人口数量的增加，维持生存的粮食需求也随之增加，在不能依靠技术进步提高单位面积产量的情况下，由于粮食需求必然导致耕地的引致需求。在初期，人口数量为 Q_1 时，耕地的需求量为 A_1，当人口的数量上升为 Q_2 时，耕地的需求量上升为 A_2。此时，耕地需求的增加将导致林地的开垦。这样，当耕地的需求量为 A_1 时，林地面积维持在 F_1 水平，当耕地的需求量上升为 A_2 时，林地面积将下降为 F_2。根据第一个假设条件，曲线 D 和曲线 S 的斜率的绝对值相等，因此，$A_2 - A_1 = F_1 - F_2$，耕地需求量的增加值刚好与林地的减少值相等。

（二）工业化初期林业土地问题的理论模型

因为农产品市场中有众多而且零散的生产者和消费者，且农产品的差别性较少，因此，工业化初期发展中国家的粮食问题，可以用图 1-3 所示的马歇尔的局部市场均衡模型来表示。

在图 1-3（a）中，D_0 和 D_1 分别表示初期和比较期的农产品需求曲线，S_0 和 S_1 表示相应时期的供给曲线。在初期，市场供需均衡点是 A 点，此时均衡价格为 P_0 均衡数量为 Q_0。而到了比较期，由于经济发展和人口、收入等市场条件的变化，农产品市场供需的均衡点移至 B 点，此时市场均衡价格和均衡数量也变为 P_1 和 Q_1。为反映发展中国家食品需求增长迅速、农业技术进步缓慢的现实，图中将需求曲线的右方位移幅度表示的较大，而供给曲线的右移幅度较小，以此粮食需求的增长快于粮食供给的增长。结果，农产品的市场均衡价格将相应上升。

因此，如果仅仅依靠市场机制，那么在粮食供给增长落后于需求增长的发展中国家，农产品价格趋于上升，农业收入也呈增长趋势。然而，处于工业化初期发展中国家的经济政策却使上述市场调节未能出现。关于这一问题我们可以用图 1-3(b)来加以说明。在该图中，以代表现代产业的工业部门为对象，并以此分析该部门劳动供求关系的变化。图中横坐标为工业部门的劳动雇佣量，纵坐标表示名义工资率。初期和比较期的劳动需求曲线分别表示为向右下方倾斜的 DL_0 和 DL_1。劳动需求是一种派生需求，在完全竞争和资本投入一定的情况下，追求利润最大化企业的劳动需求曲线就是劳动的边际收益曲线，曲线上的任何一点，都反映了在已有雇佣劳动数量的基础上，企业追加雇佣 1 个单位的劳动所能带来的

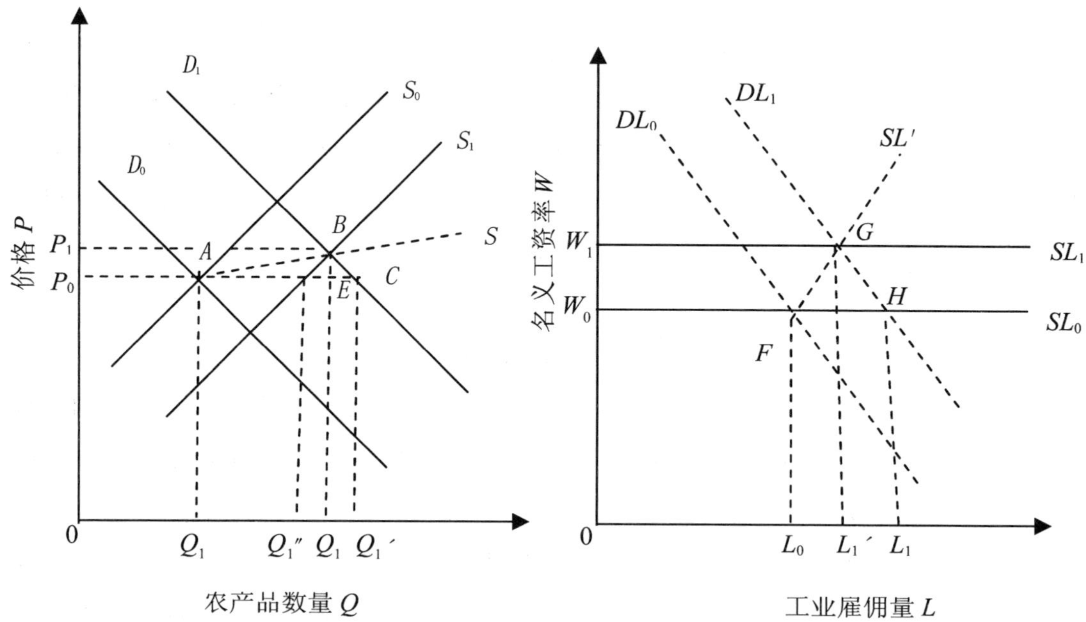

(a) (b)

图 1-3　工业化初期发展中国家粮食问题的理论模型

（资料来源：速水佑次郎. 农业经济论. 中国农业出版社，2003）

产值增加额。在某一给定雇佣量的条件下，劳动的边际收益决定于劳动以外的资本等其他生产要素的投入和生产技术水平。如果假定工业技术进步是通过新的资本投入实现的，那么劳动需求曲线从 DL_0 移至 DL_1（工资一定时雇佣增量），也可以认为是资本投入的增加引起的。

在图 1-3（b）中，劳动需求曲线与通常的需求曲线一样向右下方倾斜，而供给曲线却是一条水平的直线。这一供给曲线实际上意味着，在低收入国家，劳动供给的弹性很大，工业部门即使丝毫不提高工资水平，也会有无限多的劳动力可供雇佣。对工业等现代产业部门的劳动供给具有无限弹性的设想，乃是以李嘉图为首的英国古典学派、马克思学派以及继承了古典学派传统构建了二元经济发展模型的刘易斯等所共有的。虽然他们之间对产生无限弹性的劳动供给机制的理解不同，但是无论哪一种模型都假定工业部门在生存工资（subsistence wage）水平下可以获得无限多的劳动供给。

所谓生存工资即是根据所处社会的生存习惯，劳动者及其家庭成员维持生存和人口再生产必需的最低工资水平。换句话说，生存工资就是劳动者维持生存所必需的生活费用。在低收入阶段，它的水准很大程度上取决于粮食的价格。正因为如此，在图1-3(b)中初期的劳动供给曲线 SL_0 是一条与生存工资 W_0 高度相等的水平曲线，且初期的生存工资 W_0 与图1-3(a)中的农产品价格 P_0 相对应。如果农产品需求曲线的位移速度快于其供给曲线的位移从而导致粮食等农产品价格趋于上升的话，那么劳动者家庭的生活费用就会增加，而在名义工资保持不变的情况下，他们将无法应付生活费用的增加。于是，当农产品价格上升为 P_1 时，名义工资将从 W_0 提升为 W_1。这样，高度为 W_1 的水平线 SL_1 就成了比较期的劳动供给曲线。这种由粮食价格上涨而引起的名义工资上升，对发展中国家工业化目标会产生什么样的影响呢?

图1-3（b)显示，在初期，工业部门以 W_0 的工资水平雇佣了 L_0 的劳动，则劳动工资成本总额为面积 $FL_0 0\ W_0$，而工业总产值等于从0到 L_0 之间劳动需求曲线以下部分的面积。因此，初期工业利润就等于由 DL_0、SL_0 和纵坐标围成的面积。如果该利润全部用于工业再投资，那么随着工业资本量的增加，工业部门的劳动需求曲线将从初期的 DL_0 移至比较期的 DL_1。在这一时期，如果粮食价格不上升，工资水平保持在 W_0，那么比较期将在 H 点实现均衡。这时，工业利润等于由 SL_0、DL_1 和纵坐标围成的面积。与初期相比，工业利润增大。但是，如果粮食价格上涨导致劳动供给曲线从 SL_0 向上移动到 SL_1，那么，比较期的均衡点将移动到 G 点。在这种情况下，与粮食价格不上升时相比，工业雇佣量减少 L_1L_1'，利润减少面积 GHW_0W_1。因此，即使初期利润再投资于工业，也不能保证下一期的利润一定能够与资本积累同比例地增长。如果由于粮食价格上涨而使工资水平上升过快，工业利润甚至还有可能绝对下降。而工业利润下降将会降低企业对工业投资的积极性，最终引起工业化及整个国民经济的停滞。

恩格尔系数越大，粮食价格的上涨对工资上升的影响也就越大。因此，在经济越不发达、收入水平越低的国家，农产品价格上涨对工业化的影响越大。在这种情况下，工业化初期的发展中国家普遍采取了压低农产品价格的做法。

工业化初期经济落后的发展中国家在解决粮食问题时的最终方式与未进入工业化国家解决因生存而产生的粮食问题的最终方式有着很大程度的相似，即都通过将林地转化为耕地的做法来缓解粮食的供需紧张状况。

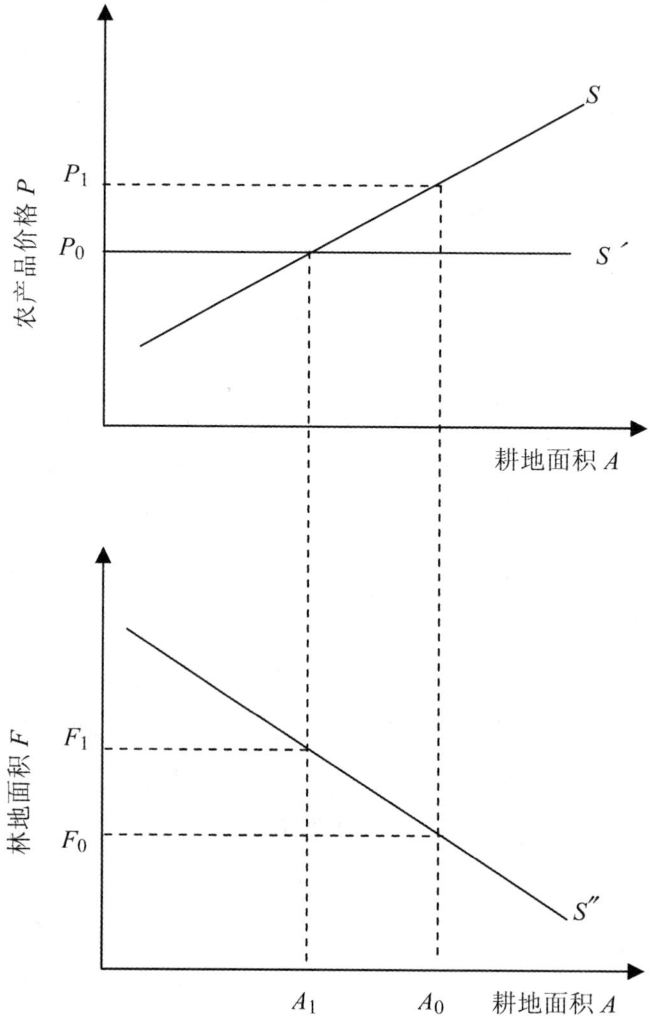

图 1-4　工业化初期林业土地问题模型

在图 1-2 中我们可以清楚地看出，单纯的人口增加导致耕地需求的上升。为维持生存，耕地需求的上升导致开垦林地的行为，进而导致林地面积的减少。而在工业化初期的发展中国家，由于人口、收入等因素导致粮食等农产品需求上涨的速度快于其供给的速度，在市场调节下，粮食等农产品的价格将上升(图 1-3)，但为保证工业劳动者的生存工资保持在 W_0 水平，政府将在政策上把农产品价格限制在 P_0 水平。这一政策对林业将产生什么样的影响？在市场调节情况下，价格上升致 P_1，这将导致农业收入增加。图 1-4 表明，在不考虑农业技术的情况下，收入增加将导致农产品供给的动力增强，进而导致耕地面积供给由 A_1 增加到 A_0。但是，政府为保证工业劳动者的生存工资保持在 W_0 水平，粮食等农产品的价格将被制在 P_0 水平，耕地的供给曲线将是一条高度为 P_0，并平行于横轴的一条水平直线 S'，此时，耕地面积也由 A_1 增加到 A_0。显然，这种增加不是粮食等农产品价格引导的结果，而是由于政府的某种激励性政策而导致的结果。由于农户通过大面积的林木采伐来增加农作物耕作面积的做法可以附带来解决农户薪材和房屋建材等问题，而且对于这些薪材和建材，政府又采用允许农户无偿或低价占有的做法。因此，当农产品的供需矛盾增加而导致耕地需求上升时，开垦林地来缓解耕地的主要矛盾就成了主要做法。图 1-4 显示，当耕地需求由 A_1 增加到 A_0 时，开垦林地的做法导致林地的面积由 F_1 减少到 F_0。

四、林业的土地问题与农业积累

事实上，工业化初期发展中国家的粮食问题和林业的土地问题是相互作用的，即在粮食问题导致林地面积减少的同时，林业也同时为农业生产提供了积累。这一问题可以用垄断市场的短期均衡模型来加以说明(图 1-5)。

采用垄断市场的短期均衡模型来说明林业为农业生产提供积累，是基于这样的假设，即转换为耕地的林地均来自于国有林。这样，林业部门对耕地的供给就具有了垄断的特征，同时，木材等林产品的供给也同样具有了垄断的特征。这一假设与现实情况基本相符。从现实的情况来看，私有林占较大比例的国家主要是芬兰、日本、瑞典、德国、法国、奥地利、美国和加拿大等发达国家，而经济水平落后的发展中国家的私有林比例较小，而且，其私有林的规模较小。例如在中国，从新中国成立到1984年这一时期，其私有林仅限于农户房前屋后自留田里的林木。因此，上述假设和现实基本相符。

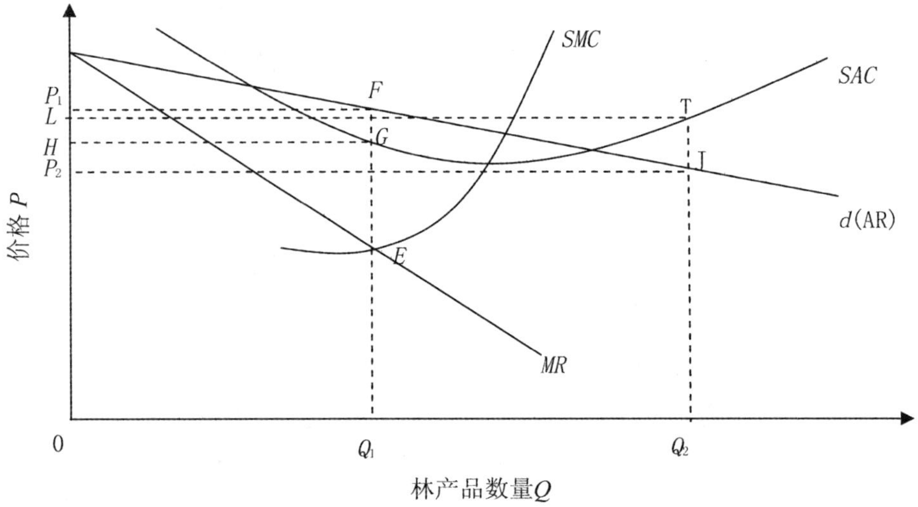

图1-5　粮食问题阶段林业对农业提供原始积累的理论模型

在图1-5中，横坐标表示林产品的数量，纵坐标表示林产品的价格。在市场经济中，林业部门为获得最大利润，也必须遵循 $MR=MC$ 的原则。由于森林本身的特性，林业部门无法在短期内调整其不变要素的投入量，林业部门是在既定生产规模下通过对产量和价格的同时调整，来实现 $MR=SMC$ 的利润最大化原则的。这样，林业部门将产量和价格分别调整到 Q_1 和 P_1 的水平。在均衡点 E 上，林业部门的平均收益为 FQ_1，平均成本为 GQ_1，平均收益大于平均成本，林业部门获得的总利润为面积 $FGHP_1$。但是，发展中国家出于其工业化政策，将粮食价格限定在较低水平。这样，政府只有通过压低或允许农户无偿占有林产品的做法产生激励，将林地转化为耕地。如果政府将林产品的价格降低为 P_2 水平，单位林产品的平均收益将为 Q_2J，而平均成本为 Q_2T，$Q_2J<Q_2T$，林业部门将亏损，其亏损总额为面积 $LTJP_2$。这一面积加上市场调节情况下的面积 $FGHP_1$，就是林业部门为农业部门提供的资本积累。

上述林业部门为农业部门提供的资本积累，事实上是在发展中国家实行工业化优先政策进而侵占农业利益的情况下，由林业部门对农业部门进行经济补偿。这一补偿部分弥补了农业部门被工业侵占的利益，同时也对林地转化为耕地的行为起到了激励作用。

第二节　农村相对贫困阶段林业的土地问题

一、经济发展中的农村相对贫困问题

与工业化初期低收入阶段的粮食问题相比，当经济进入中等收入阶段时，农村所面临的将是贫困问题。然而，中等收入阶段的贫困问题并非绝对贫困问题。与低收入阶段相比，农民经济上的贫困程度比起中等收入国家来要严重得多，但低收入阶段国家除小部分特殊阶层外，绝大多数人口都很贫穷。因此，包括农民在内，很少有人对农民的贫困状况感到奇怪。只有当国家度过了低收入贫困时期，进入了中等收入阶段时，由于工商业的发展，城市中形成了一批已经摆脱绝对贫困的人群，与他们相比，依然没有摆脱绝对贫困的农民的生活才显得格外贫穷。我们将这一阶段称之为农村相对贫困阶段。

这种相对贫困问题，与工业化过程中发展中国家经济结构的二元化现象密切相关。所谓二元经济结构是指：一方面存在着一批资本密集程度很高、并采用现代技术的大型企业；另一方面存在着众多主要依赖劳动密集型传统技术的中小企业，两者之间劳动生产率和工资水平的差距很大，而且显著的工资差距之所以长期存在，是因为学历、技术熟练程度、制度等原因，大企业和小企业之间的劳动力转移受到严格限制。

如果说支撑这种二元经济结构的底层部分是一些分散的小企业的话，那么为小企业提供劳动力，充当劳动力“蓄水池”作用的不是别的，正是农业部门。不仅对城市工商业来说，收入较低、生活困难的农民是一个无限的廉价劳动供给源，而且对整个国民经济而言，农业在劳动供给方面也起到了缓冲装置的作用。在实

行雇佣终身制和有着工会组织的大企业，即使遇到经济不景气的困境，要大批裁减员工也是十分困难的，而改变对外的用工合同则很容易。而且，由于农产品供给价格弹性和需求价格弹性较小，一旦需求减少，农产品价格下降的幅度会很大。因此，在经济不景气的情况下，一方面农业收入本身可能大幅度减少，另一方面农民工大量返乡使农村人口的贫困问题变得更加严重。

由于二元经济结构，农业与非农业、农村与城市之间的经济差距将处于扩大阶段。这是因为：一方面对于依靠廉价劳动的劳动密集型企业而言，提高农产品价格意味着工资成本的上升，这可能动摇这类企业的经营基础；另一方面，按照刘易斯的观点，由于人口的原因，农业劳动力的边际生产力即使不为零，也会小于按习惯决定的制度工资。这样，对于农村剩余劳动力，工业雇佣者只要支付制度工资，就会有无限多的劳动力从农村转移出来。因此，农民的收入在二元经济结构还在发展的阶段，其提升的空间受到了较为严格的限制。

应该指出的是，在二元经济结构的发展阶段，与以大企业职工为代表的城市人群相比，占人口总数一半以上的农民的生活贫困状况就显得十分突出，社会贫富的两极分化开始加剧，社会稳定受到威胁。因此，政府开始采取农产品价格支持和其他政策性补贴等农业保护政策，但同时更重视保护和培育现代化大型企业，因而很容易采取一些促进二元经济结构、降低农民相对收入的政策。在这一阶段，政府面临两个课题：一是如何加速工业化进程？二是如何有效地保护农产品生产并进而缓解农村相对贫困带来的社会矛盾？

二、相对贫困阶段林业的土地问题

当农村处于相对贫困阶段，由于技术等原因，粮食等农产品的生产效率较之以往时期得以提高，粮食等农产品的供给能力增强，再加上对人口再生产限制等因素，那种因人口增长并进而因单纯的生存原因导致的粮食问题已基本消失。因此，那种工业化之前因粮食问题而导致的林业土地问题也已不复存在。

但是在二元经济结构的发展中是否还存在工业化初期发展中国家的那种林业的土地问题？关于这一问题，必须结合这两个经济发展阶段的经济特征和政策特征才能有效回答。

在工业化初期，低经济水平的发展中国家在优先保证工业的政策框架下，对粮食等农产品的价格采取了低价格政策，其价格低于市场的均衡价格。这一政策导致带有农业积累功能的林业土地问题。而在农村相对贫困阶段，依然出现了林业的土地问题，即由于经济的发展，森林面积进一步减少。但是，在二元经济结构中林业土地问题产生的原因与工业化初期发展中国家林业土地问题产生的原因有所不同。

在农村相对贫困阶段，由于二元经济结构特征，政府一方面在继续推行工业优先政策的同时，并且在政策上向更广泛的非农产业（这里的非农产业不包括林业，文中的"非农产业"均是这一含义）倾斜；另一方面，虽然如何提供廉价农产品的政策课题依然存在，但政府也同时注意到了上述政策导致的农业与非农业、农村和城市之间的收入差别，以及这种差别所造成的社会矛盾。在这种情况下，农产品价格支持、农业补贴等农业保护政策开始实行。

政府推行的上述两方面政策都会产生林业的土地问题。首先，政府推行的包括工业在内的非农产业优先发展政策，在使这些产业迅速发展的同时，也消耗了巨大的以木材为主的林产品，从而使林地面积大量减少，这一减少无论在数量还是在速度上都是惊人的。其次，在政府实施农产品价格支持、部分放开农产品市场以及实施农业补贴等农业保护政策的情况下，农产品价格上升，而生产成本却在下降，农民的收入有所增加，农产品的供给动力增强。在这种情况下，农民有两种途径增加农产品的数量，一是通过农业的技术进步来增加农产品数量，二是通过扩张耕地面积来增加农产品数量。但前者必须要经历一个缓慢的过程，这对于具有迫切增收愿望的农民来说，显然不是一个合理的选择（这种不合理性至少在短期内是存在的）。因此，第二种途径，即通过扩张耕地面积来增加农产品数量就又成了农民的主要做法。而耕地面积增加的主要来源依然是林地，这其中的原因更多的是林业的农业积累功能对林地转化为农地产生了激励作用。因此，这一阶段因农业活动产生的林业土地问题是农业保护政策和林业的农业积累功能双重激励的结果。

显然，我们在农村相对贫困阶段所说的林业土地问题，是在推行非农产业优先政策和农业保护政策的双重背景下产生的林业土地问题。应该指出的是，在二元经济结构的发展过程中，由于工业用材需求的上升和森林资源的迅速减少，木材的供需矛盾加大，政府对森林资源的管制会不断加强，在粮食问题阶段那种允许无偿或低价侵占林地的做法可能会有所改变，林地转化为耕地的制度成本会不断上升。因此，这一阶段林地转化为耕地的数量和速度较之粮食问题阶段都将有所降低。

三、林业的土地问题与双重原始积累

在推行非农产业优先政策和农业保护政策的双重背景下产生的林业土地问题对经济发展的影响与工业化初期发展中国家林业土地问题的影响有着某种相似性，即这两个时期的林业土地问题都有着某种程度上的资本积累功能。但是，这一阶段的积累无论是在其产生的动因，还是在提供积累的经济领域，以及为各经济领域提供积累的程度都有所差别。

从积累产生的动因来看，工业化初期发展中国家林业土地问题对农业提供的资本积累，是在政府对粮食等农产品限价的情况下，政府为解决粮食问题而对农业的一种经济补偿。而相对贫困阶段林业土地问题对农业提供的资本积累，是价格支持等农业保护政策激励的结果；从提供积累的经济领域来看，虽然工业化初期发展中国家林业通过对农业的补偿间接地对工业提供了资本积累，但其直接提供积累的经济领域主要是农业。而在相对贫困阶段，由林业直接提供资本积累的领域除农业以外，还有工业等其他非农产业；从为各经济领域提供积累的程度来看，由于工业化初期发展中国家允许低价甚至无偿占用林地，林业对农业的资本积累功能很强，而在相对贫困阶段，由于工业用材需求的上升和森林资源的迅速减少，木材的供需矛盾加大，价格上升，而且政府对森林资源的管制也不断加强。因此，林地转化为耕地的经济成本和制度成本不断上升，林业对农业的资本积累功能开始减弱。在这一阶段，为支持工业等非农产业的发展，政府通过建立垄断性收购组织，低价获取木材等林业资源，林业开始为工业直接提供资本积累。

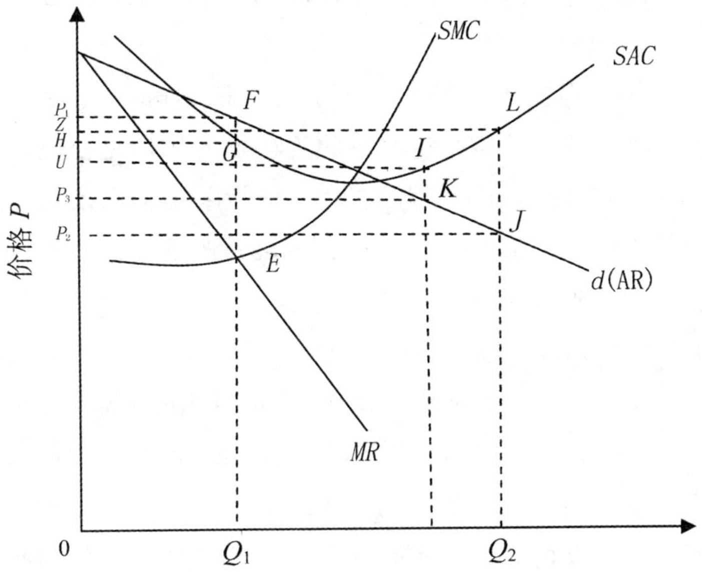

（a）农业积累功能的减弱

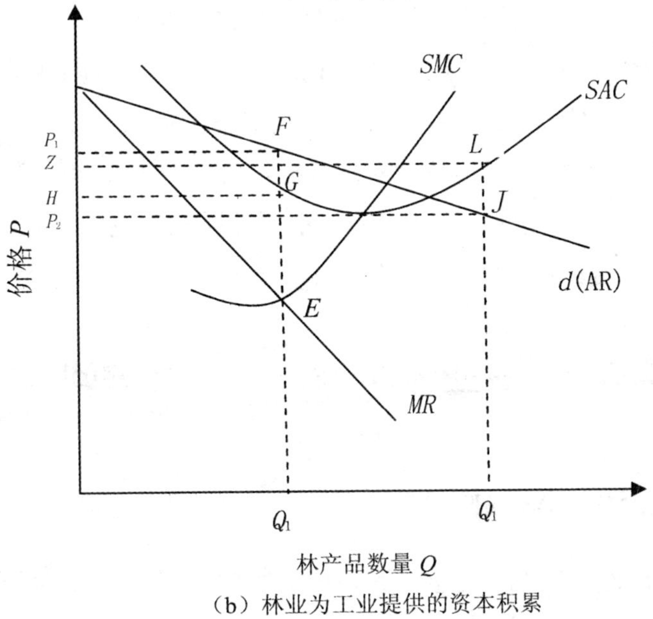

（b）林业为工业提供的资本积累

图 1-6　相对贫困阶段林业的双重积累模型

在这一阶段，林业的资本积累功能开始由农业为主向以工业为主的非农业产业转换。

相对贫困阶段由林业土地问题所产生的资本积累可以用图 1-6 来加以分析。与粮食问题阶段相似，我们假定无论是转化为耕地的林地还是工业等非农业行业使用的林产品都是国有林提供的，因此，我们依然采用垄断市场的短期均衡模型来分析这一问题。在图 1-6(a)中，处于粮食问题阶段的政府为补偿农产品限价侵占的农业利益，将林产品的价格降低为 P_2 水平，单位林产品的平均收益将为 Q_2J，而其平均成本为 Q_2L。这样，$Q_2J < Q_2L$，林业部门将亏损，其亏损总额为面积 LJP_2Z。这一面积加上市场调节情况下按照 $MR = SMC$ 原则的盈利面积 $FGHP_1$，就是林业部门为农业部门提供的资本积累。而在相对贫困阶段，由于工业用木材资源需求的上升和森林资源的迅速减少，木材的供需矛盾加大，价格上升，而且政府对森林资源的管制也不断加强，因此，林地转化为耕地的经济成本和制度成本上升。在这种情况下，木材等林产品的价格由 P_2 上升为 P_3，林业部门的亏损面积减少为面积 $UIKP_3$，林业部门为农业部门提供的资本积累变为 $FGHP_1$ 和 $UIKP_3$ 两个矩形面积相加之和，显然，这小于粮食问题阶段林业部门为农业部门提供的资本积累。在图 1-6(b)中，假定在工业等非农产业优先的政策框架下，林业部门在零利润情况下提供木材等林产品，这样，单位林产品的价格和其平均成本相等，林业部门为工业等非农部门提供的资本积累即为市场调节情况下按照 $MR = SMC$ 原则的盈利面积 $FGHP_1$。

第三节　农业调整阶段林业的土地问题

一、农业发展中的农业调整问题

与其他国家相比，富裕的发达国家在度过粮食问题贫困阶段所面临的农业问题，有两个方面的特征：一方面，从发达国家走过的路程来看，他们在解决粮食问题的过程中，农业技术已经高度发达，农业基础设施已经相当完备。因此，发达国家的农业生产率迅速提高，粮食等农产品的供给能力大幅度加强。另一方面，与发展中国家相比，决定粮食需求移动的人口和收入两个因素也在变化。在人口增长方面，1960～1998年的平均水平来看，中等收入国家的人口增长率是发达国家的2.2倍，低收入国家则是其2.6倍，但在这期间，发达国家的人口出生率却大幅度下降，其下降速度大大超过了死亡率的降低速度，因此人口逐渐趋于零增长。从收入水平来看，由于发达国家人均收入水平很高，反映收入变化对粮食需求影响效果的收入弹性会很小。因此，随着收入水平的提高，粮食需求量会逐渐趋于饱和。综合这两个方面的情况，发达国家的粮食问题已经解决。

发达国家农业问题上述两方面的特征表明，如果相应于农业生产率的提高，生产要素从需求已经饱和的粮食生产部门转移到需求还在扩大的其他部门，农产品的过剩以及与其他部门相比的报酬率下降也不至于发生。但问题的症结是，农业资源中的一大部分，如大部分的土地、灌溉排水等基础设施只能用于农业及生产特征相似的产业(如林业)，不能用于其他非农产业。而且，像劳动力这样可以转移的生产要素，由于其人力资本的价值主要体现在对农业生产的熟练程度，离开农业从事其他行业时，就可能意味着这种人力资本的价值为零，这无疑对农民来说是一大损失。因此，如果农业与其他部门之间没有足够大的收入差距，农民是不会轻易离开农业的。反之，如果劳动力的部门转移得到促进，城乡人口分布的急剧变化也会带来农村过疏、城市过密等负面效应。

综合上述表明，发达国家由于农业技术的高度发达，在粮食问题已经解决并度过相对贫困阶段之后，面临的是农产品过剩以及由此带来的与其他非农业部门相比边际报酬率下降这一问题。这一问题实质上是部门之间产品供需增长速度的差异引起的不均衡，需要通过生产要素在产业之间重新配置来予以解决，这和一般意义上产业结构调整并无本质上的差别。因此，有的经济学家将发达国家面临的农业问题称之为农业调整问题。

二、农业调整与林业土地问题的反向变化

单纯地从农业发展角度来看，与粮食问题和相对贫困问题相似，农业调整问

题的出现同样对林业产生了强烈的影响。但是这一影响的结果却与前两个农业发展阶段截然相反。

如前文所述，发达国家由于农业技术的高度发达，在粮食问题已经解决并度过相对贫困阶段之后，面临的是农产品过剩以及由此带来的与其他非农业部门相比边际报酬率下降这一问题。这一问题的出现，对林业至少产生了以下两个方面的影响：

首先，由于发达国家农产品的过剩并由此带来的农业生产的边际报酬率下降，使农业生产要素投入的动力减弱，这其中包括耕地这一最基本的农业生产要素。因此，在农业调整阶段，不会再出现粮食问题和相对贫困问题阶段所出现的将林地转化为耕地这类林业土地问题。

其次，在农业调整阶段，农业生产的边际报酬率下降是由于农业生产要素投入过多引起的。如果不及时减少农业投入，粮食供给超过需求，这将导致农产品的价格下降，从而引起农民的收入减少。因此，如果相应于农业生产率的提高，生产要素从需求已经饱和的食品生产部门转移到需求还在扩大的其他部门，农产品的供给过剩以及与其他部门相比的边际报酬率下降问题就会解决。但详细分析我们会发现，农业与各非农产业部门之间生产要素移动的流畅程度并不均衡。而恰恰是这种生产要素移动流畅程度的不均衡，才导致了农业调整阶段林业新的问题出现，即和以往林地转化为农地的情况相反，在农业调整阶段，农地开始向林地转化。为了更好地对这一问题进行解释，我们将非农产业部门划分为林业和林业以外的其他非农产业部门两部分来加以说明。

就大部分林业以外的其他非农业生产部门（如制造业、商业、信息业等）而言，由于其生产经营本身的特征，对生产要素都有其特定的要求。因此，农业生产要素向这些部门的流动具有诸多的障碍。这些障碍包括：一是非劳动生产要素的固定性。这些非劳动生产要素主要指排水灌溉等农田基础设施。这些基础设施一旦修建完成，就很难用于林业以外的其他非农业生产部门。二是农业人力资本的局限性。与生产过程相对复杂的其他行业相比，农业的人力资本更多体现在对农业生产的熟练程度，而知识以及以必要的知识水平为支撑的相对复杂的生产技能却十分缺乏，这在中年以上的农民那里体现得更为明显。这种人力资本的局限性，显然会限制农业劳动的流动。三是城乡发展制度的限制性。制造业、商业、信息产业等非农行业大多集中于城市，这在世界各国几乎都是如此。如果在城乡收入差距存在的情况下，政府不限制农业劳动力的部门转移，反而采取一些促进措施，就很有可能使城乡人口分布发生变化，这种变化有可能导致农村人口过疏、城市人口过密等负面效应。因此，政府总是在不同的时期采取不同程度的限制城乡人口流动的政策，以防止这种情况发生。这种城乡发展制度的限制性，也对农业劳动力的转移起到了阻碍作用。

但是，与上述非农业生产部门相比，林业部门在吸纳农业生产要素的过程中却有着天然的优势。这些优势包括：首先，为防止农产品过剩、农业边际报酬率下降的情况发生，如果采取缩小农业的生产规模而扩大林业规模的方式，即将农地转化为林地，那么排水灌溉等农田基础设施仍然可以发挥作用，这些非劳动农业生产要素就可以顺利地转化为林业生产要素。其次，农业生产活动和林业生产活动有着很多相似性，而且很多农林活动在农村往往并行发生。因此，劳动要素由农业部门向林业部门流动并不存在知识和生产技能的障碍，在农业劳动转移到林业部门之后，其人力资本的价值依然可以得到很好的体现。再次，由于林业部门和农业部门都处于乡村，所以劳动力由农业部门向林业部门的流动并不存在制度障碍。

上述农业与各非农业部门之间的生产要素移动流畅程度的不均衡表明，在农产品过剩、农业生产边际报酬率下降的情况下，农业生产要素向林业部门转移在经济上存在着合理性。这种经济上的合理性再加上政府政策上的引导，应该是农业调整阶段新的林业土地问题——由农地开始向林地转化的经济原因。最能对这一结论提供实证的案例莫过于美国、英国、法国等欧洲国家的退耕还林工程。

20 世纪 20 年代末，随着泡沫经济的破灭和股市的崩溃，美国经济出现了严重衰退，农产品过剩，价格下跌，农业生产极其艰难，大批农场相继破产。面对农业经济危机，美国政府意识到调整产业结构的迫切性，开始了退耕还林计划。美国退耕还林的政策措施主要有三种：一是政府收购退耕。20 世纪 30 年代初，美国纽约州制定了《休依特法案》。该法案的主要内容是：由政府投资，收购破产的农场，在荒芜的耕地上植树造林、封山育林，建立产权属于政府的林场，创造就业机会，将失业的农民吸纳为林场工人。按照这一法案，当时政府购买了逾40万hm^2的土地，进行退耕还林。二是农场主自愿退耕计划。这一计划的主要目的是通过各种鼓励政策引导农场主把一部分耕地退出生产，用于土壤保护。第一个计划为1956年出台的土壤银行计划。该计划的具体做法是：农场主将耕地存入土壤银行，银行付给一定的补助，同时对退耕的农场主给予农产品价格补贴。第二个计划是1961年制定的紧急饲料谷物计划。该计划直接目的是减少饲料谷物的库存和产量。其做法是：农场主在停耕至少20%耕地的情况下，可从政府取得停耕土地产量50%的现金或实物补助。如果停耕土地超过20%，政府的补偿比例可提高到60%。第三个计划是1965年实施的有偿转耕计划，即要求政府计划的参加者以无偿停耕一定比例的土地为条件，换取计划的各种好处，超比例退耕者政府给予一定的补贴。上述三个计划都是在农场主自愿的基础实施的。据统计，1959~1968年的10年间，仅土壤银行计划退耕地每年就有445万~1 174万hm^2。三是退耕保护计划。1985年美国政府实施"保护计划"。主要内容是对易发生土壤侵蚀耕地实行为期10年的休耕或永久性退耕还林还草。作为补偿，农业部每年向退耕农户支付一定的补助。对于永久退耕还林还草者，一次性支付种植费用总额一半的补助。到1990年，美国已对易发生土壤侵蚀的47 777万hm^2耕地全部进行了退耕还林还草或休耕。

与美国相似，欧洲发达国家在实现工业化的同时，农产品生产也开始过剩，农业比较效益下降，农民弃耕现象严重。如英国2000年约有300万~ 400万hm^2农田无人耕种。在法国，由于农产品的大量过剩和价格下跌，农场主的经济收入减少，农村已经出现人烟稀少和土地荒芜现象。在这一背景下，欧洲出现了无计划自发式的退耕还林。1956~1983年，欧洲共同体国家农业用地减少了1 100万hm^2，占耕地面积的8%，森林覆盖面积则增加了15%。2000年欧盟国家已有1 200万~1 600万hm^2的耕地退耕还林，其中法国就达200万~300万hm^2。英国在自愿的基础上，进一步出台鼓励政策，即凡愿意长期退耕还林的可签署农林协议书，政府根据协议书支付给农户125英镑/hm^2的补偿金，为期30年。这一政策无疑对退耕还林起到了促进作用。

三、需求论对农业调整阶段林业问题解释的局限

以往对上述农业调整阶段出现的林业问题，往往是从社会经济需求的角度进行解释的。这种解释的基本内容是：随着社会经济的发展，人类对森林的需求开始发生变化。一方面，工业化程度的提高对木材的需求进一步扩大，与此同时，生活水平的上升使人类对森林环境安全的需求也与日俱增；另一方面，森林的供给能力和生态环境的质量却在进一步下降。这一社会、经济的现实情况，迫使林业必须寻求新的发展模式与途径，并出现了农业调整阶段的林业问题。

这种理论的局限性在于，如果森林环境安全的需求是森林得以恢复的唯一原因，那么我们就无法解释处于粮食问题和相对贫困问题阶段的发展中国家所出现的林业问题。联合国粮农组织1990年的世界森林资源检测报告表明，1981～1990年，森林破坏的40%发生在拉丁美洲，30%在亚太地区，30%在非洲。在上述期间拉丁美洲的32个国家每年损失森林730hm^2，年毁林率约为0.9%；而在非洲的西部和中部地区，年毁林率已分别比1980年的0.6%和0.7%增加了2倍多。也是在同一期间，这些国家的林草植被遭到破坏，生态功能衰退，水土流失加剧，土壤沙化严重，并出现了江河断流、湖泊干涸等现象。这种生态环境恶化与森林资源人为减少并存的现象表明，单纯的森林环境安全的需求并不能导致森林资源的恢复。

森林环境安全需求理论不但不能解释处于粮食问题和相对贫困问题阶段的发展中国家所出现的林业问题，也同样无法有效地解释处于农业调整阶段发达国家的林业问题。美国和欧洲国家的退耕还林实践表明，这一阶段耕地向林地的转化，是在农产品过剩、农业生产边际报酬率下降的情况下，农户或农场主为防止农产品价格下降所采取的行为，这一行为更多地符合私人理性。而森林环境安全属于公共物品，因此森林环境安全需求属于社会理性的需求，它不能导致农户或农场主将耕地转化为林地这一私人行为的发生。

事实上，发生在农业调整阶段的林业土地问题是三种因素共同作用的结果，即生态环境的恶化和森林资源的减少导致了对森林生态安全的需求，农产品供给的过剩奠定了森林资源恢复的物质基础，而生产要素由农业部门向林业部门移动的流畅性为森林资源的恢复创造了条件。这三个因素缺一不可，而且只有农业调整阶段才会同时具备这三个条件，正是这三个条件的同时存在，才会使生产要素由农业部门向林业部门移动这种私人理性行为与森林环境安全的社会理性需求相吻合。因此，农业调整阶段出现的林业问题存在着某种必然性。

第二章　林业发展中的资源问题理论

所谓林业发展中的资源问题，是指随着社会经济的发展，以木材为主的林产品的需求快速增加，而林产品的供给能力却不断下降，木材等林产品供需矛盾不断加剧而造成的森林资源短缺问题。一般认为，木材等林产品供需矛盾所造成的森林资源危机开始于近代工业革命，是伴随着工业化的进程而不断加剧的。这一观点虽然不能说是错误，但却不够全面。因为上述森林资源危机的观点，实际上是将工业对木材等林产品的需求看成了单一的原材料需求并进而建立在原材料供需矛盾基础上的。但通过详细分析我们会发现，工业化本身对林业的需求并不单纯是原料的需求，产生在工业化进程中的森林资源危机也不是由单纯的木材等原材料供求矛盾所造成的。要想很好地回答这一问题，必须对工业化进程中的经济特征及林业这一部门的作用进行详细研究。

应该指出的是，森林资源的含义十分广泛，按照通行的观点，森林资源是一个陆地生态系统内以乔木为主体的森林植物群落，它既包括林木，也包括林地以及林区野生的动物和林木以外的植物。但在经济发展中被人类经济活动主动且直接利用的森林资源主要是林木资源，所以，本书中的森林资源主要是指林木资源。

第一节　工业化过程中的资本积累与政策取向

一、工业化与经济发展

发达国家经济发展成功的基本标志是实现了工业化。自第二次世界大战结束以来，工业化已成为众多发展中国家竞相实施的大政方针和计划宏图，而且极少数发展中国家和地区已初步取得了成功的经验。工业化的基本经济特征可以概括为以下几点：①工业化首要的和本质的特征，就是以机器（包括之后的电脑等日益先进的工具形式）生产替代手工生产，是一场生产技术的革命，从而也是社会生产力的突破性变革；同时，它还包含着生产组织和经济结构各层次相应的调整和变动。②工业化引起且包含了整个国民经济的发展。因为基本生产要素组合的变化，不仅表现为制造业及农业生产机械的发明和应用，而且会引起现代工厂制度、市场结构及银行制度兴起等组织的变革。这种变化将对农业、制造业等生产结构产生巨大的影响。③规模报酬递增的产业或部门，无论是产值比重还是劳动力就业比重都将逐渐在国民经济中达到优势地位，规模报酬递减的产业或部门地位逐渐下降。④工业化必须能够引起整个经济体制或社会制度的变化，以及人们的生活观念和文化素质的变化。

一个国家在实现工业化的过程中，将使整个国民经济发生质的变化，这种变化主要包括以下几个方面：

首先，工业化的过程必然造成农业部门的相对萎缩，制造业和服务业等部门的相对扩大。这种产业结构的变化，必然带来产品结构的改变，而这一改变正好和由人均收入水平提高所带来的消费需求结构的变化相适应。这不但使人们的生活质量得以提高，而且反过来又对整个国民经济增长起到了促进作用。

其次，在工业化过程中，由于发展中国家农业部门大量剩余劳动的存在，其劳动生产要素的边际报酬率将不断降低，而工业部门劳动生产要素的边际报酬率将不断上升，从而农业剩余劳动将不断转移到工业部门，这有助于农业劳动生产率的提高，更有利于社会生产力的提高。

再次，由于中心——外围这种国际格局的存在，在国际商品交换中，发展中国家处于不利的地位。发展中国家用以出口的商品主要是初级产品，而发达国家出口的商品主要是深加工产品，且初级产品对深加工产品的价格比有不断下降的趋势，这将导致发展中国家的贸易条件不断恶化。而工业化水平的提高，将有利于扭转这一趋势，改变在国际贸易中的不利地位。

此外，由于生产资本品的工业部门联系效应较强，提升工业化水平，将有利于稀缺资本的合理配置，进而取得合乎愿望的经济发展效果。

上述工业化与经济发展的关系表明，一个国家从贫穷走向富裕，工业化是其必须选择的发展道路。也正是由于这一原因，世界上大多数发展中国家或迟或早地加入了工业化进程。工业化的基本经济特征表明，工业化对国家经济的影响是全方位的。而我们在这里所关注的问题是：工业化过程对林业到底产生了什么影响？尤其从森林资源利用的角度来看，工业化过程对林业产生的影响有哪些？这种关注使我们发现，工业化过程对森林资源的影响主要来自于两个方面，即技术进步和资本形成方式的演变。

二、技术进步及其对森林资源的双向影响

在工业化的不同阶段，技术进步的类型有所不同，从而构成了对森林资源的不同影响。

(一)工业化初期技术进步的特点及其对森林资源的影响

正像马克思强调的，工业化初期的技术进步，具有用资本替代劳动的取向。以曾经是英国工业革命时期主要问题的煤矿排水为例，如果靠人力用吊桶将水提出去，当桶的数量和提水工人的数量相等后，追加一个桶的边际产品将明显下降，大概接近于零。因此，追逐利润的企业家不会花钱为每个工人购买一个以上的桶。但假设用发动机驱动的水泵，它只要用 5 个操作人员就可以抽出 100 个工人用桶提出的水。如果这个泵的成本与 100 个桶相等，企业家就愿意把单位工人资本的投资增加 20 倍而不会担心边际生产率的下降。这样一种使用资本和节约劳动的倾向似乎是工业化初期机械化的特征。由于技术进步中的这种倾向，工资率的任何上扬都将被抑制在适宜的水平，所以尽管资本/劳动比率迅速上升，仍阻止不了资本报酬率的急剧下降，以致资本的收入份额增加了。

这种工业化初期技术进步的特征，导致了机械的使用，这同时又和低收入水平阶段的需求相适应。在工业化初期的低收入阶段，消费者对标准化商品的需求是大量的，即产品的同质性很强。因此，使用机械化进行大批量生产的有效性很高。这反过来又对机械的使用起到了刺激作用。这种技术特征和消费特征，在普遍表现为供给短缺的工业化初期，导致了至少在雇佣劳动数量不变情况下的机械

规模的扩张，进而使劳动生产率提高，商品的供给能力增强。这对森林资源将产生两方面的影响：一方面，机械化的使用带来生产能力的增强，导致了包括木材在内的原材料需求迅速上升，进而导致了林木等森林资源因大量消耗而锐减。虽然森林是可再生资源，但由于林木的生长周期很长，其供给能力具有天然的弱势，而且这种长周期的特征还会使人工造林的风险预期增加，进而弱化森林人工供给的动力。这样，在林木等森林资源的消耗量大于其生长量时，森林资源问题就由此产生了，而且消耗量和生长量之间的差距越大，森林资源问题就越严重。另一方面，如果单纯地是林业以外部门原木等材料需求的上升，并不足以导致森林资源的消耗量大于其生长量这一森林资源问题的加剧，因为原木等林产品生产能力的低下可能会减缓上述森林资源问题。但是以原木为主的林产品具有很强的同质性，适用于节约劳动的机械化生产，而且这种生产同样具有在工资率被抑制的情况下增加资本收入份额的功效。因此，在机械化被其他部门采用的同时，也被林业部门采用。林业机械的采用，无疑提高了原木等林产品的供给能力，同时也加剧了森林资源的短缺。

(二)诱致性技术创新和社会需求变化对森林资源的影响

发达国家的实践证明，在工业化初期因节约劳动型技术的广泛采用而造成的森林资源问题并没有延续下去，这主要是由于两个方面的原因造成的。这两个原因分别是：诱致性技术创新和社会需求的变化。

首先，诱致性技术创新对森林资源问题起到了缓解作用。诱致性技术创新是指由于资源禀赋的变化而诱发的技术变迁。当一种生产要素的禀赋相对另一种生产要素变得更为丰富时，特定的相对要素价格会诱导出使用更多的相对丰富的生产要素和节省相对稀缺的生产要素的技术变迁。这种有偏向的技术变迁源于追求利润的企业家用相对更丰富(因而更便宜)的资源替代更稀缺(因而更昂贵)的资源来降低生产成本的努力。这种新古典经济学框架内的诱致性技术创新理论假设有一个竞争性市场，借助于这个市场，厂商生产计划中使用的要素价格反映了要素的相对丰富和稀缺性。然而，如果假定生产者能根据反映资源的社会机会成本的影子价格，认识到资源的相对稀缺性，即使这种认识非常肤浅，这个理论也能应用到自给型的非市场经济中。

当原木等林产品的供给相对于需求发生短缺时，以原木等林产品为加工对象的企业原材料成本就会上升，在市场需求不变的情况下，企业利润就会下降。企业家追求利润的努力就会产生诱致性技术创新活动，即原木等林产品的替代品开发技术和林产品的节约使用技术就会出现。这些技术的应用，无疑可以减轻原木等林产品的供需矛盾，进而缓解森林资源问题。例如，美国在 19 世纪之前，铁轨铺设中需要大量的枕木，19 世纪末铁路大约消耗全国木材的 20% ~25% 。1900 年以前，由于防腐技术的落后，枕木与地面接触腐烂很快，枕木大约 5 ~7 年就需要更换。仅 1900 年用于更换枕木的木材就消耗了 600 万 hm^2 的森林。但是随后替代品的开发解决了这一问题。现今不只是美国，世界上很多国家早已用水泥等产品替代了木材枕木。除铁路以外，发达国家的建筑、冶炼、家具制造等原先木材消耗行业的原料替代技术也已十分成熟，木材消耗量在逐渐减少。此外，随着加工技术的不断改进，木材等林产品的节约利用程度不断提高，这也使森林资源问题得到了部分缓解。

其次，社会需求的改变为森林资源问题的缓解提供了社会基础。一方面森林的大量采伐造成了生态环境的急剧恶化，另一方面随着收入水平的不断提高，人们对生态环境改善和休闲娱乐的需求也不断增强。当这一需求已不是少数人的需求而是民众的广泛需求时，解决森林资源问题的社会基础就已形成。在这种情况下，如果经济实力允许，就会采取对森林资源的开采采取较为严厉的限制性措施和出台有利于森林资源恢复的相关激励性政策。同时，森林资源保护也会在民间自发兴起。所有这些，都会对森林资源问题的缓解起到重要作用。例如，美国 1964 年制定的《天然林保护法》以及 1976 年制定的《国有林经营法》，美国、英国、法国等国家的退耕还林政策，以及在欧美国家兴起的民间环保运动都对森林资源的恢复起到了重要作用。

（三）技术进步对森林资源影响的理论模型

1. 工业化初期技术进步对森林资源影响的理论模型

根据技术进步对收入分配的影响不同，经济增长理论将技术进步区分为中性技术进步、节约劳动型技术进步和节约资本型技术进步三种类型。中性技术进步是指使利润和工资在国民收入的分配中分配比率不发生变化的技术进步。节约劳动型的技术进步是指使国民收入的分配比率有利于资本，即利润在国民收入中的分配比率相对增加。而在国民收入的分配中有利于劳动的技术进步，则被定义为节约资本的技术进步。

工业化初期大量森林采伐机械的采用，具有明显的资本替代劳动的特征。因此，关于这一时期的技术进步对森林资源的影响可以用希克斯(John Hicks)的技术进步模型进行解释。我们用 a、b、c 点资本和劳动的比率之间的比较来描述林业的技术类型(图2-1)，K 表示在生产活动中使用的资本数量，L 表示在生产活动中使用的劳动数量，T_0、T_1、T_2 三条曲线分别表示中性技术进步、节约劳动型技术进步和节约资本型技术进步这三种技术进步类型中资本和劳动的边际产量的比率关系。

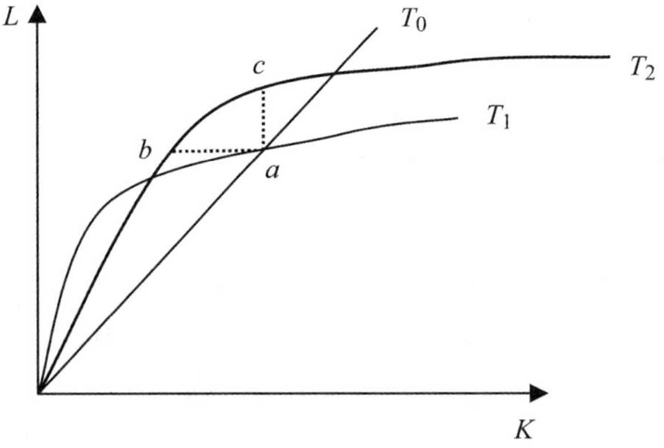

图2-1　技术进步的类型

设 $F_{K(0)}$ 和 $F_{L(0)}$ 分别为技术进步前资本与劳动的边际产量；

$F_{K(1)}$ 和 $F_{L(1)}$ 分别为技术进步后资本与劳动的边际产量。

如果 $F_{K(1)}/F_{L(1)} = F_{K(0)}/F_{L(0)}$，则该技术进步为希克斯中性。如果 $F_{K(1)}/F_{L(1)} > F_{K(0)}/F_{L(0)}$，由于 $F_{K(1)} = r$，$F_{L(1)} = w$，所以该式表明技术进步使得 r/w 提高了，即国民收入分配有利于资本，也就是说，相对于资本而言，劳动较以前相对充裕了。因此，该技术进步被称为节约劳动型的。同理，当 $F_{K(1)}/F_{L(1)} < F_{K(0)}/F_{L(0)}$ 时，技术进步则为节约资本型的。

在工业化初期，大量森林采伐机械的发明和使用，使林业生产活动中资本的投入不断增加，而劳动的投入相对减少，因此利润在国民收入中的比率不断提高。在利润的驱使下，森林的采伐速度明显加快，森林资源危机也随之到来。

2. 诱致性技术创新对森林资源影响的理论模型

正如前文所述，诱致性技术创新是指由于资源禀赋的变化而诱发的技术变迁。当一种生产要素的禀赋相对另一种生产要素变得更为丰富时，特定的相对要素价格会诱导出使用更多的相对丰富的生产要素和节省相对稀缺的生产要素的技术变迁。这种有偏向的技术变迁源于追求利润的企业家用相对更丰富（因而更便宜）的资源替代更稀缺（因而更昂贵）的资源来降低生产成本的努力。这一技术创新对森林资源的影响可用图 2-2 来加以说明。

在图 2-2 中，横坐标代表木材等林产品和其替代品的产量 Q，纵坐标代表木材等林产品和其替代品的价格和成本，AC_1 为以林产品为原材料的平均成本，AC_2 为以林产品替代品为原材料的平均成本，MC_1 和 MC_2 分别为与 AC_1 和 AC_2 对应的边际成本曲线，AC_0 和 MC_0 为森林资源相对充足时以林产品为生产资料的平均成

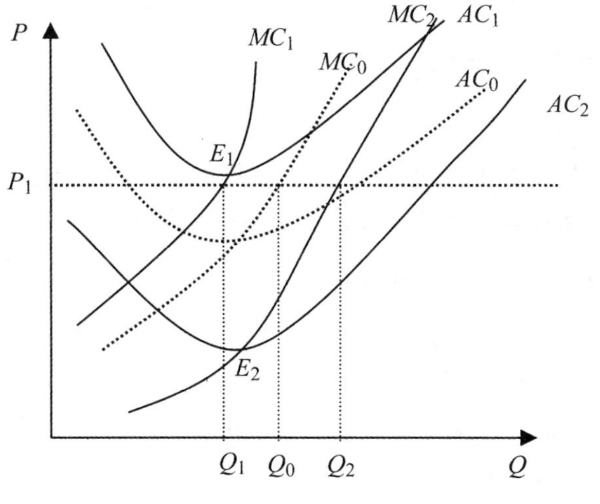

图 2-2　林产品替代品生产技术对成本利润的影响模型

本和边际成本。

当森林资源相对充足时，企业按照 $MR = MC$ 的原则，以林产品为原材料生产的产量为 Q_0，此时可以获得一定的利润。但随着森林采伐技术的改进，森林资源数量大量减少，以林产品为原材料的生产成本上升为 AC_1，此时企业的利润下降。在这种情况下，在利润的驱动下，就会诱导出使用更多的相对丰富的生产要素和节省相对稀缺的生产要素的技术变迁，即林产品的替代品就会产生，这样，以林产品的替代品为原料的生产成本就会下降到 AC_2 的水平，此时企业又重新获得了丰厚的利润。这样，诱致性技术创新就减轻了原木等林产品的供需矛盾，进而缓解了森林资源问题。

(四)霍夫曼法则与林业资源问题

工业化不仅是一个国家产业结构的转变过程，而且也是工业部门内部结构的变化过程。各国在工业化和现代化过程中，工业部门之间的结构变动，具有明显的阶段性和规律性。一般认为，工业发展过程正常地要经历三个阶段。在第一阶段，初级消费品工业如食品加工、纺织、烟草、家具等工业是主要工业部门，并且比资本品工业如冶金、化学、机械、汽车、钢铁等部门以更快的速度发展。在第二阶段，资本品工业增长加速进行，资本品工业产值在工业总产值的比重趋于上升，但这时消费品工业在产值和速度上都仍然占主导地位。在第三阶段，资本品工业比消费品工业以更快的速度增长，并渐占优势。

一般国家在工业化过程中工业结构变动的阶段性趋势的主要原因是需求结构变化和技术变化。在工业化初期，轻工业如食品加工、纺织业是满足人们最基本需要的部门。只有当基本需要得到满足之后，人们才有可能把更多资源投资于其他工业。另外，发展中国家在发展初期，资本、技术和熟练劳动力十分稀缺，而非熟练劳动力极为丰富。在这种条件约束下，发展中国家不可能迅速发展需要大量资本、技术和管理人才的资本品工业，只可能发展劳动密集、原料偏向、需要较少资本和技术的消费品工业。但随着工业化程度的提高，资本的不断积累、技术水平的不断提高，资本品工业必须加速发展。

学者对工业部门结构变动规律进行了大量研究，其中有代表性人物包括霍夫曼、盐谷佑一和钱纳里。

德国经济学家霍夫曼(W. G. Hoffman)对工业化(实际是重工业化)问题进行了开创性研究，他提出的工业化阶段理论，被称之为“工业化经验法则”，亦称霍夫曼定理或霍夫曼法则。霍夫曼认为，工业化过程中各工业部门的成长率并不相同，因而形成了工业部门间的特点的结构变化，而且具有一般倾向。这个不同的成长率是由以下因素的相互作用引起的：①生产要素(自然资源、资本、劳动力)的相对数量；②国内市场和国际市场的资源配置；③技术进步；④劳动者的技术熟练程度、消费者的兴趣爱好等。

霍夫曼选择了有代表性的8类产品进行观察分析，这8类产品分为消费品工业和资本品工业两大类。消费品工业包括：①食品、饮料、烟草等；②布匹、制鞋；③皮革制品；④家具等。资本品工业包括：①生铁、有色金属；②机械；③车辆；④化工等。为了进行观察分析，他提出一个基准——霍夫曼比率，即消费品工业净产值与资本品工业净产值之比，以公式表示为：

霍夫曼比率 = 消费品工业净产值/资本品工业净产值

霍夫曼根据20多个国家的时间系列数据分析，发现各国工业化虽然进行时间早晚不同且发展水平各异，但都表现出一个共同趋势，即资本品工业净产值在整个工业净产值中所占份额稳定上升，并呈现出大体相同的阶段性质。霍夫曼根据上述情况，将工业化过程分为四个阶段(表2-1)。

表2-1　霍夫曼工业化阶段指标

工业化阶段	消费品工业净产值/资本品工业净产值
第一阶段	5(±1)
第二阶段	2.5(±1)
第三阶段	1(±0.5)
第四阶段	1以下

第一阶段，消费品工业占优势；第二阶段，资本品工业迅速发展，消费品工业优势地位逐渐下降；第三阶段，资本品工业继续快速增长，消费品工业与资本品工业达到平衡；第四阶段，资本品工业占主要地位，认为这个阶段实现了工业化。这就是所谓的霍夫曼工业化经验法则。根据该经验法则，从20世纪20年代末看，当时达到第三个阶段的国家有英国、瑞士、美国、法国、德国、比利时、瑞典等国；进入第二阶段的有日本、荷兰、丹麦、加拿大、澳大利亚等国；处于第一阶段的有智利、印度、新西兰等国。

日本经济学家盐谷佑一利用产业关联理论，对霍夫曼工业化经验法则重新论证。他采用消费资料和资本资料的产品分类，采用总产值进行数量统计。其计算结果表明：①在较长的历史时期中，霍夫曼比率稳步下降，资本资料工业比重上升是一普遍现象；②从霍夫曼比率来看，日本在工业化时期即其重工业化阶段，下降很明显，与霍夫曼工业化经验法则吻合，但工业化水平较高的国家如美国、瑞典，按其最终产品划分的两部门比率是较稳定的，没有按照霍夫曼工业化经验法则发展，这也说明霍夫曼工业化经验法则不能反映整个工业化过程。盐谷佑一根据产业关联理论测算的霍夫曼比率，不仅论证了霍夫曼工业化经验法则的适用范围（重工业化阶段，即大体是工业化初、中期），而且还揭示了随着经济和技术的进步在现实经济生活中出现的新倾向，即在消费资料生产与资本资料生产比率稳定的情况下，重工业比率却在上升。

霍夫曼工业化经验法则表明，在工业化前期，消费品工业占优势，因此整个工业生产对地表资源的依赖程度较高，这其中就包括森林资源。因此，在工业化的初级阶段，森林资源将被大量消耗。这一推论刚好和发达国家以及发展中国家工业化初期森林资源的消耗状况相吻合。随着工业化的演进，资本品工业迅速发展，消费品工业优势地位逐渐下降，而且资本品工业逐渐占主要地位。这样，整个工业生产对地表资源的依赖程度开始逐渐降低，而对地下资源的依赖程度逐渐增加，森林等地上资源的需求压力开始减轻，森林资源得以恢复。瑞士、美国、德国、瑞典等国的森林资源的恢复基本发生在工业化后期，这也基本和霍夫曼工业化经验法则相吻合。

三、资本形成方式的演变及林业资源问题的转化

(一)资本的形成

发展经济学中资本形成理论的早期开拓者之一纳克斯(Ranger Nurkse),曾给“资本形成”(capital formation)下过一个全面的定义,即“资本形成是指社会不把他的全部现行生产活动,用于满足当前消费的需要和愿望,而是以其一部分用之于生产资本品:工具和仪器、机器和交通设施、工厂和设备等各式各样可以用来增加生产效能的真实资本(material capital)。”资本的形成既包括物质资本,也包括人力资本,但通常所说的资本形成只是指物质资本的形成。

20 世纪 50 ~60 年代,在早期发展经济学的许多论著以及很多发展中国家的经济发展政策中,物质资本或明或暗地被描述成唯一稀缺的资源,资本稀缺被看成是加速经济发展的主要障碍。例如,刘易斯就认为“经济增长理论的中心问题是要理解一个社会从 5% 的储蓄率变成 12% 的储蓄率的过程,以及伴随着这种转变而来的在态度、制度和技术方面的一切变化”。著名经济史学家、经济起飞理论的提出者罗斯托把生产性投资与国民收入的比率提高到 10% 以上看成是实现经济起飞的三个先决条件之一。著名的哈罗德 - 多马增长模型、纳克斯的“贫困恶性循环”理论以及平衡增长理论、纳尔逊的“低水平平衡陷阱”理论等均强调资本形成的重要性。

然而,第二次世界大战后几十年经济发展的事实,证明上述理论存在很大的片面性。经济发展除资本形成这一条件以外,还必须有政治、制度、社会和文化等各方面的先决条件,否则,资本的配置效率将会很低。那么,既然资本形成并不是经济成功发展的充分条件,是不是意味着资本形成的重要性降低了?其实不然。虽然经历了第二次世界大战后半个世纪的发展,少数国家和地区已经实现了工业化,但大多数发展中国家仍处于贫穷的状况。要改变这种状况,需要大量的开发投资,而这些国家的资本仍然是相对不足的生产要素。一个贫穷的国家要想变富,仍需要千方百计地筹集资本,并节约使用稀缺资本。那么,资本到底是怎样形成的呢?

纵观先进国家的工业化经验，资本形成的方式主要有以下6种：①运用行政手段动员农业剩余；②运用财政政策进行政府融资；③运用通货膨胀办法强制储蓄；④企业本身的资本积累；⑤通过金融机构和金融市场融资；⑥通过外贸和利用外资加速资本形成。

运用行政手段动员农业剩余是指工业化初期，政府运用行政手段通过直接劳动力投资、利用廉价的劳动力、征收农业税、压低农产品价格、出口农产品赚取外汇以及农民自愿储蓄等形式而形成的资本积累；运用财政政策进行政府融资是指政府通过税收、行政事业性收费、国有企业利润上缴以及举债等形式所形成的财政收入，是政府通过财政渠道而形成的资本积累；运用通货膨胀办法强制储蓄是指通货膨胀使高收入阶层的边际储蓄倾向高于低收入阶层，从而提高了社会总体储蓄倾向及可贷资金的总规模，并由于实际利率和工资率的下降刺激了企业的投资，从而实现了资本积累的目的；企业本身的资本积累是指企业将前期利润的全部或一部分转化为后期资本的过程；通过金融机构和金融市场融资是指通过金融手段筹集社会闲散资金的方式，是发达国家和20世纪70年代许多发展中国家资本形成的最主要方式；通过外贸和利用外资加速资本形成是指通过国际贸易和引进外国资本来换取设备、技术等必要资本品的一种资本形成方式。

(二)行政积累与森林资源危机

理论和实践都已证明，发展中国家为实现工业化而进行的资本积累对农业产生了十分强烈的影响。与之相似，资本积累对林业产生的影响也十分强烈(需要说明的是，在工业化理论中，虽然有些经济学家将农业的概念涵盖了林业，但其理论中论及的农业却更多地是指以粮食等农产品生产为主的狭义农业，更没有对林业的特有问题给予单独的关注)。从森林资源的角度来看，资本积累对林业产生的影响源于两类资本积累的形成方式，这两类资本积累形成方式分别对林业产生了不同的影响。为便于说明，我们将这两类资本积累划分成以政府行政手段为主导的资本积累(简称行政积累)和非政府手段主导的资本积累(简称非行政积累)。

以政府行政手段为主导的资本积累方式主要产生在工业化初期。这种积累方式对农业而言，主要表现为强制性农业生产剩余的转移对其产生的影响，但对林业而言，却涵盖了林业生产剩余转移、运用财政政策进行政府融资以及出口木材换取外汇等多个方面的影响。在林业生产剩余转移方面，发展中国家政府的主要做法往往是，一方面要求林业部门提供大量木材，另一方面采取垄断收购、限制自由市场交易的方式压低木材价格，从而使工业部门在成本降低的条件下加速发展。森林采伐和木材流通受到政府严格管制。不但国有林的采伐和木材流通受到国家的严格掌控，而且非国有林森林采伐和木材流通也要在办理严格复杂的手续并在规定的条件下才能进行，这种做法在前苏联等计划经济国家较为普遍。在运用财政政策进行政府融资方面，发展中国家政府的主要做法是，通过对林业部门征收各种税费和林业企业利润上缴的形式来形成国家财政收入，再通过财政收入对工业企业进行资金支持，进而形成企业的资本积累。从严格意义上来讲，这实质上也是对林业生产剩余的一种转移，只不过这种转移是通过财政渠道进行的。出口木材换取外汇是发展中国家政府进行工业化资本积累的另一种重要途径。一方面，由于技术水平的限制，发展中国家进行工业化的一些机械设备不能自行研制开发，必须从发达国家进口。另一方面，发达国家已经度过了通过掠夺资源来发展经济这一阶段，对森林资源开始进行全面和严格的保护，本国所需木材开始从国外进口。在这一背景下，很多发展中国家大量出口木材换取外汇，以此来购买国外的先进设备。例如印度尼西亚、马来西亚等国在20世纪90年代以前为换取外汇都曾大量地出口木材。

上述以政府行政手段为主导的资本积累方式对森林资源的影响是双重的。一方面，发展中国家为加速资本积累必然对森林资源进行大量开采，使森林资源迅速减少；另一方面对生产剩余的转移又使得林业部门无法获得充足的造林、森林管护等森林资源恢复资金，使森林资源难以恢复。这种双重影响必然导致森林资源危机的加剧。

（三）非行政积累与林业资源问题的转化

相对于以政府行政手段为主导的资本积累方式对森林资源的影响，以非政府手段为主导的资本积累方式对森林资源的影响即使不是反向的，至少也对森林资源危机起到了缓解的作用。这是因为，非政府手段主导的资本积累主要包括企业本身的资本积累和通过金融机构和金融市场融资两种方式。而这两种资本积累方式的前提是市场经济体制的成熟和经济水平的提高。通过金融机构尤其是通过金融市场融资要依靠成熟的市场体系来完成，反过来市场经济越发展，对金融体系的依赖性也就越大。同时，金融市场的融资程度还取决于经济发展水平，经济发展水平越高，金融市场的融资数量就越大。同样，企业本身的资本积累是在市场经济条件下产权独立时的经济行为，其资本积累水平取决于自身的利润水平。在经济发达国家，无论是市场经济体制的成熟程度还是其经济发展水平，都已达到了相当的高度。因此，金融方式和企业本身的资本积累已成为资本形成的最主要的方式。20 世纪 70 年代以后，包括中国在内的许多发展中国家先后开始了市场导向的经济体制改革和金融体制改革，随着改革的不断深入，以非政府手段为主导的资本积累方式正在逐渐替代以政府行政手段为主导的资本积累方式。这无疑缓解了资本积累对森林资源的压力。同时，随着经济的发展，政府对林业部门的税费征收程度开始减弱，而从其他部门获得的财政收入却大量增加，政府开始由过去的资金索取转向对林业进行资金支持，这也对缓解林业资源危机起到了重要作用。

（四）资本积累对林业影响的理论模型

如前所述，行政积累对林业的影响主要表现为：政府一方面要求林业部门提供大量木材，另一方面采取垄断收购、限制自由市场交易的方式压低木材价格，从而使工业部门在成本降低的条件下加速发展。这种做法对林业部门的影响如图 2-3 所示。在图 2-3 中，假定在工业等非农产业优先的政策框架下，林业部门只能在价格 P_2 情况下提供木材等林产品，这样，单位林产品的价格小于其平均成本，林业部门为工业等非农部门提供的资本积累即为市场调节情况下按照 $MR = SMC$ 原则的盈利面积 $FGHP_1$ 和政府垄断定价情况下的亏损面积 $LIJP_2$ 之和。

随着经济的发展，行政积累在资本积累中比重将逐渐降低，非行政积累的比重将逐渐上升，在这种情况下，如图 2-4 所示，林业的积累功能将逐渐减弱。

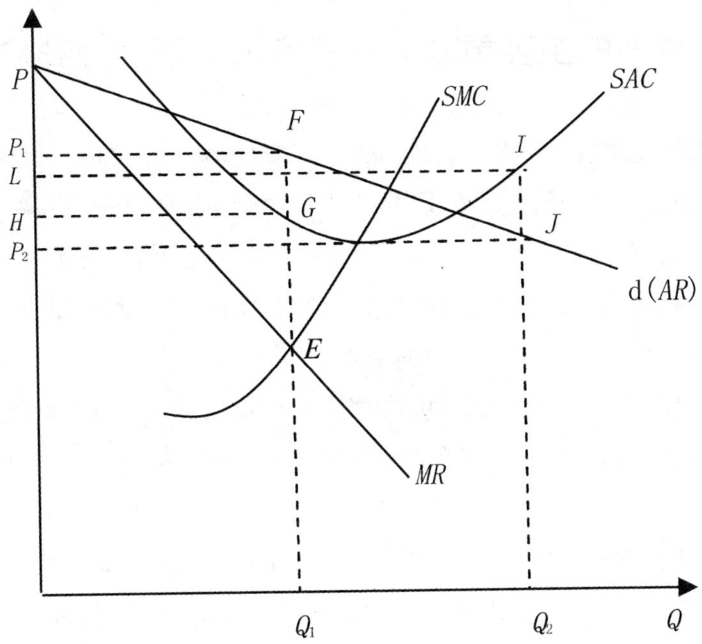

图 2-3 林业行政积累理论模型

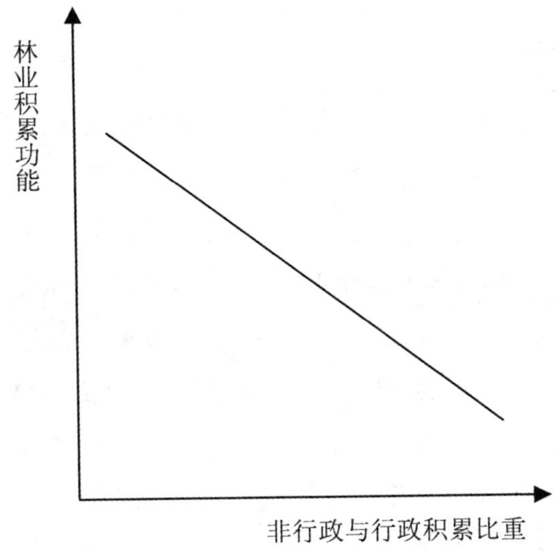

图 2-4 林业积累功能的变化

第二节　林业的主要贡献——资本形成对林业影响的实证

第二次世界大战之后兴起的发展经济学对农业和工业之间的相互关系进行了长期和深入的研究，从而产生了农业贡献理论。早在 20 世纪 40 年代，张培刚就比较系统地从粮食、原料、劳动力、市场、资金(包括外汇)等五个方面，提出并阐明了农业对工业化及整个国民经济发展的重要作用和巨大贡献。此后，美国经济学家、诺贝尔经济学获奖者西蒙·库兹涅茨在 1961 年发表的《经济增长与农业贡献》一书中又将农业对工业的作用归纳为四个贡献，即产品贡献(包括粮食和原材料)、市场贡献、要素贡献(包括剩余资本和剩余劳动力)，以及通过农产品出口获取外汇收入的贡献。

受这一理论的启发，我们发现，林业在工业化过程中也对经济发展做出了自己独特的贡献，而且上述资本形成所导致的林业资源问题与林业对工业的贡献密切相关。通过详细分析，我们认为这一贡献主要体现在三个方面，即林业的原料贡献、林业的资本贡献和林业的外汇贡献。

一、林业的原料贡献

工业革命的爆发使社会生产力获得了空前的大发展，社会对工业用材的需求量急剧增加。19 世纪中叶的欧洲蒸汽动力已开始大量用于制材业，从而导致了制材业的大发展。当时生产的工业用材，除一部分作为原木利用外，其余主要是用于各种锯材。如在美国，其 1900 年的工业加工用材的产品结构仍为：锯材 78%，纸浆 1.9%，胶合板 0.1%，其他工业加工用材为 20%。随着生产力的发展，锯材用材在全部工业用材中的比重逐渐下降，锯材(包括单板和枕木用材)原木消耗从 1951 年占世界工业用材消耗的 64.3% 降至 1973 年的 61%(表 2-2)。

1971 ~ 1990 年，发达国家木材采伐量从 12.51 亿 m^3 提高到 15.01 亿 m^3，木材实际消耗量从 12.83 亿 m^3 增加到 15.17 亿 m^3，这就为其林产工业的发展提供了原料。率先进入工业化的国家，由于人均国民收入较高，对各种纸制品的需求量

表 2-2　1951 年与 1973 年世界工业加工用材量(亿 m^3)

年份	工业用材	锯材原木	纸浆材	其他
1951 年	7.26	4.67	1.79	0.80
1973 年	13.55	8.26	3.24	2.05

注：其他包括坑木、刨花板和纤维板用材。

很大，1990 年的人均纸制品的消费水平已达 150kg/(人・年)(同年发展中国家只有 10 kg)。1971～1990 年，发达国家的纸和纸板产量由 1.19 亿 t 增加到 2 亿 t，增加了 67.5%，人造板产量由 7 116 万 m^3 扩大到 9 937 万 m^3，增加了 39.6%；尤其是刨花板产量由 2 201 万 m^3 增加到 4 437 万 m^3，增加了 1 倍多。

美国的木材加工工业首先始于制材，长期以来，锯材一直是美国林产品工业的主要产品，1899 年产量就已超过 8 000 万 m^3，1906 年达到高峰，为 1 亿 m^3，1907 年开始超过 1 亿 m^3。在美国的人造板工业中，纤维板的生产历史最早，始于 1914 年。美国的纤维板产量几乎一直居于世界首位。20 世纪 50 年代纤维板产量增加较快，1959 年比 1952 年增加 127%，在 60 年代年产量增长 34%，70 年代基本上处于稳定状态。刨花板的生产始于 1945 年，当时产量很少。1970 年的产量达到 312.7 万 m^3，比 1961 年增加 428%，1980 年又进一步增加到 626.9 万 m^3，在 1970 年的基础上又增长了 1 倍，1988 年刨花板产量达到 978 万 m^3，比 1980 年又增加了 56%。胶合板生产始于 20 世纪初，产量一直呈增长的趋势，1950～1959 年其产量增长了 1.6 倍，1969 年又在 1959 年的基础上增长 71. 5%，1988 年胶合板总产量达到 2 313.5 万 m^3，比 1969 年增加 69. 7%。美国的整个人造板产量总的来看呈上升的趋势，1988 年总产量达到 3 617.7 万 m^3。这些都要求有充足的原料支撑。

加拿大林产品结构是以锯材、纸浆、纸制品为主体，锯材曾经是加拿大林产品中的主要产品，产量、产值都居主要地位。20 世纪以来，这种现象有所改变，但锯材产品在加拿大林产品中仍占有重要位置。1965～1988 年，锯材及胶合板的用材量从 63.6% 增至 72.4%，占有了相当比重。1988 年，锯材产量为 6 905.6 万

m^3，比1965年增长了2.37倍(表2-3)。

表2-3 1965 ~1988年加拿大锯材、胶合板及纸浆消耗木材情况

年份(年)	工业用材量(万 m^3)	锯材及胶合板用材量(万 m^3)	占工业用材量(%)	制浆用材量(万 m^3)	占工业用材量(%)
1965	9 844.8	6 262.4	63.6	3 419.3	34.7
1970	11 729.7	7 565.3	64.5	4 040.7	34.4
1975	11 769.4	7 900.0	67.1	3 763.6	32.0
1980	15 422.4	11 286.5	73.2	3 957.0	25.7
1985	16 198.5	11 933.6	73.7	4 060.1	25.1
1988	17 312.3	12 538.4	72.4	4 551.5	26.3

在发展中国家中，巴西是森林资源最丰富的国家，这是促使巴西大力发展制浆造纸工业的主要原因之一。早在20世纪60年代初，巴西根据对国内外纸浆和纸市场的预测，即制定了用15 ~20年时间占领世界纸市场20%的规划，并投资35亿美元营造557万 hm^2 桉树人工林基地。1970年巴西政府又制定了全国纸浆和纸的发展规划，要求充分利用桉树人工林资源。到1985年，巴西的纸和纸板产量已达402.2万t，到1990年进一步增加到430.7万t，发展到2000年急剧增加到735.4万t。当然，从绝大多数发展中国家的林产工业现状来看，目前仍未摆脱以原材料和初级产品为主出口的境地。因此，在其国内林业主要是为初级加工产品提供原料。

印度尼西亚的特点是以胶合板工业为龙头来带动全国林产工业的发展。早在20世纪70年代初，印度尼西亚的木材工业尚属名不见经传的规模很小的产业部门。当时，全国除一些简陋的制材厂和作坊式家具厂外，几乎没有任何现代化大型木材加工企业。但是在短短的20年时间里，印度尼西亚的木材工业取得了惊人的成就，已发展成为国家的重要支柱产业，成为仅次于石油的第二大创汇产业。在印度尼西亚木材工业的腾飞过程中，胶合板工业起了先锋和主导作用。印度尼西亚拥有十分丰富的胶合板材资源，且具有充足的廉价劳动力，加上胶合板工业本身的特点适合发展中国家发展，印度尼西亚制定了优先发展胶合板工业的产业政策。1990 年的胶合板产量已达 1 050 万 m^3，该国胶合板工业每年要消耗 2/3左右的工业用材。印度尼西亚的热带材胶合板现已占据大半个世界市场，成为任何国家无法与之竞争的胶合板超级大国。印度尼西亚把家具工业作为优先发展的第二大林业产业，其丰富的优质热带阔叶材资源和橡胶木则为家具工业提供了原料保证。现在，家具产品和各种装饰用型材已发展成为仅次于胶合板的第二大产业。

通过对各国在林业资源问题阶段对木材和锯材、胶合板、纤维板等林产品的需求情况的客观描述中可以看出，处于林业资源问题阶段时，各国对林产品的需求量和消费量呈现不断增长的趋势。根据联合国粮农组织的预计，若将全世界对林产品的需求量换算成原木，今后对原木的需求将会以年均 1%（即每年 2 000 万 m^3）的速度增长。其中，发展中国家对林产品需求的增长发挥着主要作用，例如，据俄罗斯国内专家预测，到 2015 年，俄罗斯林产品消费量将迅猛增长，其中木材深加工产品消费量的增长幅度最大，具体品种包括印刷用高质量纸品、包装用纸品、卫生纸和办公用纸；据林业专家对未来几十年中国林产品需求进行的预测，到 2030 年，中国对主要林产品的需求量将达到 4.0 亿～4.3 亿 m^3，2050 年达到 5.7 亿～7.2 亿 m^3。

二、林业的资本贡献

林业不但为工业提供了原料，而且也为工业发展提供了剩余资本的积累。工业发展不但需要有原料的供应，同时也需要有雄厚的资金支持。在优先发展工业的指导思想下，农业和林业都成为工业发展的辅助行业，其自身建设的主要目的就是支持工业建设。因而，在对林产品定价和制定相应的税收政策时，都会有意识地向工业倾斜，不惜剥夺林业的利润借以发展工业。

由于森林不但为国家建设提供资源，而且对生态环境的影响也至关重要。正是由于森林资源的特殊性，许多国家都将森林资源归为国家所有，对其生产、采伐、销售实行统一规划，统一管理。土耳其早在 1937 年颁布了第一部《森林法》，其中规定了4种森林所有制形式，即国有林、公有林、基金林和私有林。1945年修改后的《森林法》又规定所有的森林归国家所有。目前，土耳其99%以上的林地及森林资源属于国有资产，林业部下属的林业管理总局负责国有林的保护、经营管理和利用。捷克斯洛伐克也于1945年开始公有化改革，将87%的私有林没收并归为国有，直到1989年捷克斯洛伐克几乎所有的森林都属于国有。

中国也是个典型的范例，在1950年6月30日发布的《中华人民共和国土地改革法》第十八条中明确规定："大森林、大水利工程、大荒地、大荒山……均收归国有，由人民政府管理经营之。"确立了森林、荒山、荒地的全民所有制。之后中央人民政府政务院又于1950年5月发布了《关于全国林业工作的指示》，规定公有林(包括国有林)应由中央人民政府林垦部或中央委托的各级林业机构经营采伐，统筹供应公私用材。其他任何机关、部队、学校或企业不得借口任何理由自行采伐。1964年5月6日，国务院批转林业部、铁道部、国家物资管理总局制定了《木材统一送货办法》。在1979年第五届全国人大常委会第六次会议通过的《中华人民共和国森林法(试行)》第五章《森林采伐利用》中，用法律规定了国家和地方的木材生产必须全部纳入国家计划，国有森林要根据国家下达的计划进行采伐，集体所有林由林业部门向社队实行订约采伐，订约收购。1984年9月第六届全国人大常委会第七次会议正式通过《中华人民共和国森林法》，对试行的《森林法》进行了补充，增加了关于严格控制森林采伐量和对森林采伐及木材实行统一管理的相关规定。此外，在《中华人民共和国宪法》中也规定了森林属于国家所有，由法律规定属于集体所有的除外。1981年3月8日，中共中央、国务院发布《关于保护森林发展林业若干问题的决定》，规定木材实行集中统一管理。在1987年下发的《中共中央国务院关于加强南方集体林区森林资源管理坚决制止乱砍滥伐的指示》要求强化执行年森林采伐限额制度，集体所有集中成片的用材林不得再分户经营。

这些法律条文和相关规章都表明：中国对森林资源的管理实行统筹规划、统一经营。林木的生产、采伐、运输、销售都由政府统一进行管理，政府作为木材的唯一需求方，形成了需求垄断，这为政府制定林价提供了便利条件。国家为了加大对工业建设的支持力度，通过压低林产品价格，转移林业利润来支持工业发展。除了在政策上通过制定各项条款．政府掌握了木材需求，通过压低林产品价格将林业利润转移到工业上，而且还通过税收的制定来加强林业利润向工业的转化。

税收是国家财政收入的主要来源，也是政府进行公共建设的重要资金保证。各个国家在林业方面都制定了相关的税费规定。通过对林业进行征税和收费不但可以增加政府的财政收入，而且可以把林业的利润向工业部门转移，加大工业建设的力度。

林业税费的制定直接关系到林业自身的建设和发展，同时也关系到工业的建设和发展。通过加强对林业的税费征收，大大减少了林业的利润，并借助各项政策规定将林业利润转移到工业建设上。就中国而言，也制定了种类繁多的相关税费。1985 年中国制定的关于林业方面的国家税收包括：原木产品税（按林农出售价 10% 征收）、农林特产农业税（按林农出售林木收入的 5% ～10% 征收）、营业税（零售木材按规定税率征收）和城市维护建设税（按国家规定计征）；各种费用包括：育林基金、更改资金、市场管理费（进入城乡农贸市场交易的按成交价 0.6% 计征）、检尺费（每立方米收 1.5 元）、林政管理费（每立方米收 1.5 元）、林区管理建设费（县、乡两级每立方米合计收 5～10 元）；此外，还有运杂费等收费。尽管之后对税收政策进行了多次调整，但各地的林业税费负担仍旧偏重，1994 年，中国将农林特产税与产品税、工商统一税中的农、林、牧、水产品税目合并，改为征收农业特产税，对生产销售原木、原竹的单位征收生产环节和销售环节共计 16% 的农业特产税，对生产销售原木、原竹的个人征收生产环节 8% 的农业特产税，同时在销售环节对收购人另征 8% 的农业特产税，加上地方农业特产税附加 10%，实际税率高达 17.6%；而且，从 1992 年起，国有林区恢复提取育林基金，提取办法由按木材销售比例改为按材积数量，每销售 $1m^3$ 原木征收 10 元，并且由省（自治区、直辖市）汇集统一上缴林业部，实行分级管理。从 1996 年开始，对国有森工企业以林区三剩物和次小薪材为原料生产加工的综合利用产品也要征收增值税，销项税按 17% 税率计算，而进项税只能以 10% 予以抵扣。过多的林业税费在很大程度上大大减少了林业的利润，经过税收和层层收费，最后落到林业生产者手中几乎所剩无几。以中国南方集体林区某县为例，该县1998年松原木平均销售价为435.91元/m^3，须交纳农业特产税等税收和省政府规定的收费96.15元，占售价的22.06%；须交纳国家规定的育林基金、维简费等林业规费86.43元，占售价的19.83%；须交县、乡、村规定的各项收费141.1元，占售价的32.37%。各项税费收入总计323.68元，占到售价的74.26%，林农手中仅落得102元，仅占售价的25.74%，再剔除各项生产费用以及人工工资的开支，林农获得的纯利润几乎为零。

国家通过制定相关的林业政策，适当压低林木和林产品的价格，并且以税收的形式巩固林业利润向工业的转移，这为工业的发展提供了大量资金支持，加固了工业发展的基础。

三、林业的外汇贡献

第二次世界大战后，世界林业产业已进入一个大发展阶段，发达国家森林资源已完全恢复并趋于稳定。而刚刚独立的发展中国家大多经济底子薄，国力较弱，为获得发展国民经济所急需的科学技术和机器设备，不得不以牺牲本国资源为代价大量出口原材料，即使一些发展较快的发展中国家和地区，用于换汇出口的也主要是劳动密集型的初加工产品。发展中国家这一时期的林业产业主要目标是为满目疮痍的国家经济积累资金，因此仍大量砍伐森林，出口原木。如森林资源丰富的印度尼西亚，此时林业发展的重点就是为经济发展获得急需的外汇，因而增加采运能力，大量出口原木。仅在1967~1970年，印度尼西亚原木年出口量就从56.02万m^3上升到784.83万m^3，增长了13.2倍，木材出口收入占全国总出口额的17.7%。至20世纪末，由于加工业不发达，广大发展中国家为了换取急需的外汇和必需的各种纸张和纸制品，仍不得不大量出口原木和初加工产品，部分发展中国家的林产品出口量呈现逐年递增的趋势(表2-4)，其中，出口的林产品包括圆木、成材、枕木、木质板、木浆以及纸和纸板等。

表 2-4　1991～1995 年部分发展中国家林产品出口量(万 m^3)

	1991 年	1992 年	1993 年	1994 年	1995 年
阿根廷	53.0	83.3	61.4	98.4	140.1
巴西	365.7	475.2	603.3	739.7	767.5
智利	856.4	863.8	804.2	950.1	1178.9

资料来源：《林产品年鉴：1991～1995》，FAO，1995

由于发展中国家出口林产品的数量不断增加，自 20 世纪 70 年代中期至 20 世纪 90 年代中期，发展中国家出口林产品的创汇额呈现明显的增长趋势，见表 2-5（此处统计的林产品主要包括原木、成材和枕木、木质板、木浆以及纸和纸板）。

表 2-5　1976～1995 年发展中国家林产品出口创汇额(亿美元)

年份	原木	成材和枕木	木质板	木浆	纸和纸板
1976	21.71	23.90	20.81	3.31	4.35
1977	23.47	23.46	21.94	2.86	4.85
1978	25.29	22.79	23.54	3.91	4.45
1979	40.00	25.31	19.13	4.89	3.99
1980	41.42	23.95	17.93	7.09	6.34
1981	26.85	22.31	23.83	9.06	9.04
1982	27.09	23.08	22.50	7.78	7.44
1983	25.28	25.71	25.06	7.56	7.66
1984	18.92	24.77	26.08	10.32	11.88
1985	18.82	23.62	27.25	8.79	12.48
1986	18.90	25.56	27.73	8.41	13.88
1987	24.75	25.53	30.22	7.00	12.68
1988	26.75	21.45	30.41	9.53	17.42

（续）

年份	原木	成材和枕木	木质板	木浆	纸和纸板
1989	27.30	24.67	30.82	9.42	15.40
1990	32.65	19.95	31.13	8.69	17.24
1991	31.88	19.47	31.69	7.77	20.31
1992	36.81	19.91	29.43	9.04	21.42
1993	34.93	21.33	35.93	7.68	17.18
1994	37.48	19.81	32.52	9.15	20.66
1995	39.17	17.64	30.17	13.56	22.21

资料来源：《林产品年鉴：1991～1995》，FAO，1995

根据表2-5所统计的数据进行计算，发展中国家出口林产品的创汇额从1976年的74.08亿元增加到了1995年的122.75亿元，30年间增加了65.70%，为发展中国家提供了大量外汇积累。由于加工技术水平的局限，这一时期林产品出口以木材和初级加工品为主，1990年发展中国家出口林产品创汇额的结构比例见表2-6。

表2-6　1990年发展中国家和地区主要林产品出口情况

国家和地区	原木(%)	锯材(%)	胶合板(%)	总出口额(亿美元)
非洲	51.5	24.11	3.76	9.58
拉丁美洲	7.62	15.52	5.88	27.44
近东	20.27	26.62	9.59	0.74
远东	19.25	19.49	40.52	91.32
其他	89.3	7.67	0.94	1.59
发展中国家合计	20.23	18.98	29.9	130.67

在发展中国家中，南美的巴西、智利和东南亚的印度尼西亚、马来西亚是最主要的林产品出口国。从目前情况看，只有巴西和智利的制浆造纸工业已发展到

一定规模。但在印度尼西亚和马来西亚，至今仍以出口初加工产品为主。

印度尼西亚独立后，急于发展国民经济，由于资金和技术力量不足，为换取急需的外汇采取出口原木和原藤的政策。1966年苏哈托执政后，加强对天然林资源的开发，林业在国民经济中的地位仅次于石油、煤矿和橡胶。在第一个五年计划期间，林业发展的重点是获得发展急需的外汇。在此期间，大量砍伐林木，大量出口原木，当时90%之多的原木用于出口，木材出口收入达全国总出口额的17.7%，仅次于石油出口额。70年代初期，印度尼西亚成为世界上最大的热带木材出口国。这种情况直到第二个五年计划期间才有所缓解。在这一期间，政府一方面强调经济增长，对原木出口进行限制，另一方面发展木材加工业，增加木材加工产品和半加工产品的出口。1978年原木出口量为1 890万m^3，占当年工业原木产量的78.1%，这一比例较之第二个五年计划之前的90%下降了近12%。而同期木材产品出口在1979年达到高峰，出口额占总出口额的13.9%。但这一时期原木出口仍然占绝大多数比例。发展到1990年，林产品总出口额为34.55亿美元，其中初加工产品高达30.83亿美元，占87.9%。

在马来西亚，木材加工企业主要生产低附加值的初级产品，原木和初级产品的出口为其创造了大量的外汇收入。1985年，原木出口额占木材产品出口的比例高达65%；到1990年，木材初级加工产品的出口创汇额占出口总额的比例仍高达80%。近几年来，马来西亚的木材深加工产品，如模具、家具、细木工板也有了相当大的发展。

在菲律宾，1984年以前林产品出口以原木、锯材、胶合板和单板为主。1984年，菲律宾的原木出口量达99.6万m^3，锯材出口量达54万m^3，原木、板材、单板和胶合板的出口额占出口创汇总额的83%。

第三节　工业化过程中林业资源问题的演变

一、关于依靠自然资源发展的反思

自20世纪50年代以来，经济增长常被看作是解决贫困的手段。但是，经济增长受到资源基础的限制，生态系统也正呈现出脆弱的迹象，这就产生了越来越多的疑问：在不破坏作为最终基础的自然系统的前提下，经济系统能否持续增长。

经济学家对这一问题的关注和研究的历史已经非常久远，从查阅的文献来看，可以追溯到18～19世纪前半期。在那一时期，古典经济学家就曾有过较为明确的论述。此后，随着工业化国家对环境污染的认识以及治理实践的深入，对这一问题研究的范围和深度都得到了迅速发展。特别是1992年联合国环境与发展大会(UNCED)之后，研究活动更是空前活跃。

(一)古典经济学家的相关论述

古典经济学形成和发展的18～19世纪(在西方经济学中，古典经济学指从18～19世纪70年代边际学派出现前的一种经济学流派)，欧洲经济正处于工业革命兴起以及农业生产率迅速增长的阶段。这一时期古典经济学家们关注的一个问题是，究竟什么决定了生活水平和国民财富的增长。

在古典经济学以前，重商主义者认为货币是财富的唯一形态，商业利润，或者更准确地说国际贸易利润是一个国家获取货币进而增加财富的来源。对重商主义的错误提出反对观点的是法国古典政治经济学的创始人皮埃尔·布阿吉尔贝尔。他宣称，农业生产为社会财富的来源。此后，重农主义者的代表人物魁奈又以"纯产品"学说从理论上论证这个观点。并进一步认为，财富的生产意味着物质本身的创造和其量的增加。在各经济部门中，他们认为只有农业才能创造物质，并使物质财富的数量增加。农产品的增长是物质创造的表现，而在农业中生产出来的产品，减去补偿生产过程中耗费的生产资料、工人和农业资本家生活资料后的余额就是物质财富数量增加的表现。因此，只有农业才是生产的。重农主义的这一观点实质上是把自然资源看作是国民财富增长的基础因素，而土地又是自然资源的最主要的构成(在古典经济学中，土地常被用来指总的自然资源)。

古典经济学的代表亚当·斯密(Adam Smith，1723～1790)继承了重农主义者关于自然资源是国民财富增长的基础性因素这一观点。在《国民财富的性质和原因的研究》(1776)一书中，斯密预言，只要有合适的市场规模和一定量的资本积累，通过劳动分工提高劳动生产率和利润率，增加资本积累，经济增长就能自行持续下去。随着运输和通讯技术的改进，又可开辟新的市场和扩大对外贸易，加强经济增长的势头。但斯密同时指出经济增长不会无限地进行下去，最后，会由于自然资源的匮乏而告停止。因为，斯密认为，一个国家一旦将它的土壤、天时和地理位置的潜力充分利用以后，就无法再前进了，但也不会倒退，不过这时工资和利润都可能非常低。

托马斯·马尔萨斯(Thomas Malthus，1766～1834)从人口的角度，对人类社会的发展前景做出了预测。在《人口理论》(1798) 一书中，马尔萨斯认为，在土地的供给数量受到限制，而农业上又存在报酬递减规律的条件下，相对于人口持续增长的趋势，存在着一种使人类的生活下降到只能维持生计的最低水平的长期趋势。这一趋势可能表现为，在维持生计的最低收入水平上，只能容许人口的再生产维持一个不变的水平。

大卫·李嘉图(David Ricardo，1772～1823)把上述斯密和马尔萨斯描述的人类社会的未来趋势命名为经济的稳定状态(stationary state)，并在他的《政治经济学与税赋原理》(1817)一书中进行了具体论述。与马尔萨斯不同的是，李嘉图认为农业能够通过扩大内涵(在一块给定的土地上进行更加集约化的耕作)或外延(开垦更多的荒地用于农业生产)的方法来增大产出，显然，这种构想代替了不变土地供给的假定。同时他认为，在任何一种情况下，土地投入的报酬都是递减的，在这一规律作用下，粮食价格将会上涨，优等土地的地租会增加，从而使地主占有这些土地生产物的更大份额，缩小了资本家和工人所占份额。当地租继续上涨到边际土地的产量只够支付所雇佣的工人的生存工资时，利润等于零，资本家毫无所获，从而整个经济情况变成一种稳定状态。

作为古典经济学的终结者，约翰·斯库尔特·穆勒(John Stuart Mill，1806～1873)在其前辈研究的基础上，注意到了知识增长和技术进步对农业和制造业的促进作用。在其著作中指出，由于技术革新，农业生产率飞速增长，从而使土地供给对经济增长的制约作用减弱。并认为，农业的报酬递减规律虽然依然存在，但技术进步已使这一规律的影响力在下降。他列举了英国的情况，在当时的英国，人均产出显然在增加，而不是下降。在注意到技术进步对人类作用的同时，穆勒并没有对人类社会未来表现出盲目的乐观。他一方面批评前辈经济学家无视技术进步的作用，把人类的未来描述成相互挤压、摩肩接踵，奋力向前的状态。另一方面指出，如果仅为了能够维持一个更庞大但并不能令人更幸福、更美满的人口数量，财富和人口的无限增长将不得不以地球上失去更大量的乐趣为代价。所以穆勒认为，理想的稳定状态应该是能够达到相对较高水平的物质繁荣的一种状态。

显然，古典经济学家们在对经济增长与环境资源相互关系这一问题的认知上并没有明显的区别和进步。他们都将土地(其实是指自然资源)供给的有限性和农业的报酬递减作为未来经济增长的限制条件，并认为在这一条件下，人类社会将进入一种稳定状态。唯一的区别或进步在于，马尔萨斯所揭示的稳定状态完全忽略了技术的作用，而李嘉图却注意到了集约化耕作的作用。到了穆勒这里，知识与技术被十分明确地提出，并指出其在创造社会财富，促进经济增长中的作用。这种进步，是随着生产力的不断提高，人们对事物认识不断深化所带来的必然结果。同样，古典经济学家止步于上述认识，也是一种历史的必然局限。

(二)新古典经济学家的相关论述

与古典经济学家的代表人物相比，新古典经济学们对人类社会未来的经济增长持有明显的乐观态度。19 世纪 90 年代，英国经济学家阿弗里德·马歇尔(Alfred Marshall，1842～1924)在早期的生产费用论和 19 世纪 70 年代产生的边际学派的理论基础上，建立了剑桥学派并成为新古典经济学的重要组成部分。关于经济增长，马歇尔的基本观点是“自然不能飞跃”，认为“经济演化是逐渐进步的”。因此，人口、技术和资源的变化都是逐渐进行的。新古典学派把人口变动作为“已知的”。把技术进步假定为独立的变量，并认为可以通过利息率的变动来调节储蓄和投资，以进行资本积累。技术进步最终会增加劳动需求，价格机制会实现经济的长期增长。

熊彼特(J. A. Schumpeter)研究了经济长期增长问题。他认为，技术创新是推动经济增长的力量。技术创新不但增加了利润，而且迅速提高了资本积累，并认为当创新工作成为大公司经理阶层的常规工作时，企业的制度形态也会随之改变，进而导致资本主义制度形态发生质的改变。因此，技术创新是从生产领域和制度领域两个层面来促进经济增长的。

新古典经济学家抛弃了古典经济家们关于经济将处于稳定状态这一观点，他们在研究长期经济增长问题时，不再把人口、自然资源等因素当成是限制经济增长的条件，而是认为价格机制、技术进步等因素可以使经济长期处于增长状态。因此新古典经济学把注意力转向微观经济分析，即着重研究资源配置问题，不再或很少探讨经济增长与资源环境的相互关系。

（三）近现代经济学家的相关论述

新古典经济学家对长期经济增长的乐观态度在20世纪50～60年代演变成对经济增长的推崇。萨缪尔森等认为，第二次世界大战之后，经济增长是西方各国的“紧迫问题之一”，也是经济学界的“第一等优先的经济论题”。自哈罗德（R. F. Harrod）和多马[①]（E. D. Domar）之后近20年的时间里，无论是西方各国的经济实际还是经济理论都存在着所谓的“增长热”。这一时期对经济增长的大量研究与新古典经济学派时期的相关研究有一个共同的特点，就是很少把资源环境作为经济增长的限制条件。在大量具有代表性的研究文献中，储蓄、投资、要素投入数量、技术进步各要素以及它们间的相互关系被认为对经济增长起决定作用。在未来学领域，虽然对资源环境问题进行讨论，但依然对未来世界的增长抱着乐观态度。其中赫尔曼·卡恩（Herman Kahn）尤为突出，在《公元二千年》（1967）一书中，卡恩等人以当时的经济和人口增长趋势为基础，结合不同国家发展的特点，来预测未来的发展。他们认为，新技术是以加速度向前发展的，“今后的三十年和三十年以后的经济大半是趋向于平稳向前发展”，“经济发展的容量和对经济发展的献身精神，以及对内部环境和外部环境的控制看起来，似乎是愈来愈没有限制了”。看来，从新古典经济学派到20世纪50～60年代的经济学家，或是无视资

---

① 哈罗德1939年发表在《经济学》上的《论动态理论》和多马1947年发表在《美国经济评论》上的《扩充与就业》等论文，标志着现代经济增长理论的开端。

源环境对经济的影响来探讨资源配置和经济增长问题，或是迷信技术等因素作用，对未来世界经济增长持有乐观的态度。

20世纪60年代后期，肯尼恩·布尔丁(K. E. Boulding)、安·厄利奇(A. Ehrlich)和保罗·厄利奇等人对经济增长提出了反对意见。70年代初，以麦多斯(Meadows)的《增长的极限》(1972)为代表，反对长期增长的声浪到达了顶点。此后，关于经济增长与资源环境的相互关系的辩论持续进行了下来。

肯尼恩·布尔丁在1966年发表了一篇著名的论文——《未来的宇宙飞船式的经济学》。在文章中，布尔丁指出主流经济学将自然环境看成是一个无限延伸的平面，能从外界获取投入物，并向外界输出，因此用CDP和CNP反映物质总流量，并认为这些流量越大越好。对此，布尔丁持否定态度。他认为，地球是一个只能接收外界的能量输入(如太阳能)和对外界进行能量输出的封闭系统。来自开采、生产和消费行为的残留物总是以各种形式与人类同在。这如同一个宇宙飞船，超出飞船本身的范围，既不存在飞船内居民可获得的资源储备，也无法向外界处理不需要的残留物。因此，地球最理想的状态是，人类的活动应致力于物质流和能量流尽可能少，以使其无限持续下去。

相隔不到5年，安·厄利奇和保罗·厄利奇于1970年和1971年两年连续出版了《人口、资源和环境》、《人口炸弹》和《怎样成为一个幸存者》三本著作。他们认为工业化国家的经济增长已超出了生态环境的最佳承载能力，“地球飞船”的超载已接近失控的程度。特别是当人口继续增加时，就可能发生瘟疫，热核战争……甚至促进人类灭亡。

布尔丁和厄利奇等人的结论虽然危言耸听，但引起的反响远不如麦多斯等人的《增长的极限》(1972)。该书以福雷斯特尔(J. W. Forrester)1971年出版的《世界动态学》为蓝本，将世界系统用一个计算机模型来模拟未来。这个模型包括：可耕作的土地数量的极限；单位耕地农业产量的极限；可开发的不可再生资源的极限；环境同化生产和消费产生的废弃物能力的极限等四个方面。模型中的每一个变量随着时间的推移，其行为相互依赖和相互作用。麦多斯等人用世界模型研究的结论是：①如果世界人口、工业化、污染、粮食生产和资源减少等保持目前的速率不变，地球将在今后100年中的某个时刻达到增长的极限。最后可能的结果是人口和工业能力的突然和无法控制的下降。②上述趋势要求建立生态和经济的平衡，这样可保持社会持续地发展下去。③为实现全球的平衡状态，行动开始得越早，成功的机会越大。

继麦多斯等人之后，又先后有梅萨罗维克（M. Mesarovic）和佩斯太尔（E. Pestel）等人提出了名为《人类处于转折点》（1974）、丁伯根（J. Tinbergen）提出的名为《重建国际秩序》（1976）两个研究报告，报告在不同程度上对多麦斯等人的研究进行了修正，但结论仍然是悲观的。

经济学家对《增长的极限》的反应大多是否定的。比较著名的批评来自于柯尔（H. S. D. Cole）、费里曼（C. Freeman）和卡恩等人。他们认为麦多斯等人的增长有限论的实质是新形势下马尔萨斯人口论的再现，错误在于所选择的经济条件、参数、基期都存在缺陷，从而使研究结论更带有假定的成分。他们同时指出：人口不具有指数增长的性质，降低人口增长的长期手段将加速经济发展；技术的发展将使未来粮食的供应采用非传统方式，食物供应不可能发生危机；价格机制的作用将使替代品不断出现，并使不可再生资源的使用得到有效控制；从长期来看，经济增长将成为消除污染的手段。根据上述理由，卡恩等人对未来世界依然抱着乐观的态度。20世纪80年代初，托夫勒（A. Toffler）、奈其比特（J. Naisbitt）等人在《第三次浪潮》、《大趋势》、《信息的财富》等著作中，从信息技术对未来的作用的角度再次支持了卡恩等人对未来世界的判断。

上述争论双方的观点处于悲观和乐观的两极，而此后的大部分研究结果却趋于两者的融合。1987年，联合国环境与发展委员会公布了一个著名的报告——《我们共同的未来》，在这个报告中首次提出了可持续发展这一概念。报告指出，发展中国家应在经济增长中扮演重要角色，并依靠经济增长获得收益，来解决贫困和不发达问题。但工业化国家的经济增长应逐步向低原材料消耗、低能耗的方向转变，并改善物质和能源的使用效率，只有这样，才可能保障环境的可持续性。报告公布5年之后，1992年在里约热内卢又召开了联合国环境与发展大会，会议就生物多样性保护、全球气候变化、森林管理等多个方面进行磋商，并采纳了《里约宣言》和《21 世纪议程》两个文件。前者是实现全球可持续发展的原则声明，后者的许多内容涉及有关发达国家向发展中国家转让资源的议题。此后，VNEP(1994)、Common(1995)、Stem (1996)、Johnson(1999)等国际机构和研究者分别就土壤侵蚀和荒漠化、长期的环境效应和收入之间关系、人口、农业和食物的可供应性等问题进行专题研究。其结论大部分证明，全球生态环境正趋于恶化，而关于经济增长与资源环境的相互关系却没有明确的结论。

(四)剩余输出理论与荷兰病的现实证明

大量的事实证明，一个国家工业化初期的经济活动，是以高度依赖自然资源为特征的。虽然自然资源具有稀缺性，但发展初期的经济增长主要依靠开发可用来生产初级品的矿物、森林和其他自然资源。经济学家 Hla Myint 提出的“剩余输出理论”曾这样描述上述经济发展初期的经济特征：在东南亚和非洲，人口密度低，有大片未被利用的土地和丰富的自然资源，当这些地区的经济在殖民主义下同国际贸易整合在一起时，一些尚未利用的自然资源因发现可用来生产外部需求很高的初级产品而开始拥有市场价值。这些自然资源首先被外国资本和企业家开发，之后又为本国资本和企业利用，成为其经济收入的主要来源。作为这个以发达国家历史经验为基础的理论的成功范例，是加拿大的自然资源开发过程。在加拿大，先是从东海岸的鳕鱼和皮货转换为内地森林里的木材，进而又转换为大平原上的小麦。在这个过程中，伴随着木材和小麦加工厂以及旨在满足本国消费需求的制造业的发展，国内市场也随着商业和交通的发展而扩大了。

然而，虽然丰富的自然资源禀赋是经济发展的一大笔财富，但有时候它却是导致经济停止的陷阱。20 世纪 70 年代石油繁荣期间，荷兰在北海发现了丰富的天然气储量，这种新资源的开发为荷兰的贸易平衡带来了很大的改善，但随后经济发展却停止了，人们将这种现象叫做“荷兰病”。此后，墨西哥、尼日利亚也出现了与荷兰类似的现象。这些现象使人们反思，一个资源基础型的经济要想有效地转换成持续增长的经济，必须找到一种将开发自然资源所获得的租金转向持续经济发展所需的人力资本和社会一般资本投资的办法。简单的开发自然资源既不能实现持续发展，也不能改善居民的生活水平。

二、工业化过程中森林资源利用政策的演变

虽然不清楚上述理论在多大程度上影响了一个国家在林业发展中的政策选择，但我们通过发达国家的实践，依然可以观察到工业化不同阶段林业政策的调整。

(一)从无限度索取到永续利用

从18世纪60年代起，欧美国家先后发生了范围广阔、影响深远的工业革命。工业革命的爆发使社会生产力获得了空前的发展，而且也促进了产业结构的巨大变化，即农业在国民经济总产值中的比重逐渐减少，工业在国民经济总产值中的比重逐渐增加。在这一背景下，社会对木材的需求急剧增加。在第一次技术革命时期，除个别国家(如德国)建立了林业产业以外，大多数国家林业仍未形成独立完整的产业部门，林业生产更多地表现为森林采伐。而且，各国政府对采伐森林资源大多采取放任甚至鼓励态度。

从19世纪70年代开始，一些工业革命比较成功的国家先后进入了工业化阶段，开始了由农业国向工业国的转化。从19世纪中后期到20世纪初，英国的农业在国民经济中的比重由22%缩小到6%，工业由34%上升为40%，服务业由44%增加到54%。德国、美国、法国等国家的国民经济也发生了类似变化。随着工业化程度的不断提高，木材需求和森林资源短缺的程度同时上升，供需矛盾加剧。在这一情况下，英国、法国、德国、美国等国家制定的林业政策具有以下明显的特点：

首先，在经营思想上确立了以木材生产为中心，以经济效益为主要目标的永续利用方针。这一点不仅体现在对现有林的经营，而且也指导着对人工林的培育。德国从18世纪末开始在“木材培育论”指导下营造的大面积针叶纯林和新西兰引种外来树种营造的针叶纯林，都是以木材生产和获取最大经济效益为主要目的。

这种经营思想也充分体现在各国在这一时期所制定的森林法中。如瑞典在1905年颁布的第一部森林法，其中新内容是“均匀采伐，永续利用”，规定“采伐

量不得超过生长量”，“林主必须切实保护森林，不得乱砍滥伐，保证采伐迹地更新”。此外，在奥地利、捷克斯洛伐克和匈牙利早期制定的森林法，美国于19世纪后期颁布的《木材培育条例》，以及日本从明治维新后长期执行的“资源政策”中，也体现了这种基本思想。德国由于开展人工造林较早，到19世纪中期已基本完成森林恢复工作，而且营造的大面积针叶纯林已暴露出很多问题，因此到19世纪后期又先后提出了“森林效益永续经营理论”和“林业政策效用论”。然而由于两次世界大战和期间发生的世界性资本主义社会经济大危机的影响，这些思想并未得到贯彻执行。

其次，对人工造林实行各种鼓励政策。由于树木生长缓慢，人工林经营周期长，而且具有一定的风险性，因此各国政府对发展人工林（包括国有林和私有林）普遍采取优惠和鼓励政策。这种政策包括资金补助、优惠贷款、减免税收、提供实物（种子和苗木）和技术指导等内容。此外，美国还采取了对造林者无偿赠与土地的政策。

第三，强调依法治林。各国相继颁布了相关的法令和条例，促进森林恢复和发展人工造林，保障森林资源的永续利用。

（二）森林资源经营政策的反复

第二次世界大战以后，由于百业待兴而又缺乏资金，为尽快恢复国民经济，各国政府不得不继续采取牺牲林业换取农业与工业的恢复和发展的政策。也就是说，在战后的经济恢复时期，林业不但未立即得到恢复，相反，为保证工农业的恢复却继续遭到破坏。这种情况主要表现在：①在战时留下的大量采伐迹地得不到更新的情况下继续进行超量采伐（采伐量超过生长量）；②采伐木材的目的是解决薪炭材或增加粮食生产。

日本在第二次世界大战后为了满足复兴经济和解决粮食问题及就业问题，对国内森林资源继续进行破坏性采伐，致使森林的荒废程度不断加剧。到1949年，全国需要更新造林的采伐迹地累计已达150万hm^2，荒废林地约30万hm^2，区域荒废的林地23万hm^2。而采伐的木材，至1951年仍有40%以上是用作薪炭材。有鉴于此，日本政府于1948年开始实施造林补助金制度，1949年发展水源涵养林，1950 年成立国土绿化推进委员会，1951 年确立了对全国森林经营管理起监督促进作用的“森林计划制度”，1954 年又制定了《发展防护林临时措施法》。日本林业的恢复实际上到 1955 年才宣告结束，即战时和战后初期造成的大量采伐迹地到此时才完全更新造林完毕，1956 年薪炭材消费比重降至 28.5%。

联邦德国在第二次世界大战后初期，由于经济完全崩溃，为了恢复生产和重建家园仍不得不继续进行超量采伐。如在 1946 年，其采伐量高达 6 130 万 m^3，过伐 2 430 万 m^3，而且在采伐的木材中薪炭材约占 37.5%。薪炭材比重居高不下的情况一直延续到 50 年代初期，直到 1952 年，联邦德国和民主德国的薪炭材采伐量依然占总采伐量的 22% 左右。

芬兰在 20 世纪 30～60 年代一直处于农产品极度匮乏的状态。为了实现粮食自给，政府长期实行奖农政策，1945 年颁布的《土地获得法》和 1950 年制定的《林垦法》都是以毁林为代价来增加农产品生产。这些法律规定，凡毁林农垦者都可得到政府补助。这种情况一直延续到 1969 年政府颁布《农田休耕法》，即粮食实现自给以后才得以改变。

（三）多效益经营思想的萌芽

第二次世界大战之后世界经济在度过了短暂的恢复期后，从 20 世纪 50 年代开始的 20 年间，发达国家的经济获得了空前的发展，各主要工业国的国民生产总值年均增长率一般达到了 5%～6%，个别国家（如日本）甚至高达 16%～17%。这一时期为满足木材的需求，工业化国家一方面采取集约经营措施提高林木生长量，另一方面发展木材的综合利用提高利用率和开发替代品技术。同时在林业政策上进行了以下调整：

首先，林业经营继续以木材生产和经济效益为主，但已广泛执行分类经营方针。20 世纪 50～70 年代初，在国外林业经营中起主导作用的仍是 18 世纪起源于德国的“森林永续经营理论”。由于该理论追求纯经济效益，强调以生产木材为主要目的，因此非常符合当时的森林经营者急于大量生产木材以满足工业高速发展需求的愿望。瑞典 1948 年诞生的第二部《森林法》在世界林业大发展阶段的产业政策中就颇具代表性。这部《森林法》产生于瑞典制浆造纸工业飞速发展，其他木材工业部门也急于扩大生产，所有用材部门都希望得到稳定而廉价的原料的时代，因而它的中心思想是强调林业应更多地提供工业用材。《森林法》重申森林采伐量不能超过生长量，并进一步提出应把林业作为一种能产生工业利润的产业来经营，林地必须用于生产木材。

在此阶段中，工业高速发展带来的城市集中、公害加剧及生态环境恶化等问题，使人们对发挥森林多种效益的重要性已有所认识。美国国会1960年通过的《森林的多种利用及永续生产条例》，联邦德国1965年开始推行的“森林效益国”政策即是在这种背景下出台的。但从当时他们的实际做法看，仍以木材生产为优先发展的目标，针叶材产量和木材销售量都在成倍增长。

为了缓和森林利用中经济效益与环境效益的矛盾，许多国家采取了分类经营的方针，即将林地划分为用材林和非用材林。用材林主要用于生产木材，非用材林一部分是由于林地生产能力低，不适合用于生产木材，另一部分虽生产能力达到用材林标准，但为发挥防护和其他社会功能而将其划为各种防护林、国家公园、自然保护区或特殊用途保留林，不再作为生产木材之用。从发展趋势来看，用材林的面积在逐渐减少，国家公园和自然保护区则不断增加。由于用材林担负着提供木材的主要任务，所以林业发达国家多对其采取集约经营的方式，以提高森林单位面积的木材产量。

其次，营林、森工走向综合。在过去，由于森林资源十分丰富，木材原料供应充足，森林工业企业对造林态度冷淡。但在最近几十年，特别是第二次世界大战以后，由于木材资源日益短缺，木材价格不断上涨，森工企业为求得自身的生存和发展已越来越多地注意经营林木，从而为实现森工与营林综合经营开辟了道路。

森林工业走上与营林综合经营道路的主要原因有以下几点：一是森林资源急剧减少，已产生木材原料枯竭的危险，威胁到企业投资者的利益；二是为保证加工工业的生产，必须保证原料源源不断地供应；三是人工林提供的木材径级虽小，材质稍差，但通过改进加工工艺和设备已能生产出满足要求的产品；四是科技发展大大缩短了林木培育周期，使造林成为森工企业有利可图的事业；五是几十年来木材价格的猛烈上涨更加激发了森工企业营林的积极性。

由于纸浆生产可用小径材，适宜使用速生材，用材林也容易规划经营，所以纸浆公司首先采用了综合经营的方式。随后，一些大型制材和胶合板工业企业也相继走上这条道路。

据美国官方统计，1970 年美国的公司林面积已占用材林面积的 13%，1977 年提高到 14.1%。1950～1959 年日本的纸浆公司共造林 9.3 万 hm^2。加拿大森林多属国有，由于实行公有森林私人经营的管理体制，许多木材加工企业都租赁了大面积的森林，从事从营林到加工的一条龙经营，如全国最大的林产工业企业——麦克米伦公司租赁森林几百万公顷，进行从营林到采伐，一直到生产出各种林产品的一条龙最佳效益经营。

瑞典私有林占全国森林的 74%，除 25% 的公司林林权比较集中外，其余 49% 均为小私有林主所有。小私有林主经营面积小，财力单薄，技术水平低，提高经营集约强度困难。为此，瑞典各地成立了林主协会，并在全国设置总会，统一销售林主生产的木材，协会还集中林主财力建立木材加工企业，组织合作造林和采运，使林权分散的私有林也走上了林工结合的道路。前苏联的林业和森工虽是分治体制，但无论是主管营林工业的林业委员会还是作为产业部门的森工部，都同时从事营林和森林工业活动，只是侧重点有所不同而已。

再次，调整森林工业政策。自 20 世纪 60 年代初以来，工业化国家普遍对森林工业政策进行调整，把解决木材不足的重点从单纯扩大采伐量逐步转向发展木材综合利用。木材综合利用率和单位工业用材产品产值成为衡量一个国家木材工业水平的重要标志之一。70 年代初，联邦德国和瑞典的木材综合利用率已分别达到 84% 和 83.8%，芬兰为 75%，美国、苏联和日本也有较大进展。在工业发达国家，木材加工剩余物（板条、板皮、截头、碎单板和锯屑等）已相当多地用于生产纸浆和人造板，如北欧国家加工剩余物的工业利用率（不包括能源利用），在 1972～1974 年已达到 85%，美国（1970 年）和苏联（1975 年）也分别达到了 46.6% 和 30.8%。

随着木材综合利用的发展，人造板和制纸、造纸工业成为这一时期发展最快的两个现代化工业部门。1950～1973年，美国、瑞典、联邦德国和加拿大的木材采伐量增长分别为15.2%、43.4%、15.9%和62.3%，但在同期这些国家的人造板生产量分别增长了6.03、4.1、10.6和7.45倍，木浆生产分别增长1.75、18、0.86和1.27倍，纸和纸制品生产分别增长1.34、3.17、2.5相0.97倍。

在此期间，苏联森工内部的投资结构也发生了明显变化。在20世纪60年代以前，采运工业投资在森工总投资额中历年都占60%以上，林产工业投资仅占30%左右。到了70年代末，前者已降至40%左右，后者已增加到50%以上。其他东欧国家也都出现了类似情况。随着对加工业投资的大幅度增长，林产品结构亦发生巨大变化，如1950～1973年苏联木材采伐量仅增加15.8%，而人造板产量却增长了8.62倍，纸和纸制品增长了4.9倍。

各国森林工业的调整还表现在优化产品结构，大力发展深加工产品和附加值高的产品。压缩薪炭材和初级产品比重，从而使刨花板这一技术密集、成本低廉、原料要求不高和用途广泛的产品得以快速发展，锯材和人造板各种二次加工产品产量也迅速扩大。

第四，对人工造林采取鼓励政策。造林是一项在短期内难以产生经济效益并具有一定风险的事业，因此为发展人工林，改善木材供需矛盾，各国政府都广泛采取经济和技术扶持政策。

联邦德国、日本、新西兰和澳大利亚等国之所以能在短期内恢复被破坏的森林资源并得以稳步发展，进而建立现代化林业，主要原因之一是他们都制定了一整套的林业保护与扶持政策。财政和技术上的扶持尤为突出，这主要表现在两个方面：一是对国有林免税。这些国家规定任何单位和个人都需向国家上缴固定财产税，一般财产税款按固定资产的5%计算。有人估计，联邦德国的国有林财产（林地及地产）至少价值460亿～500亿美元，政府免收这笔财产税，等于1年投资20多亿美元用于国有林建设。二是对小私有林主进行资金补助和技术指导的侧重点放在鼓励小私有林主造林上，因而提高了小私有林主的造林积极性。

第五，对私有林采取扶持政策。除个别国家外，大多数工业发达国家私有林都占很大比例。私有林往往位于社会条件和自然条件较好的地区，树木生长快，劳动力密集，但由于林权分散，经营单位细小，难以合理规划林区道路和有效利用大型机械。此外，私有林生产的木材批量多而小，很难与木材加工厂进行旗鼓相当的合作。因而，各国政府都非常重视扶持私有林，制定了许多关于私有林的扶持政策。政策内容主要包括以下两个方面：一是在经济和技术上给予扶持，鼓励营造人工林，帮助私有林提高经营水平。如芬兰、瑞典、联邦德国、日本、美国、加拿大等都从法律上规定，国家以无偿或低息有偿等形式资助林主发展造林。二是推行私有林合作化政策，林权分散是诸多国家私有林的共同特点，为有利于森林集约化经营并帮助林主进行木材的产销活动，美国、日本、芬兰、联邦德国等国家长期坚持推行私有林合作化政策，鼓励小私有林主组成各种协会，进行合作。如美国的“标准林场”，芬兰、瑞典的林主协会，日本建立的森林组合等都在引导协助私有林沿集团化、协作化方向发展上发挥了重大作用。私有林合作生产不仅提高了生产效率，解决了农村林业劳力不足的问题，重要的是经营强度的提高加快了森林木材蓄积量的增长。私有林木材产量的增加弥补了国家木材消费的不足，改善了林主经济收入，也使国家有财力去承担亏损严重的自然生态保护及提供休憩旅游的任务。林主的素质影响林业的发展水平，这些国家的政府每年都有培训林主的预算，每年对部分林主进行培训。

第六，以外养内政策。英国、日本、联邦德国等国家继续采取以外养内政策。经过几十年努力，日本、联邦德国的森林资源已有很大恢复，其森林覆盖率已达到相当水平，英国为恢复自己的森林资源也作了很大努力。但由于幼龄林多，不能利用，也为了保护本国资源，这三个国家继续采取以外养内政策。

1952～1972 年，英国、日本和联邦德国的林产品进口量一直占世界林产品总进口量的 30% 以上，其中日本进口量增长最快，英国和联邦德国的进口量所占份额在 20 世纪 60 年代有所下降。日本主要进口原木，实际上早在 1962 年日本即已成为世界最大的原木进口国，1962～1972 年原木进口量从 316.1 万 m^3 上升到 4 919.8万 m^3，增长了 15.5 倍；原木进口量占全球原木进口量的比例由 1962 年的 44.8% 上升到 1972 年的 54.6%，超过全球原木总进口量的一半。与此同时，日本又利用部分进口木材加工成林产品后出口，既弥补了进口的一些亏空，又保护了本国森林资源。

总之，在此阶段，随着全球经济的恢复和高速发展，林业的发展有一个飞跃，上了一个新台阶。其发展的主要特点在于：①发达国家的森林资源相继恢复，并大力营造人工林。②实现森林永续利用已成为各国森林经营的指导思想，森林经营目的仍以发挥经济效益为主，但发达国家已开始重视森林的多效益利用，并实施分类经营原则。③能源结构的改变和技术发展促使工业化国家的林产品结构发生巨大变化，工业用材比重大幅度上升，薪炭材比重明显下降，木材综合利用水平显著提高，各种附加值高的产品获得了优先发展。④森林资源丰富的发展中国家基于自身的资源优势，开始发展自己的民族工业，但初级产品和半成品占很大的比重，为取得国民经济的发展，他们仍不得不继续采取大量采伐和大量出口原木的政策。

第三章　林业发展中的生态问题理论

在工业化进程中，由于工业化初期生产力水平低下，科学技术落后，林产品替代品少等原因，加之林业在原料、资本、外汇等方面对工业化做出的贡献十分突出，人们对森林资源采用粗放型经营和掠夺式采伐。这一做法使得森林资源大量减少，资源问题日益严峻，同时也导致生态状况不断恶化，生态问题日益显现并逐渐突出。在林业发展进程中生态问题经历了由萌芽阶段向凸显阶段的转变。本章在对生态问题进行深入的经济学分析之后，将以人们对生态问题的认识过程和经济发展的不同阶段为主线，分析生态问题由萌芽阶段向凸显阶段的发展过程，进而说明经济发展和生态建设将会协调发展，林业的生态功能将会逐步得到重视。

需要指出的是，生态与环境之间是有区别的，关于二者之间的关系有很多种说法，本书认为生态一词可以在更高层面上运用。这是因为生态是与生物有关的各种关系的总和，包括生物与环境之间的相互关系，生态已经将环境包括在内了，可以说生态是整体，而环境作为部分纳入其中。在此基础上探讨的生态问题即指由于人类不合理的活动，导致基本生态过程即生态结构与功能的破坏和生命维持系统的瓦解，从而危害了人类生存的问题。

第一节　生态问题的经济学分析

随着近些年来全球人口不断增加，资源逐渐减少，生态状况日益恶化，生态问题逐步得到人们的重视，进而成为人们研究、讨论的重点问题和热点问题。人们试图从生态学、社会学、伦理学、哲学等各个角度探讨生态问题，本章将从经济学角度对其进行深入分析。

一、生态的公共物品特征

生态是一个不可分割的整体，其作用的发挥是以保持生态整体性为前提的，一旦生态被分割为各个部分，其功能就会大大削减，甚至完全消失；良好的生态可以改善人们的生存环境，提高人们的生活质量，同时也会附带产生社会效益和经济效益；改善生态的投资者可以是具体的，但是其消费者却无法落实到具体的个人。

上述对生态自然属性的描述概括起来即为，生态具有整体有用性、用途多样性、功能持续性以及环境共享性。

正是由于生态具有这些自然属性，其大部分价值并不是在市场上通过等价交换实现的，也不能通过市场价格来反应。这不仅因为生态的价值难以量化，更重要的是因为生态具有效用非竞争性和消费非排他性，经济学上称之为公共物品性。

生态具有公共物品的特征主要是因为其具有效益外部性。外部性是指个人或经济单位所承担的收益和成本是另外的个人或经济单位行为的直接后果，而自身没有付出成本或得到补偿的任何情况。许多具有公共物品性的产品都具有较强的外部性。外部性有正的外部性和负的外部性两种类型：当社会成本小于私人成本时，称为正的外部性；而当社会成本大于私人成本时，称为负的外部性。企业或其他生产部门为了自身的私利而疯狂地掠夺自然资源，造成了生态状况的恶化和生态系统的失衡，但他们并不会因此付出相应的成本；而政府为了恢复生态却需要支付较高的成本，致使社会成本大大高于私人成本，这就产生了负的外部性。由上述生态的自然属性可以看出，生态在技术上或经济上不可能把不支付费用而需要消费的人排除在外；并且无论增加多少消费者，也不会因此而减少其他消费者的消费，或者说一个人对生态的消费并不会减少其他人对生态的消费。生态具备公共物品(public goods)最基本的特征——效用非竞争性和消费非排他性，所谓消费非竞争性是指物品的社会边际成本不会因消费者人数的增加而增加，即其社会边际成本为零；效用非排他性是指不能够，或者说从成本—收益的角度看不能经济有效地排除潜在消费者从这类产品中受益。此外，生态还具备公共物品的几个派生性质：

第一，生态消费的被动性。处于生态系统中的人自觉或不自觉地就对生态进行消费了，这种消费是不能进行选择的。不论你愿意与否，也不论你是否有这种消费需求，只要处于生态系统中，就自然而然成了生态的消费者。就消费者而言，其对生态的消费是被动的，但同时又是必需的。

第二，生态需求的无弹性。生态的效用非排他性，为潜在的消费者提供了不必付费而直接享受生态的可能性。按照“经济人”假设，人们的决策都是以自身利益最大化为前提的，既然存在不必支付费用而可以直接获取收益的可能性，人们就会选择不支付费用，进而也就产生了公共物品消费中普遍存在的“搭便车”现象，导致了生态需求价格弹性为零。

如图 3-1 所示，Q^* 代表人们对生态的需求数量。由于生态的自然属性，人们的生存离不开生态系统所提供的生态，不会因为其价格的高低而决定是否消费或消费多少；另一方面由于生态具有公共物品性，人们不必为消费的生态实际支付费用，人们对生态的消费总是既定区域范围内提供的生态，所以其需求曲线就表现为一条垂直于横坐标的直线，说明价格的变动对生态的需求没有影响。

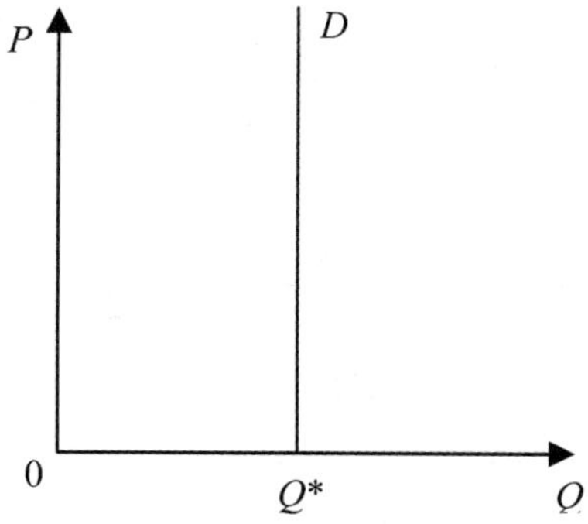

图 3-1　生态需求曲线

第三，生态产权的不明晰性。产权包括所有权、使用权、处置权和剩余收益索取权等。由于生态具有消费非竞争性和效用非排他性，社会公众可以共享其使用权。其所有权也常存在主体缺位的情况，归属很难确定，从而导致剩余收益索取权及与之相关的交换、处置和资本化的权利无法明确。产权界限的模糊，致使生态的交易很难通过市场来实现。由于交易双方的主体不明确，各自代表的利益也就无从谈起，使得市场这一有效的资源配置方式失去了其应有的效率和效果，对生态交易变得无能为力。

生态的公共物品性使得具有生态功能的森林资源在一定程度上也具备了公共物品性，森林是陆地上最大的生态系统，当其发挥生态功能时，其所产生的生态效益对整个生态状况的改善起到了重要的作用，然而这种生态效益的发挥并不会得到消费群体的直接经济补偿，这时收益的外部性就产生了，同时森林的生态功能也具有产权不明晰性和消费被动性等特征。

二、生态需求的经济学特征

生态的自然属性决定了生态系统与人类的生存和发展密切相关，而公共物品特征又使人类对其需求有着某种独有的特征。

（一）生态需求的基本表现

由生态的自然属性可以看出，生态系统对人类的生存和生活有若至关重要的影响，其不但为人们的生活提供了空间，也为人们的生产经营活动提供了载体。人们对生态的需求主要体现在以下几个大的方面：

第一，生存环境改善的需求。人类生存总要依赖于特定的环境和空间，人类在这个特定的环境和空间中进行各种生产和生活活动，通过自己的劳动创造出生产资料和生活资料，创造出社会财富，并不断繁衍生息。生态质量的好坏直接影响人类的生存状态。

第二，生活质量提高的需求。随着历史发展和社会进步，人类的生活状况越来越好。现在人们生活的目标不再是单纯的吃饱穿暖这些最基本的要求，而是要不断提高生活的质量。在人类社会形成之初，生态状况接近自然状态，很少打上人类活动的印记，但是物质极度匮乏，人们的生活质量非常低；经济的发展和社会的进步使人们的物质需求日益得到满足，但生态状况却遭到了严重的破坏，人们的生活质量从生态角度来说仍旧较差。如今人们不必再为填饱肚子而整日奔波，闲暇时间越来越多，就愈发渴望能够回归大自然，渴望享受高质量的生态。

第三，社会可持续发展的需求。生态作为可持续发展的一个重要影响因素起着至关重要的作用。生态为经济建设和社会发展提供了基本保障，良好的生态状况将会推动经济和社会稳步、协调发展；反之，经济和社会的发展也会促进生态状况的逐步改善，最终达到经济、社会和生态之间的和谐，实现可持续发展。

上文从较为宏观的方面阐述了人们对生态的需求愿望，生态和人们的生产、生活休戚相关，人类的一切活动都离不开生态。这一表象的分析使人们对生态的需求有了初步的了解，但是，人们对生态的需求愿望能不能形成一种有效的需求仍值得进一步探讨。

(二)生态需求的博弈

需求是指有机体因某种生理或心理因素的缺乏，产生的一种不平衡感或缺失感，而力求去平衡或去满足的内部心理状态。有效的需求需要具备两个基本的条件，即购买欲望和实际购买能力。任何一个条件没有满足，都难以形成有效的需求，因而从产生购买欲望到实际发生购买行为需要一个过程：

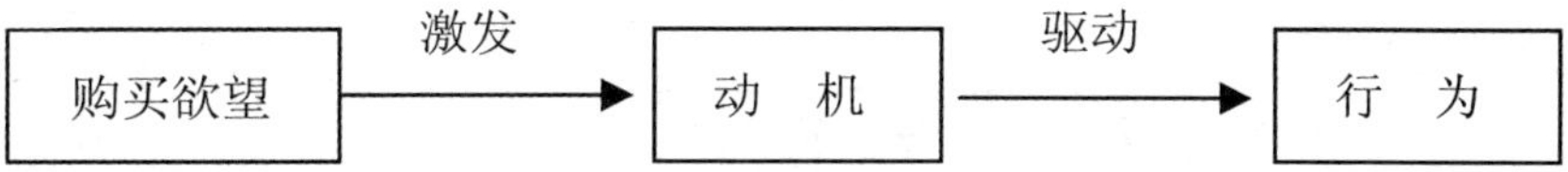

图 3-2 有效需求的形成过程

由图 3-2 可知，从产生购买欲望到发生实际购买行为要经过激发和驱动两个关键的环节。购买欲望通过激发变成了购买动机，购买动机再通过驱动就引起动作，发生了购买行为，这种驱动实质上就表现为实际的货币支付能力，即实际购买能力，只有实际支付了货币之后才能形成有效的需求。由于生态具有公共物品性，消费者的理性会导致“搭便车”现象产生，为了使自身效用达到最大化，消费者都会选择自己不实际支付费用而免费享有他人支付所创造的生态，这种“搭便车”现象的产生可以用博弈论模型来加以论证。

在设定这一博弈论模型时，首先要做出基本前提假设：

第一，此模型只考虑两类生态的消费者：一类是从生态系统中获取资源，并向生态系统中排放废弃物的企业(用参与者 A 表示)；另一类是除企业之外的其他消费者，主要是消费生态的居民(用参与者 B 表示)。

第二，令参与者不支付费用时(用 F 表示)可获得的最大效用为 2；其支付费用时（用 E 表示）则会损失 1，最终获得的效用为 1。

第三，若企业和居民都愿意为获得高质量的生态而支付一定数量的货币，则二者的各自效用会达到(1，1)；若双方只有一方愿意为此支付费用，另一方不必为此支付费用而可以免费消费生态时，则获得效用分别为(1，2)或(2，1)；当二者都不愿付费进行消费，而都想免费获利时，将达到各自效用的最大化，即(2，2)。

第四，当二者都不支付费用时，并不影响生态的供给，此时将由这一模型之外的政府来提供生态。

由此可设定如图 3-3 所示的博弈论模型。

		参与者 A	
		E	F
参与者 B	E	(1，1)	(1，2)
	F	(2，1)	(2，2)

图 3-3 "搭便车"现象的博弈论模型

博弈是指一些个人、团队或其他组织，面对一定的环境条件，在一定的规则约束下，依靠所掌握的信息，同时或先后，一次或多次，从各自允许选择的行为或策略中进行选择并加以实施，并从中各自取得相应结果或收益的过程。图 3-3 中 E 表示为了获得对生态的消费将支付一定的费用，即需求愿望将会转化为有效需求，此时产生 1 单位的效用损失；F 表示不必支付任何费用，而可以免费获得对生态的消费，在这种状况下，对生态的需求只是停留在需求愿望阶段。可以看出，仅以参与者 A 为例，当参与者 B 选择 E 时，即参与者 B 愿意为获得对生态的消费而支付一定的费用时，若参与者 A 也选择决策 E，则其自身获得的效用为 1；若参与者 A 选择决策 F，则其自身可以获得效用为 2，作为一个理性的"经济人"，参与者 A 就会选择决策 F，即不支付任何费用而直接免费享受生态的消费。当参与者 B 选择 F 时，即参与者 B 不愿意为获得对生态的消费而支付一定的费用时，若参与者A选择决策E，则其自身获得的效用为1；若当参与者A也选择决策F，则其自身可以获得效用为2，同样参与者A也会选择决策F，还是不会支付任何费用。也就是说，不论参与者B做出何种选择，对于参与者A来说其最佳的决策都是选择决策F，即不支付费用而免费消费生态，换言之，参与者A对生态的需求只是停留在需求愿望阶段，而未能通过实际支付货币形成有效的需求。同样，对参与者B也存在同样的情况。那么参与者A和参与者B都会不支付费用，“搭便车”现象便产生了。

此外，购买欲望只是人们内心的一种愿望，当人们有能力并愿意为此付出货币时，这种需求愿望才会转化为有效需求。购买欲望与需求是有区别的，二者之间并非总是同步、同量的。在一定时期内对一种物品的需求量总是要小于对这种物品的需要量。因为有时没有转化为需求的条件，只能是形成潜在的需求。因此，从严格意义上来说，对生态的需求只能是一种需求愿望，而未发展成现实的需求购买行为，并不是真正意义上的需求。

（三）生态需求愿望的无差异曲线

人们对生态的需求只是一种需求愿望，影响这一需求愿望的不仅包括生态的质量，同时也包括人们的经济条件。在同一需求愿望程度下，现有的生态质量和现有的经济收入水平之间存在着一定的关系；不同的生态质量和收入水平又会影响人们对生态需求愿望的程度。

通过对生态需求的经济学特征分析可知：人们对生态的需求只是一种购买欲望或者说只是一种需求愿望，不会通过真正支付货币进而形成一种有效的需求。从某种意义上说，人们对生态的消费有时并不是自身自主做出的选择，而是由政府在替代民众选择，因为政府通过对企业或个人征收的各种税费最终有可能会有部分用于对生态保护和建设，进而提供更良好的生态，但是并没有哪一个个体会自愿掏自己的腰包来消费生态，人们对生态的有效需求难以形成。

人们不愿意自己出资来消费生态，并不意味着他们没有消费生态的需求愿望，相反由于生态系统不仅是人们依赖的生存环境，而且能够给人们带来美的享受和身心的愉悦，生态状况的好坏直接关系到人们生活质量的好坏，因而人们时刻都对生态有需求愿望，只是这种愿望会受到各种因素的制约。下面着重探讨一下现有生态状况等级和人们现有的收入水平对生态需求愿望产生的影响。

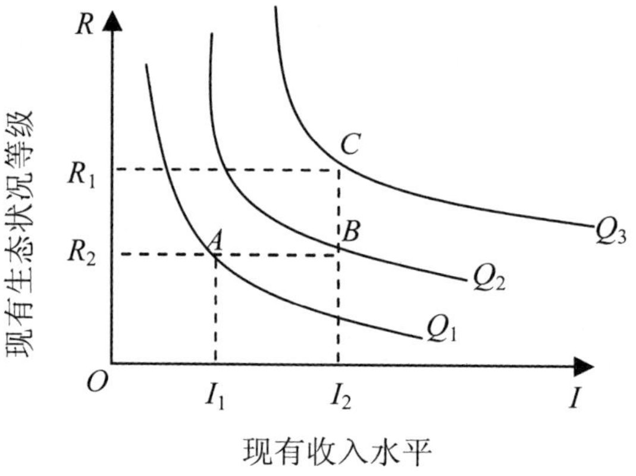

图 3-4　生态需求愿望无差异曲线

（资料来源：王爱民．环境产品的政府双重垄断分析．社会科学，2005，8）

如图 3-4 所示，纵坐标代表现有生态状况的等级，沿着纵坐标的方向生态状况逐渐变差，即处于 R_1 水平时生态状况要比在 R_2 水平时更差；横坐标代表人们现有的收入水平，沿着横坐标的方向收入水平越来越高，即处于 I_1 时人们的收入水平要低于 I_2 时的水平。Q_1、Q_2、Q_3 则代表三条不同程度需求愿望的无差异曲线，在每条无差异曲线的各点具有相同的需求程度，并且这三条无差异曲线按照离原点距离的远近，Q_3 的需求程度最高，Q_1 的需求程度最低。当生态状况处于 R_2 水平时，若现有收入水平为 I_1，则人们对生态的需求愿望为处于 Q_1 上的 A 点，若现有的收入水平为 I_2，则人们对生态的需求愿望为处于 Q_2 上的 B 点，可知在现有生态状况等级一定的情况下，人们现有的收入水平越高，其对生态的需求愿望也就越强烈；当人们的收入水平仍为 I_2，若现有生态状况处于一个相对较差的情况，即位于 R_1 时，人们对生态的需求愿望为处于 Q_3 上的 C 点，达到一个需求程度更高的无差异曲线水平，可见在人们现有收入水平一定的情况下，现处的生态状况越差，对生态的需求愿望会更加强烈。图 3-4 形象地描绘了现有生态状况等级和现有收入水平对生态需求愿望的影响，现有收入水平越高，现处的生态状况越差人们对生态的需求愿望也就越强烈。通过此图能得出与环境库兹涅茨曲线相同的结论，即收入水平越高，人们对生态的需求愿望越强，解决生态问题的经济实力也越强，生态状况有所好转的可能性也就越大。

同时，也应该注意到，虽然现有生态状况等级与人们收入水平之间存在着这样的关系，但这并不能说明人们对生态的需求愿望会得到最大的满足。这是因为在经济尚未发展到一定程度之前，人们不会主动支付货币来消费生态。这一时期主要还是依靠政府代表人们来实现对生态的消费，换言之，政府是生态有效需求的主体。当然这一结论带有一定的时期性，当经济发展到相当高的程度时，个体也有可能成为生态有效需求的主体。在这段时期内，只有在政府支付能力范围内才能使人们对生态的需求愿望得到满足。

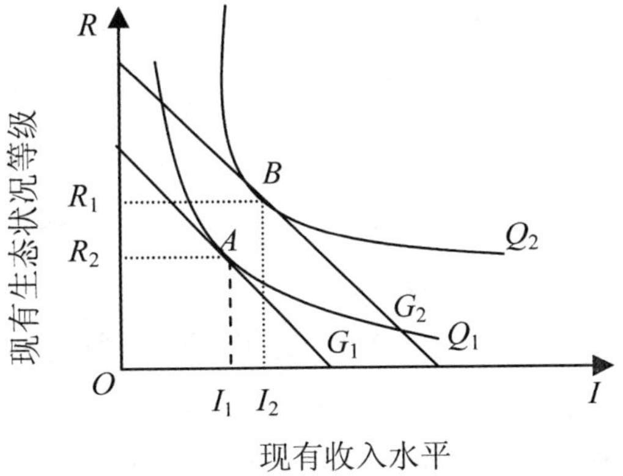

图 3-5　政府支付能力与生态需求的关系

图 3-5 中增加了两条预算曲线，预算曲线主要是指政府对生态需求的实际支付，分别用 G_1、G_2 表示，并且处于 G_2 时政府对生态的有效需求要大于在 G_1 时的有效需求。由此可见，政府对生态消费的支付能力也将影响人们对生态需求愿望的满足程度。当预算曲线为 G_1 时，人们对生态的效用满足度只能为 Q_1 及其以下的程度，即便此时社会公众对生态的需求愿望达到了位于 Q_2 的 B 点，其需求愿望的程度提高了，但由于其大大超过了预算曲线 G_1 所能提供的范围，在现实中是得不到满足的，只有当预算曲线也相应提高到 G_2 的位置时，这种需求愿望才能得以实现。

（四）恩格尔系数与生态需求的实现

如前所述，与私人物品相比，由于受公共物品特征的限制，生态需求在多数情况下很难通过市场交换的手段来实现。当没有相应的机制提供生态时，公众的生态需求只能停留在需求愿望的层面上。这时有两个因素对这一需求愿望产生较为强烈的影响。首先，生态需求愿望的强弱决定于环境质量的变化。公众生存依托的原环境质量越高，其需求越表现为生态环境以外的其他物品或服务，而对生态环境的需求愿望则越弱。相反，当原环境的质量很低或质量不断降低时，生态环境对公众的效用就会不断增强，其需求愿望也会随之提高。现实中的这一现象可以看成是边际效用递减规律在生态环境上的具体表现。其次，公众的收入水平变化也对生态需求愿望产生强烈影响。公众收入水平越低，其恩格尔系数越高，越是必须首先满足基本生活需求，而生态需求愿望较弱。相反，在公众收入水平不断提高的情况下，恩格尔系数越低，剩余收入将导致公众的生态需求愿望不断增强。

恩格尔系数的下降事实上是经济实力提高的结果。当人均 CDP 达到 1 000 美元左右，第二产业的产值比重达到50%左右时，即达到了倒 U 曲线的拐点。根据日本、中国台湾及东南亚等国家和地区的发展经验表明，只有达到人均 GDP 3 500 ~3 800 美元时，才能保持一种平稳状态，此时对生态建设的投入也才能稳定，林业建设才能进入生态治理大于破坏的阶段。也就是说，在经济发展的初期阶段、人均财富比较少的时候，生态状况是随着经济的增长而不断恶化的，此时生态状况处于曲线的左侧；随着经济继续增长，生态压力达到最高，接近曲线顶端临界点，经济发展到中等收入水平时，生态状况开始变好，转向曲线的右侧，即公众的生态需求愿望才能得到实现。

三、生态由外生变量到内生变量的转变

通过对生态需求愿望无差异曲线的分析，可知生态质量与经济水平之间存在着一定的关系，并且生态与经济之间的联系越来越紧密，随着经济增长方式的不断演进，生态不再是独立于经济系统之外的既定条件，而是逐步向经济增长的内生变量转化。

（一）经济增长方式的演进

在发展经济学领域，已有的可持续增长研究主要是采用新古典增长的经济学工具，生产率被假定为按外生的不变比率增长。但是随着社会的不断进步，经济增长模式也在不断演变，新的经济增长模式将技术进步视为经济增长的内生变量，认为技术进步是经济增长的决定性因素，但是这一理论却忽略了资源、环境以及制度等因素对经济增长的影响。一种因素是否为内生变量，或者说能否从外生变量转化为内生变量，与经济增长方式密切相关。从经济发展历程来看，经济增长方式主要经历了以下几个阶段：

第一，粗放型经济增长方式。这种经济增长方式主要出现在经济发展的初期。这一时期，经济发展基础薄弱，各种资源尚未得到充分利用，土地、资本、劳动力是经济发展最主要的推动力，加大对这三者数量上的投入，很容易使经济增长呈现出速度快、数量多、产值高的态势。在这种增长方式下，经济增长的内生变量就是资本、土地和劳动力。

第二，集约型经济增长方式。这种经济增长方式主要出现在经济发展有了一定基础之后，对资源的开发和利用已经达到了一定限度，单纯地依赖掠夺式开采和简单的人力、资金投入已经难以实现经济的快速增长，这时就需要考虑如何能有效地利用资源，在不影响经济增长的前提下，减少生产要素投入数量，提高生产要素质量。由于资源的稀缺性，更是决定了要关注下一代的生存条件，关注可持续发展的重要性。随着知识经济的发展和科学技术的不断进步，人们越来越意识到科学技术能创造财富，是经济发展的强大推动力，作为生产力源泉之一的科学技术可以从经济增长的外生变量转化为内生变量。此阶段，资本、劳动力、土地和技术（知识）成为经济增长的内生变量，实现经济增长的高质量、高效益，有利于实现经济的可持续发展。在这一阶段后期，制度学派有学者称制度对经济发展也起到十分关键的作用，建议把制度也纳入经济增长的内生变量。

第三，绿色型经济增长方式，也有人称之为知识生态型经济增长方式。这种经济增长方式一般出现在经济发展到较高水平，人们开始追求生活质量的阶段。它是一种将经济效益和生态效益结合在一起的新型增长方式，把生产力的另一源泉——生态也从经济增长的外生变量转化为内生变量，从而兼顾了经济增长与生态安全，使经济、社会和生态的可持续发展有了可靠的保证，实现和谐的人地关系。在这种经济增长方式中经济增长的内生变量扩展为资本、劳动力、土地、技术(知识)以及生态五个方面。

绿色型经济增长方式是一种健康的、合乎科学的、经济发展和环境保护相协调的、能够实现经济、社会、生态的可持续发展的经济增长方式，是一种真正的"合理性的经济增长方式"。它既继承了集约型经济增长方式的优点，又更加兼顾经济增长与生态建设之间的关系，利于实现以下目标：一是经济增长的高质量，二是人与自然的和谐发展，三是人与人之间的和谐发展，包括同代人之间以及代际之间的和谐。

在经济增长方式的演进过程中，生态逐渐由经济增长的外生变量纳入到经济系统之中，转变为经济增长的内生变量，这是客观条件变化的必然趋势。

(二)生态转变为内生变量的必然趋势

人类社会的发展经历了不同的历史阶段，传统经济学不考虑资源环境的稀缺性，不将生态归为经济增长的内生变量，而我们现今的研究更倾向于把生态看作是经济增长的内生变量，这是一种进步，但并不能说明传统经济学就是错误的，任何阶段的经济思想都是与当时的客观条件相适应的。发展到绿色型经济增长方式阶段，生态已经实现了由经济增长的外生变量到内生变量的转变，但这个过程不是一蹴而就的。最早以生态问题作为研究对象的经济研究可以追溯到 20 世纪 50 年代，自称为制度学派的卡普对公害问题进行了比较全面的探讨，同期，以克纳赛为首的美国未来资源研究所出现了以环境作为资源的素材对经济进行分析。中国生态经济学家刘思华把生态作为经济增长的外生变量的传统理论称之为"生态外因论"，并于 1999 年提出了"生态内因论"，即良好的生态状况是直接作为生态经济再生产过程的必要组成部分而存在的，并内置于经济增长过程中，成为经济增长的重要的内生要素。由于良好的生态日益成为一种短缺的资源要素，将其视为经济增长的内生变量是进一步完善经济增长理论的必然。

从亚当·斯密奠定的经济理论开始，经济学领域一直存在两种基本观点：一是人类发展的资源存在着某种稀缺；二是人类发展需要有效的配置稀缺资源。今天，一方面如何解决过剩劳动力的就业问题已经成了全球的主要矛盾。另一方面，日趋衰减的自然资本则成为经济增长的关键制约因素，持续的经济增长越来越受到自然资本的束缚和制约。

在绿色经济增长方式到来之前，“资源—产品—污染排放”这一过程是单通道的，表现为线性的关系，如图 3-6。

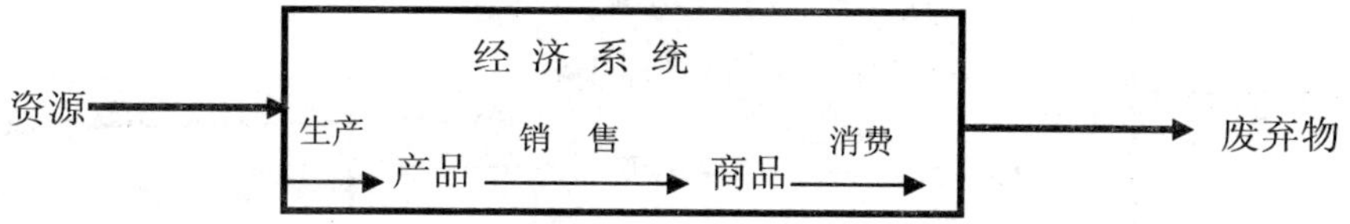

图 3-6　线性关系图

资源进入经济系统后经过生产、销售、消费等一系列过程，最终以废弃物的形式投放到生态系统中。就生态系统而言，自然资源数量减少了，而废弃物的数量增加了，尽管大自然有一定的自我修复能力，但也无法阻止污染物对生态的破坏，进而导致生态问题的产生。这种线性经济的特征是高开采、低利用、高排放，在这种线性经济中，经济系统越做越大，而外面的生态系统则变得越来越小，仅仅是通过把资源源源不断地变成废物来实现经济的数量型增长。

生态发展成为经济增长的内生变量，这对传统的经济发展方式提出了挑战，循环经济正是在这种背景下提出的，它是对 200 多年来传统经济发展方式的一种变革和突破。循环经济的提出，一定程度上融合了经济与生态，试图将二者之间的冲突最小化，它是对工业化之后的线性经济的一种超越，它改变了传统经济的那种人与自然之间的交换模式。

所谓循环经济，就是把清洁生产和废弃物的综合利用融为一体的经济。本质上是一种生态经济，它要求运用生态学规律来指导人类社会的经济活动。简而言之，循环经济是按照生态规律利用自然资源和环境容量，实现经济活动的生态化转向，它是实施可持续战略必然的选择和重要保证。如图 3-7 所示，循环经济是一个闭合的循环往复过程，它要求把经济活动组织成一个“资源—产品—再生资源”的反馈式流程，其特征是低开采、高利用、低排放。循环经济与以往的线性经济模式有着重大区别，它增加了对经过经济系统排放到生态系统中废弃物的再生利用。但不能简单地把循环经济等同于对废弃物品的再生利用，仔细观察我们就会发现，图3-7与图3-6的区别除了对废弃物品进行再生利用进而形成一个闭

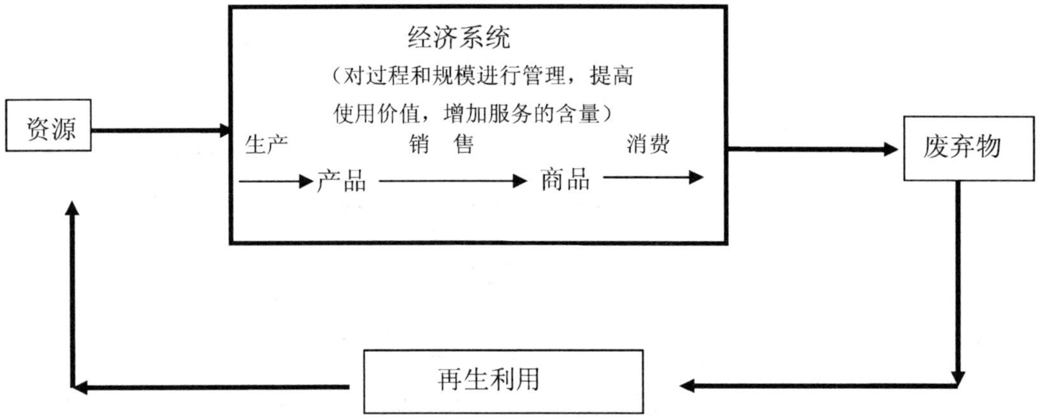

图3-7 循环经济模式

合的循环系统外，在经济系统内，还强调了对生产过程和经营规模进行管理和控制，努力提升产品的使用价值，而不是立足于交换价值，同时生产者也不是推销产品而是推销服务，循环经济有可能使服务质量达到最优，从而实现从生产优先社会向服务优先社会或真正意义上的后工业社会即服务社会的转变。“减量化、再利用、再循环”是循环经济最重要的实际操作原则，循环经济是生态从外生变量向内生变量转化的最直接应用。

土地、资本、劳动力是进行生产活动必不可少的要素。在农业社会，土地和劳动力是最重要的生产要素。土地为人们的生产经营活动提供基本的物质保障，劳动力投入在生产力不发达的情况下显得尤为重要，但当时人口稀少，土地贫瘠，于是诸如鼓励生育，毁林开荒的指导思想应运而生。发展到工业社会初期，土地和劳动力仍旧是重要的生产要素，但相比之下资本要素显得更加重要，加大

资本投入力度，推动机器大工业的发展进而加快经济发展。这时期生态没有得到足够的重视，并不是说生态不重要，而是在当时的条件下，自然资源和生态的提供是相对充足的，尽管生态状况也遭到了严重的破坏，但尚未超出人们的承受范围，因而传统经济学未把生态看作是经济增长的内生变量，是与当时的客观条件相适应的。

今天，我们提倡把生态纳入经济增长的内生变量也有其客观条件。随着前期经济发展对自然资源的不断开发和利用，甚至是掠夺式的开采使用，给今天的生态问题埋下了伏笔。如今，水土流失、土地沙化、泥石流、地震、洪涝、旱灾这些自然灾害时有发生，由于人与生态之间的不协调造成的SARS和禽流感等疫情也不断出现，生态状况不断遭到破坏，已经不像以前那样非常适合人们的生产经营活动了。因此，满足社会经济可持续发展的生态同其他要素一样也是一种稀缺性的资源要素。技术虽能解决一部分资源替代的问题，但不能从根本上解决资源的稀缺，对生态能力的持续也显得无能为力。生态再也不是独立于经济系统之外、特定不变的外在因素了，而是与经济发展相互影响、相互制约的内在因素，并且将生态由经济增长的外生变量转化为内生变量对经济发展具有重要的指导意义。因而，此时将生态归为经济增长的内生变量是有其合理性的。

第二节　社会经济发展与生态问题

人类诞生以前，生物圈保持着良好的循环状态，生命物种不断繁衍生息。发展到采猎社会后期，由于采猎工具不断进步，导致了捕杀动物的增加，人们对自然环境的依赖很强，但由于当时人们的力量相对弱小，对生态造成的后果也甚微。到了农业社会，生态平衡也基本保持在良好状态，尽管这一阶段曾出现过人为破坏生态的行为，例如钻木取火、刀耕火种、兽皮制衣等，但这些行为只是局部的、轻微的利用自然的行为，是人类进步的必要保障，并未对生态构成威胁。工业革命发生后，随着人口迅速增长和生产力不断发展，人类“征服自然”的能力急剧增强，对生态状况破坏的行为逐渐增多，力度也不断加大。在人类社会的发展进程中，生态问题随着经济发展和人们对生态认识的深入不断出现新的变化。

一、生态问题的萌芽

生态问题实质上是经济发展，特别是工业化和生态保护之间的矛盾问题，是人和生态相互依赖、相互融合的关系失调。一是人类索取资源的速度超过资源本身提供能力的增长速度，其替代品的再生速度和向生态系统排放废弃物的数量超过生态的自我修复能力；二是自然资源的补给、再生需要时间，一旦超过极限，便不可逆转。生态的利用及其影响一般是一个长期过程，破坏生态的行为和生态状况的恶化之间的时间间隔也很长，人们追求短期经济效益的行为就使得对生态的保护和建设没有得到足够的重视。

所谓生态问题的萌芽阶段并不是指生态状况开始出现恶化的时期，而是指经济有了一定程度的发展但仍相对落后，生态状况恶化现象已经出现，人们已经意识但尚未深刻意识到生态对人类进步以及经济发展的重要性，还未大规模地对生态状况的恶化进行治理的阶段。

自人类诞生之日起就与生态系统紧密相连，生态状况与人类行为密切相关。在传统社会时期，没有现代科学技术、农业是国民经济的主体、社会结构僵化而缺少弹性、人们信奉消极无为的思想观念成为当时的主要特征。经过经济“起飞”准备阶段的过渡以后，经济“起飞”阶段又出现了新的特征。

（一）实现经济“起飞”的条件及其基本特征

在经历了经济“起飞”准备阶段这个漫长的过渡阶段之后，经济增长就进入了“起飞”阶段，经济“起飞”是指一个国家或地区在工业化初期的较短时间内，突破了不发达经济的停滞状态，实现基本经济结构和生产方式的剧烈转变，经济高速增长。罗斯托在其六阶段经济发展理论中将一些国家的经济“起飞”时间确定为：英国在18世纪末，法国和美国在19世纪中叶，德国在1850～1875年，日本在19世纪最后25年，加拿大在19世纪末20世纪初。就世界范围来看，进入20世纪以后，尤其是第二次世界大战以后，随着战后经济逐步恢复，社会发展日趋稳定，又有一批国家相继进入了经济“起飞”阶段。“起飞”阶段是经济发展中的关键阶段，在经济发展过程中具有分水岭的意义。之所以说“起飞”阶段至关重要，是因为一个国家或地区能够通过“起飞”阶段的建设从贫困走向繁荣，从停滞走向发展，摆脱纳克斯提出的“贫困恶性循环理论”的困境和莱宾斯坦提出的“低水平均衡陷阱”的桎梏，但是要想实现经济“起飞”必须要满足以下几个条件：

第一，较高的资本积累率。当生产性投资即经济中的净投资在国民收入中的比重达到10%以上时才有可能实现经济的“起飞”。

第二，建立能带动经济增长的主导部门体系。“起飞”一般是由一个或多个主导部门的发展推动的，主导部门的发展又带动了相关辅助部门的发展。主导部门就是那些具有革新创造性的部门或者是能够利用新的未开发资源的部门，因而这些部门的经济增长比较快，而且发展也比较有后劲。在进行主导部门的选择时要选择那些供求弹性比较大、产业关联度比较强的行业或部门，这样会带来更大的关联效应。

第三，进行社会、政治和经济制度的变革。经济发展不是一个孤立的过程，而是与政治、社会的同步发展紧密相连的，只有三者协调一致，互相配合，才会实现经济的“起飞”。

与传统社会阶段相比，经济“起飞”阶段，在经济发展、科学技术、教育文化、政治基础等方面都取得了进步，但都未达到先进水平。这一时期，新工业扩张迅猛，经济再生产不断扩大；新工业的发展又促进了城市地区和其他现代化工业企业的进一步扩张；这种扩张导致了人们收入的增加和储蓄率的提高；新技术不断在工业和农业中应用，农业生产率革命性的变化是“起飞”成功的必要条件。此外，政治发展相对稳定，国家对经济发展能够进行一定干预，在某种程度上能够发挥指导作用；人们对于自然的态度不再是消极无为，而是提倡自觉发挥主观能动性；产生了一个日益扩大的企业家阶层，他们把扩大的投资引导到私人部门，这些条件都在一定程度上推动了经济“起飞”的进程。

（二）生态问题的萌芽阶段

根据对生态问题萌芽阶段的界定可知，在这一阶段经济发展已经取得了初步成就，但尚未为解决生态问题奠定坚实的经济基础；生态状况恶化的现象已经出现，尽管生态问题引起了部分人的关注，但尚未普遍引起人们的高度重视；并且此阶段的生态问题有着区别于凸显阶段的特征。下面将从这三个方面逐一地进行阐述。

第一，经济发展取得初步成效，但尚未积累足够资金解决生态问题。在经济“起飞”阶段，人们对经济发展的需求仍是主导需求，依然十分关注经济建设。经济“起飞”的主要目的就是要摆脱经济停滞不前的状况，使得经济能够取得突飞猛进的进展，以抵消人口增长对经济发展的削弱，使经济增长因素对人口增长的刺激作用有所下降，从而使得人均收入水平有所增长，进而摆脱“低水平均衡陷阱”的制约。针对“起飞”阶段经济水平低下、生活状态落后、发展后劲不足等情况，相对于生态需求来说，人们对经济发展的需求显得更为迫切和强烈。因而，处于这一阶段的人们着重考虑如何实现经济利益而忽略对生态的保护有其一定的合理性。

从西方发达国家来看，在其处于经济“起飞”阶段时，经济活动在这一时期异常活跃，处于经济“起飞”阶段的国家最基本的特征就是经济飞速发展。英国是世界上较早进入经济“起飞”阶段的国家，早在 18 世纪末就进入了经济的“起飞”阶段。英国的 CDP 由 1700 年的 10 709 百万国际元(在多边购买力评价比较中将不同国家货币转换成统一的货币，以 1990 年为标准，下同)增加到 1820 年的 36 232 百万国际元，在 120 年内增长了 2. 38 倍；而在上一个百年内，英国的 GDP 由 1600 年的 6 007 百万国际元增加到 1700 年的 10 709 百万国际元，仅增长了 0. 78 倍。可见，英国在经济“起飞”阶段实现了经济的快速发展，在同一时期英国的 GDP 超出了其他国家，如图 3-8。

由图 3-8 可见，在 1820 年，英国的 CDP 是德国的 1. 38 倍，意大利的 1. 61 倍，日本的 1. 75 倍，美国的 2. 89 倍。除了几个规模大或经济基础好于英国的国家外，英国的经济实力已经进入了世界前列，并超过了整个非洲 31 010 百万国际元的 CDP 值。剔除人口因素的影响，英国的人均 GDP 也由 1700 年的 1 250 国际元增长到 1820 年的 1 707 国际元，增长了 0. 37 倍，而上个百年只增长了 0. 28 倍；在 1820 年英国的人均 GDP 仅次于荷兰，位居世界第二位。

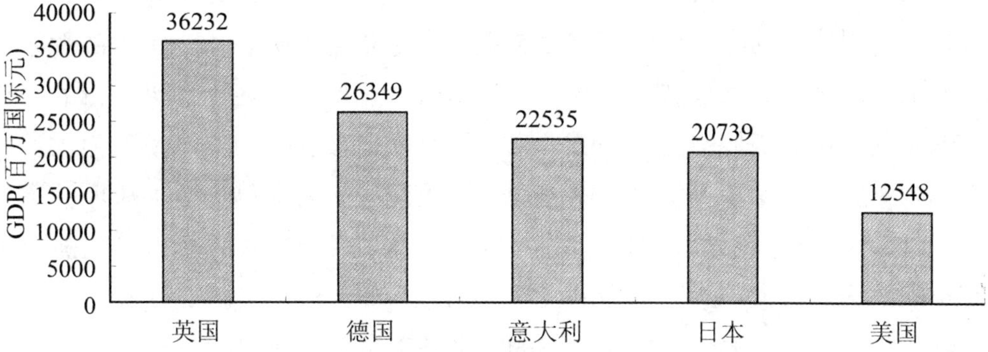

图 3-8　1820 年几个主要国家的 GDP 比图

（资料来源：安格斯·麦迪森．世界经济千年史．北京：北京大学出版社，2003）

同样，当美国和日本等国家进入经济“起飞”阶段时，经济发展也十分迅速。到 1890 年美国工业产值就达到了 95 亿美元，跃居世界第一位，美国经济的成功“起飞”不但为其创造了财富，而且也为其大国地位奠定了基础；日本经历了明治维新之后，经济发展十分迅速，1885 ~ 1900 年，日本制造业的国内净产值由 8 600 万日元猛增至 36 500 万日元，增长了 3.24 倍，年平均增长率高到 10.1%，同期，其国民生产总值的年均增长率也高达 7.6%。

由上述经济“起飞”阶段的特征可知，这一阶段需要大量的资本积累和大规模开发自然资源，第二产业占据主导地值，主要实行粗放型的经济增长方式，依靠大量资本和资源的投入来换取经济的快速增长。尽管这一时期经济建设取得了很大的成就，但是对于解决生态问题无疑还是杯水车薪。

第二，人们的生态意识有所进步，但对生态的需求尚未占据主导地位。所谓生态意识是指人们在生产活动的基础上获得的对人类与自然环境相互关系的认识，是根据社会和自然的具体可能性，最优解决社会和自然关系问题方面所反映的社会和自然关系的观点、理论和感情的总和。生态意识在人类远古时期已经产生，并随着历史条件的变化而发展，在人们还没有对生态有足够的认识以前，非理性的人类行为在所难免。发展到经济“起飞”阶段，人们对自然资源的开采和对生态系统的破坏发展成为一种理性的行为，这是因为尽管已经有人意识到生态的重要性，但是由于这一时期经济与生态更倾向于相互冲突、相互矛盾的关系，根据当时的实际情况和发展要求，人们还是不得不选择以破坏生态为代价的经济增长方式。这一阶段人们对生态的需求主要为对生态系统的物质能量的需求，这种需求归根到底还是源于经济发展的需要，可以说经济需求仍为这一时期的第一需求。另外，尽管这一时期人们的行为对生态造成了严重破坏，但是并未超出当时生态空间的限制和人们忍受能力的极限，加之高额经济利益的驱使和人们改善自身经济条件的迫切需要，人们对生态的需求并不是十分强烈。

林业发展较为发达的德国在处于经济“起飞”阶段时，认识到了生态的重要性，将林业的经营思想由单纯地追求经济利益转变为持久满足社会对木材和其他林产品的需求时，兼顾为社会其他方面服务；而单一追求经济快速增长的美国从进入经济“起飞”阶段直至19世纪下半期，政府没有制定任何保护森林和发展森林的政策，而有关林业方面的政策都是强调木材供应。德美两国在这一阶段的林业政策从一定程度上体现了人们对生态已经有了初步的认识，但是迫于现实的需要仍旧以经济建设为首要需求，林业也主要是以提供木材为主要任务。

第三，萌芽阶段生态问题的具体表现。生态状况的变化始终与人类的行为有着密切的联系，随着经济增长速度不断加快，经济规模日益扩大，致使资源的开采量和投入量急剧增加，资源的存量以惊人的速度递减。煤炭、矿山、森林等重要资源的过度开采，动植物的生存环境遭到严重破坏，加之人口增长和工业化进程的加快，引发了一系列生态问题。以美国为例，1850～1910年，人口增长与城市化加剧了对森林、草原、农田、野生动物及其栖息地等自然资源的疯狂掠夺。北美大陆的森林覆盖率从60%下降到25%。当今，仍有许多国家依然处于经济“起飞”阶段，经济的发展、人口的增加、城市化进程的加快以及利用自然手段的进步，使得厄尔尼诺现象、“温室效应”、土地沙化、地面沉降、物种减少、生态失衡等一系列生态问题随之发生。

在生态问题萌芽初期，由于人口相对稀少以及人们所掌握的控制与破坏生态的能力相对有限，加之此时生态的自我修复能力比较强，人类对生态系统的开发离生态空间的承载极限还有一定距离，相对于稀少的人口及有限的开发能力而言，生态资源可以说是无穷无尽。然而，随着人口激增，人均资源消耗量与废物排放量的剧增，人类活动对生态造成的破坏十分严重。尽管也有一些有识之士意识到如此下去经济发展将会受到生态状况的制约，但是由于此时人们对经济的需求仍旧是主导需求，加之生态的恶化程度尚未超出人们的承受极限，关键还是由于当时的经济发展水平还没达到能够彻底解决生态问题的程度，生态问题始终未得到足够的重视。尽管人们已经有了一定的能力进行生态建设，但是这种建设的投入会影响经济的发展速度，甚至可能会出现得不偿失的情况，因而人们对生态的需求仍只能停留在需求愿望阶段，没有强大的经济实力促使其成为有效的需求，生态问题也不可能得到有效的解决。

二、生态问题的凸显

随着经济的进一步发展，开始步入经济稳态发展阶段。处于这一阶段，经济水平、社会保障、文化程度等各个方面都有了很大程度的提高，人们对生态的保护意识不断增强，对生态的需求也日益增加，生态需求开始逐步转变为人们的主导需求。生态问题凸显阶段就是指经济已经发展到了相当高的程度，人均 GDP 也进一步增加，在这种情况下人们保护生态的意识逐渐增强，对生态的需求更加全面，并上升为主导需求，解决生态问题已经具备了各方面条件。

(一)经济稳态发展阶段的特点

走向成熟阶段、高额群众消费阶段和追求生活质量阶段可以归结为经济增长的稳态发展阶段。在经历了一段较长时期的经济持续增长的“走向成熟”阶段，新工业加速扩张，老工业日渐衰退，经济结构不断发生变化，新的思想和体制以及先进的科学技术不断得到应用，人类社会就进入高额群众消费阶段(The Age of High Mass Consumption)，在这一阶段中，主导部门逐渐转向耐用消费品和服务行业，劳动力结构也会发生变化，白领人口的比重会不断上升，社会不再把现代技术的进一步扩展和经济发展作为压倒一切的首要目标，而是把日益增加的资源用于社会福利和社会安全，并且有越来越多的资源被引导到耐用消费品的生产和大众服务的提供上来。之后的追求生活质量阶段，人们更加注重追求闲暇和娱乐，而不把收入增长看得最重要。在经济稳态发展阶段，由于经济已经发展到相当高的程度，人们对经济的需求日益淡化，对生态的需求却变得强烈起来。

（二）生态问题的凸显阶段

伴随着经济的发展，各个方面都发生了相应的变化，对生态问题的影响也与萌芽时期有所不同。这里仍旧从经济发展、人们对生态的认识程度以及生态问题在凸显阶段的表现三个方面进行阐述，并且随着全球化进程的加快，发达国家的发展历程为发展中国家提供了重要的借鉴，人们对生态的认识程度不断加深，并就生态的重要性等问题达成了共识，在此基础上提出了可持续发展理论。

第一，经济发展已经达到一定程度，基本具备解决生态问题的经济实力。在经济稳态发展阶段，经济发展速度会有所减缓，但仍呈现上升的趋势。仍以美国为例，从第一次世界大战结束到1929年，除了20年代初有一短暂的萧条阶段外，美国经济出现了一段相对稳定的发展时期。在经历了经济大危机和第二次世界大战之后，1947年到1953年的7年时间内，美国国民生产总值的平均年增长率为3.9%，并且这一阶段，人均国民生产总值也有一定幅度的增长。在一些发达国家步入经济稳态增长阶段之时，全世界的经济发展也取得了辉煌的成绩。按1990年国际元计算，全世界GDP从1913年的27 048亿国际元增加到1998年的337 256亿国际元，在80多年的时间里增长了11.5倍。至1998年，按1990年国际元计算，西欧人均GDP已达17 921国际元，东欧已达5 461国际元，经济最为发达的美国已达27 331国际元。

追求生活质量的阶段是人类社会发展的第二次突破，人均GDP仍旧呈现不断增长的趋势，但人们的追求不再仅仅局限于物质方面，而更加重视休闲和娱乐。这一阶段的内容极其丰富，美国及其他发达国家和世界人民都把“人与自然和谐”作为追求生活质量和实现可持续发展的终极目标。美国在20世纪50年代完成高额消费阶段的任务后，人均GDP仍旧呈现不断增长的趋势。

由图3-9可以看出，美国人均GDP呈不断增长的趋势，并且近些年来增长幅度有所加大，人们物质生活水平已经达到了相当高的程度，生活状况不断好转，

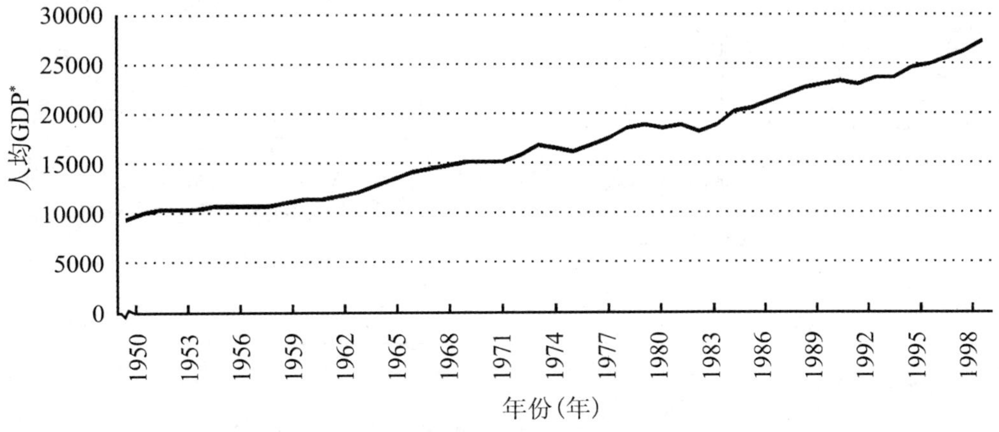

图 3-9　1950～2000 年美国人均 GDP 增长趋势

注：人均 GDP 以 1990 年国际元计算

（资料来源：安格斯·麦迪森．世界经济千年史．北京：北京大学出版社，2003）

人们的经济需求得到了充分的满足。

这一阶段经济的发展并不仅仅表现在 GDP 的增加，产业结构也发生了重大的变化，逐渐由第二产业占主导地位转变为第三产业占主导地位，经济增长方式也过渡到绿色型经济增长方式，减少了对资源的开发利用，同时也减少了对生态状况的破坏行为。

第二，人们的生态意识不断进步，生态需求发展为全面需求，并成为人们的主导需求。这一阶段，人们能够得到的物质供给远远超过了人们的需求，对经济的需求会变得相对弱化。在人们衣食无忧之时，人们会考虑如何提高生活质量，如何更惬意地享受生活，甚至在当代人生活质量提高时，如何满足下代人的生存和发展，对生态的认识逐步深化并且更加理性。此时，人们对生态的需求不单单局限于向生态系统索取物质能量，而且包括人们的生理、生活对良好生态状况的需求。并且与以前所探讨的人们对生态的需求愿望不同，此时人们对生态的这种全面需求不仅仅是停留在需求愿望阶段，而是具备了一定的支付能力，能够形成有效的需求。

如图 3-10 所示，当生态状况等级处于 R 点，人均收入为 I_1 时，人们对生态

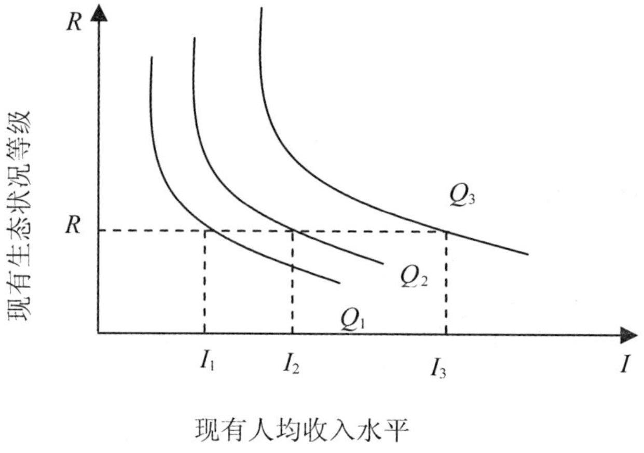

图 3-10　生态需求无差异曲线

的需求为 Q_1；人均收入为 I_2 时，人们对生态的需求为 Q_2；人均收入为 I_3时，人们对生态的需求为 Q_3；由此可见，生态质量一定的条件下，随着人均收入水平的增加，人们对生态产生的需求更加强烈。这一结论与图 3-4 所探讨的生态需求愿望的无差异曲线基本一致，所不同的只是此阶段人们的需求有可能成为能够实际支付的有效需求。尽管生态具有公共物品性，但此时无论是政府还是个人都具有较强的经济实力，随着人们生活水平的提高，消费者对商品消费的结构会发生变化，对生态状况的要求会越来越高，加之人们思想观念的进步和环保意识的增强，人们愿意承担生态税等利于改善生态状况的税收，甚至有可能愿意承担为消费生态而实际支付费用，这时人们对生态的需求远远超过了对经济发展的需求，生态问题已经凸显出来。

第三，凸显阶段生态问题的具体表现。由于这一时期，经济发展已经达到了一定的高度，经济不再是解决生态问题的主要制约因素，这时对生态的破坏不再是由于生产活动对资源的大量开采和使用，而转移到人们的过度消费行为。由于经济高度发达，人们对投资和消费的需求不断增强，消费者的消费热情高涨，而商家对消费者的消费预期也比较有信心，在双方乐观情绪的鼓舞下，商家制作了大量广告来鼓动消费者消费更多的商品，甚至高水平、高质量的消费已经成为一种生活理念渗透到社会价值之中。这种高消费需要有大量的物质支持，同时由于产品更新换代的速度加快，以及消费观念的变化，被人们淘汰下来的产品也就越来越多，这带来了较为严重的废弃物处理问题。有资料表明：在工业化国家，燃料燃烧释放出导致酸雨的硫化物和氮氧化物占全球排放量的3/4，世界上绝大多数的化学废气是由工业化国家的工厂生产的，其空调机、烟雾辐射和工厂释放了90%的破坏臭氧层的物质。处于追求生活质量阶段的高消费不仅给本国带来了生态问题，而且这些民众消费的产品有相当一部分是来自于发展中国家，由于发展中国家的经济基础较为薄弱，为了加快本国经济发展的步伐，不惜以生态来换取经济的发展，就这样把环境污染和生态破坏问题又引入了这些发展中国家，进而导致全球的生态问题更加凸显出来。

但此时在解决生态问题上，人们可以表现得更加有所作为。经济的发展带动了科技、教育、文化等各个方面的发展，科学技术的不断提高为解决生态问题提供了现实路径；信息技术的发展推动了产业结构的转型，污染物的排放量不断减少；人们受教育程度的提高也使生态保护的意识不断增强且深入人心。这些都大大提高了人们解决生态问题的可能性和可行性，因而各国都更加重视对生态的建设和保护。发达国家的典型代表美国，在经历了经济“起飞”阶段之后，至1910年北美大陆的森林覆盖率为25%，到1992年美国的森林覆盖率已恢复至33%，这一时期对森林资源的保护工作取得了一定的进展，使森林覆盖率有了大幅回升。森林资源十分丰富的瑞典、芬兰等国，也十分重视保护本国的生态，保护森林资源。瑞典森林面积逾2 600万hm^2，森林覆盖率达60%，人均拥有森林3.2 hm^2；芬兰森林总面积逾2 300万hm^2，森林覆盖率达69%，人均拥有森林5 hm^2，是欧洲人均森林最多的国家。

(三)可持续发展与生态问题

在部分发达国家进入经济稳态发展阶段时，从世界范围来看经济发展积累了大量物质财富，人们已经具备了一定解决生态问题的能力，并且随着人均收入水平的提高，人们对生态的需求变得更为强烈，更加重视人与生态之间的和谐发展。尤其是进入20世纪90年代，发达国家对生态的深刻认识促使发展中国家也逐步意识到了生态的重要性，保护生态、保护环境的观念已得到了共识，正是在这种条件下，可持续发展理论应运而生。

有人曾如下描述资源、人口、生态、社会和经济这五者与可持续发展之间的关系："资源是可持续发展的起点和条件，人口是总体可持续发展的关键，生态是可持续发展的终点和目标，经济和社会发展则是宏观可持续发展的途径和调节器。"随着人口的迅速膨胀和人们进行物质变换能力的不断增强，尤其是第二次世界大战后工业化突飞猛进发展对生态造成的严重破坏，使人们不得不反省自己传统的发展方式是否有利于子孙后代的延续发展。可持续发展最早是由生态问题引起的，要实现可持续发展归根结底是为了创造有利于当代人以及后代人全面发展的环境。

可持续发展理论正是针对盲目追求生活质量不断提高的生产和消费方式所带来的不可持续的发展前景而提出的全新发展理念。它把人口、资源、生态、经济和社会发展视为一个整体，从全局和长远的角度来考虑发展问题，追求长期而永久的人类利益，把人类的全面发展与生态的保护和永续利用有机结合起来。可持续发展理论的提出代表由黑色工业文明向绿色生态文明转折的开始，从发展过程中人与自然的关系来看，可持续发展就是追求发展过程中的"生态可持续性"，发展应该不损害和不超过生态系统的更新能力。从经济角度来看，可持续发展的核心是经济发展，经济发展是社会其他方面进步的基础和前提，也是解决生态问题的基本保障。在实现经济增长时，不应再以资源的浪费和生态的破坏为代价换取经济总量的增加，而应追求不破坏自然资源和生态状况的绿色经济增长方式。这种增长不但能够保证当代人经济福利的增加，又不会对后代人追求经济福利的增加造成损害。但是可持续发展理论对于发达国家和发展中国家却有不同的意义。

对于发达国家来说，其在工业化初期，世界经济的总量还很小，世界资源刚刚开始大规模开发，生态的承载能力也足够大，能够吸收工业生产中排放的废弃物，这为发达国家快速实现工业化提供了便利条件。如今，这些发达国家经济发展已经达到相当高的程度，科技、教育、文化、卫生、福利、保障等各个方面都得到了相应的发展，已经具备了解决生态问题的条件，相对于发展中国家来说，比较容易实现经济、社会和生态的可持续发展。因而，无论是就历史的合理性还是就现实的紧迫性而言，发达国家在可持续发展中都应该承担更多的责任和义务。

对发展中国家来说，这种可持续发展的意义更大。发展中国家经济增长的外部环境不同于发达国家经历工业化时期的外部环境，如今世界经济总量已经非常庞大，但资源和生态的许多方面已经显示出不堪重负的迹象。同时其在发展的初期内部环境也不容乐观，生产力水平低下、资金和技术短缺、人口膨胀、自然资源管理体制落后、市场机制不发达等，这就使得发展中国家更难发展起来。正因为如此，许多发展中国家相继进入了经济衰退、人口爆炸和生态状况恶化的恶性循环。如果发展中国家按照发达国家曾经历的过程进行工业化，不计后果，不惜代价，进行粗放式的发展，过度破坏资源和生态，走先破坏后治理的路子其结局将更难收拾，可能带来世界资源生态系统崩溃的后果。同样，如果不顾客观实际，把可持续发展的高标准强加到他们头上，既不合理也不可行。发展中国家的生态问题大多数是由于经济发展缓慢或发展不足而引起的，发展中国家增长型经济仍处于资金短缺阶段，政府的经济实力有限，加之这一阶段人口增长迅速，经济的增长很大部分需用来满足新增人口的需要，因而难以对生态建设进行大量投资。同时，发展中国家的科学技术研究相对落后，在技术上对发达国家有很强的依赖性。因此，发展中国家仍以经济发展作为首要目标。目前，尽管不少国家制定了可持续发展战略，并设计了一系列法律制度来予以保障，但是由于发展中国家经济水平低、人口素质不高、公众的环保意识薄弱、政府措施执行不力等原因，这些战略的执行未收到良好的效果。对发展中国家应适当降低标准，实现弱可持续发展，使他们尽可能在短时间内轻装上阵，充分发挥后发优势，实现生产力水平的提高，满足人们基本的生存需要，逐步获得可持续发展的各方面条件。所谓“弱可持续发展”，并不是说发展中国家的发展可以完全不顾生态后果，而是指应把发展置于首位，为了发展可以适当降低对生态要求，减轻他们在保护全球生态中的责任和义务。

三、林业发展与生态状况的改善

可持续发展理论的提出，强调了和谐和可持续的理念，这一理论的提出以及生态状况恶化的现实迫切要求生态的改善。林业建设与生态建设密切相关，相辅相成，一个地区的森林覆盖率高低不仅直接影响到当地的小气候，甚至在很大程度上决定该地区的环境质量和生态状况。

林业是与生态密切相关的产业，这主要是由于森林是陆地生态系统的主体，对生态的影响十分巨大，发展林业是生态文明建设的重要组成部分，同时也是维护国土生态安全的基础。之所以认为林业有这样重要的作用是因为人类面临的一系列生态问题如温室效应、生命物种减少、水土流失、沙漠化扩大、土壤退化、水资源危机、大气污染、酸雨等都与森林有直接或间接的关系。森林资源不断减少，生态不断恶化，使得生态平衡受到了破坏，引发了众多生态问题。解决森林保护、培育以及可持续发展等一系列问题，将会有利于生态的改善。

森林是人类赖以生存的一个巨大的自然资源，是陆地上面积最大、分布最广、组成结构最复杂、物种资源最丰富的生态系统，对维持生态平衡、延续人类发展起着极其重要的作用。森林是林业的基础，其功能具有多样性，其中大部分功能都与生态系统相关，致使林业具有生态功能；同时森林也是国民经济发展所依赖的重要自然资源，为国民经济发展提供基本的资源保证。正是基于林业的生态效益，更深入地说是森林的生态功能，提出了林业是生态建设的主体的观点。

森林的生态功能主要有以下几个方面：

第一，森林的涵养水源功能。森林能够涵养水源是一个无争的事实，由于树冠、树根以及枯落物的特殊作用，森林能够吸收大量的降雨以至降雨不至于完全挥发，还可将大量水源保存于地下，在一定程度上可以缓解全球的水资源危机。此外，森林对地表径流和河川水温也会产生一定的影响。

第二，森林的保持水土和防风固沙功能。防护林的建设在防风方面做出了重大贡献，由于树木的自然生产特征，使森林在保持水土流失、固沙阻沙方面起到了一定作用，阻止了荒漠化进程的加快，并在一定程度上改善了土壤板结状况。

第三，森林的固碳功能。由于世界人口增加和大量工业制造产生的含碳的废气物排放量的增加，空气中的含碳量急剧增加，这将严重威胁到人类的生存。森林是陆地生态系统的最大的碳储备库，在进行光合作用的时候释放出氧气。据研究表明森林每生产 10t 干物质，可吸收 16t 二氧化碳，释放 12t 氧气，森林每生长出 $1m^3$ 的蓄积量，大约可吸收固定 350kg 的二氧化碳。空气中碳含量的减少，就会减轻温室效应和厄尔尼诺现象给人类带来的危害，使空气质量得到提高。

第四，森林保持物种多样性的功能。近些年来，随着生态状况的逐步恶化，许多珍贵的动植物都濒临灭绝。这导致了生态物种之间的不平衡，对生态系统会产生破坏作用。森林是地球生命系统的基因库和能量库，在维持生命物种多样性和储存能量方面具有独特的作用，绿色植物通过光合作用可以将太阳能转化为化学能，动物依靠这些化学能转换为机械能和热能，来完成生命的主要过程。

第五，森林减弱噪声的功能。噪声对人们的工作、学习、休息和身体健康都产生不利的影响。随着工业的高速发展和城市人口的迅速膨胀，噪声也愈来愈强烈。森林植物通过对声音的吸收和反射作用，能阻隔、减弱噪声对人类的危害。

总之，森林在防止水土流失、改良土壤、涵养水源、净化水质、防风固沙、净化空气、减少噪音、维持碳平衡、调节全球气候等方面都能够起到良好效果。没有森林，生态系统就会受到严重破坏，生态的质量就会大大降低，人们的生存就会受到严重威胁。加快林业的发展，大力推动其生态功能的发挥，对改善生态能够起到有效的促进作用。

林业既是一项基础产业，也是一项重要的公益事业，充分发挥林业生态效益有利于生态的改善。但是，林业的生态效益并不是从一开始就得到了重视，在林业发展进程中，林业的经济效益在较长的时期内一直处于主导的地位。在经济发展的初期，由于经济水平低下，人们利用自然的能力有限，最容易获得的木材便成为人们首选的资源，其不但为工业直接提供原材料，而且还为工业的发展提供资本和外汇的支持。木材的生产和提供在相当长的时期内担任着林业的首要任务，在这一思想的指导下，毁林开荒、乱砍滥伐的现象层出不穷，森林覆盖率不断下降，水土流失、土地荒漠化、生命物种减少等生态问题应运而生，对生态造成了严重的破坏。因而，若想改善生态，必须要加大对林业生态效益的支持力度，使其真正成为林业经济效益和社会效益的基础，推进生态的可持续发展。

第三节　经济发展与生态建设的冲突与协调

人类历史上经历了两次产业革命，第一次是人类由采猎社会过渡到农业社会的农业革命；第二次是由农业社会过渡到工业社会的工业革命。这两次革命都使人类所使用的生产工具有了很大的进步，大大提高了生产力，增强了人类改造自然和利用自然的能力，促进了经济的发展，改善了人们的生存状况。然而，从生态的角度来看，从最初的直接依赖自然资源，转变为利用自然资源直至掠夺自然资源，这两次革命对生态状况形成了一定程度的破坏。

一、经济发展与生态建设的相互关系

许多国内外学者都试图揭示出经济发展与生态建设之间到底存在着怎样的关系，其中对这一问题论述较为深入的是美国经济学家、诺贝尔奖获得者库兹涅茨。经过大量统计分析之后，库兹涅茨于 1955 年提出了环境库兹涅茨曲线，尽管这一提法后来遭到了种种质疑，但是迄今为止环境库兹涅茨曲线却较为清晰地描述了生态质量与人均收入水平之间的关系。尽管由于各国的具体情况千差万别，环境库兹涅茨曲线有可能表现为略似 N 形或 L 形，但一般情况下，环境库兹涅茨曲线都表现为倒 U 形曲线。

环境库兹涅茨曲线，纵坐标表示生态的退化程度，沿着箭头的方向生态退化指数增高，生态质量越来越差；横坐标表示人均收入状况，沿着箭头的方向表示人均收入水平增高。从图 3-11 可以看出，在经济发展过程中，生态也同样存在先恶化后改善的情况。在经济发展初期，由于经济活动水平较低，对生态的破坏也较轻微；在经济起飞、制造业大发展的阶段，资源的消耗大大超过资源的再生，生态严重恶化；经济发展一段时间之后，尽管生态仍旧会随着人均收入水平的增加而出现恶化的趋势，但生态恶化的速度会大大减少；在经济发展到高级阶段，

经济结构改变，对生态破坏严重的产业被停止生产或转移，经济发展带来的积累为解决生态问题奠定了经济基础，同时科学技术也不断提高，人们的生态保护意识也增强了，生态会随着经济的发展不断得到改善。

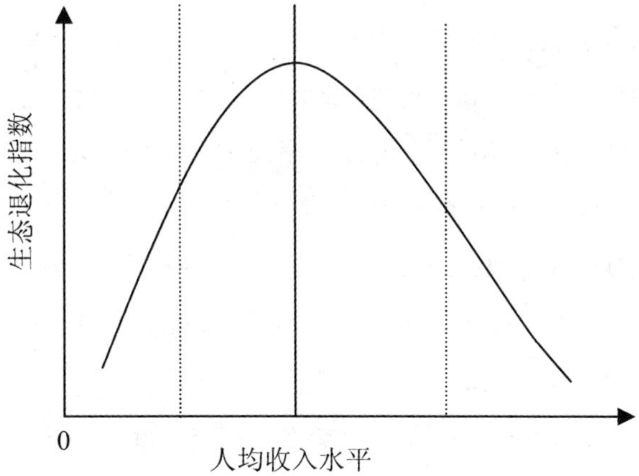

图 3-11　环境库茨涅茨曲线

经济发展和生态建设之间的关系会随着所处的经济发展阶段的不同而有所不同。图中倒 U 型曲线上升的左半边就是经济发展与生态相冲突时期的表现；而倒 U 型曲线下降的右半边就是经济发展与生态协调发展时期的表现。但是倒 U 型曲线的出现并不是唯一依赖于人均 GDP 的增长，而与技术进步、人口增长、教育发展等相关因素都有关系。实际上，随着经济发展水平的提高，科学技术、文化教育以及人们的生态保护意识都会不断进步，人们对经济发展的理解也会变得更加理性。

生态建设和经济发展之间紧密相连，生态是经济发展的基础，为经济发展提供最基本的资源保障，同时由于生态承载能力的有限性，生态又会制约经济的发展。经济发展对生态的变化起到主导作用，经济发展处于不同的阶段会对生态产生不同的影响，然而生态问题的最终解决一定程度上还要依靠经济的发展。

在经济发展的初期阶段以及其后的一段时间内，经济增长与生态建设之间存在着某种冲突。尽管这是人们所不愿看到的，但其在当时的经济条件下又具有一定的必然性。在经济发展的初期，科学技术不发达、教育水平落后、人口增长迅速，这些问题都决定了要想实现经济增长，只能依靠大量开采、利用自然资源。这种向自然界无休止的索取必定会造成对生态的破坏，向生态的承载能力提出挑战。经济增长与生态保护之间出现了矛盾，一方的实现必定以另一方的损失为代价。经济平衡与生态平衡之间的矛盾主要表现为具有增长型机制的经济活动对生态资源需求的无限性和具有稳定型机制的生态系统对生态资源供给的有限性之间的矛盾。自然生产力的供给可理解为“环境承载力(carrying capacity)”，最早柏拉图在《第五章　法则篇》中写道：“所谓最适宜的市民人口数量是无法确定的，一块土地必须能够足以供养既定数量的人口，并供给舒适感与食物。”生态经济学家P. R. Ehrlich将环境承载力定义为：“一定区域内维持某种生物数量不致减少的能力。”随后Roughgarden又对其进行了补充：“用有机体总数测度的某个环境内可更新资源数量。”1992年，荷兰地球之友协会又提出了环境空间(environment space)的概念，Spangenberg将其定义为：“是一个想象的具有环境上限和社会下限的某种机会空间。”可见，就生态系统而言，资源、生态的供给是有限的，但是经济发展对其需求却是无限的，这就造成了经济增长与生态建设之间的冲突。

由于生态的公共物品性，产权界定不清晰性和严重的外部性，使得市场这一有效的资源配置方式，在对生态资源进行配置时失去了应有的效能。“搭便车”现象的产生使得价格的制定非常困难，即便制定出来也不能准确地反映真实的供需状况。当市场出现失灵时，最好的弥补措施就是纳入政府管理。但是政府干预与市场调节的目标有时是存在偏差的。市场是通过供求关系来公正、公平地反映商品的价格；而政府调控则带有一定的主观性，通常要考虑社会、政治、环境等各个方面，受人为因素的影响十分强烈，加之寻租行为的产生，使得政府命令或调控政策在执行过程中发生扭曲或篡改，因而政府干预在解决经济和生态的关系问题时也是失效的。

在经济增长与生态建设存在冲突的阶段，大多数国家选择了优先推进经济增长，这并不意味着他们没有意识到生态的重要性，只是在那种条件下选择发展经济具有必然性。纳克斯提出的“贫困恶性循环理论”为这一选择提供了理论依据。当一国处于经济发展初期阶段时，生产力水平相对低下，经济状况比较落后，生活水平较差，科学技术水平低，若想谋求经济增长，只能依靠不断加大资本品，以及包括自然资源在内的各项要素的投入。同时由于其自身的经济实力和科技水平都比较落后，不可能依靠科技力量来实现对资源的合理开采和有效利用，而只能是对自然资源进行掠夺式开采，过度加以利用。人们的这种掠夺式开发、利用的行为又会使生态受到更大的压力，有时候甚至超过了修复和再生的可能性，最终造成对生态的破坏，引发一系列诸如资源短缺、土地荒漠化等生态问题。而恶劣的生态不能很好地为经济增长提供丰富的资源和良好的发展空间，经济增长就会受到生态的制约，失去资源基础和良好的发展空间经济就会陷入进一步贫困的状态，经历了一个“贫穷—生态恶化—贫穷”的恶性循环。这并不是说人类在解决经济与生态之间的冲突时是无能为力的，要探寻一条跳出这一“恶性循环”的道路，最直接也是最有效的方法就是加大经济建设力度，促进经济迅猛发展。

二、经济发展与生态建设的协调

经济与生态的协调是指经济的发展只有与生态的发展保持协调，才能保持经济的持续稳定发展。经济发展与生态建设是一个问题的两个方面，长期只注重一方面而忽略另一方面必将导致社会发展的停滞。发展经济需要按客观规律办事，不能只顾短期经济利益，而一味破坏生态；也不能不顾经济实力的制约，盲目进行大规模的生态建设，而使未来的经济发展缺乏动力。需要有一个长远的战略思想，将目前的经济利益和长远的经济利益以及长期的生态效益结合起来，将经济发展与生态建设结合起来。

良好的生态条件，可以为经济发展提供坚实的基础，提供丰富的资源，同时也可以提高生态系统的自我修复能力，容纳经济发展中产生的更多的废弃物，推动经济的快速发展；经济实力的增强，又会带动许多方面的发展，可以提高人们的生活水平。增强人们的环保意识，推动科学技术的进步，解决生态问题的能力也会得到提升，经济发展不会自动解决生态问题，但会提高解决生态问题的能力。有人曾将经济与生态之间的关系表述为：“人类社会的经济过程就是对生态系统的开发利用过程”，“开发利用”的方式和程度直接影响了经济发展与生态建设之间的关系。对生态系统的合理开发、利用和节约并举可以促进经济和生态的协调发展。

经济发展带来生态问题，同时又增强了解决生态问题的能力，生态问题的解决又为经济持续、稳定发展打下了基础。环境库兹涅茨倒 U 型曲线下滑的右半边就是经济增长与生态建设协调发展时期的表现。可见，对良好的生态的收入弹性最终为正的。就一个国家而言，当经济发展达到一定程度以后，随着国民收入的增加，用于解决生态问题的资金投入和技术投入都会随之增加，从而抵消了经济增长过程中带来的生态问题产生的后果。国民收入增加得越多，人们对高质量生态的需求也更强烈。

有人曾作过这样的测算：发达国家在人均 GDP 达到 3 000 美元以后，才开始大规模的生态建设；而且通常认为，当人均 GDP 达到 4 000 ~ 5 000 美元时，生态质量才会出现好转，即位于环境库兹涅茨曲线的顶峰位置。究竟当人均 GDP 达到多少时，经济发展和生态建设之间会协调发展，即环境库兹涅茨曲线的峰值达到多少更为合适？若人均 GDP 必须达到测算的 4 000 ~ 5 000 美元才会出现经济发展与生态建设的协调发展，现在的发展中国家需要多长时间才能达到这一水平？在达到这一水平前，发展中国家是否还能忍受生态恶化带来的损失？西方发达国家的成功经验告诉我们，加快经济建设，推进经济“起飞”，在短期内积累大量财富，首先摆脱经济贫困，然后在经济发展过程中注重教育、科技、政治、文化等相关方面的协调发展，最终能够有能力彻底解决一度产生的生态问题。鉴于这些国家在经济发展过程中对生态造成的严重破坏，有人提出经济建设应与生态建设并行发展，抑或更加偏重于生态建设。那么这种新型的发展道路能不能帮助人们摆脱“贫困恶性循环”呢？经济发展有利于生态问题的解决，并且在很大程度上决定着生态问题解决的效果。但并不仅仅是因为经济增长，人们解决生态问题变得相对容易，而是因为经济增长引发了一系列变化，其首先满足了人们生存和生活的物质需求，人们的生活状态有所改善；资金的充裕使得研究和创新工作能够更容易展开，科学技术不断进步；人类征服自然的手段更加先进，不再是以前的强取豪夺，生产效率大大提高；人们受教育的水平不断提高，环境保护意识逐渐加强；发展观念的转变，使得人们对生态的需求更加强烈。这一系列变化，使得生态问题在经济处于一定发展水平时变得容易许多，也就是说，并不是经济发展就能解决生态问题，只有当经济发展到一定程度，能够带来上述一系列变化时，解决生态问题这一目标才会比较容易实现，这样经济发展和生态建设才可能协调统一起来。若从一开始就加强对生态的建设，而忽视经济建设，或是将二者齐头并进，最好的结果就是保护好生态，经济发展却处于停滞或倒退；甚至会出现生态建设和经济建设“双输”的局面。这样的发展道路是不会实现可持续发展的。可见，若想摆脱“贫困恶性循环”，就应以经济建设为突破点，优先推动经济发展。

对发展中国家来说，经济与生态相协调的中心是经济发展，因为生态问题的解决最终还要依靠经济的发展。就西方发达国家的发展经验来看，无论其人口密度大小、资源禀赋情况、生态状况好坏，几乎大部分国家都经历了以生态为代价大力发展经济的阶段，但其目前的生态问题的严重程度远远轻于发展中国家，人口膨胀、资源短缺、森林减少、水体污染、土地荒漠化等现象大多出现在发展中国家，贫穷和经济不发达是产生生态退化的重要原因。发展中国家的发展道路贴切地说是“先发展，后治理”的发展模式。在发展过程中，尽量避免不可逆转的生态损失。不可逆转的定义是对于某种生态损失而言，由此带给人们的收益远远小于逆转这种损失所需的费用。虽然发展过程中允许产生一定程度的生态损失。但不能允许无谓的损失，不能允许得不偿失的损失，应以适度的生态损失换取高效的经济增长，以较小的生态损失换取较强的生态治理能力。经济发展和生态建设之间的协调发展，除了包括经济发展之外，还包括生态发展和人类自身的发展。这种协调发展是指在以人类为核心和主体的全球生态经济系统中，人类通过不断理性化的行为和规范，以协调人类社会经济活动与生态的关系，协调经济发展与生态建设的关系，协调人类和生物圈的和谐统一，协调人类的持久生存，世代福利与资源分配的眼前与长远关系，从而实现全人类寻求的总体目标的最优化。

生态质量的好坏受经济水平的严重制约，并且受由经济发展引发的产业结构变革、科学技术进步、消费水平与方式的转变、环境法规与管理完善、环境意识增强等影响。这为我们降低环境库兹涅茨曲线的峰值，提前实现经济发展与生态建设的协调发展提供了可能。通过对这些因素进行严格调控，弥补经济系统对解决生态问题的投入不足，完全有可能在低于环境库兹涅茨曲线峰值人均 GDP 4 000 ~5 000 美元的情况下，提前实现生态的良性循环，跨越传统的单纯依靠经济实力解决生态问题的思路。

通过对生态改善与经济发展进行综合决策很可能在环境库兹涅茨倒U型曲线的左侧就实现生态与经济的协调发展。综合决策主要是指转变单纯考虑经济的决策方式，在决策过程中把生态与经济进行统筹考虑。首先，要深入研究这项决策的宏观背景和运行环境，将关于经济和环境的单项决策都融合于一项统一的综合决策之中；其次，改善生态保护的社会氛围，不仅仅要加强制定完善的生态保护的法规体系和相关的经济激励措施，更重要的是建立政府、企业和社会公众良性互动的管理机制，形成全社会自觉保护生态的良好风气，从自我认知上意识到保护环境的重要性；最后，要利用市场机制，规范和发展环保产业，与命令型环保管理相比，经济手段更能有效地起到保护环境的预期效果。环保产业不但能收到一定的经济效益，更重要的是能够运用市场机制有效地起到保护环境的作用。但这一做法实际操作起来很有难度，如何实现政策之间的相互协调，以及有效激励措施的制定仍需进一步思考。

三、生态建设与林业经营思想的转变

可持续发展战略的提出，使生态建设的地位凸显出来，生态建设作为国家发展的一个重要方面，被纳入国家发展的整体规划中来。林业是生态建设的主体，随着生态建设重要性的不断增强，林业的经营思想也随之发生转变，林业的生态功能越发显得重要。

在生态建设大规模开展之前，林业以提供木材、发挥林业的经济效益为主要任务。发达国家的历史经验表明：工业化是落后国家经济增长的核心，要实现现代化和经济增长，必须经历工业化阶段。对于处于工业化阶段的国家来说，经济建设是各国发展的首要任务，人们对生态的需求不是十分强烈。林业在此阶段主要是通过毁林开荒等手段为农业提供耕地，进而为工业发展提供所需原材料；或是通过提供木材以及林副产品直接为工业提供原材料，并从资本和外汇等方面大力支持工业发展，从而推动经济建设的开展。因而，此时林业的经济效益显得尤为突出，这一点在工业化阶段各国的林业经营思想当中都有所体现。德国、美国、法国等国家都曾采取过森林永续经营思想，以木材的生产和供应为最主要的任务。

中国林业总产值占国民生产总值的比重总体上呈现不断增加的趋势。由于中国在20世纪50年代末至60年代初经历了“大跃进”、三年自然灾害和国民经济调整，对林业造成的破坏比较严重，这一阶段林业总产值占国民生产总值的比重有所下降，此后，这一比重一直呈现增长的势头。这说明林业的经济功能在这一阶段表现得十分突出。林业经济功能的发挥在这一阶段林业经营思想中占据主导地位，但是林业生态功能的重要性也引起了人们的重视。人们已经认识到林业的生态功能能够为农业的发展提供良好的小气候，对于改良土壤、涵养水源、防风固土等能够起到良好的作用。但是这种认识并未形成系统的经营思想，也未将林业的生态功能纳入林业经营的范围。

随着经济的不断发展，人们对生态与经济之间关系的认识越来越深入，并且更加理智。在生态平衡与经济平衡之间，主导的一面，一般说应该是前者，因为生态平衡如果受到破坏，这种破坏的损失就要落在经济的身上。生态平衡是经济平衡的基础，只有在保持生态平衡下的资源利用才谈得上是合理利用，才是最符合长远经济效益的利用。经济发展至关重要，决定了人类生活水平的高低，而生态状况决定了人类能否生存发展，人类社会物质资料的生产和再生产归根到底是从生态系统中获取各种资源，加工成人们所需要的生产资料和生活资料，人类的一切活动都是在最大生态系统即生物圈中进行的，人类和生态系统之间的物质交换是人类生存和发展的永恒的自然基础。在认识深化的基础上，人们逐步开展生态建设并不断扩大其规模。

随着生态建设规模的扩大，林业的生态功能越来越得到人们的关注，此时林业经营思想也相应发生了一定的变化。随着全球生态问题的日益严重，加之人们对林业生态功能的认识不断加深，林业的生态功能不断渗入到林业经营思想当中，林业分工论和近自然林业以及生态林业论等经营思想的提出都强调了林业生态功能对林业发展的重要性，以及对生态保护的重要作用。

随着经济快速发展，社会财富急速增加，伴之而来的是森林资源遭到严重破坏，生态逐步恶化，人类的生存环境受到了严重的威胁。人口、资源和生态之间的矛盾日益加剧，人们认识到经济、社会和生态的可持续发展至关重要，不但影响当代人的生存条件，而且直接决定了子孙后代的生存。在这种背景下，林业可持续经营理论应运而生。林业可持续经营理论就是指森林生态系统的生产力、物种、遗传多样性及再生能力的可持续发展，以保证有丰富的森林资源与健康的环境，满足当代和子孙后代的需要。林业可持续经营思想是与可持续发展理论相适应的，只有实现了林业的可持续经营，才会保障人类的生存，为经济的可持续发展提供有力保障。

随着生态建设的逐步开展，林业经营思想由单一的发挥林业经济功能转变为综合发挥林业多种功能，并着重突出林业生态功能，这一转变将林业的生态功能也纳入了林业经营的范畴，将会更好地指引林业生态功能的发挥，促进生态建设的快速发展。

第四节　发达国家林业典型经营模式

从20世纪60年代起，发达国家即进入了飞速发展的时期，人们生活日渐富裕起来。对于经济发达国家而言，这一时期不再是通过毁林开荒来解决温饱的粮食问题阶段，也不再是通过砍伐森林来提供原材料的工业化发展阶段，而是严重的森林破坏所引起的生态问题阶段。在这一背景下，人们对林业的经营模式进行了探索。20世纪60年代后期，联邦德国在“林业政策效益论”、“船迹理论”、“和谐化理论”的基础上，又创立了“森林多功能理论”。这一理论很快被美国、日本、瑞典等国家所接受，为林业经营提供了丰富的理论基础，从而翻开了森林多功能经营新的篇章。在这一理论的影响下，经济发达国家根据各自的社会经济和林业发展状况，分别采取了不同的林业经营模式。

一、森林经济、社会和生态三大效益一体化经营模式

（一）理论渊源和现实背景

森林的经济、社会和生态三大效益一体化经营模式产生于德国，因此，也被

称为德国经营模式。在漫长的历史长河中，德国林业以其特定的自然历史条件，以及不断丰富创新的林业经营思想史，在一定程度上引领着世界林业经营发展的进程。众所周知，森林永续经营理论、法正林理论、近自然林业理论、森林多功能理论等，都源自于德国，这些理论的发展和深化为森林的经济、社会和生态三大效益一体化经营模式奠定了坚实的理论基础。

德国位于欧洲大陆中部，在公元前2000年前后进入农耕时代，和东方的农业文明一样，都是建立在毁林开荒的基础之上。通过砍伐森林来获得更多的土地种植农作物，以获得更多的食物，而木材作为用材的比例却极低。德国的原始森林曾覆盖国土面积的75%，但到了19世纪，由于大量毁林开荒，森林覆盖率减少到20%。

17世纪前期，德国的制盐业和矿冶业开始兴起并发展起来，各国君主为保证自己的企业有源源不断的燃料和原料供应，纷纷制定了新的《森林条例》。这也是德国历史上最早的关于恢复森林的指令。17世纪中期，德国因制盐、矿冶、玻璃、造船业等工业的发展，对木材的需求量猛增，开始大规模采伐森林。这种对经济利益的追求，给森林带来了前所未有的灾难性破坏，从而导致了18世纪初的“木材危机”(也被称作“能源危机”)。1713年，汉里希·冯·卡洛维茨首先提出了森林永续利用原则，并指出：“努力组织营造和保持能被持久地、不断地、永续地利用的森林，是一项必不可少的事业，是这个国家最伟大的一门艺术和科学。”此后，整个德国掀起了一场恢复森林的运动。卡洛维茨也因此被德国人奉为“森林永续利用理论”的创始人。这一理论的出现也为近代林业的兴起与发展拉开了序幕(董智勇，1992)。1795年，哈尔提希(Hartig G. L. 1764～1837)提出了“木材培育论”，其中心思想是追求纯经济利益，以获得木材为目的的森林永续经营。该理论在18世纪德国造林工作中起着主导作用。到1826年，洪德斯哈根(J Christian hurdeshagen，1783～1834)在其专著《森林调查》中，创立“法正林”学说以及森林经理的法正蓄积法。这标志着森林永续经营理论的形成，并成为欧美国家100多年来实施经营同龄林和追求森林资源永续的理想森林结构模式，对各国林业发展产生了巨大影响。可见，这一时期的主要特点是为满足工业日益增长的木材需求而进行的森林资源单效益利用。

1867 年，奥托·冯·哈根提出了著名的“森林多效益永续经营理论”：经营国有林不能逃避公众利益应尽的义务，而且必须兼顾持久的满足木材和其他林产品的需要和森林其他方面的服务目标。继他之后，恩特雷斯于 1905 年在《林业政策》中又提出了森林多效益问题的“森林的福利效益”，即森林对气候、水分、土壤和防止自然灾害的影响，以及在卫生和伦理方面对人类健康的影响，进一步发展了森林多效益永续经营理论。1933 年，在德国正准备实施的《帝国森林法》中明确规定：永续地、有计划地经营森林，既以生产最大量的用材为目的，又必须保持和提高森林的生产能力；经营森林要尽可能地考虑森林的美观、景观特点和保护野生动物；必须划定休憩林和防护林。后来因第二次世界大战的爆发，此法未能颁布实施。19 世纪末到 20 世纪初出现的这些林学家成为森林科学的真正奠基人，为现代林业的经营提供了理论依据和理论根基，并为森林的经济、生态、社会效益一体化经营思想打下了坚实的基础。第二次世界大战后，由于林业单纯追求经济利益和战争对经济的影响，造成了大面积森林的毁害，导致国家必须扶持林业，经营明显向总体效益转化，并由此产生了“林业政策效益理论”。这一理论是由德国林业政策学家第坦利希提出的，并指出林业应服务于整个国民经济和社会福利。同时，由“拯救阔叶林委员会”出版的《未来属于混交林》，集中了 200 多位科学家的观点、言论。他们认为“以经济为目标的人工林发展方针已经成为一个退化的纲领”，并向政府提出了高额资助营造阔叶林和混交林，把针叶林改造为阔叶林和混交林，对阔叶林至少取消 50 年地产税等具体意见，促进了林业政策转向森林的多效益经营。自此以后，德国确立了林业为木材生产和社会效益服务的双重目标。20 世纪 50 年代，出现了“船迹理论”与“和谐(协同)理论”两种截然不同的主张，在林学界引起了一场激烈的争论。船迹理论突出木材生产效益，认为随着木材生产可以带动森林其他效益的产生，如同前进中的船一样会产生一片向两旁扩展的波浪。该理论实际上是一种唯心主义观点，其核心是三大效益兼顾，木材生产优先。而和谐化(协同)理论是坚持永续的原则及经济、生态、游憩效益协同发展，把木材生产和其他效益同等对待。显而易见，和谐化理论适应当今社会的发展潮流，而且适用于发达国家对社会及生态的迫切需求。20 世纪 60 年代，可以被称作是生态觉醒的时代，德国开始推行森林多功能理论，实行多效益经营的模式。多效益林业的指导思想不单纯着眼于森林经济效益，其经营目标既着眼于生产木材和林产品，又要考虑到保持水土、改善环境、保护野生动植物资源及森林游憩和体育活动的需要。这一理论很快被美国、瑞典、日本、印度等许多发达国家所接受，在全球掀起一个“森林多功能理论”的浪潮。经济效益、社会效益和生态效益一体化经营模式正是在这一背景下产生的。

(二)经济效益、社会效益和生态效益一体化经营模式的内涵

1975 年，联邦德国公布了《联邦保护和发展森林法》，由此德国开始正式实行经济效益、社会效益和生态效益一体化经营模式，即采取永续、经济和公益三结合原则。这一模式的基本内涵是：①保证森林的永久性、持续性和均匀的利用效果，满足人们对木材和林产品的长远需求，永久保证森林对气候、水土、空气的保护效益及游憩；②企业以最小的开支取得最大的经济效益；③尽可能保证森林发挥最大的生态效益，以及通过改善森林结构，确保其经济效益。这种模式适用于木材需求压力不大、森林资源比较丰富且分布比较均匀的情况，核心是三大效益一体化经营。这种经营模式被誉为林业标准经营模式，但三大效益一体化经营模式的实施必须具备严格的条件，如森林资源分布和淘汰要很均匀、集约化程度高、国家经济实力要雄厚以及独特的经济扶持政策等。因此，实行这种经营模式的国家少之甚少。

在具体实行三效益一体化经营中，联邦德国吸取以往森林经营的经验和教训，采取了近自然林业经营模式。

由于在 18 世纪末到 20 世纪的造林运动中，联邦德国大部分地区的天然林被改变为人工针叶林，致使天然林几乎全部消失。大规模地营造针叶林导致了德国林分结构发生了巨大的改变。14 世纪初，其阔叶林的比率为 60% ~70%，然而到 20 世纪初，其针叶林的比率上升为 60% ~70%。人工纯林稳定性差，抗灾力弱。1972 年的风灾刮倒 2 900 万 m^3 林木后，1990 年的风灾又刮倒 7 500 万 m^3 林木，20 世纪 80 年代初发生的森林“新灾害”(大气污染所致的酸雨等灾害)使得 50% 以上森林受损。由此，造成林业投入和产出长期严重倒挂，并且林业投资亏损一直呈上升趋势①。盲目地单一营造人工纯林，这显然是林业发展的一个时期特征。

20世纪80年代后期以来，联邦德国林业开始向“近自然林业”转轨，“近自然林业”即是在经营中使地区性的主要乡土树种得到明显表现，它不是回归到天然的森林类型，而是尽可能使林分建立、抚育、采伐的方式同潜在的天然森林植被的自然关系相接近；要使林分能够进行接近生态的自然发生，达到森林生物群落的动态平衡，并在人工辅助下，使天然物质得到复苏。近自然林业提出了林业新方针：林业通过顺应自然向生态目标转变，要求加强森林的稳定性、自然多样性，要求为森林多种用途的利用保持自然力，要求促进资源的经济利用。这一方针也成为欧洲共同体国家共同的林业发展方针。近自然林业的主要措施包括：①保持地力，任其自然发展，不进行人工施肥；保留枯枝落叶和植被，不排水；采取保护性森林采伐方式和集材方式；②在针叶纯林中引入阔叶树种和混交林树种；从生态稳定性和未来安全性考虑，使林分达到足够的树种多样性；③建设稳定、多价的异龄林；④采用天然更新方法和延长更新时间；⑤对自然干扰采用生物预防措施，采用机械或生物技术防止灾害，只在森林濒危时方可采用化学防治方法；⑥适当地、节制地开发道路，避免抚育和采伐时损伤土壤和林分，建设不扰乱森林的游览路线。近自然林业强调了恢复天然林，使阔叶林、混交林保持相当的比例，建立和发展顺应自然的人工林，保持和建立稳定的生态系统，保证了森林经济、生态、社会三大效益一体化的林业经营模式顺利实施。

二、森林多效益主导利用经营模式

森林多效益主导利用经营模式大致与一体化经营模式形成于同一个历史阶段。这种经营模式是以林业分工论和多效益理论为指导，采取不同林种侧重于发挥某些效益并采用不同的经营形式的一种林业发展模式。法国、新西兰、澳大利

---

① 1967年，联邦德国地区经营国有林每公顷亏损39马克；1986年每公顷亏损达115马克；1995年每公顷亏损达132马克。

亚、前苏联等国家在实施这一经营模式中，取得了显著的成果。这种经营模式以法国和新西兰较为典型。

（一）法国森林多效益主导利用经营模式

法国林业具有2 000多年的发展历史，它也是世界上近代林业发展得最快的国家之一。第二次世界大战后，法国为了加速恢复在战争中被破坏的森林资源和满足对木材日益增长的需要，制定了大力造林、扩大森林资源的林业发展战略，即以造林为手段，恢复和重建森林资源。通过国民林业基金会的扶持，使得全国定点营造了高产用材林200万hm^2，森林面积增长速度比战前快5倍，仅用40多年的时间，全国森林面积达到了1 512.7万hm^2，森林的覆盖率增加了7%，由战前的20%增加到了27%。虽然法国国有林只占10%，但它在森林经营方面起着主导作用。20世纪60年代初，法国林业基本上实现了恢复高产用材林的造林目标，但由于林业经营粗放，森林质量差，林权分散，林地散碎，很不适应国民经济发展的需要。因此，1963～1964年法国又制定了森林集约经营的发展战略，即在继续增加森林资源的同时，加强经营管理，实行集约经营，提高森林质量。这一时期法国林业工作重点，除提高国有林集约经营水平外，还要大力组织私有林进行计划经营。这一发展战略对提高法国整个林业经营水平起到了重要的推动作用。

20世纪70年代后，随着工业的迅速发展，生态环境日趋恶化，人们对森林的生态效益和社会效益的要求越来越高。法国林学家B·马丁等人总结了各国森林资源管理理论，提出了“木材培育论”，指出人类应该从传统林业的桎梏下解脱出来，建立一个专门培育木材的企业。在面积不大，但立地条件优越、交通方便的林地，采用科学的营林方法，营造速生丰产林，追求木材高产、高效和高利润，而让其他类型的森林充分发挥其生态效益和社会效益。该理论对法国林业经营思想的转变起了很大的作用，森林全面经营方式逐渐向木材培育、公益森林和多功能森林这三大块经营演变。

法国从1978年起对林业经营进行了调整，即进行森林多效益主导利用的经营思想，采用“三大模块”的经营模式。这种经营模式的具体方式是：①木材培育，唯一目的就是追求更多、更快、更好地生产木材。最基本的原则是采用良种选育和栽培技术相结合的方法，二者相互补充，缺一不可；②公益森林，发挥森林的生态效益和社会效益，以满足社会日益增长的需求；③多功能森林，提供大径材的用材林，主要是发挥森林经济效益，同时也发挥森林生态效益和社会效益，它占全国森林面积的绝大部分(前两种模块林地相对较少一些)。这种对不同地区、不同林分、不同树种，突出其主导功能，兼顾其他功能，以发挥森林多效益来满足社会的各种需求的经营模式在法国取得了良好的效果。

(二)新西兰森林多效益主导利用经营模式

新西兰素有“绿色岛国”的美誉，其一年四季气候温和湿润，温差变化小，降雨充沛且分布均匀，土壤肥沃，林业发展的条件可谓得天独厚。加之新西兰决策者坚决实行独特的林业“分类经营”为指导的多效益主导利用的经营模式改革，从而也造就了新西兰的人工林奇迹。如果说德国是从原始的毁林开荒、放牧到资本主义工业化的掠夺性采伐，破坏森林的过程可谓岁月漫长，而新西兰却只用了一百多年时间就走完了他们历经的道路。

20世纪初，随着移民的增多和国民经济的发展，新西兰森林资源遭受了严重的破坏，使生态环境恶化，水土流失严重，保护和发展森林资源已是刻不容缓。1922年开始了大规模人工造林，并出现过两次造林高潮和一个相应的停滞时期。第一次造林高潮是在1922～1936年，在新西兰的部分地区进行人工造林，造林面积达27万hm^2，这次造林也为60年代新西兰木材出口的繁荣局面打下了基础。1936～1960年是一个相应的停滞时期，人工造林速度减慢，由于第一次造林树种(北美黄杉)选择不当，再加上第二次世界大战所带来的经济萧条等因素，在这20多年的时间里新西兰的造林基本上停滞下来。自60年代起，由于新西兰的决策者清醒地认识到大力发展人工造林，不但对出口创汇起到极大的促进作用，而且对国内的失业人口也能提供很好的就业机会。因此又掀起了第二次造林高潮，与第一次造林相比较又有很大的区别，即在全国范围内对人工林的营造进行规划，国有林的经营方针主要是大力发展人工林，实行短轮伐期的集约经营，并建立用材林基地；保护和发展天然林，充分发挥其生态效益和社会效益，兼顾其经济效益。而且这次造林树种主要选择了辐射松，该树种生长快，每公顷年生长量可达 17 ~ 23m^3，轮伐期可缩短到 25 ~ 35 年。因而形成了以辐射松为主的新的森林后备资源和木材生产基地，每年可为国家提供 980 万 m^3 的木材，占全国木材产量的 95%，其中超过 270 万 m^3 用于出口，为国家换取了大量的外汇。从生态方面来看，也可以说，人工林已完全代替了天然林所承担的木材生产任务，从而保护了天然林，使天然林的生态效益和社会效益得以体现。

20 世纪 80 年代后进行的林业改革，使新西兰林业走上了分治经营的道路，并形成了具有新西兰特色的林业发展模式。即从森林多效益向森林多效益主导利用经营方向转移，实行以“林业分工论”为指导的多效益主导利用经营模式。它的突出特点是工业人工林迅速崛起，实行集约经营，并将国有林划分为商品林和非商品林。商品林主要是工业人工林，以满足市场的木材需要为主。非商品林主要是天然林，以发挥其生态效益为主。而且工业人工林也实行了在生态平衡基础上的经营，保证了三个世代的人工林未发生地力衰退。从而在短短几十年，营造了 110 万 hm^2 的人工林，年供给木材 1 000 万 m^3 左右，造就了占有林地面积仅 14% 的人工林提供全国木材产量 95% 的奇迹，从而使一个缺材国一跃成为木材自给有余并能大量出口的木材生产国。

三、森林多效益综合经营模式

这种模式是属于前两种模式的中间类型，以森林永续利用为指导，充分发挥森林多种效益，实行综合经营。瑞典、美国等国实行这种经营模式。

瑞典是一个森林资源丰富的国家，国土面积为 4 100 多万 hm^2，其中森林面积为 2 340 万 hm^2，森林覆盖率为 57%。林业也是瑞典的国民支柱产业之一，在经济发展中占有重要地位。为了更好地了解瑞典的林业经营情况，有必要对其林业发展的历史背景作简单的叙述。

16 ~ 17 世纪，这个时期是从限制采伐森林到自由采伐森林的开始。当时炼铁业是瑞典的第一个工业部门，需要大量的木材做燃料。由此炼铁业也就成为第一个有利可图的生产部门，从而打开了木材的经济利用价值。这一时期森林利用的特点主要是作为燃料和焦油工业原料，制材工业和制浆造纸工业只是后半期才发展起来。

从19世纪40年代到19世纪末，是森林的自由采伐和森林工业的蓬勃发展时期，瑞典开始了工业化的历程。由于制材工业的迅速发展，世界资本主义经济对木材的需要量激增，导致了瑞典森林的大幅度减少，大部分森林变为疏林或劣质林。其主要的特点是：大规模的自由采伐，森林工业迅速发展，锯材是木材利用的主要形式；森林经营粗放，造林规模小，效果差；森林管护的法制不健全。

20世纪前50年，瑞典林业经营进入了一个新阶段。先后颁布了两部对保护森林有重要意义的法令，并建立了林业委员会。1903年通过的第一部《森林法》，规定采伐量不得超过生产量，林主必须切实保护森林，禁止乱砍滥伐，确保采伐迹地更新等。为了确保《森林法》的实施，1905年，瑞典成立了林业研究所，各省也成立了相应的林业委员会，负责监督私有林的经营管理和《森林法》的实施。1948年，颁布了第二部《森林法》，重申了采伐量不得超过生长量，还进一步提出，把林业作为一种能产生工业利润的产业来经营，林地必须用于生产木材，并对林主提出了更高的要求，如保证更新质量、及时防治病虫害等。这个时期最大的特点是：林业法制逐步健全；林业机构的职能得到明确；森林经营得到了足够的重视；林业科研得到了相应发展。

由于瑞典林业经营的传统指导思想是森林永续生产，即木材永续生产。林业经营的核心是木材年采伐量不得超过年生长量，采伐迹地必须及时更新。林业的投资，包括造林、抚育、林道建设等大部分由木材实现的收入来支付，所以林业经营主要以木材生产为主。20世纪60年代后，随着环境逐渐恶化，生物多样性逐年减少，环境、森林资源保护和对游憩影响等问题受到了普遍关注，人们迫切要求全面发挥森林的经济、社会和生态三大效益，因而传统的单一木材生产的森林永续经营思想受到了极大的冲击。1975年瑞典颁布了《森林多种用途规定》，强调所有林地必须考虑环境保护和其他效益综合利用，即以森林永续利用为指导思想，充分发挥森林的多种效益，实行综合经营模式。国有林的经营方针是在考虑国家的整体利益、发挥多种效益、保证永续利用的原则下，争取经营利润，同时关注林区人口的就业问题，注意自然保护及公众的其他利益。

美国位于北美洲中部，气候地域差异明显，土地类型复杂多样。森林面积 2.98 亿 hm^2，占土地总面积的 33%，人均拥有森林面积达 1.12 hm^2。美国近 100 多年以来，森林资源的兴衰消长同移民开发、经济发展以及人类对林业的认识程度密切相关。

随着欧洲移民大量涌入美国，19 世纪中叶，美国森林资源已遭受极其严重的破坏。毁林开荒、建筑房屋、生产用材等耗费了大量的木材，加之资本主义工业化的迅速发展，吞噬了大片的原始森林。这一时期的主要特点是只采伐不更新。1891 年，是美国森林经营活动的历史性转折点。在关于修改《土地法》的附件中，授权总统在国家领域内根据国家的需要和社会的利益，将用材林或其他森林资源宣布为保留林。这些保留林便发展成为以后所形成的美国国有林。保留林的出现，表明了美国国有林经营活动的正式开始。并为美国林业资源的保护和发展都起到了积极的作用。19 世纪末，由于受德国“永续经营”的影响，美国开始学习并借鉴了其多年经营经验，从而对自己原有传统森林永续生产指导思想进行了修正，把永续生产的重点放在了调整蓄积量上，即在特定的时期和环境内允许采伐量超过生长量。

第二次世界大战后，为满足恢复建筑设施用材的需要，国有林成了主要的木材来源。从而使得国有林面积急剧下降，农业生产、环境等都受到了相应的影响。同时，人们也清醒地认识到森林在保证农业增产、保护生态环境、保护生物多样性及提供游憩场所等方面的重要作用。显然需要重新评价国有林的作用，并制定新的经营规划。1960 年，美国制定了《森林的多种利用永续生产条例》，即用法律形式把森林多种利用和永续生产的原则确定下来，使其在美国林业中占主导地位，并实行森林多效益综合经营，把森林的经营目标从单纯获取木材转为游憩、放牧、生产木材、保护集水区、保护野生动物等综合经营。它标志着美国林业的发展进入了多种利用的新阶段。为了发挥森林的生态效益和社会效益，美国森林公园和自然保护区面积不断扩大，而用材林面积逐渐减少。尽管用材林面积减少了，但森林蓄积量却增加了。这说明，美国国有林这种经营模式取得了良好的经济效益。

1970年后，美国的林业经济学家M·克劳森、R·塞乔博士等人着手进行林业分工研究。他们认为，现代集约林业与现代化农业有一定的相似之处，如通过集约林业来生产木材，森林的潜力是相当巨大的，并提出了森林多效益主导利用的经营思想，对森林永续利用理论提出了挑战。到80年代，美国林学家J·F·富兰克林提出了“新林业”理论，主张把森林生产和保护融为一体，特别是保持和改善林分及景观结构的多样性。新林业理论避免了传统林业生产与纯粹自然保护之间的矛盾，找到了一条美国林业发展的合理道路。

四、林业经营模式的区别与联系

全球森林资源的持续减少和生态环境的不断恶化，是当今人类社会生产和发展面临最为严重的威胁之一。就目前而言，森林的多效益一体化、多效益主导利用和多效益综合利用三种经营模式可以被认为是世界林业的主要经营模式，也是现今大多数国家主要实施的林业发展战略。通过研究发达国家典型林业经营模式的发展变化，有利于从中吸取经验和教训，有利于正确地经营和管理森林，使林业的发展能够逐步满足人类对林产品及森林多效能日益增长的需要。

森林多效益一体化、多效益主导利用、多效益综合利用三大经营模式均源于森林多效益经营模式。由于受特定国家社会经济发展水平、文化背景、森林资源现状等的影响和制约，各国采用了侧重点不同的经营模式。可以说，三大经营模式是多效益经营模式在不同国家的衍生和发展。虽然三者都基于多效益经营模式，但各自有着不同的特征：多效益一体化经营模式，是把木材生产和其他效益等同对待，即保证森林各效益的永久性、持续性和均匀性，以满足社会对木材等林产品以及森林生态功能的需求，并通过森林生态系统结构的改善发挥最大的生态效益和经济效益。所以其实施必须具备严格的条件（如森林资源分布和淘汰要均匀、集约化程度高、国家经济实力雄厚以及独特的经济扶持政策等）。森林的多效益主导利用经营模式则突出其主导功能，兼顾其他功能，以发展森林多种效益来满足社会各种需求。是以林业分工论和多效益理论为指导，实行“林业分类经营”的原则，侧重于发挥某些效益的经营形式。其主要思想是：由于社会对森林的三大效益的需求不同，所以森林各功能的利用潜能各异，森林经营者应该根据供给与需求、自然与技术潜能将林地的利用做出主次之分，以森林的最大效益的发挥决定优先权，以主导利用的方式确定经营单位的性质和经济循环方式。达到局部上分而治之，整体上合而为一的效果。所以，它的实施适合于森林资源少和财力有限的国家。而多效益综合利用模式，是以森林永续利用为指导，充分发挥森林的多种效益，实行综合经营。它的实施既要注重发挥某些效益，又要充分从全局考虑整体的效益。所以说，它是前两种模式的中间类型。

上述三种模式在具体实施上虽然各有特色，但其指导思想却基本一致，即林业经营要实现经济、生态和社会效益三者之间的协调和统一。耐人寻味的是，这三种典型的林业经营模式均产生于经济发达国家，并在发达国家进行了相对完整的实行。之后，一些经济相对欠发达国家才开始逐渐接受这些经营思想和经营模式，但实施程度上与发达国家相比还存在很大差距。这说明经济发展水平与林业经营模式之间存在某种必然的联系。

第四章　林权政策演进的一般规律

随着工业化进程的推进，林业发展经历了土地问题、资源问题以及生态问题阶段。在林业土地问题阶段，森林资源的稀缺性开始显现，森林资源逐渐由无产权的自由进入状态转变为对林权进行初始界定；在林业资源问题阶段，森林资源的稀缺性日益凸显，加之各国林权初始界定状况以及经济发展特征不同，林权政策演进呈现出不同的路径依赖，主要表现为以国有林为主和以私有林为主两种典型类型；发展到林业生态问题阶段，人们对森林资源的需求日益多元化，森林资源的稀缺性更加突出，林权政策呈现出新的特征。

第一节　林权及相关概念界定

国外学者并未直接对林权概念给予明确界定，而是以分析林权的权力构成的方式界定了林权的内涵。早在 1992 年 Schlager 和 Ostrom(1992)二人就提出了林权由进入权(或称为使用权)、收益权、管理权、排他权和转让权所组成的一个权利束。二者的研究成果对探讨林权的权利构成做出了重大贡献，这一研究成果也先后被 Peter Glück(2002)以及 Tran Ngoc Thanh 和 Thomas Sikor(2006)等人在进行相关研究时多次引用。Thomas Sikor 和 Tran Ngoc Thanh(2007)在分析越南中心高地林地分配过程中实施放权政策的具体模式时更加详尽地阐述了林权所包括的具体权利。国内学者对于林权概念界定尚未达成共识，目前对林权的表述主要有以下几种：一是依据《中华人民共和国森林法》等相关法律文件的规定，将林权表述为依法确认的森林、林木和林地的所有权和使用权；二是将林权表述为依法对森林、林木、林地享有的占有、使用、收益和处分的权利；三是将林权表述为森林、林木或者林地的所有者和经营者对森林、林木、林地依法享有的占用、使用、收益或者处分的权利，刘宏明将“所有者和经营者”更加具体化为自然人、法人或者其他组织。此外，国内还有一种观点认为，应将林地产权称之为“山权”，而林权仅指林木产权，这通常被理解为狭义的林权。

由于目前国内外对林权概念的界定尚未达成共识，以产权理论为依据明晰林权概念就成为研究林权政策演进的首要问题。产权是指由于产权客体的存在以及对产权客体的使用所引起的产权主体之间相互认可的行为关系，本质上反映的是人与人之间的关系。产权由产权主体、产权客体和产权权能三部分组成，在界定林权概念时也应从这三个方面着手。由此，林权应理解为林权主体对森林资源的所有权、使用权、收益权和处置权等一组权利束。在这里，将林权客体界定为森林资源，不仅包括森林、林木、林地，还包括依托于森林、林木、林地的野生动植物和微生物；林权主体在不同国家、不同时期有着不同的具体表现形式，主要包括国家、集体、社团、社区、农户、农场、公司等多种形式。

与其他稀缺资源的产权相比，林权是一个更加复杂的概念。这主要是由于作为林权客体的森林资源包含的内容十分丰富，不仅包括森林、林地、林木，还包括野生动植物和微生物，而且，森林资源除了具有经济功能之外，还具有较强的生态功能和社会功能，同时兼具私人物品、公共资源以及公共物品等多种物品属性。处于不同经济发展阶段，人们对森林资源的需求有所变化，在制定林权政策时对森林、林木、林地的关注程度有所不同，因而林权概念所涉及的林权客体的范围一直处于一个动态变化过程。通常情况下，在林业土地问题阶段更加注重林地产权，林木产权往往依附于林地产权之上；在林业资源问题阶段，对林木资源的关注程度更加凸显，甚至出现林地和林木产权分离的现象，并且对森林作为一个完整的生态系统所发挥生态功能的关注程度逐渐增强；发展到林业生态问题阶段，林权客体逐渐将森林资源所包括的内容都纳入其中。这可以通过当前各国对林权问题进行研究的现状加以印证，发展中国家多是探讨林地和林木的产权问题，发达国家则更加关注建立适当的林权政策以保护生态多样性等问题。

林权政策演进过程实际上是随着制度环境变化，林权利益相关主体为了追求潜在利润对林权进行重新配置的过程。这里的“林权利益相关主体”不仅包括当前林权政策所规定的林权主体，而且还包括潜在的林权主体，即在林权政策演进后即将成为林权主体的部分。

第二节　林业土地问题阶段的林权政策

在处于粮食问题阶段和农村相对贫困阶段时，尽管导致林地转变为耕地的原因和转变的数量有所不同，但是林地转变为耕地的趋势未发生改变；发展到农业调整阶段，耕地逐渐开始转变为林地。本节谈到的林业土地问题阶段仅指经济发展水平比较低的前工业化时期和工业化起步阶段。在这一时期内，森林资源逐渐由无产权的自由进入状态转变为对森林资源进行初始的产权界定状态，此时的林权客体主要表现为林地资源。

一、森林资源的无产权状态

在经济发展水平十分低下的漫长历史中，森林资源一直处于无产权的自由进入状态。据有关资料显示，在历史早期，有人居住的陆地上约2/3是茂密的森林，其面积约为90亿hm^2。由于当时森林生态系统比较完整，森林资源的自我修复能力比较强，保障了森林资源的持续供给，因而森林资源的绝对量比较丰富。另一方面，由于当时林木砍伐技术十分低下，人们对森林资源的开发利用程度非常有限，保障了森林蓄积量维持在一定水平。从人们对森林资源需求的角度而言，这一时期人们对森林资源的需求都是基于自身生存的需要，主要是利用林木来建造房屋和劳动工具，或是将林木作为薪材使用，人们更加关注的是森林资源生活和自身生产用途，故人们对森林资源的需求量相对有限。

综观森林资源的供给和需求，这一时期森林资源未显示出稀缺性。新制度经济学派认为，资源的稀缺性是建立产权的基本前提，当森林资源十分丰富时，由于有足够的数量来满足所有人对森林资源的需求，人们对森林资源的消费不具有竞争性，单个主体在利用森林资源时不会产生很强的外部性，因而不存在为了将外部性内在化而建立产权的动机。此时，人们可以根据自身需求任意获取森林资源，因此，这一时期的绝大多数国家对森林资源几乎都采取了自由进入的方式。例如，加拿大在前工业化时期的很长一段时间里，木材几乎没有任何经济价值，特别是在森林资源比较丰富的北部地区，其林业活动基本上是满足生存需求，利润最大化并不是其林业活动的动力和动机。因而，对森林资源并未界定产权。

二、林权的初始界定

由于工业化前期森林资源并未表现出明显的稀缺性，也未有明晰的林权界定，此时森林资源具有典型的公共池塘资源特征，人们通过尽可能多地占有和利用森林资源来排除其他人对森林资源的消费。特别是随着人口数量不断增加，人—地关系开始紧张，可利用土地的数量不能满足人口增长的需要，将林地转变为耕地的需求日渐强烈。因此，在农业生产技术十分有限的情况下，增加耕地提高粮食产量就成为主要途径。由于资金积累十分困难，劳动力数量的增加又会削弱粮食产量增长所发挥的作用，因而增加耕地投入量更成为提高粮食产量的主要手段。为了增加耕地面积，采取大规模毁林开荒的手段而不是开发未利用土地，这主要是因为将林地转变为耕地会产生更大的效用。一方面，由于长期堆积的枯枝落叶层能够大大增强土壤肥力，有助于提高粮食产量；另一方面，砍伐的林木可以用于建造房屋和制造劳动工具以满足人们的基本生存需要。为了增加耕地投入数量，人们对森林资源的消费具有明显的竞争性，大规模毁林开荒行为致使森林面积大量减少，然而“毁林”的目的是用于“开荒”，很少程度上是出于对林木资源的需求。因而，这一时期林地资源的稀缺性较林木资源的稀缺性更为突出，林权政策的制定也多围绕林地资源产权展开，甚至许多国家都是在本国的土地政策中涉及林权政策。

由于在林业土地问题阶段，森林资源特别是林地资源的稀缺性已经开始显现，为了更好地配置森林资源，各国逐渐开始界定林权。在西班牙，由于长期以来林区居民享有使用和消费森林资源的权利，在初始界定林权时仅将林地和林木资源的产权赋予给林区当地的居民，而未向居住在林区之外的任何主体赋予林权。林区大面积的森林资源既不归国家所有，也不归林区内的某一个个人所有，而是由居住于特定村庄的群体共同所有，但这种林权类型并不是通过法律形式确定的，而是依靠对林地和林木资源习惯性的使用权利和其他非正式的制度规范确立的。印度尼西亚在获得独立之后，在很大范围内将森林资源界定为国有林权，政府完全享有森林资源的所有权、使用权、控制权和管理权，严格控制着林地的利用方式和利用程度，甚至在一个更广泛的范围内决定社区、个人和合法实体之间的关系。与印度尼西亚相类似，印度大部分森林资源均为国有林权，所有决策权和制定权都集中于林业部门，林地和林木资源的使用者和地方利益相关者在林权政策的运作过程中很少有发言权。除了国有林权和共有林权，私有林权也是在林权初始界定时一种林权形式，但由于这一时期界定林权的技术和经验尚未成熟，界定私有林权的成本较高，因而私有林权的比例相对有限，大部分森林资源多界定为国有林权或共有林权的形式。

三、林权政策的基本特征

在林业土地问题阶段，大规模毁林开荒行为使得森林资源的稀缺性开始显现。由于林权界定技术和经验的匮乏，该阶段的林权政策主要表现出如下特征：第一，该阶段的林权政策主要针对林地资源，林木资源居于从属地位。实际上，对林地进行产权界定的过程是一个土地资源配置过程，许多国家借助土地改革来完成对林地产权的界定，附着于林地之上的林木多根据林地产权建立相应的产权结构，故而这一时期林地和林木产权多是相统一的。第二，由于界定林权需要花费成本，在经济发展水平十分低下的情况下，界定林权的技术非常有限，初始界定的林权政策主要以归属权为核心，强调林地和林木归谁所有，对于林权的权利束中各具体权能的配置比较模糊。第三，由于具有较高排他性的私有林权进行界定的困难程度最高，尽管私有林权占有一定比例，但是国有林权、共有林权等带有不同程度公有林权性质的林权形式仍占据绝对优势。第四，在经济发展水平较低时期，整个制度体系都处于初步建立阶段，正式产权制度的建立十分困难，因而这一时期的林权政策多以信仰、使用习惯等非正式制度为主，强制性程度较弱。

第三节　林业资源问题阶段的林权政策

在林业资源问题阶段，林权政策随着外在环境的变化发生相应改变，并呈现出一定程度的路径依赖。实际上，林业资源问题在工业化初期已经有所显现，之后逐渐占据主导地位，这种情形一直持续到工业化中期和后期。正如本书第二章所述，在经济发展中被人类经济活动主动且直接利用的森林资源主要是林木资源，林木资源在林业资源问题阶段的重要性十分突出，此阶段林权政策更加偏重于对林木资源的产权界定。

一、林权政策演进的动因

工业化初期是经济发展速度较快的阶段，许多国家在这一阶段顺利实现了经济的“起飞”，并逐渐过渡到工业化中期和后期。在这一过程中，由于林木资源不仅能够为工业发展提供原材料，还能提供大量的资金和外汇积累，而且林地也是转变为耕地和建设用地的主要来源，人们对森林资源的需求不断增加。由于人们对木材的消耗量急剧增加，森林资源大面积减少，稀缺性逐渐增强，林权需要进一步明晰。林产品特别是木材市场化程度的不断完善，也对明晰林权起到了推动作用。

（一）森林资源稀缺性逐渐增强

发展到林业资源问题阶段，不仅薪材、房屋建造材料、劳动工具材料的需求日渐增加，而且对其作为工业原料、提供资金和外汇积累的手段的需求也逐渐增加；同时由于城市化进程的推进，对林地转变为耕地和建设用地的需求也不断增加。森林资源在这一时期快速减少，据联合国环境规划署的报告显示，有史以来全球森林资源已经减少一半，仅1990～2000年十年间全球森林资源每年就减少近千万 hm^2。由于人们对森林资源的需求不断增加，随着森林面积逐年减少，森林资源的蓄积量越来越不能满足人们的需求，森林资源的稀缺性逐渐增加，这可以从影响林木资源需求和供给两个方面的因素来进行分析。

1. 林木资源经济价值凸显

在林业土地问题阶段，人们对林木资源的需求主要侧重于利用其建造房屋或制造劳动工具等与人们生存密切相关的方面。随着工业化进程的推进，林木资源的经济价值日益凸显，这可以用具有较高经济价值的工业用原木的生产量来加以反映。所谓原木是指未经加工的木材，包括薪材和工业用原木，其中薪材是指用于煮饭、取暖或能量生产等方面作为燃料的未加工的木材，主要用于满足人们的生存需要，经济价值相对较低；工业用原木包括锯材原木、胶合板材、造纸材以及其他工业用原木，主要用于工业生产，具有很高的经济价值。因而，林木资源经济价值的提高可以用原木生产结构的变化来予以反映。

20 世纪中后期，大部分发展中国家处于工业化初期阶段，工业化导致工业用原木的需求大大增加，而对薪材需求的比例却呈现下降趋势，在需求的引导下，原木的生产结构相应发生了变化。表 4-1 展示了智利、印度尼西亚、巴基斯坦和越南四个发展中国家原木生产中工业用原木产量比例的变化趋势。由于历年工业用原木产量比例的变化趋势不是十分明显，故对每三年的工业用原木产量占原木总产量的比例计算简单算术平均数。如表 4-1 所示，4 个发展中国家的工业用原木产量比例都有了不同程度提高，薪材和木炭产量的比例有所下降，这表明发展中国家对林木资源经济价值的需求不断增加。

表 4-1　部分发展中国家工业用原木生产比例

	智利	印度尼西亚	巴基斯坦	越南
1982 ~ 1984 年均值	57.3%	18.6%	5.0%	13.3%
1985 ~ 1987 年均值	60.6%	18.9%	5.8%	15.8%
1988 ~ 1990 年均值	62.3%	21.5%	7.3%	15.5%
1991 ~ 1993 年均值	67.6%	21.2%	8.7%	13.8%
2004 年	69.2%	29.8%	9.5%	19.8%

资料来源：根据《FAO 林产品年鉴 1982 ~ 1993》、《FAO 林产品年鉴 1991 ~ 1995》、《世界森林状况 2007》数据计算得来。

除了个别发展中国家自身原木生产结构中工业用原木产量比例不断提高之外，从整个世界工业用原木的总产量而言，这一时期发展中国家工业用原木产量占整个世界工业用原木产量的比例也呈现不断增长的趋势(图4-1)。

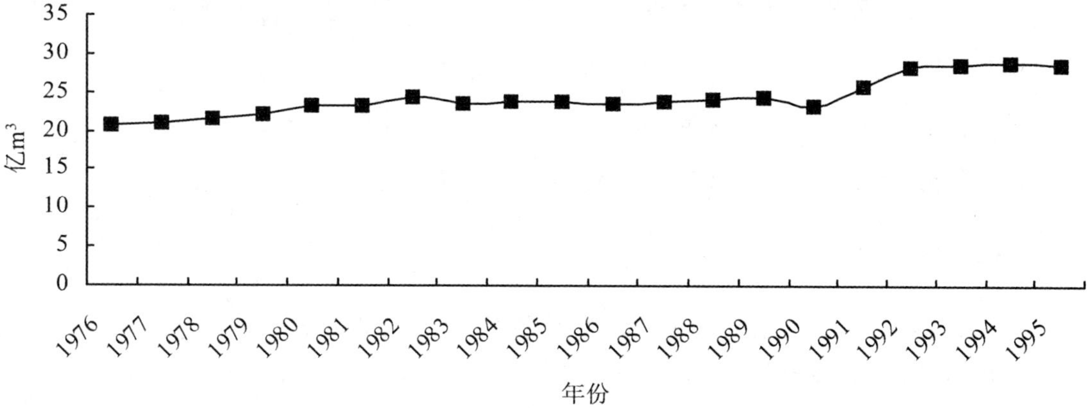

图4-1　1976～1995年发展中国家工业用原木产量比例变化趋势图

资料来源：根据《FAO林产品年鉴1976～1987》、《FAO林产品年鉴1982～1993》、《FAO林产品年鉴1991～1995》数据计算得来。

由于林木资源不仅能为工业发展提供工业原料，而且能够提供资金和外汇积累，人们对林木资源经济价值的需求逐渐增强，而对其生活用途的需求则相对弱化。林木资源的经济价值一旦显现，人们对林木资源经济价值的需求趋于无限，而林木资源的供毕竟是有限的，对林木资源需求的无限性和供给的有限性势必会增强林木资源的稀缺性。

2. 人口数量不断增长

经济发展较快的时期通常伴随着人口数量的快速增长，在20世纪中后期，处于林业资源问题阶段的大部分发展中国家都保持了较高的人口增长速度。表4-2反映了部分发展中国家在这一时期的人口增长速度，增长率多维持在10%左右。

表 4-2　部分发展中国家人口增长率　　单位:%

时间	智利	南非	印度	马来西亚	土耳其	巴西	印度尼西亚	巴基斯坦	越南	尼泊尔
1976～1980	7.04	9.49	8.18	12.76	9.78	12.77	8.77	12.49	10.12	9.11
1981～1985	7.35	10.51	11.04	10.42	8.60	9.30	6.63	13.69	8.72	10.72
1986～1990	6.24	11.59	10.07	10.24	11.53	4.50	7.72	13.35	8.72	5.72
1991～1995	8.40	11.25	9.74	13.23	9.88	7.67	8.59	15.88	11.41	18.50

资料来源：根据历年《世界经济年鉴》数据计算得来。

人口数量的增长对林木资源和林地资源的需求都会产生重要影响：一方面，人口数量的增加导致薪材、房屋建造材料以及劳动工具制作材料等与人们生存密切相关用途的需求的增加，而且也会导致对工业品需求的增加，进而导致对林木资源作为工业原料需求的增加；另一方面，人口数量的增加导致对住房、公共设施等建设用地的需求增加，同时对将林地改变为耕地以提高粮食产量的需求依然存在。尽管人口数量增加在一定程度上会增加林业生产的劳动力投入量，但是由于林木生长过程受自然因素的影响比较大，人工干预影响其产量的功效较小。人口数量的增加对森林资源需求产生的影响远远大于对增加森林资源供给产生的影响，因而，人口数量的增长是造成森林资源减少的一个主要原因。

3. 城市化进程不断推进

城市化进程通常以人口城市化率来衡量，所谓人口城市化率是指城市人口占人口总数的比例。从国际经验看，工业化中期是城市化水平发展最快的时期。例如，日本于 1947～1975 年处于工业化中期阶段，同期城市化率从 28% 提高到 75%，28 年间提高了 47 个百分点，平均每年提高 1.67 个百分点；韩国的城市化率从 1960 年的 28% 提高到 1981 年的 56%，平均每年提高 1.33 个百分点。通常情况下，处于林业资源问题阶段的国家都伴有较高的城市化率增长速度，表 4-3 反映了 1995～2004 年部分发展中国家城市化率水平及其增长速度。

表 4-3　部分发展中国家的城市化率及其增长速度　　单位:%

年份	1995	1999	2003	2004	1995～1999 年增长率	1999～2003 年增长率
巴西	78.2	80.7	83.1	83.6	3.2	3.0
马来西亚	53.7	56.5	63.9	64.4	5.2	13.1
印度尼西亚	35.4	39.2	45.6	46.7	10.7	16.3
中国	30.2	33.8	38.6	39.6	11.9	14.2
印度	26.8	28.1	28.3	28.5	4.9	0.7

资料来源：根据《世界经济年鉴 1996》和《世界经济年鉴 2006》数据整理、计算得来。

城市化进程的推进大大增加了对林木资源的需求，同时也增加了对将林地直接或间接转变为建设用地的需求。城市中人口密度比较大、公共设施相对齐全，建设城市过程中住房、道路及其他公共设施的建设规模不断扩大，房屋建造、装修装饰、家具制造以及早期铁路修建过程中枕木的大量使用都增加了对林木资源的需求。城市化进程更突出的影响表现在将林地间接转变为城市建设用地，这主要是因为城市多形成于人口相对集中、经济相对发达、交通相对便利的区域，通常情况下这些地方都是工农业发展比较迅速的地区，因而城市建设用地需求多是通过占用耕地面积来满足的，而粮食生产对耕地的需求仍旧存在，因而耕地面积的减少又会引发毁林行为，最终导致林地面积减少。

通过上文分析，可以做出如下假定：①假定城市建设用地都是由耕地转变而来；②假定农业生产技术水平既定，耕地仍旧是粮食生产的主要投入品，因而耕地需恢复到原有水平以保障粮食生产；③假定减少的耕地面积全部由林地弥补；④假定林地和林木产量之间存在着简单的线性关系，而不考虑林地质量对林木产量的影响；⑤假定价格不变。第①和③假定相结合，结果即相当于林地直接转变为建设用地，因而无论是林地直接或间接转变为城市建设用地都不会影响最终结果；第②条假定也较符合当时的情形，即便是农业技术有所进步，也不可能完全替代耕地的投入，因而即便不是完全弥补减少的耕地面积，但仍旧有增加耕地面积的必要，耕地面积恢复数量的差异不会严重影响分析问题的结果，故假定耕地面积恢复到原有水平。

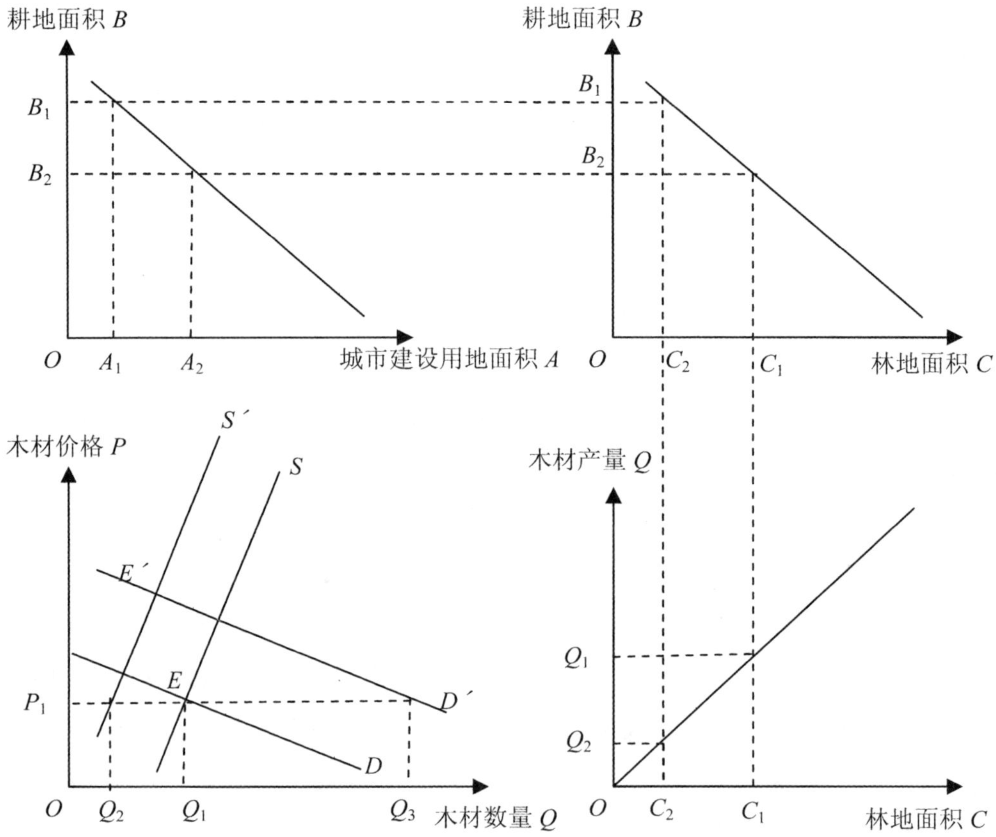

图 4-2　城市化进程对森林资源稀缺性的影响

图 4-2 反映了城市化进程对森林资源稀缺性的影响。在假定条件下，耕地面积与城市建设用地面积、耕地面积和林地面积之间是完全负相关的关系，因而是一条夹角为 45°的向右下方倾斜的直线；林地面积与木材产量之间是正相关关系，是一条向右上方倾斜的直线；由于林木的生长周期比较长，因此木材供给价格弹性较小，又由于木材的用途比较广泛，而且随着经济发展替代品不断出现，因而其需求价格弹性较大，故木材供给曲线较陡峭，需求曲线较平坦。城市化进程的

推进使得城市建设用地的需求由 A_1 增加到 A_2，为满足这种需求，耕地面积相应由 B_1 减少到 B_2；由于耕地投入仍旧是粮食生产的主要生产要素，因而耕地面积的减少势必会减少粮食产量，而粮食产量与人们的基本生存密切相关，是必须予以保障的，因而增加耕地面积进而保证粮食产量的需求仍旧存在。若想使得耕地面积由 B_2 恢复到 B_1，相应林地面积就要由 C_1 减少到 C_2；由于林地面积和木材产量之间是简单的线性关系，林地面积的减少使得林木产量由 Q_1 减少到 Q_2；由于林地面积减少导致的木材产量减少使得林木供给曲线由 S 移动到 S'，当价格仍旧维持在 P_1 水平的情况下，木材供给数量仅为 Q_2，另一方面由于城市化进程推进引发的房屋建造、装修装饰、家具制造以及铁路枕木对木材需求的增加导致木材需求曲线由 D 移动到 D'，在价格为 P_1 的情况下，木材需求数量为 Q_3，木材的供给明显小于需求，木材供需缺口即为 Q_3-Q_2。

4. 伐木技术和造林技术的进步

伐木技术和造林技术是影响森林资源供给的主要因素，林木采伐技术的提高，一方面会导致人们利用林木资源的能力增强，增加当前的木材供给，短期内缩小木材的供需缺口；另一方面更深远的影响是，运用大机械伐木的高效率会使得人们对林木资源经济价值的需求进一步膨胀，导致掠夺式采伐，进而使得森林蓄积量逐渐下降，不利于对林木资源的可持续利用。这个过程可以用下式来表示：

$$S_{t+1}=S_t+G_t-Q_t$$

其中，S_t表示时间 t 森林蓄积量，G_t表示时间 t 林木生长量，Q_t表示时间 t 林木采伐量，S_{t+1}表示时间$(t+1)$森林蓄积量。在时间 t 内，单纯利用劳动力而不采用任何机械设备进行伐木时，人们采伐林木的数量是十分有限，此时 $G_t>Q_t$，即林木的生长量大于采伐量，则 $S_{t+1}>S_t$，森林蓄积量呈现增长的趋势；若在时间$(t+1)$提高林木采伐技术，大量机械设备应用于林木采伐使得采伐林木的能力逐步增强，林木的采伐量不断增加，即 $Q_{t+1}>Q_t$，而林木生长量增加速度十分有限，那么 $Q_{t+1}/Q_t>G_{t+1}/G_t$，即林木采伐量的增长速度大于林木生长量的增长速度，也就是说林木的采伐量逐渐接近林木生长量，这种状况持续下去，到时间$(t$

$+i$)，$i \geqslant 1$ 时，林木采伐量就会超过林木生长量，$G_{t+i} < Q_{t+i}$，此时，$S_{t+i+1} < S_{t+i}$，森林蓄积量开始下降。可见，伐木技术的进步会导致森林蓄积量大大减少，影响到森林资源的可持续利用。

为了保障木材的持续供给，大多数国家积极发展人工林，以期通过增加森林面积来提高森林蓄积量。飞播造林、病虫害防治以及林木管护等技术的进步对于提高森林面积和蓄积发挥着一定作用。但由于林木生长过程受自然因素的影响比较大，并且投资回收期相对较长，对森林营造和管护技术的研发投入带来的收益较小，因而此时多将技术研发的重点侧重于林木采伐方面。

人们对森林资源经济价值需求的增强、人口数量的增长、城市化进程的推进以及技术的不断进步都是影响森林资源需求和供给的主要因素，但是影响程度、影响途径以及产生影响的方向并不相同。对森林资源经济价值需求的增强导致人们对森林资源的需求迅速膨胀；人口数量的增长会增加林业生产的劳动力投入，但这对增加森林资源供给的影响十分微弱，更主要的影响还是体现在对林木资源需求的增加；城市化进程的推进，一方面增加了对林木资源的需求，另一方面减少了林地面积使得林木资源的供给更加有限；尽管造林技术的进步对于增加森林面积和蓄积发挥着重要作用，但应用更为广泛的伐木技术会在更大程度上增加当前的木材产量，从而减少森林面积和蓄积。综合而言，在林业资源问题阶段，森林资源大面积减少，而对森林资源的需求日益增加，森林资源稀缺性不断增强，进而引发人们对森林资源的竞争愈发激烈，明晰林权更有利于提高森林资源的配置效率。森林资源稀缺性的不断提高使得林权界定与保护的边际收益增加，人们在林业土地问题阶段界定林权过程中积累的知识和经验促使林权界定和保护的边际成本有所减少，在这种情况下，界定林权的边际收益大于边际成本的可能性增大，因而在林业资源问题阶段界定林权的活动变得频繁，处于公共领域的森林资源的比例逐渐减少。值得注意的是，虽然森林资源的稀缺性是界定林权的重要前提，但是将林权界定为何种类型还要受其他因素的影响。

（二）森林资源市场化程度增强

市场化程度可以理解为市场通过价格机制在一个经济体资源配置中发挥作用

的程度。从世界经济发展的经验来看，随着工业化进程推进市场化程度也不断增强。衡量森林资源的市场化程度可以用国际木材市场的交易量、国内木材市场交易量以及林业投资主体中非国有成分所占比重等指标来衡量。

经济发展的不均衡在世界范围内日益突出，据统计，世界上最富的20%和最穷的20%人群之间的收入差距逐渐拉大,这一比例1960年为30: 1,1990年为60: 1，1999年为74: 1，2003年已达到80: 1，发达国家和发展中国家经济发展的不均衡导致对林木资源的需求呈现很大差异；另一方面，森林资源在世界范围内的分布具有明显的区域性特征，全球森林主要集中在南美、俄罗斯、中非和东南亚，这4个地区拥有全世界60%的森林，而世界上有62个国家的森林覆盖率不到10%。由于各国(或各地区)经济发展水平的不均衡导致对森林资源的需求程度存在很大差异，一国范围内森林资源需求与供给的非均衡性越强。各国在经济发展水平和森林资源上的重大差异，导致国际市场上木材交易的数量越来越多。

20世纪中后期，绝大多数发展中国家都处于林业资源问题阶段，这一时期发展中国家原木、成材、木质板、木浆、纸和纸板的总出口价值呈现明显增长趋势，图4-3反映了1976～1995年发展中国家出口林产品总价值的变化趋势：除20世纪80年代前半期出现小幅下降之外，整体上呈现增长的趋势。发展中国家林产品出口总价值的增长在一定程度上体现了世界范围内森林资源市场化程度的增强。

如果说各国之间以及国内各地区之间经济发展水平和森林资源分布的不均衡促使木材交易的动机增强，那么道路交通的便利、交通工具和通讯工具的发达大大减少了林木资源的运输成本，这也为增强森林资源的市场化程度提供了有利条件。不仅世界范围内森林资源市场化程度有所增强，一国(或地区)范围内森林资源的市场化程度也有不同提高，林业投资主体日益多元化，森林资源市场化程度的增强为林权界定提出了新的要求。

森林资源稀缺性不断增强，享有林权的主体将会获得更多的潜在利润，人们对森林资源的争夺愈发激烈，在这种情形下进一步明晰林权更有助于对森林资源的合理利用；而森林资源市场化程度的增强则在很大程度上为私有林权的建立提

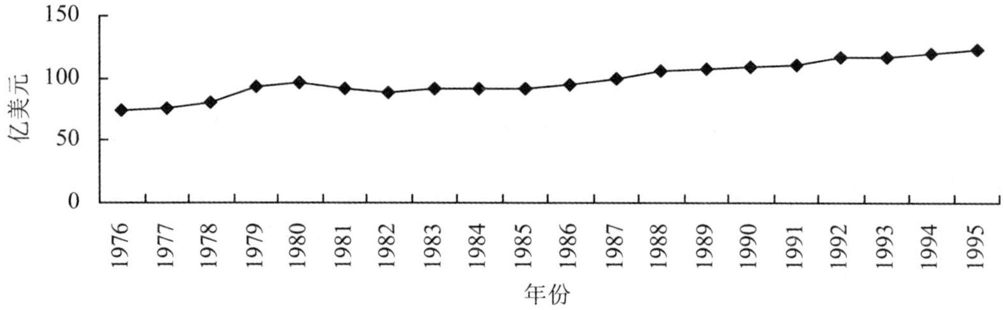

图 4-3　1976 ~ 1995 年发展中国家林产品出口总价值

资料来源：根据《FAO 林产品年鉴 1976 ~ 1987》、《FAO 林产品年鉴 1982 ~ 1993》、《FAO 林产品年鉴 1991 ~ 1995》数据计算得来。

供了重要的前提条件。

二、林权政策的类型

在林业资源问题阶段，由于森林资源稀缺性逐渐增强和森林资源市场化程度不断提高，明晰林权成为这一阶段的典型特征。但这并不意味着在任何一个国家明晰林权都采取私有化倾向。据《2005 年全球森林资源评估报告》称，全球 84. 4% 的森林是公有林，13. 2% 的森林是私有林，在所调研的 229 个国家和地区中，公有林比例超过 50% 的国家占 74%，私有林比例超过 50% 的国家占 26%。在世界范围内，绝大多数国家都采取多种林权形式并存的林权政策，只有少数国家采取单一的林权形式，例如印度尼西亚、土耳其实行国有林权政策；纽埃岛、库克群岛和基里巴斯岛实行私有林权政策。在林业资源问题阶段，林权政策表现为三种不同的类型。

（一）以国有林权为主的林权政策

一些国家在林业土地问题阶段对林权进行初始界定时，将大部分立地条件好、蓄积量丰富的森林资源界定为国有林权。发展到林业资源问题阶段，对林木资源的需求大大增加，国有林立地条件好、生产能力高等优越条件能够在更大程度上保障木材供给，而且采用国有林权的形式通过国家对木材生产进行控制和调拨，能够缩减森林资源配置的时间和成本。因此，大多数国家在此阶段林权公有的程度得到了固化。此外，这些国家在初始界定林权时国有林权的比例很高，进行林权私有化的成本势必较高，因而这一时期继续沿用了国有林权为主的林权政策。例如，在加拿大，殖民统治时期林权多界定为皇室所有，殖民统治结束之后，国有林权的比重仍达到90%以上，尽管在部分地区将森林资源的经营权下放，但国家仍旧掌握着绝对的控制权，随时可以将经营权收回；由奥斯曼帝国转变而来的土耳其，林权形式一直未发生大的改变，国有林的比重高达99.9%，只不过不由政府直接经营，而是多数由大规模的国有森林公司来经营，并且不允许流转给个人。另外一些国家在林权初始界定时国有林的比重并未占有绝对优势，但由于本国私有林主的实力十分有限，不能承担足额供给林木资源的重任，只能由国有林来供给林木资源，虽然在林权结构中国有林权的比重可能未超过50%，但是各种政策都倾向于保护和扶持国有林权，日本为这一类型的典型代表。历史上日本的森林覆盖率高达90%以上，但是由于工业化过程中人口快速增长和对森林资源的过度利用，人均有林地面积仅为不足0.2hm^2，私有林规模比较小，私有林主面临着严重的造林资金不足的困境。恢复期日本造林面积不断增长，但私有林造林面积却出现了下降的趋势，尽管通过建立利益分成机制成立森林合作组织在一定程度上能够有效缓解私有林主所面临的困难，但是这个过程需要较长时间才能完成。因而这一时期日本将林权政策倾向于扶持国有林来满足对林木资源的需求。例如制定了“国有林长期生产计划”和“国有林生产力增长计划”，并放宽对木材的采伐限制，不再需要获得许可证，只需在采伐前向有关林业部门通报即可，还通过鼓励进行皆伐作业的形式扩大国有林的采伐量。而未对私有林提供资金、技术等方面的扶持。

国有林权的绝对优势和私有林主实力相对微弱是实行以国有林权为主的林权政策的主要原因。此外，政治体制和经济体制也会对林权形式产生重要影响。前苏联和保加利亚、南斯拉夫等东欧社会主义性质的国家都采取了国有林权为主的林权政策，甚至国有林权是本国唯一的林权形式。

(二) 以私有林权为主的林权政策

在林业资源问题阶段，并不是所有的国家都制定国有林权为主的林权政策，还有一大部分国家在这一时期制定以私有林权为主的林权政策来保障林木资源的供给，这主要是由于以下几个原因导致的。

第一，相比较而言，实行私有林权为主的林权政策的国家在初始界定林权时，通常将立地条件较好、生产力强的森林界定为私有林权。例如，德国在进行林权初始界定时，将分布于生态状况恶劣、脆弱或敏感地带的森林界定为国有林权，而将分布于立地条件较好，实现林木经济价值成本较低地区的森林界定为私有林权。同样，在瑞典，立地条件较差的北部地区的森林多界定为国有林权，立地条件较好的中南部地区的森林多界定为私有林权。

第二，私有林的规模较大，或通过对规模较小的私有林进行合作经营的模式促使其发挥规模效益。在实行私有林权为主的林权政策的国家中，森林资源的丰富程度存在很大差异，私有林的规模也不尽相同，如瑞典的森林覆盖率高达近70%，人均森林面积 $3hm^2$ 多，私有林主平均拥有林地 $50hm^2$，私有林规模较大；与其相类似，芬兰森林覆盖率高达73%，人均森林面积也多达 $4.3hm^2$，私有林主平均拥有林地达 $35hm^2$。瑞典和芬兰的私有林规模较大，便于私有林主实现规模经营。相比较而言，德国、法国和美国等国家森林覆盖率仅为30%左右，人均森林面积不足 $1hm^2$。在德国人均森林面积仅为 $0.1hm^2$，私有林主多达100多万个，平均拥有林地不到 $5hm^2$，只有2%的私有林主拥有森林面积超过 $50hm^2$；在法国人均森林面积约为 $0.3hm^2$，私有林规模也非常小。在私有林规模较小的国家通常采取合作经营的方式发挥规模效益，如德国从19世纪中期开始就走上了私有林合作化的道路，集中开展林木砍伐、树木种植与维护、道路修建与保养、技术推广服务、营林资金筹集以及木材运输销售等活动，提高了森林经营管理的效率。。

第三，私有林权制度安排运行的时间较长，私有林主已经掌握丰富的造林、营林经验。在德国的私有林地区，当地私有林权从1050年前开始形成，在近1 000年中都没有发生变化，私有林权的可继承性使得当地农民对祖先遗留下来的私有林已经形成习惯性的权利，林权纠纷问题已经基本不存在，这使得私有林权制度的执行成本大大降低，这种情况德国表现的最为突出。在瑞典，私有林权制度安排实行的较长时间里，私有林主亲自参与育林、采伐、集材、运输等林业生产经营活动，具有丰富的生产管理经验。私有林主长期以来享有对森林资源的产权，使其对森林资源的使用形成习惯性权利，在此过程中积累的丰富的造林营林经验为实行以私有林权为主的林权政策提供了重要条件。

第四，私有林主对林业收入的依赖程度较强。由于私有林主享有林权的时间较长，而且私有林的立地条件较好，获得林业的经济价值相对容易，因而私有林主对林业经济收入的依赖程度较高。据统计，在瑞典有 70% 的私有林主将林业收入作为生活收入的一部分。

由于在这些国家私有林比国有林具有更明显的优势，更能承担提供木材供给的重任，因而这些国家在制定林权政策时对私有林权的限制较少，而且对私有林权给予更多的优惠和扶持。美国、德国、法国、芬兰和瑞典等国都在法律上给予私有林权最大程度上的保护，私有林主在遵守法律规定的前提下有自主经营森林的充分权利，不受其他任何干预。除了法律上给予私有林权充分的保障之外，国家还通过宣传教育、财政补贴、低息贷款、税收优惠、技术推广以及全部或部分承担私有林区公共设施建设等措施扶持私有林来为本国工业发展提供工业用材和林副产品。尽管这些国家为私有林的发展提供了宽松和便利的条件，但是要求私有林主不能随意改变林地用途，而且私有林主在销售一定数量的林木资源之后，必须在原有林地上重新植树以保证木材供给的持续性，并严格按照法律规定进行林木砍伐。这些国家通过对私有林权的政策扶持使得私有林在更大程度上承担木材供给的重任。在瑞典，国有林的比重仅为 17%，其他社区、教堂等公有林权占 7%，私有林比重高达 76%，其中私有林又分为农民家庭庄园式的私有和公司私有两种类型，仅家庭庄园式的私有林主庄园就提供了全国 60% 的木材生产；在德国，私有林权形式占 46%，但提供每年木材供给的 60%；在芬兰，58% 的私有林提供了全国 80% 的工业用材。

（三）转型期国家林权政策的变化

转型期国家在这一时期多进行了林权政策的调整，并且表现出两种不同的演进路径：一种是继续保持国有林权为主的林权政策，以俄罗斯为典型代表；另一种是林权私有化程度不断增强，私有林权的比重不断增加，以罗马尼亚为典型代表。

前苏联为了发展工业化和农业集体化取消了私有林权，规定所有森林资源均归国家所有，林业的经营管理和利用方式都趋于向集中化发展，国有林权是唯一的林权形式。前苏联解体之后，俄罗斯延续了国有林权的林权政策，尽管通过租赁的方式将部分经营权下放到地区政府或具体的租赁者身上，但森林、林地和原木生产仍由国家控制，联邦政府直接负责对森林资源的管理。与俄罗斯相类似，波兰也延续了以国有林权为主的林权政策，有79%的森林资源仍实行国有林权。

罗马尼亚共和国成立之后随即开展工业化建设，为了能够集中力量满足工业发展对林木资源的需求，将共有林和私有林全部收归国有，国有林权的比例由29%转变为100%，成为1948～1989年间罗马尼亚唯一的林权形式。之后，随着国家转型，林权形式开始多样化。1991年罗马尼亚制订了一项将森林归还给私人的政策，私有林权的比例大大增加，到2004年国有林权的比例下降到67%，共有林和私有林的比例分别增加到25%和10%左右。与罗马尼亚相类似，捷克于1945年将87%的私有林权没收为国有之后，到1990年后，随着经济转型又将没收的森林重新归还给原来的主人；斯洛伐克从1948年开始实行森林资源国有化，发展到1989年国有林权达到99.6%，随着社会变革及森林资源私有化的实施，到1994年私有林权的比例恢复到17%；拉脱维亚、立陶宛以及斯洛文尼亚等国都在转型期开展了森林资源私有化进程。

在林业资源问题阶段，对林木资源的需求大大增加，森林资源的稀缺性逐渐凸显，享有林权往往意味着掌握了获得潜在利益的可能性。西方产权学派认为，当资源的稀缺性凸显时，私有林权的制度安排具有更高的效率，但该结论是与西方国家市场经济的高度发达为前提的。由于各国森林资源禀赋以及森林资源市场的情况存在差异，私有林权并不是在任何国家都是最佳的林权制度安排，而且在特定领域、特定时期国有林权制度安排比私有林权制度安排更有效率。因而，在林业资源问题阶段，不仅存在着以国有林权为主的林权政策，同时也存在着以私有林权为主的林权政策，即便是转型期国家林权政策的演进也以这两种林权政策类型为主。尽管这一时期采取了不同的林权政策，但可以得出的结论是，这一时期林权政策的制定都是以持续供给木材为出发点的。

三、林权政策的特征

由于森林资源的稀缺性更加凸显，林业资源问题阶段的林权政策呈现出与林业土地问题阶段明显不同的特征：

第一，对林权的界定更加明晰。由于森林资源稀缺性更加凸显，需要对林权进行更加明晰的界定，林权明晰是指林权各具体权能在林权主体之间的分配与界定。林权明晰是一个相对的概念，不管是私有林权还是公有林权，在某些条件下是明晰的，在另一些条件下则可能是不明晰的，随着林权制度环境的变化，原本明晰的林权形式也可能变得不再明晰。因而，不能把明晰林权简单地理解为就是林权私有化的过程，而是林权各具体权能在林权主体之间进行配置和明确的过程。例如，芬兰在制定林权政策时，将确定私有林区林木资源砍伐数量的权利赋予给政府部门，限制了私有林主对森林资源的收益权，私有林主在政府规定的采伐数量范围内享有对森林资源的收益权。此外，在实行以私有林权为主的国家中，对林权所包含的处置权多在国家与私有林主之间进行分配，国家限制私有林主将林地转变用途。

第二，林权政策的制定以林木资源为核心。在林业资源问题阶段，林木资源的稀缺性十分凸显，林权政策的制定是以满足林木资源的持续供给为核心的。例如德国、芬兰等国都要求私有林主砍伐林木必须以适度砍伐和及时更新为前提以保障林木资源的持续供给。此阶段制定的林权政策往往忽略森林资源的多种功能，而只关注森林资源的经济价值。

第三，通过法律、法规等正式制度对林权予以制度化。在林业土地问题阶段，常常通过习惯习俗、意识信仰等非正式制度对林权进行初始界定，发展到林业资源问题阶段，由于森林资源稀缺性凸显以及界定林权的经验和技术的积累，对林权的界定和保护逐渐转变为通过法律、法规等正式制度的形式来进行。这一时期各国先后颁布《森林法》等法律或其他法规来为林权提供保护。

第四节　林业生态问题阶段的林权政策

为了推动本国经济的快速发展，处于林业资源问题阶段的国家通常对林木资源进行过度砍伐利用，造成了生态状况急剧恶化，经济发展和生态建设之间的矛盾日益突出。发展到林业生态问题阶段，随着经济水平不断提高，人们对森林发挥生态功能的需求逐渐上升到主导地位，森林资源的公共物品特征日渐凸显，林权政策也发生相应改变。目前已经进入林业生态问题阶段的国家主要为美国、日本、德国等老牌资本主义国家，因而本文主要以发达国家为例来分析林业生态问题阶段的林权政策。

一、林权政策演进的动因

由于人们对森林发挥生态功能的需求逐渐上升到主导地位，森林资源的稀缺性进一步增强，林权政策的制定转变为侧重于森林生态功能的发挥。随着经济发展，不仅林产品市场的市场化程度有所增强，而且森林发挥生态功能所产生的森林生态产品市场以及林权交易市场的市场化程度也都有所提高，这为林权政策的制定提供了一个新的制度环境。

（一）森林资源稀缺性进一步增强

在林业生态问题阶段，美国等国森林面积和蓄积呈现双重增长的趋势，从绝对量上而言，森林资源的数量稳步增加。据统计，1995 年至 2005 年，美国的森林覆盖率由 23.2% 增加到 33.1%，瑞典的森林覆盖率由 59.3% 增加到 66.9%，意大利的森林覆盖率由 22.1% 增加到 33.9%。然而，由于这一时期对森林生态系统发挥生态功能的需求大大增加，需要增加更多的森林资源存量恢复已遭到严重破坏的森林生态系统。从这个角度而言，这一时期森林资源的稀缺性进一步增强了。

1. 环境保护意识的增强

在林业资源问题阶段，出于为工业发展提供木材供给的目的，对林木资源进行了大规模砍伐利用，森林面积和蓄积大量减少，导致生态状况遭到严重破坏，泥石流、雪崩、洪水等自然灾害频繁发生。在经历了多次自然灾害之后，人们开始意识到保护生态环境的重要性，相应的，对林业发挥生态功能的需求逐渐上升。林业生态功能的发挥是以森林作为一个完整的生态系统为前提的，减少对林木资源的消耗，保障森林的面积和蓄积对于发挥林业的生态功能发挥着重要作用。图4-4反映了20世纪末发达国家原木产量增长率的变化趋势，从中可以看出，原木产量的增长率明显降低，甚至一度出现了负增长趋势，这表明发达国家砍伐林木的数量大大降低。

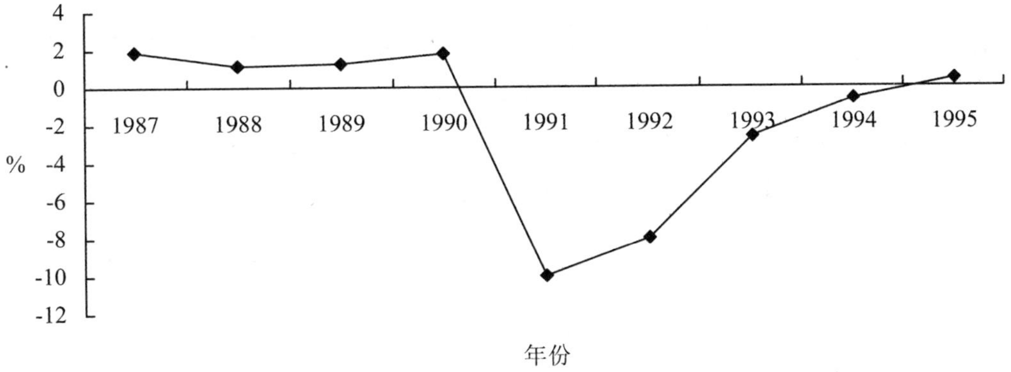

图4-4　美国原木产量变化趋势

资料来源：根据《世界森林状况》(2005)整理得来。

人们环境保护意识的增强有助于推动森林面积和蓄积的增加，即便是这样，与人们日益增长的对林业发挥生态功能的需求相比，森林资源的数量和质量还有待于大大提高。此外，环境保护意识的增强使得人们对于自身居住场所使用的建造、装修材料以及家具饰品等环保性能的要求不断提高，对房屋建造材料和家具制作材料等的选择更注重于其环保性能。由于木制建筑在吸音性、吸湿性、绝缘性、无辐射等方面的独特优势，加之防蚁、防潮、防火等技术日趋成熟，木制建筑的优越性逐渐显现出来。而且据加拿大木业协会的研究结果显示，木制建筑与混凝土建筑相比，从林木砍伐、房屋建造、使用到拆除的整个建筑周期中，对环境造成的破坏程度很小，因而，木制房屋在德国和新西兰等国已经成为建造节能环保建筑的首选。出于改善自身居住环境的需要，人们对木制房屋和实木家具的需求不断增长，这又导致对林木资源的需求有所增长，这种情况在近些年来表现得更加明显。

2. 对林业经济效益的依赖程度下降

在林业资源问题阶段，林业经营者通过砍伐林木来实现林业的经济效益，这种方式使林业经济效益和生态效益之间发生了很大冲突。随着经济不断发展，人们的生活水平大大提高，对保护森林以促使林业发挥生态功能的需求逐渐增加，生态需求逐渐上升为主要需求。而且，随着一国产业的升级，无论从国家的角度还是从农户的角度，对林业产生经济效益的依赖程度都有所降低。1997 年发达国家林业产值占国民生产总值的比例为 1%，而同年发展中国家的这一比例为 2%，林业收入在农户家庭收入中的比例也呈现下降的趋势，农户对林业经济效益的依赖程度大大下降。人们对林业经济效益依赖程度的下降大大减少了对林木资源的砍伐，图 4-5 和 4-6 分别描述了美国和日本原木产量减少的趋势。

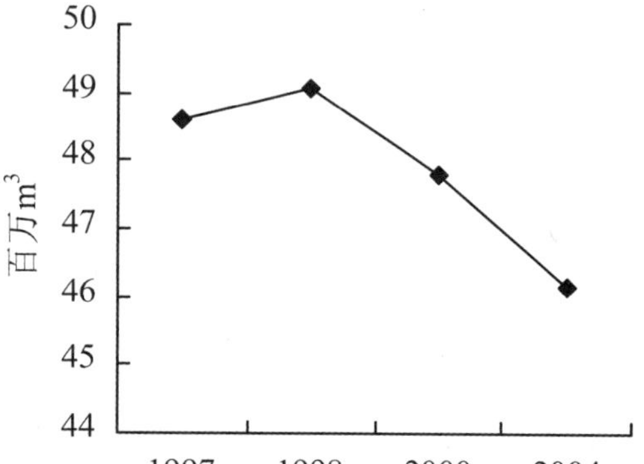

图 4-5　发达国家原木生产量增长率变化趋势

资料来源：根据《世界森林状况》(2005)整理得来。

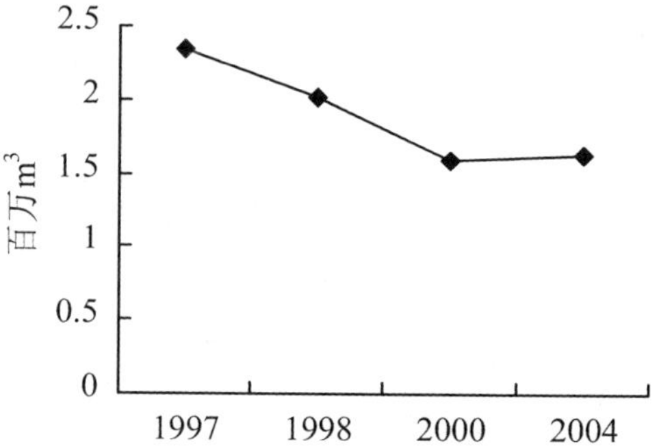

图 4-6　日本原木产量变化趋势

资料来源：根据《世界森林状况》(2005)整理得来。

实际上，进入林业生态问题阶段的国家多呈现了本国原木产量减少的特征，发达国家对林业经济效益依赖程度的降低与本国林业技术的进步和国际木材贸易市场的发展有着密切的联系(下文将详细阐述)。随着森林面积和蓄积的不断增加，生态状况逐渐好转，获得林业经济收益的途径逐渐转变为以发展森林旅游等第三产业为主，获取林业经济收益途径的转变有助于林业经济收益和生态效益的协调。

3. 诱致型技术进步

森林资源绝对数量的减少以及资金的相对充裕使得技术进步逐渐由传统型向诱致型转变，传统的技术创新侧重于对砍伐林木的新技术和新设备的研发，而诱致型技术创新则侧重于对节约林木资源利用量的研发。这一时期的技术进步主要表现在四个方面：一是提高森林保护的技术；二是缩短林木生长周期的技术；三是延长木材使用寿命以及综合利用的技术；四是生产木材替代品的技术。日本、芬兰、德国、瑞典、美国等发达国家在这些方面的技术水平均达到了相当的高度。尽管诱致型技术创新在林业资源问题阶段已经有所显现，但是应用和推广的程度十分有限，发展到生态问题阶段，由于人们对林业生态功能的需求日渐增加，对诱致型技术创新的需求也越发强烈。影响木材供给的一个主要因素就是林木的生长周期比较长，林木生长的长周期导致木材供给的周期也比较长，远不能满足对木材日益增长的需求，因而，缩短林木生长周期技术的采用能够在一定程度上缓解这一矛盾。提高木材的综合利用率，充分利用现有的木材资源，能够减少预期对林木资源的需求，以芬兰为例，其对木材的高综合利用率减少了对木材的大量需求，林木采伐后，较粗的部分运往木业分部下属工厂，生产锯木材或胶合板；较细的部分和树梢、枝丫等运往造纸厂制浆造纸；制浆后的废料如树皮、浆渣可燃烧，用于造纸能源；木材加工及胶合板生产的废料木屑则可以作为浆厂的原料。另外一种节约木材利用的技术就是开发木材的替代品，通过先进技术减少水泥、塑料等替代品的成本，进而减少对木材的需求。

假定木材和木材替代品市场都是完全竞争的(实际上垄断市场结构也不影响

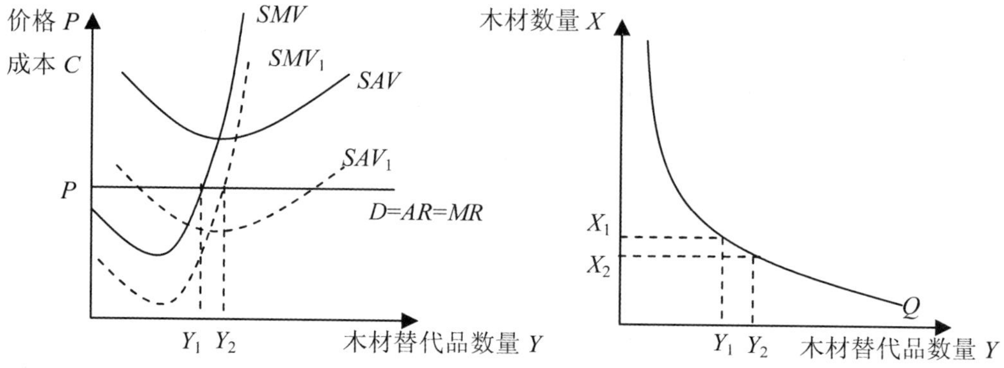

图 4-7　生产替代品的技术创新对木材需求量的影响

对木材需求数量减少的趋势，只不过减少的数量会有所差异），图 4-7 反映了生产木材替代品的技术发生变迁对木材需求量产生的影响。当开发木材替代品的技术有了新的进步会促使木材替代品的生产成本由 *SAV* 下降到 SAV_1 的水平，相应边际成本由 *SMV* 下降到 SMV_1 水平，这使得原本不能获得经济利润的决策现在变得有利可图，并且根据 $MC = MR$ 原则做出的决策，木材替代品的数量由 Y_1 增加

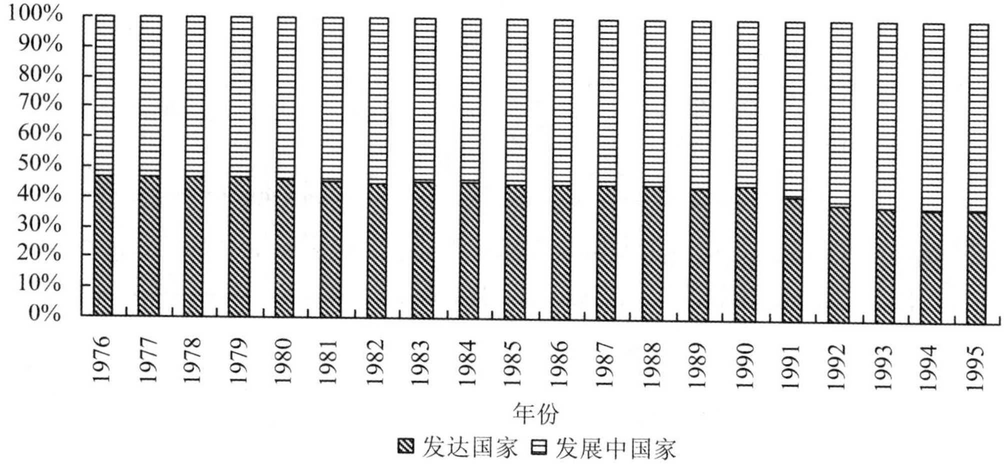

图 4-8　发达国家原木生产量增长率变化趋势

资料来源：根据《*FAO* 林产品年鉴 1976 ~ 1987》、《*FAO* 林产品年鉴 1982 ~ 1993》、《*FAO* 林产品年鉴 1991 ~ 1995》数据计算得来。

到 Y_2，因而对木材的需求量会从 X_1 减少到 X_2。

林业诱致型技术进步大大提高了木材的出材率、综合利用率以及对木材的替代率，这些因素导致发达国家对木材的消耗量出现了稳步下降趋势。图 4-8 反映了 1976～1995 年间原木消费量构成中发达国家和发展中国家的比例，可以看出，发达国家原木消费量的比重逐渐下降，由 1976 年的 46.76% 下降到 1995 年的 36.83%。对木材消耗量的下降有助于保障森林的面积和蓄积，促进林业生态功能的发挥。

从人们环境保护意识不断增强、对林业经济效益的依赖程度逐渐下降以及诱致型技术进步的角度而言，对林木资源的砍伐数量不断减少，森林面积和蓄积有所增加，从表面上看，似乎森林资源的稀缺性已经有所缓解。但是，在林业生态问题阶段人们对林业发挥生态功能的需求上升到主导地位，而森林面积的增加在很大程度上是由于人工林面积增加导致的，天然森林占森林面积的比重仍比较低。天然林和人工林在发挥生态功能方面发挥的作用存在很大差异，天然林是一个相对完整的生态系统，对于调节气候、涵养水源、保持水土、防风固沙，特别是为野生动物提供栖息地，保护生物多样性等方面发挥着重要作用；相比较而言，人工林的树种结构比较单一，生长周期较短，发挥生态功能的程度较弱。人工林面积的快速增长并不能很好地满足人们对林业发挥生态功能需求的增长，因而这一时期森林资源的稀缺性并未减弱，而是进一步增强了。

（二）市场化程度进一步增强

发展到林业生态问题阶段，森林资源的市场化程度进一步增强，这不仅体现在国际和国内木材交易市场的发达，而且林权交易市场已经形成，并且市场化程度也逐渐增强。

随着经济全球化的发展，国际林产品贸易市场的市场化程度进一步增强，各国纷纷对林产品贸易政策进行调整，特别是对进出口关税进行调减，全球林产品贸易总量和贸易金额不断增长，贸易种类日益丰富，参与林产品贸易的国家与日俱增。林业生产和林业投资的全球化，改变了发达国家从发展中国家进口木材原料和向发展中国家出口木材产品的单向贸易模式，形成了木材原料和木材产品同时向发达国家和发展中国家双向流动的新模式，林产品的市场化程度不断增强。不仅木材等林产品市场的市场化程度逐渐增强，而且林权市场的市场化程度也不断提高，特别是在林地和林木资源产权统一、私有林主规模较小的日本、德国等发达国家，林权交易十分频繁。通过进行林权交易，规模较小的私有林权逐渐流转给规模较大、资金丰富、基础设施完善的私有林权或流转为共有、国有林权，这更好地保证了林业的持续经营。

森林资源市场化程度的增强带来的直接影响当属对林产品价格的影响，当需求大于供给，价格就会上升；当供给大于需求，价格就会下降。林产品的价格直接影响了林权主体的收益。由于林权主体之间的边际成本并不一致，在同一价格水平下有的林权主体会丧失继续经营的兴趣，而另一些林权主体则会增加扩大经营规模的兴趣，因而林权交易市场得以发展。

二、林权政策的类型

林业的多功能性在林业生态问题阶段得到了人们的广泛重视，为了更好地保证林业生态功能的发挥，必须限制对林木资源的砍伐以保存一定的森林面积和蓄积量；另一方面，经济发展对林木资源的需求仍然存在，需要通过砍伐林木来得以满足。在这种情况下通常对森林实行分类经营。其中，以提供木材供给为主的森林具有很强的私人物品特征，主要通过市场对其进行配置。以发挥生态功能为主的森林具有很强的公共物品特征，通常由政府来进行管理。为了实现林业多种功能之间的协调，不同国家根据自己的国情采取了不同的林权政策。

(一) 以国有林发挥生态功能的林权政策

在林业生态问题阶段，一些国家森林资源国有化的趋势明显增强。实行以国有林为主发挥生态功能的政策主要是由于以下几个方面的原因决定的。

1. 森林资源的生态功能具有明显公共物品特征

当森林主要执行生态功能时，其公共物品特征十分明显（详见第三章相关论述），公共物品的非排他性和非竞争性特征往往会导致市场失灵，若单纯由私有林权来保障林业发挥生态功能往往会导致森林资源供给数量的不足。这是因为，私有林主营造和管护森林资源以保障其发挥生态功能的行为带有很强的正外部性，由于生态产品的消费者可以通过“搭便车”进行免费消费，私有林主获得的个人收益十分有限，甚至为零。而私有林主保障林业发挥生态功能的活动可以大大改善整个社会的生态状况，获得的社会收益十分巨大。因而，私有林主保障林业发挥生态功能活动产生的社会收益要远大于私人收益。V_p、V_s、C_p分别代表私有林主营造和管护森林资源以保障林业发挥生态功能的私人收益、社会收益和私人成本，由于该行为具有明显的外部性，$V_p < V_s$，如果私有林主的私人成本 C_p 大于私人收益 V_p，则私有林主采取该行为的积极性十分微弱，进而社会收益也不会得以实现。

即便是私有林主营造森林并发挥其生态功能，但是其提供的数量往往不能满足社会公众的需要。见图 4-9，*MPR* 和 *MSR* 分别代表私有林主的边际收益和社会的边际收益，私有林主根据 *MPR* = *MC* 的原则决定提供 Q_1 数量森林发挥生态功能，而根据 *MSR* = *MC* 的原则决定的数量应为 Q_2，$Q_2 - Q_1$ 的差额即反映了私有林主提供森林资源的不足。

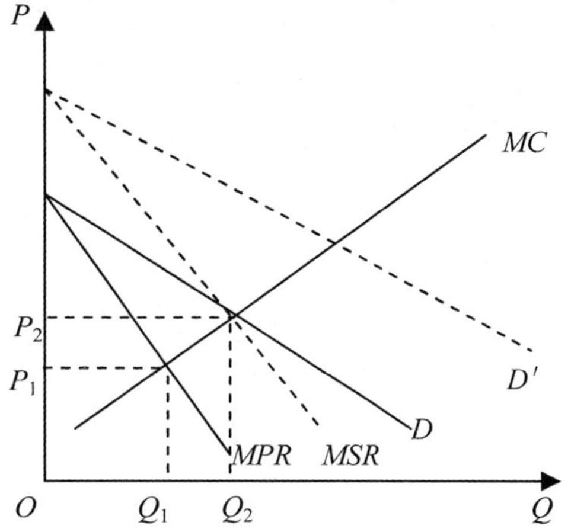

图 4-9 私有林主保障林业发挥生态功能

林业发挥生态功能具有的外部性和公共物品特征是采取国有林权政策发挥生态功能的主要因素。

2. *私有林主对林业经济效益的依赖程度降低*

随着经济不断发展，人们的收入水平逐步提高，收入结构也发生了很大变化，人们对林业经济效益的依赖程度不断降低。特别是在私有林规模相对较小的日本、德国等国家，由于木材价格下降、私有林主造林经费有限、营林劳动力不足等诸多原因，私有林主对继续经营林业逐渐失去兴趣。林业收入给私有林主、特别是小规模私有林主带来的边际效用逐渐降低，私有林主多将森林作为继承给子女的财产，而不再十分关注其增值，因而无意采用先进的林业技术和建设林道等基础设施，对森林资源的管护和经营比较松散。由于这些原因，私有林的质量和产量都呈现大幅下降的趋势。在这种情况下，为了保障对林木资源的持续供给，特别是发挥林业的生态功能，国家或是引导私有林主之间的合作，或是购买私有林为国有，由政府组织营造和管护，特别是对有重要价值的林木、野生动物资源、湿地等，国家通常全资买下建设国家森林公园、自然保护区、野生动物保护区，由国家财政全额拨款进行建设，并严加管理和保护。

3. 国家财政实力增强

之所以采取由国家购买私有林以发挥林业生态效益的模式，除了由于本国私有林质量出现下降之外，还有一个主要的原因是由于本国财政实力十分强大。根据国际货币基金组织《政府财政统计年鉴(2007)》公布的2006年数据计算，被统计的51个国家的财政收入占GDP比重平均为40.6%，21个发达国家的平均水平为45.3%，30个发展中国家的平均水平为35.9%。其中，税收收入占GDP比重的平均水平为25.4%，发达国家的平均水平为29.5%，发展中国家的平均水平为21.3%。表4-4反映了2006年部分发达国家和发展中国家财政收入占GDP的比重。

表4-4 财政收入占GDP比重的比较

	发达国家					发展中国家				
国家	法国	德国	英国	意大利	瑞典	印度	泰国	智利	伊朗	巴基斯坦
比重	50.3%	43.8%	41.6%	45.4%	55.3%	21.9%	22.0%	27.8%	30.7%	35.8%

资料来源：《中国财政收入规模的国际比较》http://www.mof.gov.cn

从表4-4可以看出，同年，发达国家财政收入占本国GDP的比重远高于发展中国家的比重，而且发达国家的GDP总量比发展中国家GDP总量也要高得多，因而发达国家财政收入实力十分强大。这为国家购买私有林提供了坚实的物质基础，也是私有林公有化的一个主要原因。

森林的公共物品特征、私有林主对林业经济效益依赖程度降低以及国家财政实力的强大导致国有林的比重大大增加，表4-5展示了美国林权结构变化的趋势。

表4-5　美国林权结构变化趋势

	1969年	1970年	1977年	1987年	1992年	2003年	2005年
公有林权	28.38%	28.61%	28.07%	27.02%	34.62%	42.57%	42.38%
私有林权	71.62%	71.39%	71.93%	72.98%	65.38%	57.43%	57.62%

注：公有林权包括联邦政府所有和州及地方政府所有之和；私有林权包括公司所有和个人所有之和。

当美国进入林业生态问题阶段之后，公有林权的比重呈现不断增加的趋势，之初公有林权比重的增长趋势相对缓慢，20世纪60年代末至80年代末近20年时间里，公有林权的比重基本未发生大的变动；自20世纪80年代末开始，美国公有林的比重快速增长，从1987年的27.02%增加到2005年的42.38%，近20年时间增长了56.85%。在日本、德国等国家也都出现了国家购买私有林以发挥森林生态功能的情况，国有林比重呈现不同程度的增长。

既然国家财政实力比较强大，可以通过购买私有林转而由政府组织经营来实现森林的生态效益，为何发达国家没有购买全部的私有林，而仍有一部分森林处于私有林权状态，甚至在一些国家私有林权的比重反而呈现了增长的趋势，这需要对实行私有林权政策的原因进行深入分析。

（二）制定私有林权政策的原因

在林业生态问题阶段，人们对林业发挥生态功能以改善生态状况的需求大大增加，同时也十分重视林业的经济效益和社会效益，积极发展多功能、集约化林业，强调兼顾林业的多种功能。在对林业多种需求同时存在的情况下，私有林权仍在某些领域发挥着重要的作用。

1. 私有林是木材供给的主要来源

以发挥经济效益为主的森林具有很强的私人物品特征，加之木材市场逐渐完善，通过市场交易可以对林木资源起到很好的配置作用。因而，私有林权的制度安排有助于私有林主在市场条件下按照自身利益最大化原则，适时、适量地提供木材供给。发展到林业生态问题阶段，由于国有林需承担发挥生态功能的重任，对国有林的采伐数量大幅度减少，由私有林承担着提供木材供给的重任。2006年，美国私有林的比例为57.6%，由于联邦和州政府对私有林采伐没有强制性采伐限额限制，当年美国国内木材采伐量4.25亿m^3中有92%来自于私有林，私有林几乎承担了用材林供给的全部责任；同年，日本的私有林比例占58%，年产木材量为1900万m^3，占当年木材产量的68%；尽管加拿大是一个公有林比例高达92.1%的国家，其林业公司、个人或共同体所有的民有林仅占约6%，但生产锯材和纸浆所用原木的19%产自私有林，而且79%的薪材、77%的糖浆等药剂产品以及采油树的大部分均由私有林提供。

2. 长期实行私有林权政策的路径依赖

就当前已经处于林业生态问题阶段的发达国家的情况而言，私有林权制度安排由来已久，芬兰、瑞典、德国、法国等国私有林的雏形可以追溯到11世纪，长期私有林权政策的执行使得私有林主已经习惯于享有林权。尽管私有林主对林业经济收益的依赖程度逐渐降低，但是私有林主享有林权的习惯使得其不愿放弃私有林权，而更倾向于把森林资源当作自己的一项财产予以保留。若将私有林转变为其他林权形式，势必会遭到部分私有林主的反对。而且私有林还肩负着提供木材供给的重任，因而私有林权必须予以保留，这也是国家为何不能将私有林权全部购买的原因。

3. 国家对私有林的扶持

尽管为了保障林业发挥生态功能，国有林的比重呈现了增长趋势，但私有林比重在一些国家仍占据绝对优势：美国私有林比重为57.62%，日本私有林比重为58%，奥地利私有林比重为80%，瑞典私有林比重为76%，芬兰私有林比重为51%。为了更好地协调林业经济效益和生态效益之间的关系，促进私有林发挥生态功能，这些国家从各方面对私有林给予扶持。

上文在探讨以国有林发挥林业生态功能问题时，指出以私有林为主来发挥林业生态功能将导致提供生态产品数量的不足，造成这一问题最主要的原因是$V_p < C_p < V_s$，若国家通过对私有林主进行补贴和扶持，增加私有林主获得的收益，只要$V_p \geq C_p$，私有林主就有积极性进行造林护林，并在一定程度上保障林业发挥生

态功能。因此，各国纷纷采取各种措施对私有林予以扶持和鼓励：对私有林主提供财政补贴和信贷支持用于造林、林道建设、抚育间伐、病虫害防治、高性能林业机械的购置、木材综合加工利用、信息网络建设等；通过减征、免征等税收优惠政策减轻私有林主的负担；建立森林保险组织等风险防御体系以增强私有林主抵御风险的能力。日本、瑞典、美国等国都通过对私有林提供经济和非经济支持的方式来促使私有林发挥生态功能。

为了积极引导私有林发挥生态功能，国家对私有林主的补贴和扶持必不可少，在国家提供补贴和扶持的情况下，私有林主的造林营林积极性会有所提高。但是，国家为私有林主提供的扶持政策能够持续的时间直接影响了私有林发挥林业生态功能的效果，一旦国家停止对私有林主的政策扶持，私有林主获得的收益必然会有所减少，持续经营林业的积极性会大大衰退，甚至荒废经营。

由国有林来发挥林业的生态功能是一项有效的措施，但是依靠中央或联邦政府以及地方政府对森林进行直接的管护与经营，需要花费更多的精力和资金；以私有林来发挥林业的生态功能，需要国家提供足额和长期的补贴及支持。共有林权在一定程度上能够弥补二者的不足，但自身也存在很大的缺陷，因而共有林权的实施仍处于探索过程中。

三、林权政策的特征

在林业生态问题阶段，促进林业多功能的协调发展是林业发展的重点。在发挥林业经济利益的同时，更要注重发挥林业的生态效益和社会效益。在此阶段林权政策表现了新的特征：第一，此阶段林权政策的制定以保障林业多功能协调发展为核心，发挥林业生态功能并不是单纯依靠植树造林就能完成的，更重要的是保护森林生态系统的完整性。因而，在制定林权政策时，无论是制定国有林权政策还是制定私有林权政策，保障森林生态功能的政策倾向性都较强。第二，对林权的保障更加制度化、规范化。林权的清晰界定只是林权发挥激励作用的最基本条件，对林权给予法律上的保护能够保障林权的稳定性，因而，将习惯性使用森林的权利予以法制化和规范化更利于对林权的保护。

第五节　经济发展与林权政策演进的关系

林权政策演进是实现低效率林权政策向高效率林权政策转变的过程，对林权政策效率的判定并不能根据采取的林权类型进行评判，而应在特定社会经济环境下，林权政策将潜在利润予以内在化的程度来进行衡量。也就是说，并不一定私有林权效率高，共有林权和国有林权等公有林权类型效率就低，而应根据林权政策所应用的领域和所处的社会经济环境来分析林权政策的效率和效果。林权政策之所以会发生变迁主要是因为一项林权政策会随着经济发展呈现出生命周期性特征。一项林权政策实施之初呈现效率不断提高的趋势，当达到一定程度之后，由于此林权政策与已经变化了的社会经济环境的相适应性逐渐弱化，其效率不断降低，因而，林权政策演进就产生了。上文分析了处于不同林业发展阶段林权政策演进的影响因素，林业需求的转变、人口数量的变化、城市化进程的发展、技术的不断进步以及森林资源相对价格的变化都是影响森林资源稀缺性的主要因素；在森林资源稀缺性增强的同时，森林资源市场化程度也在不断提高。森林资源的稀缺性是影响林权政策制定的主要因素，实际上，经济发展是影响林权政策演进的最根本因素，随着经济不断发展，人口、技术、市场化程度、经济结构以及城市化进程都会发生相应改变，进而影响到森林资源稀缺程度的变化。因而，经济发展从根本上决定了林权政策的演进。处于不同经济发展阶段，社会经济环境都会随之发生改变，对森林资源的需求也会有所不同，既定的林权政策为了适应社会经济环境的变化需适时发生调整。

在 IAPP 的规范物品理论中，按照竞争性和排他性程度的不同，将物品分为四种：公共物品、集体物品或俱乐部物品、公共池塘资源和私人物品（见图 4-10）。同一物品在不同制度安排条件下、不同需求条件下、不同文化条件下、不同审美条件下或是发挥功能不同，物品的性质也会发生转变。在林业发展的整个过程中，由于经济发展导致对林业的需求发生了变化，森林资源的属性也发生了变化。在林业土地问题阶段，人们需要将林地转变为耕地以保障农业生产。十分丰富的森林资源具有典型的公共池塘资源的特征，无产权或公有林权的林权制度安排使得森林资源快速减少；发展到林业资源问题阶段，为了满足工业发展对林木资源作为工业原料、资金积累和外汇积累的需要，人们对林木资源经济价值的需要日益凸显，木材及其他林产品具有典型的私人物品特征，森林资源的市场化也有所增强，部分国家私有林权的比例有所增加；到林业生态问题阶段，人们对森林作为整体提供生态功能的需求上升到主导地位，林业多种功能协调发展，此时森林资源兼具私人物品、俱乐部物品和公共物品的多种特征，为了满足对森林资源的不同需求，往往采取多种林权形式相结合的政策。

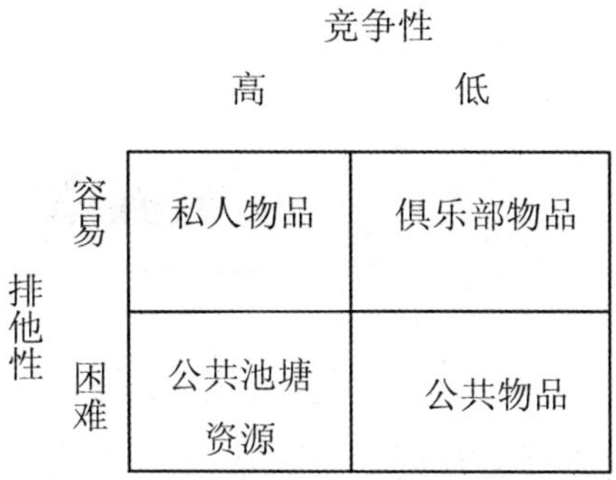

图 4-10　物品的分类

经济发展是林权政策演进的根本原因，同时，各国的政治体制、森林资源禀赋、林权初始界定情况以及意识形态和习惯习俗等非正式制度对林权政策的制定也发挥着重要作用。

第五章　中国林权政策演进

中国林权政策演进过程基本遵循了林权政策演进的一般规律，但也表现出中国独有的特色。在新中国成立之前以及成立之初的漫长时间里，对森林资源的利用主要表现为毁林开荒。尽管也颁布过一些护林植树的诏令和条文，但这一时期主要是对原始林的开发利用，林权政策尚未引起足够重视，仅有的对林权的界定主要依附于土地政策的相关规定。新中国成立之后，工业化进程逐步推进，经济发展速度明显加快，对森林资源的需求不断增加，林权政策也相应进行了多次调整。

第一节　中国林业土地问题阶段的林权政策

在新中国成立之前以及成立初期的漫长历史时期内，林业发展呈现了较为明显的林业土地问题阶段的基本特征，森林资源逐渐由无产权状态过渡到对林权进行初始界定。

一、林权界定模糊时期

自远古时期直至清朝末年，由于各种原因导致的毁林行为降低了森林覆盖率，而人口却呈现了快速增长的特征，森林资源逐渐匮乏使得林权逐渐由自由进入形式转变为开始初步界定状态。但由于森林资源几乎没有经济价值，林权仍旧一直处于十分模糊的状态，并引发了进一步毁林行为。

（一）此阶段林权的基本类型

樊宝敏等人运用回推法推测远古时期的中国森林覆盖率约为60%～64%之间，可见，中国在历史上是一个森林资源比较丰富的国家，而且当时的人口总数低于140万，森林资源禀赋较好，此时，森林资源处于无产权的自由进入状态。发展到清朝后期，中国的森林资源覆盖率下降到15%～17%，而人口总数增长到4亿人左右，森林资源变得相对贫乏，界定林权的需求开始萌生。

晚清时期，林权类型分为官有林和私有林两种，官有林主要是指朝廷和各级官府占有的森林，以皇室林和军垦林为主，主要是满足皇室狩猎、避暑、游览、陵墓修建等方面的需求，也有一部分是为了保护河岸和道路而种植的河防林和护路林。私有林带有明显的封建私有性质，大小官吏和地主占有绝大部分，此外还有少部分是商人、寺庙和氏族或村寨占有的山林，而农户占有的山林比例微乎其微。实际上，这种林权界定没有相应的法律加以保障，林权政策十分模糊。然而，即便是如此模糊的林权界定只是存在于部分地区，东北、西北、西南等大面积原始森林基本上都处于无主的状态，尽管皇室规定凡是无主的森林都为官有林，但实际上基本处于无产权界定的自由进入状态。

（二）林权界定模糊的原因

各个历史时期所发生的战乱是造成森林资源减少的一个主要原因。政权的统一、分裂、更迭多是通过战争方式实现的，林木资源是当时较容易利用的制造兵器和工具的原料，因而战争对武器和运输工具的需求引致对林木资源的需求。另一方面，人口大量增长导致对薪材的需求不断增加，无序的樵采行为破坏了大量森林资源。同时，人口的增长加之地主土地规模的扩大，使得平原地区的耕地逐渐不能满足需求，大批无地农民被迫上山毁林开荒。到了清朝晚期，沙皇俄国、日本、德国等较为发达国家为了保证本国的工业化发展，以签订不平等条约或是直接强取豪夺的方式侵占和破坏中国的森林资源。此外，皇室为了满足私欲而砍伐森林、大兴土木，以及由于自然因素或人为原因导致的森林火灾都造成了森林资源存量的减少。在上述各因素共同作用下，中国的森林资源急剧减少，表5-1反映了从上古时期到清朝末期中国森林资源覆盖率逐渐降低的变化趋势。

限于当时的生产力水平，人们只能单纯地利用森林资源，而无力营造和管护，仅仅依靠森林的自我修复能力慢慢恢复，因而，森林资源匮乏的情形日益严重。森林资源的不断减少导致对其进行产权界定的需求不断增强，但是以下原因

表 5-1　中国森林资源覆盖率的变化

时期	远古时期	上古时期	秦汉时期	魏晋南北朝时期	隋唐时期	五代辽宋金夏时期	元朝时期	明朝时期	清朝前期	清朝后期
森林资源覆盖率(%)	60~64	46~60	41~46	37~41	33~37	27~33	26~27	21~26	17~21	15~17

资料来源：樊宝敏，董源．中国历代森林覆盖率的探讨[J]．北京林业大学学报，2001，23(4)：26.

注定林权界定势必会产生界定不清晰的情形：一方面由于森林资源匮乏并未体现出非常明显的经济意义上的稀缺性，也就是说，尽管森林资源的总量和人均数量都有所减少，但这一时期人们对森林资源的需求仍旧局限于对林木自身用途的需求。例如皇室占有森林主要是为了能够在其间狩猎、游览或是建造陵墓，而私人占有森林资源主要是为其提供薪材、建造房屋的原材料或是将其视为财富的象征，森林资源的经济价值尚未明显显现；另一方面，封建社会或半殖民地半封建社会的社会体制决定了对私有产权的保护能力十分有限，加之技术方面的限制，清晰界定林权的成本非常大。皇室只是默许了私有林权，并未通过建立相应法律的方式对私有林权予以保护。

二、未成功的林权明晰过程

林权长期处于模糊状态使得人们对森林资源的破坏进一步加剧。由于穷苦农民的数量与日俱增，农民迫于生计纷纷来到林区进行毁林开荒以种植农田、建造房屋，而且大多采取粗放型的“火田耕作法”，即放火烧山后再行耕种，三四年后撂荒，再另选地段烧垦。这种破坏性地利用森林资源的方式导致森林资源进一步减少，由 1840 年的 1.59 亿 hm^2 减少到 1849 年的 1.57 亿 hm^2。

辛亥革命之后，中国先后经历了南京临时政府统治时期、北洋军阀政府统治时期和南京国民政府统治时期，而且在国民党政府统治时期还存在着革命根据地和解放区。森林资源逐渐减少的趋势给新政府的林业管理提出了挑战，各个政府都希望能够通过明晰林权以减少对森林资源的过度利用。清朝皇室统治被推翻，原有的皇室森林必须重新界定产权。北洋军阀政府和国民党政府都将林权划分为国有林权、公有林权和私有林权三种类型。其中，将归中央政府所有的森林称为国有林；地方政府和有关部门所有的森林称为公有林；私有林的界定与晚清时期没有太大区别。这种界定林权的方式与发达国家林权类型的划分非常类似，而且政府还通过制定专门的《森林法》来保障林权的界定。在革命根据地和解放区，林地和林木的产权是分离的，私人在私有林地通过付出劳动种植的树木、或有能力经营但未付出劳动而占有的天然林、或在公地上栽植的树木，林木产权均归私人所有；凡是界定不清以及范围较大的森林资源都归国家所有。

表面看来，这一时期林权界定相对清晰，而且《森林法》中对相关细节进行了明确规定。但是，由于林权界定的外部条件尚未成熟，无法对已界定的林权给予有效的保障，各项政策并未真正得以落实。政府对林权明晰的努力并未收到预期效果，因而将这一阶段称之为“未成功的林权明晰过程”。造成林权无保障的原因主要有以下几个方面：一是频繁的战争导致林权的无保障。这一期间，国民党对中国工农红军进行了五次“围剿”，日本也发动了侵华战争，为了取得战争的胜利，国民党和日军都曾放火烧山造成森林资源的大量减少，面对这种不可抗力，林权的激励作用微乎其微。二是人口的快速增长给林权的保障也带来了压力。1911～1949 年，人口数量从 3.74 亿增加到 5.42 亿，增长了 44.9%，人口的快速增长给林业发展带来了更大的压力，特别是在一些田少山多的地区，一年所产的粮食仅够三四个月食用，农民迫于生存的压力上山开垦，面对这种情形，政府只能是听之任之，对林权的保护根本无从谈起。三是人为因素导致的林权纠纷现象严重。由于战争等原因，政府无力管护国有林及公有林，故将其下放给商人经营从而收取名目繁多的勘测费、领照费、验照费、保证金、山份、木植票费、木税等等来为政府提供财政支持以积极备战。按规定发放森林证应由林务机关进行勘测，但由于偏僻林区常有土匪骚扰，加之勘测技术十分有限，使得勘测活动耗时费力，因而勘测人员大多怠于履行职责。勘测人员或在远处探望估测，或向当地人探询山河地形，即制表绘图上报，领导机关也不复查核实，造成一块林地重复发放多次的情形经常发生，林权纠纷十分严重。

战争频繁、贫苦农民数量剧增、勘测技术的局限以及勘测环境的恶劣决定了林权界定的外部条件尚未形成，不能保证林权的稳定性和可靠性，因而林权的激励作用荡然无存。这一时期的造林数量远远小于对林木资源的砍伐数量，据国民党四川省建设厅调查，大渡河流域毁林垦荒面积自泸定到咱喊约 1.86 万 hm^2，自美乐到富林约2.88 万 hm^2，流沙河两岸约2.1 万 hm^2。而在东北地区，1916～1929年间，仅东线林场就采伐原木 47.47 万 m^3，枕木 77.79 万根，板材 247.35 万 m^3，由于采伐无度，30 年内中东铁路两侧 20～30 公里范围内的森林已被砍伐殆尽。

三、以土地改革推进林权变迁

新中国成立之后，为了解放农村生产力和发展农业生产，同时也为了增强广大农民对中国共产党的拥护和支持，中国政府开始以“耕者有其田”为目的进行土地改革。在对土地进行分配时，林地以及与之相联系的森林和林木产权也出现了私有化趋势。在这里需要明确的是，在中国，森林产权、林地产权以及林木产权是相互独立又相互联系的，因而，将林权的三个主要客体分别讨论有助于对林权政策形成深入的理解。鉴于历史文献中林权政策相关用语的历史局限性，除了引用原文以外，尽量将其转变为当前对其界定的含义，例如“山权”、“地权”一定程度上即为林地产权；“山林所有权”则带有林权的含义，而“林权”更侧重的是“林木产权”。

（一）土地改革时期的林权政策

从法律层面而言，1950 年6 月颁布的《中华人民共和国土地改革法》对林权的相关规定主要有：“大森林、大荒地、大荒山等，均归国家所有，由人民政府管理经营之”；“没收和征收的山林、茶山、桐山、桑田、竹林、果园、荒地等，应按适当比例，折合普通土地统一分配之”。可以看出，大森林为国有产权，没收和征收的“山林”则划分给农户实行私有林权。在具体执行过程当中，根据“树随地走”的原则，林木产权也进行私有化。通过土地改革运动，将地主的山林分配给农户所有，封建地主私有林权逐渐转变为农户私有林权，这一时期，林权客体相对统一，林地、林木和森林作为一个完整的整体进行林权界定，林权的各具体权利分割性较弱，林权的权利束相对完整地界定给林权主体。而且，对农户权利的限制和干扰较少，对其将林地用于其他用途和采伐林木的行为没有任何限制，并且在山区和初级市场允许农民与农民、农民与国家及商人之间买卖木材。

(二)农户私有林权的政策效果

尽管私有林权作为一种林权类型长期存在，但是建国之前林权主体以官吏、地主等为主，他们占据了绝大部分森林资源。表5-2反映了福建省林权的基本状态，其数据依据对建瓯市阳泽、房村和霞抱三个乡进行典型调查的数据计算得来。结果表明，仅占总户数5.82%的地主和富农占有62.12%的杉木林，而占总户数87.22%的中农、贫农和雇农仅占有23.94%的杉木林。因而，以前的私有林权又称为封建地主私有林权。

表5-2　福建省林权状况　　单位:%

私有林权主体	地主	富农	中农	贫农	雇农	小商贩	工商业者等	祠堂寺庙
户数占比	3.56	2.26	29.27	51.20	6.75	2.56	4.40	—
杉树数量占比	58.15	3.97	12.83	10.31	0.80	3.13	10.70	0.90

资料来源：熊大桐等，中国近代林业史[M]. 北京：中国林业出版社. 1989：223.

土地改革使农民获得了更多的森林资源，同时也获得了相对完整的私有林权。但是结合以往经验和当时情况，大多数农民对农户私有林权的稳定性持怀疑态度，期望尽快获得收益。因而，这一时期毁林开荒、大量伐木行为有所增加，农户造林护林积极性也未被调动起来。综合来看，产生了如下政策效果：

第一，伐木数量大大增加。由于农民对农户私有林权的稳定性持有怀疑态度，尽可能在短期内获得收益的动机大大增强。同时，由于初级市场允许农民进行木材交易，这样砍伐的林木即便自己消费不了也可以通过市场途径尽快变现。所以，农民开始大量、快速地砍伐林木以尽快获得既得利益，突出地表现在这一时期森林覆盖率、活立木蓄积和林分蓄积都呈现出下降趋势(见表5-3)，而同期木材产量却呈现逐年增加的趋势。

表 5-3　森林资源各评价指标比较

时　期	有林地面积(亿 hm^2)	森林覆盖率(%)	活立木蓄积(亿 m^3)	林分蓄积(亿 m^3)
1949 年	1.20	12.50	116	108
20 世纪 50 年代	1.13	11.81	110	102

资料来源：中国林业统计年鉴

图 5-1 反映了 1949～1952 年全国木材产量的变化趋势，从图中可以看出，全国的木材产量呈现逐年增长的趋势，特别是 1951～1952 年之间更是呈现了快速的增长，再一次证实了人们急需将林木收益快速变现的心理。

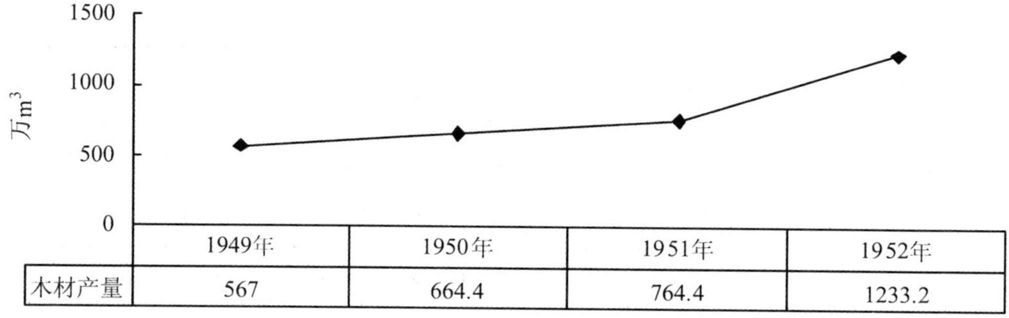

图 5-1　1949～1952 年全国木材产量变化趋势

第二，林地逐渐转变为耕地。农民砍伐大量林木以快速变现，法律并没有对砍伐迹地的用途加以限制，农民有权决定继续种树还是转作他用。1949～1952 年，全国人口增长速度基本保持在 2% 左右，快速增长的人口数量对耕地数量产生了更多需求，故产生了林地转变为耕地的需求。另一方面，林木的生长周期比较长，投资回收期也比较长，种植林木与农民期待尽快获得收益的心理是相悖的。尽管林地转变为耕地的数据难于获得，但是，这一时期耕地面积逐年增加（见图 5-2），林地面积则出现了下降趋势，这也可以间接反映林地逐渐转变为耕地。

第三，农户造林积极性不高。正如上文分析，农户快速变现林木收益的心理

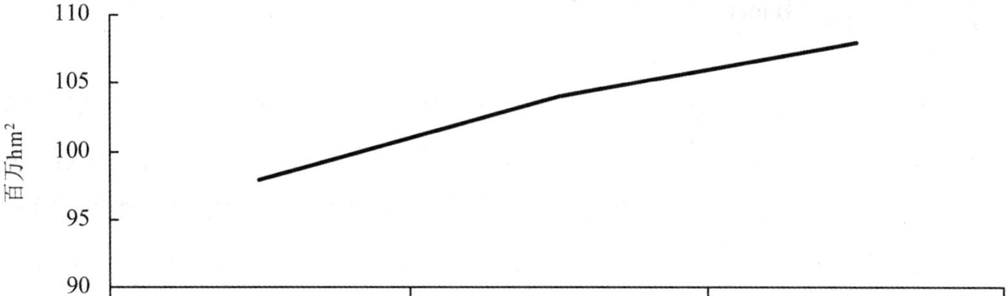

	1949年	1950年	1952年
耕地面积	97.88	104	107.918

图 5-2　1949～1952 年耕地面积变化趋势

和人口增长导致对耕地需求的增加，这些因素都导致这一时期农户的造林积极性不高。土地改革运动增加了农户占有林地面积的数量及比重，农民造林积极性未被调动起来使得这一时期全国范围内的造林面积都十分有限。1949～1952 年全国造林面积总和仅为 170.73 万 hm^2，而 1955 年一年全国的造林面积就为 171.05 万 hm^2。

在新中国成立之前的漫长历史时期，林权政策的演进在很大程度上受政治体制改变、习惯习俗等方面的影响：随着封建社会转变为半殖民地半封建社会，皇室林转变为国有林和官有林，私有林几乎没有发生太大改变；当半殖民地半封建社会转变为新民主主义社会时，封建地主私有林权逐渐转变为农户私有林权。

第二节　中国林业资源问题阶段的林权政策

自 1953 年开始，中国借鉴前苏联的经济发展模式，开始实行第一个五年计划，从此中国开始走上了工业化道路。由于林木资源可以作为工业原料，同时能够为工业发展提供资金和外汇积累，因而工业发展对林木资源的需求大大增加，随着社会经济环境的不断变化，中国实行林权政策演进以更好地保障木材的供给。发展到工业化中期，全球化趋势明显增强。一方面提供了通过国际市场供给木材的途径，另一方面各项环境保护方面的国际公约对保护中国的生态状况也产生了重大影响。

与大多数国家采取的公有林权和私有林权的分类有所不同，新中国成立后中国实行的林权类型主要有国有林权、集体林权和私有林权三种，国有林权的主体是国家，包括中央政府和各级地方政府；集体林权的主体为农村集体经济组织，一定程度上带有共有产权的性质；私有林权的主体是个人，包括农户、私有企业等。由于国有林权和集体林权的排他性程度相对较弱，带有公共产权的性质，通常情况下将二者统称为公有林权，与个人所有的私有林权相对照。

一、界定公有林权以保障木材供给

中国刚开始进入工业化初期时，工业发展对木材的需求急剧增加。根据当时的情况，政府采取公有林权形式来保障木材供给，这一情形从 1953 年一直持续到 1981 年实行林业“三定”政策。

(一)私有林权转变为公有林权的动因

由于工业化的开展对林木资源的需求激增，农户私有林权未能有效地保障经济发展对林木资源的需求，林权政策的演进势在必行。综合而言，林权公有化程度增强的原因主要有以下 5 个方面：

(1)工业发展对林木资源需求急剧增加。自 1953 年宣布开始实行第一个五年计划，中国就确立了优先发展工业的经济发展战略，当时生产力水平十分低下，技术水平也十分落后。像大多数国家处于林业资源问题阶段初期时一样，中国也选择利用木材作为工业原料，同时将林木资源作为资金积累和外汇积累的主要工具，而一家一户的小规模经营很难满足对林木资源需求的急剧增加。

(2)农户私有林权并未对农户造林护林行为起到很好的激励作用。这主要体现在两个方面：一方面由于农户对私有林权的稳定性有所质疑，多数农户不愿造林，而是选择尽快伐木，将林木的价值快速兑现；另一方面大多数农户单凭借自身能力无力造林。建国初期的土地改革不仅实现了土地农民私有，在此基础上各种农具、耕畜等也相应分配给农户，使得原本有限的生产工具更加分散。农户凭借自家的劳动工具和劳动力很难进行造林护林，对林间道路、水利设施等基础设施的建设更是望尘莫及。

(3)农户毁林行为的潜在影响因素仍然存在。一方面土地改革时期2%的人口增长速度产生的惯性使得这一时期人口增长速度依然较快，同时，家庭劳动力不足的情况也是导致增加人口的动机。事实上，1953～1975年中国人口增长速度的确基本保持在2%左右的水平；另一方面，城市化进程推进是导致林地减少的又一个原因。建国初期中国的人口城市化率水平非常低，仅为10%左右。自1950年至1960年人口城市化率的增长速度基本保持在5%左右的水平，到1960年人口城市化率已高达19.7%。城市化进程的推进使得林地直接或间接转变为建设用地，导致林地面积减少。人口快速增长和城市化进程推进都是导致林地面积减少的重要影响因素，农户私有林权制度安排在经济发展水平较低的情况下会加速林地向耕地和建设用地的转变。采取公有林权的形式，从国家层面对土地利用进行统一规划能够在一定程度上缓解这一趋势。

(4)外汇储备和市场开放程度决定了不能通过国际市场提供木材供给。木材供给不外乎通过国内市场和国际市场两个途径来提供。中国这一时期对国外市场并没有完全放开，经济发展主要立足于国内范围，即便对国际市场完全放开，中国也没有足够的外汇储备用于进口木材。因而，这一时期的木材供给主要依靠国内木材生产来提供，制定合理的林权政策来调动林业经营者造林护林的积极性对于维持木材的持续供给发挥着重要作用。

(5)基于前苏联经验形成的对社会主义的基本认识。前苏联社会主义建设的经验在当时给中国人民带来了很大的鼓舞，在很长一段时间内中国的经济建设都在因循前苏联的发展路径。鉴于前苏联社会主义建设的经验，无论是政府还是人民对社会主义都形成了这样一种认识：即建设社会主义首先要实现生产资料公有制。在发展工业的同时，对农业、手工业和资本主义工商业进行社会主义改造，以期逐步实现生产资料的社会主义公有制。这无疑是实行林权公有化十分重要的原因。

综上可知，工业发展导致对木材需求快速增长，可以通过国内和国际两个市场来提供木材，但限于中国当时的外汇储备水平和市场开放程度，只能主要依靠国内市场来满足木材供给。因而，提高木材供给能力是这一时期制定林权政策的主要目的。在农户私有林权制度安排下，农户不愿也无力造林的现实以及人口增加带来林地减少的压力使得农户私有林权在提高木材供给能力方面的作用十分微弱，因而对林权公有化的需求有所显现。

（二）林权逐步公有化的过程

基于上述原因，在当时的历史条件下实行林权公有化是一个理性的选择，这种公有化过程不应是一蹴而就的，而是一个循序渐进、逐渐适应的过程，中国的林权公有化过程表现出明显的阶段性特征。

1. 农户私有林权基础上的统一经营

农户为了提高劳动生产效率，在保持农户私有林权的基础之上，自愿组合成林业生产互助组。政府随即抓住这一时机因势利导，在互助组的基础上采取将农田、山林入股，耕畜、农具等折价入社并参与分红的办法，组成林业初级合作社。1955 年 11 月，政务院颁布的《农业生产合作社示范章程草案》中明确规定：成片的林木一般应逐步过渡到由合作社经营。农户私有的林木应根据以下原则，按照不同的情况分别处理：一是零星树木归农户自己所有、自己经营；二是需要经常投入劳动的，如果园、茶山、桐山、竹林等由合作社统一经营，由合作社支付合理的报酬；三是对松树、杉树等成材林经本主同意，可以由合作社统一经营，合作社所得收益扣除护林、采运、运送成本和应得的报酬外，其余部分都归林主；四是新栽的幼树交给合作社统一经营，林主应得报酬可以有收益后再付，也可以由合作社按照所费工本收买，转为合作社共有。农民除保留自留山、自留林、自留树以外，其余山林连同耕畜、农具一样作价入社，由合作社统一经营。在初级合作社阶段，农户私有林权的性质并未发生根本性变化，只是森林、林地、林木作为生产资料进行折价入股并享有据此获得收益的权利，同时采取合作社统一经营、农户共同劳动的经营模式。而且还保留自留山、自留地和自留树由农户自己经营。

2. 农户私有林权转变为集体林权

经历三年多初级合作社时期，农民对这种经营模式逐渐适应，政府开始大力推进高级合作社的建立，加速林权公有化进程。1956 年颁布的《高级农业生产合作社示范章程》中规定：除少量零星树木仍属于原农户私有外，幼林、苗圃、大片的经济林和用材林都需要根据收益大小及当时的材积等作价，转为合作社集体所有。在这一时期，对于林木入社问题带有明显的强制性，除院旁、宅旁、坟盘子内、自留地内等特定范围内的零星树木之外，其余林木都必须折价入社，但仍在一定程度上保留原林主对林木收益的获取权，合作社需从林木收益中给本主一定比例的报酬。但是取消了以林地入股参与分红的政策，林地无偿归农业生产合作社集体所有。农户除了对特定范围内的零星树木享有产权之外，农户私有的森林、林地以及其他林木的产权都已经完全转变为合作社集体所有。国有林权和集体林权在这一时期占据绝大部分比重，林权的公有化程度不断增强，而且由初级社向高级社的转变仅仅用了不到两年时间就在全国范围内得以实现。

3. 集体林权掩盖下的国有林权

在一些地区尚未完全实现初级社向高级社的转变时，河南省遂平县即出现了由 20 多个高级社进一步合并而形成的大社，政府推行林权公有化的热情备受鼓舞。1958 年通过了《关于在农村建立人民公社问题的决议》中规定：人民公社带有全民所有制成分，并且这种成分将在不断发展中继续增长，逐渐代替集体所有制。按照“一大二公”的要求，将高级社所有的森林、林木、林地全部归人民公社所有；一些地方在初级合作社和高级合作社时期需偿还折价款的折价山林，全部低价甚至无偿归人民公社所有；在并社过程中自留地、零星果树等都将逐步“自然地变为公有”。高级社合并为人民公社的过程，公有化的速度令人吃惊。1958 年 8 月人民公社的比重仅为 30%，到了 9 月，仅仅一个月的时间人民公社的比重就上升到 98%，除西藏自治区之外基本实现了人民公社化。而且，公有化的程度更加彻底，农户对零星树木的私有产权也逐渐“自然地变为公有”，至此农户私有林权已经完完全全地转变为人民公社所有这一特殊的集体所有形式。之所以称之为“特殊的集体所有形式”是因为人民公社“政社合一”的性质决定了“人民公社集体所有”的外衣下掩盖的是国家对农户的绝对控制。例如，栽植的树种、栽植的时间、栽植的方式、栽植的劳动投入以及林木的砍伐、销售等一系列林业生产活动都受到人民公社的严格控制。因而，人民公社时期的林权类型实际上是高度集体林权形式掩盖下的国有林权。

4. 人民公社回归为真正集体所有

从初级社的建立到高级社合并为人民公社仅仅用了 5 年时间，快速的林权公有化过程带有讽刺意味地证实了新中国成立初土地改革时期农民对农户私有林权稳定性产生怀疑的正确性。在这一过程中积累了许多问题，例如在一些地区处理山林入社问题时，违反了农民入社必须坚持自愿互利的原则：有的折价不合理，有的拖欠折价款，有的甚至变相无偿划归为集体所有；高级社时期将林地无偿转变为集体所有；人民公社时期更是直接将折价山林低价或无偿归为集体所有。政策的不连续性以及对农民利益步步侵蚀使得农民的生产积极性受到很大打击。为了挽回局面，1959 年中共中央起草了《关于人民公社管理体制的若干规定（草案）》，规定人民公社实行“三级所有，队为基础”的体制，确定生产队为人民公社的基本核算单位，并且恢复了农户的自留地制度。1961 年颁布的《中共中央关于确定林权保护山林和发展林业的若干政策规定（试行草案）》（即“林业十八条”）专门针对确定和保护林权问题作了相应规定，一方面承认高级合作社时期的林权政策，包括个人对零星树木的私有产权。另一方面规定人民公社以来和以后新造的各种林木实行“谁种谁有”的原则，对农户自行栽植的林木的私有林权予以认可。1962 年的农业六十条的规定中对林权界定的原则是根据森林资源分布特征的不同尽量下放林权，易于分配到生产队的平原、丘陵地区，可将当地山林面积的 5% ~20% 分配给农户自己经营；森林资源分布均匀的山区尽量分配给生产队；而在分布不均匀的山区，不能分配给生产队的则由生产大队集体经营。同时，林地产权也随之下放到生产队，林地和林木产权实现分离。

1966 ~ 1976 年“文化大革命”时期，人为因素对林权政策产生了很大影响，而且带有很强的随意性和偶然性。在这种情况下林权政策十分混乱，无一定之规，并且在各个地区之间的差异很大。在这一特殊历史时期结束之后，为了改变森林资源管理的混乱局面，中共中央于1979年颁布了《中华人民共和国森林法(试行)》，首次以法律的形式对林权问题进行明确规定："根据宪法关于现阶段生产资料所有制的规定，森林属于社会主义全民所有和社会主义劳动群众集体所有；人民公社社员在房前屋后和生产队指定的地方种植的树木，归社员个人所有；机关、团体、部队、学校、厂矿、农场、牧场等单位，在当地革命委员会指定的地方种植的林木，归本单位所有。"同时规定："不准将国有林划归集体和非林业单位，不准将集体所有林划归个人，不准平调社队的林木和社员个人的树木。"可以看出，这次颁布的《森林法(试行)》是以保护国有和集体林权为基本宗旨的。

林权公有化过程是在社会主义改造和公社化运动中完成的，带有明显的强制性制度变迁特征，农民利益在这一过程中一度被忽视，农民的生产积极性受到严重挫伤，积累的一系列问题为公有林权的发展埋下了隐患，以致逐渐演变成为公有林权向私有林权转变的诱因。

(三)公有林权的政策效果

农户私有林权不能满足工业发展对林木资源需求的快速增长是林权公有化的主要原因，在长达近30年公有林权占绝对主导地位的漫长时期，公有林权政策的确为经济发展做出了贡献，提供了大量的木材，也为工业发展积累了资金和外汇。但另一方面，林权公有化过程中对农民利益的忽视成为公有林权发展的隐患，公有林权政策严重挫伤了农民的生产积极性。

1. 公有林权政策对经济发展的贡献

通过实行公有林权政策，国家或集体掌握着造林、营林的控制权，在很大程度上可以避免农户私有林权政策下农户不愿造林或无力造林的局面，从国家层面上保障工业生产所需木材。林权公有化的过程实际上是一种典型的强制性制度变迁过程，行政命令和政治运动的实施效果会很快体现出来，同期数据能够较好地反映公有林权的政策效果。

第一，木材及主要木材加工制品产量持续增加。在生产力比较低的情况下，木材是工业生产的主要原料，木材的充足供给是工业发展的重要保障。公有林权政策有利于对劳动力和伐木工具进行统一调配，提高伐木效率，保障木材供给。

在1970年之前木材产量呈现出明显的波动性，1958年和1966年出现两次明显的木材高产期，1970～1980年木材产量继续保持高位运行并呈现出平稳增长的趋势。为了使木材产量的变化趋势更加明显地展现出来，将每五年的木材产量进行平均，木材产量的变化趋势如图5-3所示。由图可见，这一时期木材产量呈现明显上升的趋势，公有林权政策提高了砍伐林木的能力和效率，增加了木材的供给量，有力地保障为工业发展提供原料。尽管中国从1950年就开始进口木材，但在1980年之前木材进口量非常少，国内市场是提供木材的主要途径。

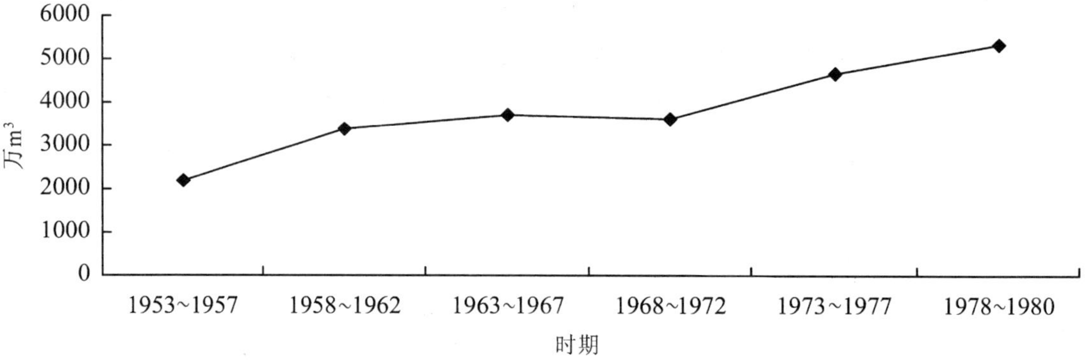

图5-3 木材产量变化趋势

不仅木材产量呈现出明显的增长趋势，锯材、胶合板、纤维板、刨花板产量也都呈现不同程度的增长趋势，图5-4至图5-7分别反映了各自产量的变化趋势。

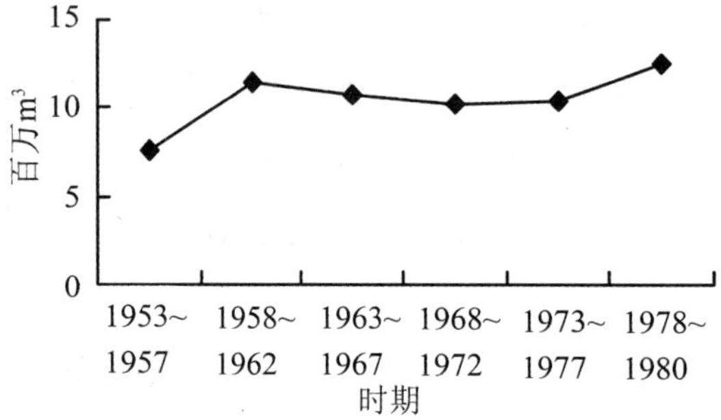

图5-4 锯材产量变化趋势

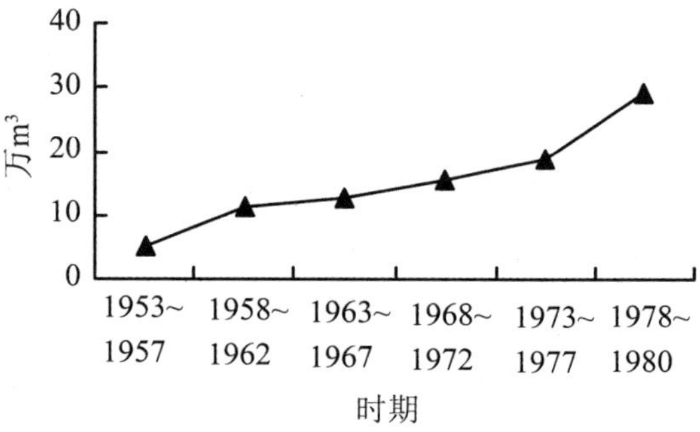

图5-5 胶合板产量变化趋势

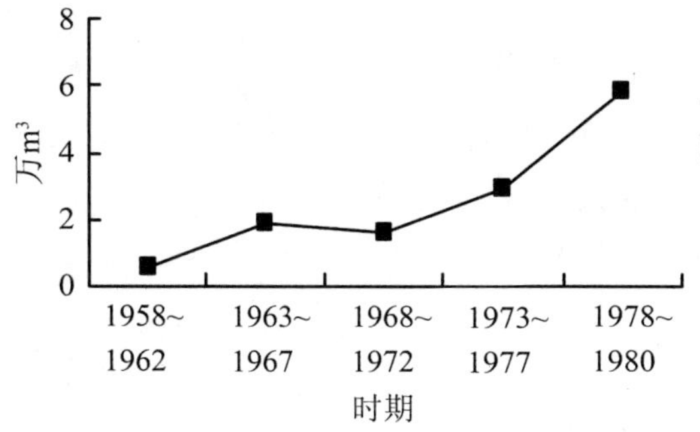

图 5-6　刨花板产量变化趋势

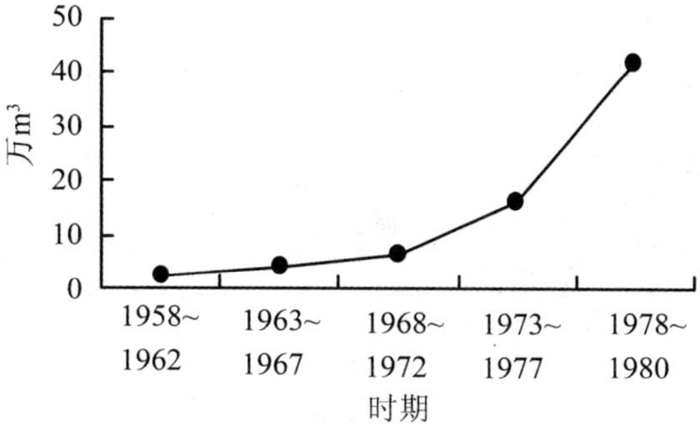

图 5-7　纤维板产量变化趋势

同样也采用计算五年算术平均数来代替五年平均水平的办法，计算结果表明：尽管增长特征各有不同，但总体上都呈现出增长的趋势。特别是胶合板和纤维板呈现明显增长趋势，而锯材的产量则有一段时期内处于下降的状态。

第二，营林生产主要指标呈波动性增长特征。木材产量的增加在一定程度上反映了对现有林木资源的利用程度不断增强。由于林木生长周期比较长，若不及时予以更新和造林，当前砍伐能力越强则意味着以后木材产量越少，因而造林和及时抚育更新对木材持续供给有着重要影响。与产量指标的处理方法一致，同样计算每五年的算术平均数来反映造林面积、迹地更新面积、育苗面积和幼林抚育面积的变化趋势(见图 5-8、5-9、5-10、5-11)，明显表示了林木资源的供需关系。

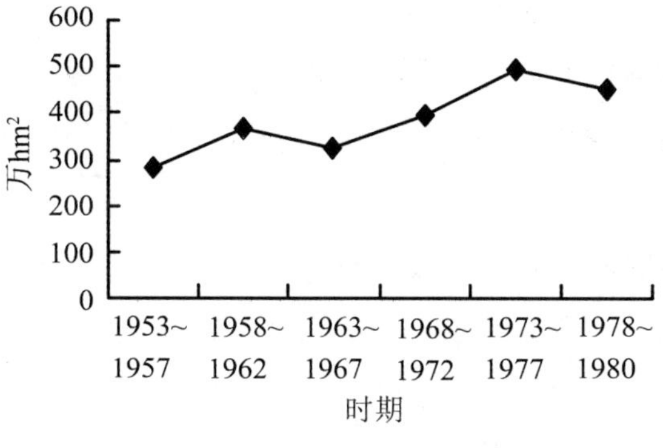

图 5-8　造林面积变化趋势

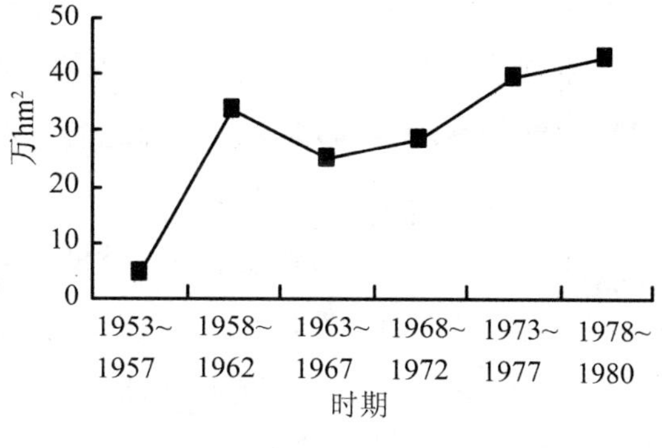

图 5-9　迹地更新面积变化趋势

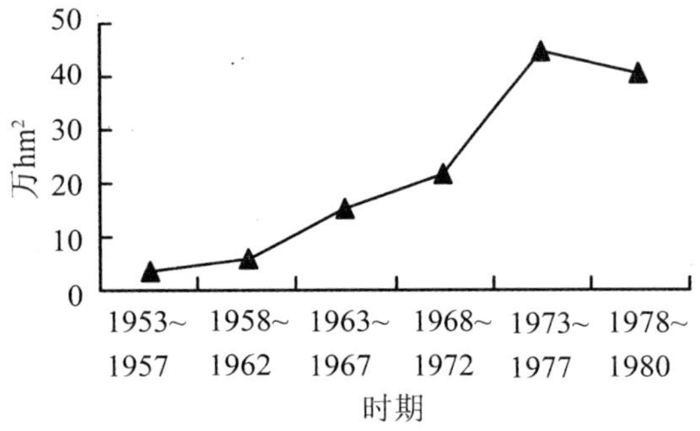

图 5-10　育苗面积变化趋势

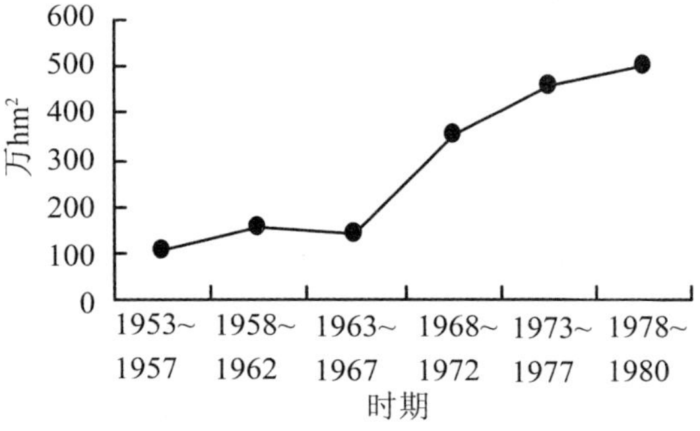

图 5-11　幼林抚育面积变化趋势

为了保证国内木材生产满足工业生产的需要，20 世纪 50 年代中国政府提出了“以营林为基础，普遍护林、大力造林、采育结合，永续利用”的方针。公有林权政策将劳动力和劳动工具进行整合提高了生产效率，各项营林指标在这一时期的确呈现了明显的增长趋势。为了巩固取得的成就，20 世纪 60 年代中央政府又提出“以营林为基础，采育结合，造管并举，综合利用，多种经营”的方针，但由于国家和集体对林业经营和管理的严格控制，农民的生产积极性受到打击，消极怠工现象多有发生，除了育苗面积之外，其余三项指标都有明显减少的特征。60 年代中后期国家将林权逐渐由人民公社下放到生产队，各种营林活动逐渐恢复。尽管各项营林指标在这一时期都呈现出不同程度的波动性，但从总体趋势而言仍旧表现出增长的趋势，为以后木材供给奠定了基础。

木材产量呈现持续增长的趋势意味着林木砍伐量不断增长，而同一时期内各营林指标却呈现了阶段性波动的特征。在二者综合作用下森林覆盖率也呈现出明显的波动性，如图 5-12 所示。

第三，土地统一规划缓解了林地的减少。新中国成立初至 1978 年 29 年时间里中国人口增长了 77.11%，而在 1978 年至 2007 年同样也是 29 年时间里，人口增长了 37.26%。在工业化起步阶段，受资金短缺的制约，劳动力成为工业发展的主要投入要素，经济发展对劳动力需求的增加以及按工分和人均进行利益分配的方式都推动了人口的快速增长。人口增长导致对耕地需求的增长以及城市化发

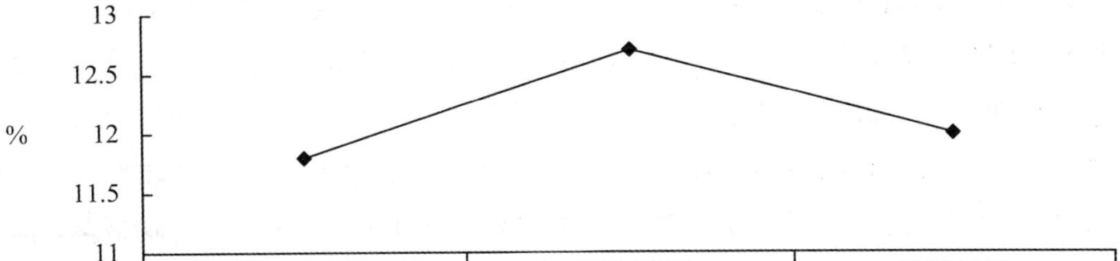

	1950-1962	1973-1976	1977-1981
森林覆盖率	11.8	12.7	12

图 5-12　森林覆盖率变化趋势

展对建设用地需求的增加都会对林地产生压力，这也是农户私有林权难以有效解决的一个问题。

实行公有林权政策，将耕地、林地等农业用地和建设用地都划归为国家或集体所有，从国家层面对土地用途进行同一规划能够在一定程度上缓解农户私有林权政策下林地转变为耕地的趋势。人口增加派生对耕地的需求增加，城市化进程导致对建设用地的需求增加，而工业生产对林木资源需求的快速增加决定了林地面积不能大规模减少，因而政府把开垦荒地作为缓解林地转变为耕地或建设用地的主要途径。图 5-13 反映了这一时期开垦荒地的数量，可以看出，在林权公有化程度逐渐增强的过程中开荒面积迅速增加，而在将林权逐渐下放给生产队的过程中开荒面积呈现了逐渐减少的趋势。

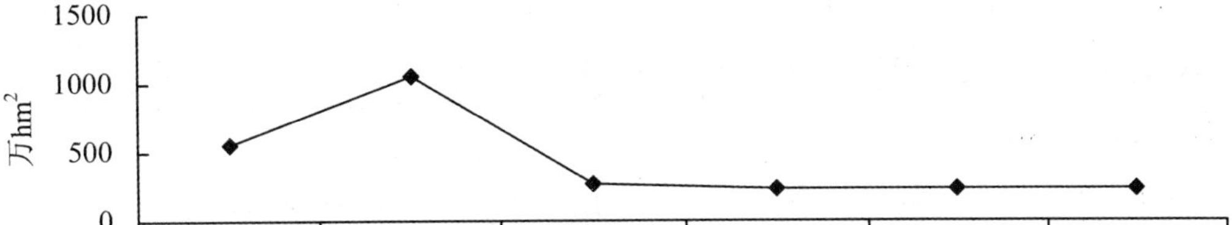

	1953-1957	1958-1962	1963-1965	1966-1970	1971-1975	1976-1980
开荒面积	550	1056	274	224	235	233

时期

图 5-13　开垦荒地面积的变化趋势

开荒面积的增加能够缓解林地向耕地的转变，既有助于满足人们对粮食的基本需求又保障工业发展对林木资源的需求。尽管相关统计年鉴中耕地面积的数量在这一时期呈现明显下降的趋势，但是，毕于运、郑振源(2001)和封志明、刘宝勤(2005)等人的研究都表明，在这一时期，由于诸多原因使得统计年鉴中的数据要小于实际耕地面积，实际耕地面积甚至呈现出上升的趋势，对其修复的结果如图5-14所示。在耕地面积增长的同时，粮食单产也呈现出不断提高的趋势，由1953年1320 kg/hm^2 提高到2745kg/hm^2，二者共同作用使得粮食产量增长迅速(图5-15)。出现了除三年自然灾害期间之外，人均粮食产量逐渐增长的局面，这为经济发展提供良好的社会环境。

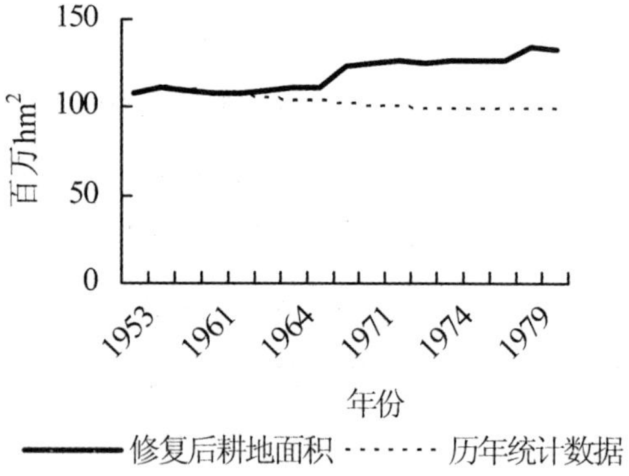

图5-14　耕地面积实际数与统计数的比较

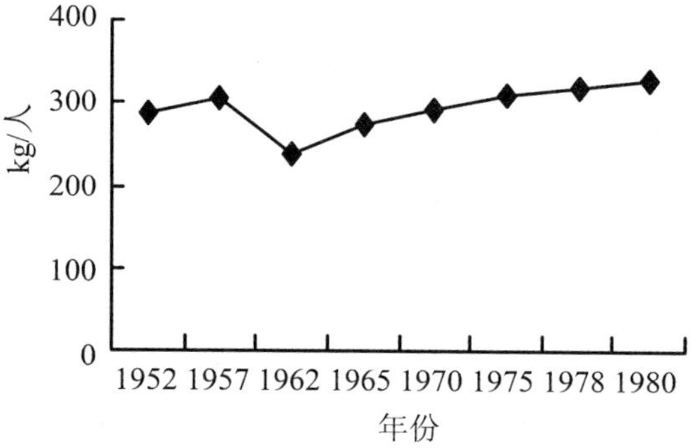

图5-15　人均粮食产量变化趋势

开荒面积的增长缓解了林地面积减少的压力，林地面积由1973～1976年的25 760万hm^2 增加到1977～1981年的26 713万hm^2，林地面积增加为提高木材产量提供了基本保障。

第四，提供大量资金积累。由于工业生产所需要的木材主要由国内市场提供，所以这一时期中国几乎没有木材出口，因而也没有为经济发展积累更多外汇，但是通过公有林权政策为经济发展提供了大量的资金积累。在公有林权政策下，国家控制着木材的生产和配置，实行对全国农村木材的计划生产和统购统销，即由国家木材经营部门统一组织全国木材的收购、分配、订货和调运，统一管理全国木材市场，并采取木材价格管制，制定低于市场均衡价格的低收购价。然后将统一收购的木材以较低的价格，甚至是无偿调拨的形式提供给工业部门。通过这种方式为工业发展提供了大量的资金积累。

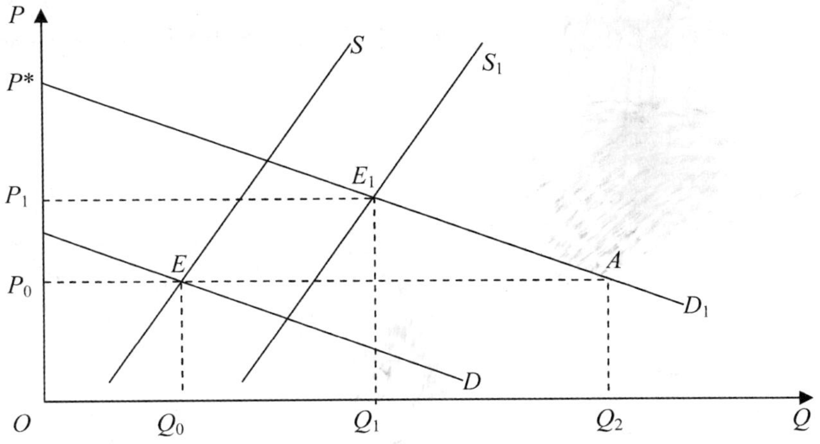

图 5-16　林业生产经营者为工业提供资金积累的过程

图 5-16 揭示了国家通过制定限制价格以使得林业为工业发展提供资金积累的过程。S 和 D 分别代表初始的供给曲线和需求曲线，同前文论述的一样，由于林木生产周期比较长，故供给曲线相对陡峭；E 代表初始市场均衡状态，P_0 和 Q_0 分别代表初始均衡时的均衡价格和均衡产量。工业发展对木材需求急剧增加，需求曲线由 D 平移到 D_1；同时，公有林权政策使得木材的供给量也大大增强（第一点中已有论述），供给曲线由 S 增加到 S_1。若由市场发挥调节作用，则新的均衡点为 E_1，相应新的均衡价格和均衡产量分别为 P_1 和 Q_1，在这种情况下，P^* P_1 E_1 所组成的三角形面积即为消费者剩余的部分，由于工业部门是木材的主要需求者，这里假定消费者剩余全部由工业部门获得。但现实情况并非由市场来进行调解，而是由国家制定低于市场均衡价格的木材收购价格，假定其为 P_0，此时的消费者剩余则变成由 P^* P_0A 组成的三角形面积，与价格机制进行资源配置相比，消费者剩余增加了的 P_1 E_1AP_0 所组成的梯形面积即为林业生产经营者为工业发展

提供的资金积累部分。国家不仅通过控制木材市场、压低木材价格来转移林业经营者的生产者剩余，而且制定了名目繁多的税费，包括农业税、农林特产税、所得税、产品税、增值税等税收以及育林基金、市场管理费、检尺费等一系列收费，大概要占到售价的30% ~60%。与其相比，农业生产的税费仅占10% ~20%。国家通过收取高额税费直接获取林业经营者的剩余利润，转而补贴给工业部门。

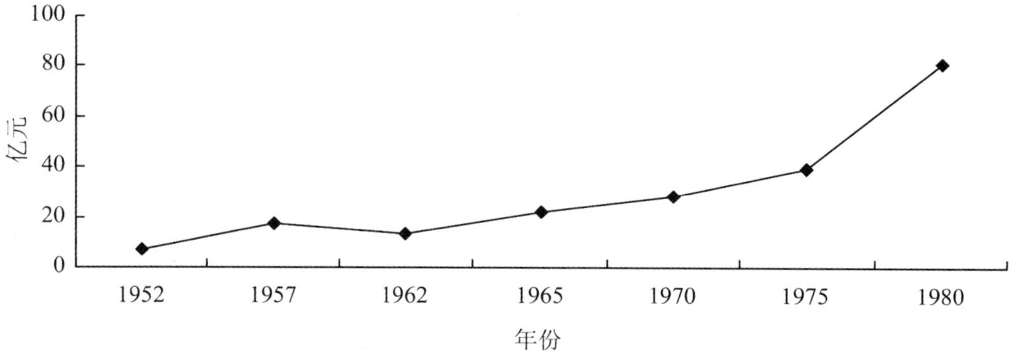

图5-17　林业产值变化趋势

一个值得注意的问题是，实际上林业产值在这段时期内一直呈现了增长的趋势，见图5-17所示，除了在20世纪60年代初期有所下降之外都呈现比较明显的增长趋势。有人可能会发出这样的疑问，既然林业为工业发展积累了大量的资金，自身的产值为何还呈现了如此明显的增长趋势？

实际上，这一问题从木材产量变化率对林业产值占国民生产总值比重变化率的弹性角度分析会更透彻。Q 为木材产量；O 为林业产值占国民生产总值的比重，用林业产值占农林牧渔业产值的比重与第一产业占三大产业比重的乘积近似代替；则 $E=(\triangle O/O)\div(\triangle Q/Q)$ 即可表示木材产量变化率对林业产值占国民生产总值比重变化率的影响。选取1952年、1957年、1962年、1965年、1970年、1975年以及1980年的相关数据进行弧弹性的计算，结果如下表所示：

表 5-4　弹性系数值

时期	1952～1957	1957～1962	1962～1965	1965～1970	1970～1975	1975～1980
弹性系数	0.51	2.24	0.23	0.59	0.09	1.93

除1957～1962年和1975～1980年两个时期弹性系数在2左右之外，其余大部分时期弹性系数明显小于1，甚至1970～1975年的弹性系数仅为0.09，这说明木材产量变化率对林业产值占国民生产总值比重变化率的影响很小。这从另一个角度反映了林业为工业发展提供了资金积累。

通过上文分析可以看出，公有林权政策在工业化刚开始的时期的确对经济发展起到了推动作用。通过将林权实行公有化，统一经营、管理和配置森林、林地及林木资源，不仅增加了木材及其制品的供给量，提高了造林面积，缓解了林地面积的减少，而且为工业发展提供了大量资金积累。但是，实行公有林权政策的后期，经济发展水平逐步提高，20世纪60年代末70年代初中国已经逐渐进入工业化初期的后半段，在新的经济发展形势下，公有林权政策的弊端日益显现，原有的隐患也逐渐显露，对农民的生产积极性造成很大的打击，从造林面积和育苗面积等指标也可以看出，在20世纪70年代中后期有了明显下降的趋势。

2. 公有林权政策的隐患日益凸显

当经济发展进入工业化初期后半段时，以增加木材供给为主要目的的公有林权政策的隐患逐渐显露，弊端日益突出，农民的生产积极性受到严重挫伤。尽管从各总量指标来分析，公有林权政策的确使林业为工业发展提供了大量的原材料和资金积累，但是绝对量增长的背后却隐藏着各种隐患。通过增长率和结构指标等相对指标或人均指标进行更加深入分析发现，各种迹象都表明农民的生产积极性受到很大打击。

第一，各指标增长速度的不同变化趋势。通过上文分析可以看出，无论是木材及木材加工品、造林及抚育更新面积以及林地面积等总量上都呈现出不同程度的增长趋势。但是，在总量增长的同时，不同指标在不同时期的增长率却有明显的变化。由于这一时期强制性制度变迁特征非常明显，行政命令和指令计划通常以很快的速度显现出效果，政策的多变导致政策效果的波动性很强，因而各项指标历年的增长率也都表现出非常明显的波动性，很难从中总结出规律。为此，根据经济发展水平和林权政策特征进行时期的划分，并选取各时期的平均水平进行比较不失为一个很好的办法。首先，结合经济发展水平的不同和林权公有化程度的变化过程将实行公有林权的时期划分为五个阶段：1953～1958 年；1959～1965 年；1966～1970 年；1971～1975 年和 1976～1980 年。由于历年的增长率波动性非常强，因而几何算术平均法不能很好地反映这一特征，故选取各时期历年增长率的简单算术平均数作为这一时期的代表。利用该方法对各指标的增长率进行计算之后发现如下特征：反映农民造林积极性的造林面积和迹地更新面积的增长率自 20 世纪 70 年代初呈现明显的下降趋势，到 20 世纪 70 年代末期甚至出现了接近零增长或负增长趋势（见图 5-18）；木材和竹材产量的增长率自 20 世纪 60 年代后半期到 20 时期 70 年代初时仍呈现上升趋势，发展到 20 世纪 70 年代中后期则呈现明显的下降趋势，但增长率仍大于零（见图 5-19）；而几种主要木材加工品产量的增长率在 20 世纪 70 年代呈现了明显上升的趋势，这意味着这些木材加工品的产量以更快的速度在增长（见图 5-20）。

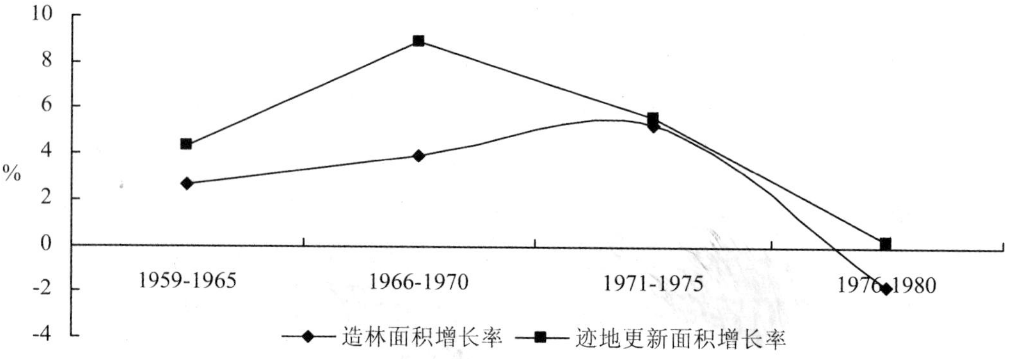

图 5-18　造林面积及迹地更新面积增长率变化趋势

不同类型指标增长率的不同变化趋势在一定程度上反映了国家在这一时期对经济发展的态度，“优先发展工业”、“以农补工”等政策的实施使得农民的利益受到侵犯，农户个体利益和国家利益之间的冲突越加严峻，农民的生产积极性受

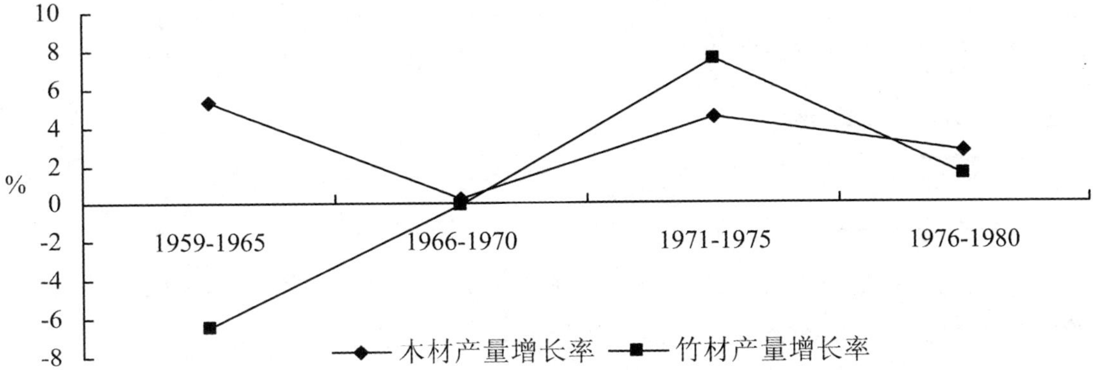

图 5-19　木材产量和竹材产量增长率变化趋势

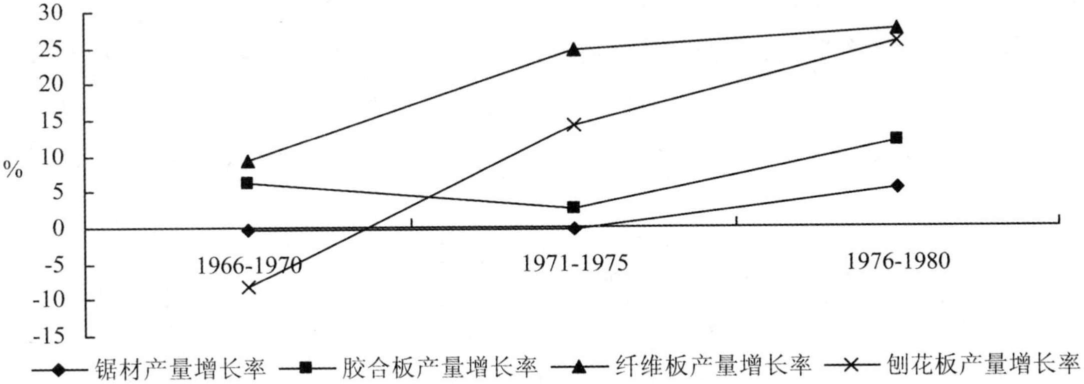

图 5-20　木材加工制品产量增长率变化趋势

到很大程度挫伤。

第二，对林地的利用程度下降。公有林权政策实行之初，通过开垦荒地缓解了林地面积的减少，大力开展植树造林使得有林地面积由 1950 ~ 1962 年的 1. 13 亿 hm^2 增加到 1973 ~ 1976 年的 1. 22 亿 hm^2。但是第一次(1973 ~ 1976 年)和第二次(1977 ~ 1980 年)森林资源清查的数据表明，该时期林地并未得到很好利用。

表 5-5　林地方面指标的变化

时　期	有林地比重	无林地比重	宜林荒地面积(亿 hm^2)	宜林沙荒地面积(亿 hm^2)
1973～1976 年	47.32%	33.31%	0.78	0.06
1977～1981 年	43.17%	37.93%	0.85	0.12

林地主要包括有林地、灌木林地、疏林地、未成林造林地、无林地以及苗圃等几种类型，有林地面积占林地面积的比重能够反映对林地的利用效果。对两次森林资源清查结果进行比较发现，有林地的比重下降了 4 个百分点，而无林地的比重上升了 4 个百分点。不仅如此，宜林荒地和宜林荒沙地的面积都呈现不同程度的增长，这些特征都表明农民的生产积极性受到了挫伤。

第三，林木资源稀缺性增加。尽管林地面积总量上有所增加，但是由于未对林地进行有效的利用，有林地面积反而出现了减少的情形，森林覆盖率相应也有 12.7% 下降到 12%，而且人均森林面积和人均森林蓄积都呈现了下降的趋势，见表 5-6。

表 5-6　森林覆盖率及人均指标的变化

时　期	森林覆盖率(%)	人均森林面积(hm^2/人)	人均森林蓄积(m^3/人)
1973～1976 年	12.70	0.13	9.30
1977～1981 年	12.00	0.12	9.10

农民个体利益和国家利益之间的冲突导致农民的生产积极性受到很大打击，造林、营林的效果明显下降，而且对林地的利用程度也大不如前，随着经济不断发展，公有林权政策的弊端逐渐显现，并成为林权政策再一次变迁的主要诱因。

二、林地公有基础上的林权私有化

随着经济不断发展，公有林权的弊端日益显现，急需建立一个将外部经济内在化的机制来调动林业生产者的积极性。由于社会经济条件的变化，制定林权政策的外部制度环境也随之改变，林权政策变迁的条件已经逐步具备，公有林权逐渐演变为私有林权，但是鉴于以往私有林权的政策效果，国家对现行私有林权给予了不同程度的限制。

（一）公有林权转变为私有林权的原因

公有林权转变为私有林权，一方面是由于随着经济发展公有林权原有的体制弊端逐渐显现。另一方面是由于经济发展以及森林资源状况的变化导致林权政策变迁势在必行。

1. 公有林权的制度缺陷

无论是国有林权还是集体林权，由于产权的排他性较弱，在具体经营过程中都不可避免地会产生委托—代理问题。在中央政府与各级地方政府之间、中央政府与国有林业企业之间、集体与农民之间等都普遍存在着委托—代理关系，根据委托—代理理论可知，由于现实生活中信息不对称现象普遍存在，对代理人的绩效评定十分困难，一旦以行政命令式的“强制合同”来代替激励合同势必会挫伤劳动经营者的积极性。由于集体与农民之间的委托代理关系直接决定了林权政策的实施效果，因而这里仅以集体与农民之间的委托—代理关系为例进行分析。

在实行公有林权时期，农民进行统一劳动。劳动时间、劳动内容、劳动形式都由集体统一控制。在这种情况下，农民的劳动实质上是一种“团队工作”的性质。尽管每个农民都能够独立选择工作的努力水平，但是由于创造出一个共同的产出水平，每个农民对最终产出的边际贡献依赖于其他人的努力程度，因而在参加集体劳动的各个农民之间形成一个囚徒困境的博弈。从作为委托者的集体的角度来考虑，集体希望通过设计激励机制使农民的生产积极性受到保护以完成预期的工作。但是，由于农民的劳动实际上具有“团队工作”的性质，因而以劳动成果为考核标准十分困难，以劳动投入作为考核标准成为一个相对令人满意的选择。农民的劳动投入又分为劳动投入的数量和劳动投入的质量两个方面，对于集体而言，观测农民劳动投入的数量要比观测其劳动投入的质量容易得多。限于当时的技术水平，单纯考核农民投入的数量是一个现实的选择，因而在实行利益分配时实行“工分制”。在集体和农民之间的委托代理中存在着集体与农民之间的博弈和农民相互之间的博弈两种博弈关系，具体见图 5-21 和图 5-22 所示。

		集体组织	
		监督	不监督
农民	努力	（α-a，na-c）	（Π-a，na- d）
	偷懒	（β-b，nb- c）	（Π-b，nb-d）

图 5-21　农民和集体组织之间的博弈

公有林权在处于人民公社阶段实际上是高度集体林权形式掩盖下的国有林权，农民在这一阶段没有退出集体组织的权力，因而农民之间的博弈由初级社阶段的重复博弈演变为一次性博弈。在这个基本判断之上，为能清晰说明这一问题，首先要对博弈模型进行基本假定：第一，农民个体之间的劳动投入数量是一致的，且对劳动投入的选择是一致的。第二，集体组织的监督行为可以使农民的劳动产出更真实地反映出来。这里的监督行为不仅指对农民劳动投入数量的考核，更主要的是对劳动投入质量的考核，而不监督主要是指仅对劳动投入的数量进行考核，而未对其质量进行考核的行为。不监督行为会导致对农民劳动产出的考核出现扭曲。第三，农民努力工作的产出要比偷懒的产出更多，相应努力的成本要大于偷懒的成本。第四，限于当时的技术水平，集体组织进行监督的成本要远远大于不进行监督的成本。第五，不考虑其他成本的影响，集体组织的收益即为集体的总收益扣除分配给农民的收益以及进行考核的成本之后的余额。第六，集体中农民的数量为 n。

		农民 A	
		努力	偷懒
农民 B	努力	（Π-a，Π- a）	（Π-a，Π- b）
	偷懒	（Π-b，Π- a）	（Π-b，Π- b）

图 5-22　农民之间的博弈

基于上述假定，α 和 β 分别代表农民在努力工作和偷懒时的产出，且 $\alpha>\beta$；相应，a 和 b 分别代表农民在努力工作和偷懒时的成本，同时 $a>b$。在集体组织进行监督的情况下，农民劳动的产出能真实地表现出来，而当集体组织不进行监督时，农民劳动的产出扭曲为按劳动投入数量衡量的 Π。因为假定农民之间的劳动投入数量是一致的，所以在没有监督的情况下，所有农民的产出都被衡量为

Π；c 和 d 分别表示集体组织进行监督和不监督时的成本，同样 $c>d$。

在农民和集体组织的博弈中，由于集体组织的收益为集体的总收益扣除分配给农民的收益以及进行考核的成本之后的余额，且农民的劳动投入数量是一致的，则在监督的情况下，若农民选择努力，集体组织的收益即为 $n\alpha-n(\alpha-a)-c$，进行简单运算后为 $na-c$；同理，在监督的情况下，若农民选择偷懒，集体组织的收益即为 $nb-c$；在不监督的情况下，若农民选择努力，集体组织的收益即为 $na-d$；在不监督的情况下，若农民选择偷懒，集体组织的收益即为 $nb-d$。在这个博弈中农民面临着集体组织进行监督和不进行监督两种情形：当集体组织进行监督时，农民选择努力还是偷懒取决于 $\alpha-a$ 和 $\beta-b$ 之间的关系，当 $\alpha-a>\beta-b$ 时，农民会选择努力；反之，农民就会选择偷懒。当集体组织不进行监督时，由于农民的劳动产出都被按照劳动投入的数量进行衡量，无论努力或是偷懒均为 Π，则由于 $a>b$，$\Pi-a<\Pi-b$，农民的最佳选择即为选择偷懒。同样，集体组织也面临着农民努力和偷懒两种情形：当农民努力时，由于 $c>d$，则 $na-c<na-d$，集体组织的最佳选择即为不进行监督；当农民偷懒时，$nb-c<nb-d$，集体组织仍旧选择不进行监督。因此，不监督对集体组织而言是一个占优均衡，在此情形下，农民的最佳选择为偷懒，(偷懒，不监督)成为一个均衡。

农民之间的博弈是一个典型的囚徒困境博弈，当农民 A 选择努力时，农民 B 的最佳选择是偷懒；当农民 A 选择偷懒时，农民 B 的最佳选择仍旧是偷懒，偷懒对于农民 B 而言是一个占优均衡。同理，对于农民 A 而言偷懒也是一个占优均衡，因而，偷懒是在按“工分”进行利益分配机制下的最佳选择，(偷懒，偷懒)成为农民之间博弈的均衡。

可见，在权力高度集中的集体林权政策下，由于委托—代理关系的存在，信息不对称和技术水平的限制使得考核农民劳动投入质量的成本异常高。集体组织从理性出发选择按“工分”考核农民劳动投入的数量，在这种既定的制度安排下，农民之间出现囚徒困境博弈，偷懒成了农民的最优选择，“搭便车”现象日渐明显，农民的生产积极性受到很大挫伤。上文对执行公有林权政策的政策效果的分析更直观地表明了这一点。公有林权政策的内在缺陷越来越不适应经济发展的需要，不仅以“工分制”为基础的利益分配机制挫伤了农民的生产积极性，而且政府制定限制价格将林业生产的潜在利润转移给工业部门对农民而言也是一个打击。

2. 社会经济条件以及森林资源状况的改变

随着经济发展，公有林权内在机制导致农民生产积极性受到挫伤，这是引发林权政策演进的主要原因。同时，经济发展带来的一系列影响改变了制定林权政策的外部环境。

首先，人均粮食产量的增长降低了在私有林权政策下林地转变为耕地的概率。在经济发展过程中除了集中力量优先发展工业，对粮食生产也一直给予高度关注。政府在保证耕地面积的同时还应用新技术来提高粮食单产，人均粮食产量从 1952 年的 288.13 千克增长到 1980 年的 326.69 千克。人均粮食产量的增长能够缓解人们对耕地需求的增加，进而能够降低私有林权政策下林地转变为耕地的概率。

其次，森林资源经济意义上的稀缺性日益凸显。森林资源稀缺性不仅体现在人均森林面积和人均森林蓄积的减少，更主要的是经济发展对林业经济依存度逐渐提高，使得森林资源经济意义上的稀缺性日益凸显。据统计资料显示，自 1979 年林业产值占国民生产总值的比重上升到 1.12% 之后，之后几年这一比重一直呈现上升的趋势，在 1984 年达到 1.61%。森林资源稀缺性的增强使得明晰林权的需求更加突出。

再次，农民在长期林业生产过程中积累了丰富的经验。在公有林权政策期间，集体统一调配农民进行林业生产，技术的采用和长期的生产实践过程使得农民积累了丰富的林业生产经验，并掌握了林业生产技术，为林权私有化提供了条件。

此外，农业实行家庭承包责任制的成功为林权私有化提供了成功的经验，直接推动了林权私有化的进程。

（二）林权私有化的过程及政策效果

建国初期，随土地改革而实行的私有林权导致的毁林开荒现象使得政府在决定再次实行私有林权时对私有的程度有所保留。同时，由于在 20 世纪 70 年代末开始的农业家庭联产承包责任制也保留了土地的国家或集体所有，因而，再次实行私有林权时，国家和集体保留了森林和林地的所有权，只将林木产权和林地使用权分配到农户。1981 年 3 月，中共中央发布《关于保护森林发展林业若干问题的决定》，提出要“稳定山权林权、给社员划定自留山，并落实林业生产责任制”。在保证既定林权界定基础之上，将存在争议和纠纷或是尚未界定林权的部分予以明晰；根据各地区自身特征，按照不同比例或面积划定自留山给社员经营；同时，划定责任山并承包给个人经营，承包年限一般为五年、十年、二十年。

由于国家和集体保留了林地所有权，农户不得擅自改变林地的用途，这进一步阻止了林地向耕地的转变。与建国初期实行的私有林权带来的政策效果不同之处在于，一方面提高了农民的造林积极性，造林面积由 1981 年的 411 万 hm^2 增加到 1985 年的 833.68 万 hm^2，迹地更新面积、育苗面积和幼林抚育面积等也都有不同程度的增长。另一方面，农民毁林行为更加高涨。尽管 80 年代初期计划内木材消耗量为 6 800 万 m^3 左右，但同期计划外木材消耗量却为 22 610 万 m^3 左右，占消耗总量的 76.9%，而计划外木材消费量多来自于农民的非法毁林。造林积极性高涨和毁林行为加剧并存成为这一时期私有林权政策效果的典型特征，但二者在本质上并不矛盾。建国初期实行私有林权，由于农户对私有林权政策的稳定性持有怀疑态度以及人口增长给耕地带来的压力导致农民大量进行毁林开荒，之后林权公有化过程在某种程度上证实了农民对私有林权政策稳定性的怀疑，当林权再次私有时，农民的怀疑心理依然存在，因而尽快砍伐林木、获得当前收益仍是农民的最佳选择。即便认定这一政策是稳定的，但是对承包期的规定仅为 5 年、10 年和 20 年，尽管与农业的承包期相比相对较长，但与林木的生长周期相比还是较短，要想获得更多的收益必须尽快砍伐现有林木以栽植新的林木。另一方面，1981 年全国农民人均纯收入仅为 233.44 元，在对林业经济依存度高的山区，农民的人均收入水平更低，尽早砍伐林木将其经济收益变现能够即时提高家庭生活水平。再有一个因素是，1985 年开放木材市场，允许农民和集体的木材自由上市，实行议购议销，政府对木材的长期限价政策扭曲了木材的真实价格，市场的放开使得木材价格明显上涨，经济利益的刺激成为导致这一时期毁林行为的又一个主要影响因素。在以上四个因素的综合作用下，这一时期农民的毁林行为大大增加。由于国家和集体保留了林地的所有权，农民无权随意将林地转变为耕地，为了在较短承包期内获得更多的收益必须及早栽植林木，因而这一时期农民的造林、护林积极性也较高。从某种程度上而言，这一时期带有"毁林造林并重"的特征。

尽管这一时期，农民的造林积极性得到了提高，但是大量毁林行为使政府对私有林权的效果提出了质疑，为了避免情况进一步恶化，国家决定停止分山到户的林权政策改革。

三、多种林权实现模式共存

自1981年中国开始实行林业"三定"工作以来，通过划定自留山、责任山的形式将林地使用权和林木产权逐渐向农户过渡，但是由于前文所述四个原因的综合作用使得农民毁林行为大大增加，特别是在竹林资源广泛分布的南方地区，由于竹林生产周期较短，变现后在承包期内再次获得收益的可能性更大，因而乱砍滥伐的情况更加严重。为了防止对林木资源的过度利用，自1987年开始，一些地方政府把分下去的林地重新收回由集体统一经营，而另一些地方政府则根据自身情况仍旧实行私有林权。这一时期各地区都在探讨适合本地具体情况的林权实现模式，无论是国有林权还是集体林权实现模式都呈现出多元化特征，形成了多种林权实现模式共存的局面。

(一)多种林权实现模式并存的原因

林权类型主要包括国有林权、集体林权和私有林权三种。20世纪80年代以前，中国的国有林通常由林业部门、或委托地方政府、或由国有林业企业进行经营；集体林主要由农村集体经济组织进行经营；私有林主要由农户进行家庭经营。同一类型林权的实现模式比较单一，随着经济发展，林业发展的外部环境发生了变化，林权实现模式多样化的局面开始出现。

1. 木材供需矛盾趋缓

中国经济发展在20世纪80年代末90年代初明显趋缓。1989年中国GDP增长速度仅为4.1%，1990年下降为3.8%，第二产业的产值结构比例甚至出现了下降的趋势，经济发展速度趋缓导致对木材需求的增长也有所缓解。同时，这一时期人口城市化率的增长速度比较平稳，从1987年的25.3%增长到1997年的31.9%，长达11年的时间仅增长了6个百分点。而且主要是1996年和1997年增长速度比较快，前期增长比较缓慢，与之前经济高速发展阶段相比，此阶段对木材需求的压力有所减轻。另一方面，改革开放政策的实施使得国际市场成为木材供给的一个主要来源，进入20世纪90年代，中国进口木材的数量不断增加（见图5-23）；同时，对木材的节约量和替代品数量也不断增长（见图5-24）。综合而言，这一时期木材的供需矛盾日趋缓和。

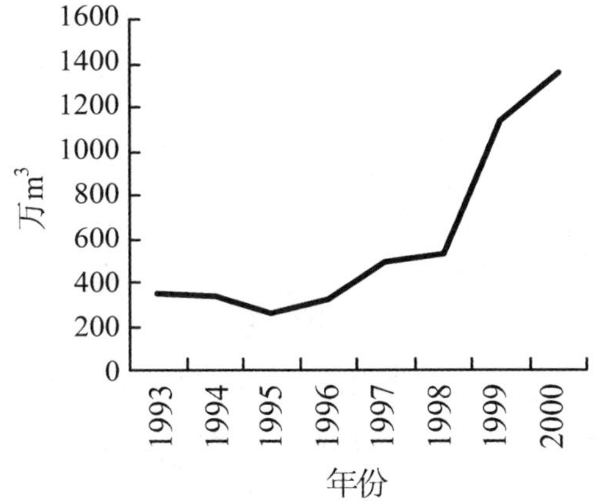

图5-23 中国木材进口数量的变化

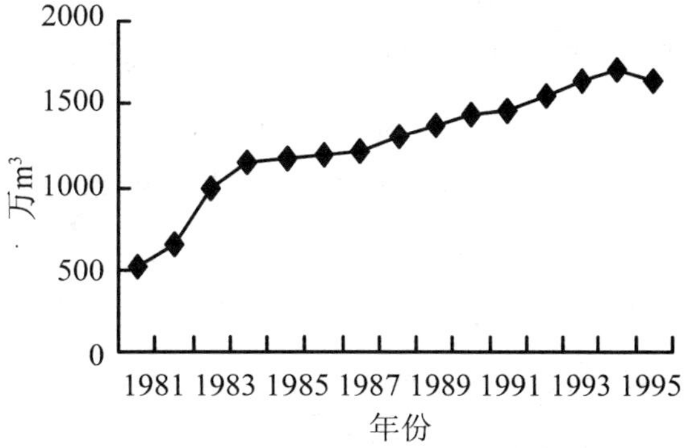

图5-24 中国木材节约和代用合计数量的变化

这一过程如图5-25所示。对木材需求的减少表现为需求曲线由 D 下降到 D'；从木材供给的角度而言，改革开放政策的实施促使木材供给渠道日益丰富化，通过进口从国际市场上获得木材大大增加了木材的供给量，表现为供给曲线由 S 增加到 S'。当木材价格固定为 P_0 的水平下，上述因素的影响使得木材供需缺口由 $Q_D - Q_S$ 缩小为0。木材供需矛盾趋于缓和，林权政策严格以木材供给为核心的策略可以有所放松，这为各地实践不同的林权模式提供了宽松的环境。

2. 集权向分权转变的大环境

在改革开放之前，中国实行中央高度集权的计划经济体制，采取自上而下的指令性计划制度；改革开放之后，这种高度集权的计划经济体制有所转变，地方政府和林业部门在国家宏观调控下享有更多的林业经济管理自主权。在经济体制由集权向分权转变的大环境下，各省以及各地方部门可以根据自身的具体环境制定相应的经济发展政策和林权政策，在改革开放之后，各省经济发展呈现不同的特征，经济发展的差距逐渐拉大，各省根据自身的经济情况和当地森林资源禀赋特征制定林权政策，因而这一时期呈现了多种林权实现模式共存的情况。

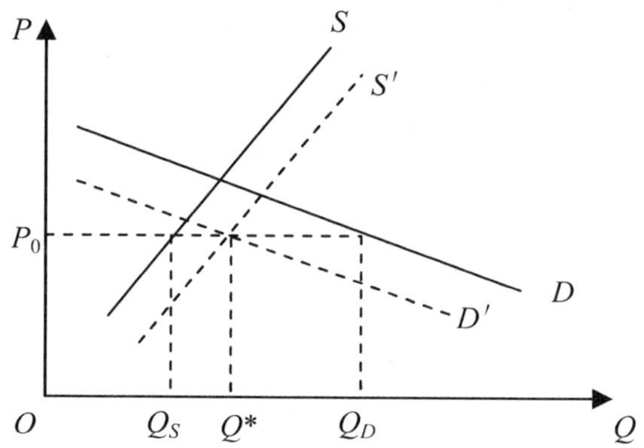

图 5-25 木材供需矛盾趋于缓和的过程

3. 市场经济体制的逐步建立

在长达 40 多年的工业化初期阶段，木材市场几乎一直处于国家控制之中：1953～1979 年全国实行木材统购统销制度，木材价格由国家统一控制，基本处于一种僵化状态。在 1980 年之后，南方和北方的木材市场出现了分化：南方集体林区先后经历了有管制的议购议销、开放木材市场、恢复管制，直至 1993 年才再一次放开木材市场；北方则实行计划调拨体制，之后逐渐允许少量木材通过市场交易，直至 1998 年木材市场才全部放开。木材市场的放开改变了林权政策的制度环境，木材价格由政府统一控制转变为由市场供需关系决定，这为私有林权政策的实行提供了前提条件。为了在市场经济条件下获得更高的利益，各个林业经营主体积极探索不同的林权实现模式。

（二）共存的林权实现模式

自 1981 年实行林业“三定”政策以来，农民在很大程度上获得了林地使用权和林木所有权，但由于各地经济发展水平和森林资源禀赋存在很大差异，各地都在积极探索适合本地实际情况的林权实现模式。国有林权的实现模式主要有场长目标承包经营模式、职工个人或分户承包经营模式、联户或合伙承包经营模式、阶段劳务承包模式、分场或工区经营包干模式、家庭林场经营模式、股份合作经营模式、租赁经营模式以及森工企业集团公司模式等；集体林权的实现模式包括家庭经营模式、集体统一经营模式、合作经营模式、租赁经营和承包经营模式以及股份制企业模式等。这里仅对几种典型的林权实现模式予以简单介绍。

1. 承包经营模式

承包经营模式是指在保留必要的统一经营的同时，以职工、林农及其家庭分散经营为主的经营模式，具体包括联户承包、家庭承包和抵押等方式。其中，家庭经营模式是指以农户家庭为林业生产经营的基本单位，将部分所有权、使用权和收益权等赋予农户的一种经营模式。该模式将生产过程中的劳动者、经营者和受益者统一起来，调动了广大农民植树造林的积极性，充分利用了家庭内部的劳动力；但家庭经营模式的规模较小，资金少且分散，不利于集中采伐和对剩余物的综合利用。

2. 租赁经营模式

租赁经营模式是指国有林业企业把一部分生产资料租赁给集体或职工个人经营，或是国有林场、采育场或乡村林场租赁农户的自留山或责任山的经营形式。租赁期一般是一个轮伐期，在租赁期内由承租方进行造林及管护，期满向出租方缴纳一部分租金。

3. 乡村集体林场模式

乡村集体林场是集体林权实行统一经营的典型模式，实行按劳分配的分配制度，并向村行政组织上交公共积累。在实行林业“三定”之后，南方集体林区未承包给农户的林地大多采取乡村集体林场的模式，到 1988 年底，全国共有乡村林场 11.1 万个，经营面积 0.11 亿 hm^2，其中有林地面积 0.08 亿 hm^2，森林蓄积 2.7 亿 m^3。但由于行政干预过多、管理体制僵硬、资金匮乏等原因，乡村集体林场的经济效益不佳。

4. 合作模式

林业合作模式有联户经营、折股经营、股份合作制和跨所有制跨行业的联合等多种具体形式。农户以资金、劳动力、技术以及林地使用权等为条件进行合作经营，优势是可以进行资源整合，实现规模效益；但也存在着产权不清、分配制度不合理等缺陷。合作造林模式是20世纪80年代末90年代初建立社会主义市场经济体制以后的产物，在自愿互利的基础上，双方签订合同，进行合作造林。福建省三明市是实行林业股份合作制模式的典型地区，1984～1998年，福建三明率先提出“分股不分山、分利不分林”的林业股份制改革，组建村股东会。但在实践中，由于绝大部分的股东会和村两委是重合的，股东会由村委会管理，因此，林木林地所有权和经营权未被分离，林农个人的股权虚置，权益得不到落实，改革中没有得到应有的成效。

5. 股份制企业模式

随着商品经济的发展和社会化大生产的开展，新出现了一种企业财产组织形式——股份制，股份制企业的全部资本都是由全体股东共同出资，并以股份形式构成的企业，主要包括股份有限公司和有限责任公司两种类型。随着现代企业制度的建立和完善，林业经营也开始采取股份制企业模式。

6. 企业集团模式

企业集团是由若干具有内在联系的企业，基于共同的利益和一致的目标，在平等、互利和互惠的原则下，依据共同达成的联合协议、合同或章程，自愿组成的经济组织形式。林业企业集团实际上是林、工、商一体化经营的深化发展，在20世纪80年代初，广西就组建了南宁林工商联合公司，该公司坚持以营林为基础、以林产工业为主导、以商业为纽带，实行林工商联合，产供销一条龙经营。随后，在全国各地相继组建起林业企业集团。

（三）多种林权实现模式共存的政策效果

林权的集权化程度不断降低，各地有权根据当地的具体林情探讨不同的林权实现模式，对造林面积、木材产量以及森林蓄积量等方面产生了不同的影响。

第一，林业产值快速增加。由于各地有权根据当地的经济发展水平和具体林情制定相应的林权政策，因而，这一时期各地以发挥林业经济效益为主要目的，对多种林权实现形式进行探讨，促使林业产值不断增加，见图5-26所示。中国林业总产值由1986年的201.19亿元增加到1999年的886.3亿元，13年间增长了3.4

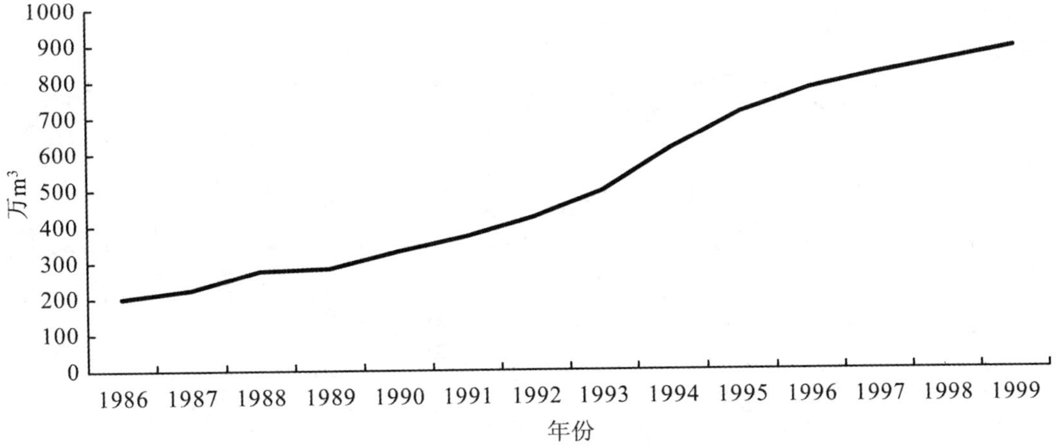

图 5-26　中国林业产值变化趋势

倍。这表明这一时期对多种林权实现形式的探讨，在很大程度上推动了林业经济效益的发挥。

第二，木材产量波动变化，木材初级加工制品量明显上升。这一时期，由于各个地方根据自身特征对林权的具体实现形式进行多种探索，对木材砍伐和利用采取不同的政策，导致这一时期在全国范围内木材产量呈现出波动变化特征（详见图 5-27）。对木材进行加工所生产的胶合板、纤维板和刨花板等木材初级加工制品的产量却呈现明显增长的趋势，见图 5-28 所示。

第三，对林地的利用程度增强。由于各地根据当地具体情况制定林权政策，改变了全国范围内实行同一林权政策的弊端，在一定程度上激励了林业经营主体造林护林的积极性，使得这一时期对林地的利用程度大大增强。对林地的利用程度可以用有林地占林地的比重、无林地占林地的比重以及宜林荒山荒地占林地的比重等指标来反映，图 5-29 反映了 20 世纪 70 年代末至 20 世纪 90 年代末对林地利用程度的变化。从图中可以看出，自 1989 年开始，有林地占林地的比重明显上升，由 1977 ~ 1981 年的 43.15% 增加到 1994 ~ 1999 年的 60.37%，增长了 38.89%；同期，无林地占林地的比重由 37.92% 减少到 21.66%，减少了 42.87%。表明这一时期对林地的利用程度不断增强。

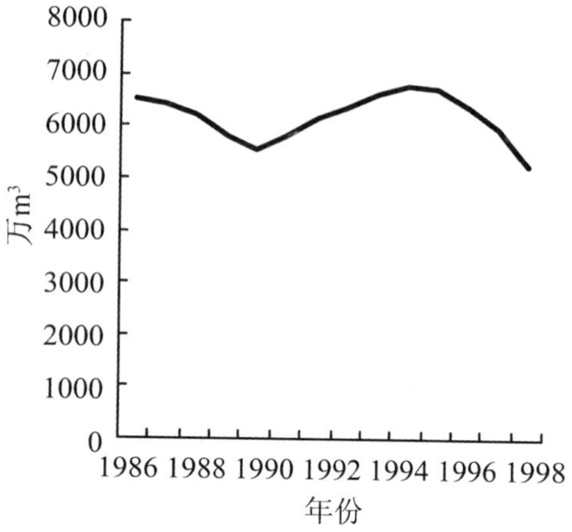

图 5-27 1986～1999 年木材产量的变化

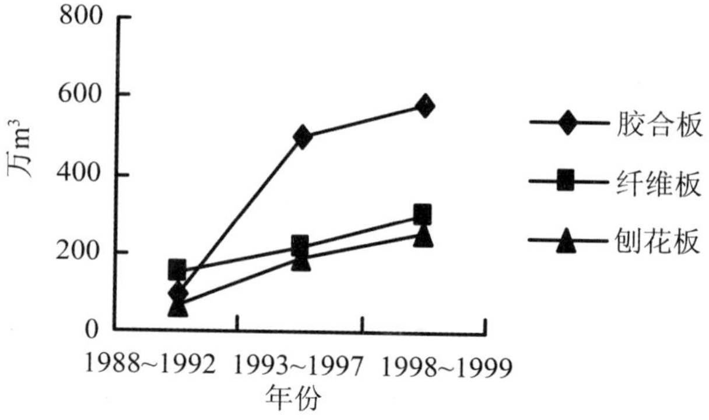

图 5-28 1986～1999 年初级木材加工制品数量变化

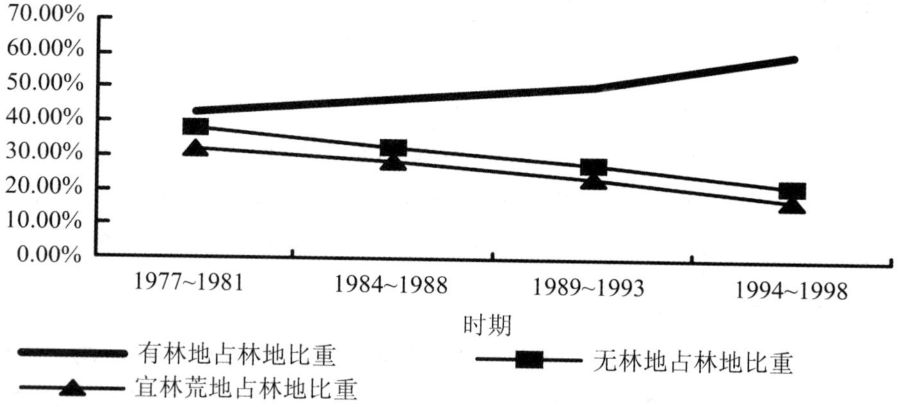

图 5-29 对林地利用程度的变化趋势

第四，森林面积和蓄积双增长。由于这一时期的林权政策在一定程度上调动了林业生产经营者造林护林的积极性，增加了对林地的利用程度，因而，这一时期有林地面积呈现明显的增长趋势，由 1977～1981 年的 1.15 亿 hm^2 增加到 1994～1998 年的 1.59 亿 hm^2，增加了 38.26%；林分面积由 1977～1981 年的 1.01 亿 hm^2 增加到 1994～1998 年的 1.34 亿 hm^2，增加了 32.67%；森林覆盖率由 1977～1981

年的12.00%增加到1994～1998年的16.55%，增加了37.92%。同时，由于进入20世纪80年代后期，中国政府将林业经营方针转变为“由采伐利用天然林为主转变为以营林为主；由单一木材生产为主转变为多种经营、综合利用；由粗放经营为主转变为实行集约经营、科学管理；由林业部门为主转变为全社会办林业，全民搞绿化”，林业发展的重点也逐渐转变为以保护和管理现有森林资源为中心，扭转了森林资源下降的趋势。故而，这一时期森林资源蓄积也有所增加，活立木蓄积由102.61亿m^3增加到124.88亿m^3，增加了21.70%；林分蓄积由90.28亿m^3增加到112.67亿m^3，增加了24.80%。

尽管这一时期，对多种林权实现形式的探讨推动了林业产值的增加、木材初级加工制品产量的增长、对林地利用程度的增强以及森林面积和蓄积的双双增长，但是这种林权制度安排仍然存在着诸多隐患。这一时期很多村逐步通过林地租

表5-7　森林面积和蓄积变化趋势

时　期	有林地面积(亿hm^2)	林分面积(亿hm^2)	活立木蓄积(亿m^3)	林分蓄积(亿m^3)
1977～1981	1.15	1.01	102.61	90.28
1984～1988	1.24	1.07	105.73	91.41
1989～1993	1.34	1.14	117.85	101.37
1994～1998	1.59	1.34	124.88	112.67

赁、合作经营、划拨、改变森林用途等方式将部分林权转移到村庄外的个人、组织或者村庄内少数人手中。但由于当时林权价格偏低，农户对林权的重视程度不够，而且林权流转程序和签订的合同并不十分规范，导致林权不清、利益分配不明晰等问题，为以后的林权纠纷埋下了隐患。

第三节　中国进入林业生态问题阶段的林权政策

自1992年可持续发展理论提出以来，环境保护问题在世界范围内，特别是

在发达国家引起了高度重视，在这种国际环境下中国也于1995年正式把可持续发展作为国家的基本发展战略。1998年，中国发生了特大洪涝灾害，这为中国的生态问题敲响了警钟，林业生态功能得到了高度重视，1999年中国又制定了《全国生态环境建设规划》，强调了保护和建设生态环境的重要性。在21世纪初，中国林业发展进入了一个新的阶段，森林资源不仅要满足社会对木材等林产品的需求，同时要满足改善生态状况、保障国土生态安全的需要。因而这一阶段对林木经济价值需求不断增加的同时，对森林生态价值的需求也逐渐增强，与西方发达国家的林业生态问题阶段有所不同，21世纪初期，中国林业兼具林业资源问题和生态问题阶段的双重特征。

一、影响林权政策的因素分析

（一）对林业的经济性需求仍呈现增长趋势

从国家层面而言，木材市场仍旧存在着供求缺口，对林木资源的需求不断增加。经济发展以及随之相伴而生的人口增长和城市化进程推进大大拉动了对木材的需求：首先，中国经济持续、稳定增长导致对木材需求增加。进入21世纪中国经济增长仍旧保持在10%左右的速度，第二产业的产值结构比例也基本维持在47%左右，工业发展对林木资源的需求仍旧存在；其次，人口数量增加导致对木材的需求增长。尽管进入21世纪人口增长速度明显下降到低于1%的水平，到2007年人口增长率仅为0.52%，但1998~2007年10年中人口总数仍增加8503万人，人口增长导致对木材加工制品以及以木材为原料的工业品的需求不断增加，进而派生出对林木资源更多的需求；再次，城市化快速发展导致对林木资源的需求增长。进入21世纪后，人口城市化率从2000年的36.2%增加到2007年的43.1%，保持了3%左右的增长率，城市化进程的加快推动了对房屋建造、装修装饰、家具制造以及道路、水利等基础设施建设等多方面的需求增加，从而引致对林木资源需求不断增加。

从木材供给的角度而言，国外木材市场以及节约代用技术的进步在一定程度上增加了木材的供给：一方面，进口木材逐渐成为供给木材的一个主要途径，尽管在新中国成立之后，中国一直有木材进口的行为，但在20世纪80年代之前数量非常少，1981～1998年18年间原木进口合计量仅为0.91亿m^3，而1999～2006年8年间原木进口量合计为1.78亿m^3，并且呈现逐年增长的趋势(见图5-30)，若将进口的锯材、单板、刨花板、纤维板、胶合板按照一定标准(每m^3锯材消耗原木按1.43 m^3计算；每m^3刨花板、胶合板和纤维板消耗原木分别按2.0 m^3、2.3 m^3和2.0 m^3折算)折合成原木数量，则进口的原木数量合计数将会更大。另一方面，技术进步使得节约和开发木材替代品的能力增强，相应缓解了木材的供需矛盾，中国自20世纪70年代后期就开始注重节约木材和替代木材的技术，木材的节约量和代用量也呈现逐年增长的趋势。

尽管进口木材和提高木材节约代用技术有助于增加木材供给，但是通过进口木材缓解国内对木材的需求并不是一个长久之计。一方面随着进口原木数量的不断增加所需的外汇也不断增多，用于进口木材的外汇由1997年的15亿美元增加到2004年的50亿美元，这对于处于工业化中期阶段的中国而言仍是一个较为沉重的负担。另一方面全球一体化程度不断增强和环保意识逐渐强化使得环境保护组织对中国大量进口木材的行为施加很大压力，甚至认为中国木材需求的增加将会破坏亚洲发展中国家的森林保护行为，因而，依靠进口木材满足国内木材需求的道路不会走得很远。目前中国的技术水平仍旧十分有限，木材节约量和代用量之和仅为木材供给量的10%左右，而且在木材生产、流通、加工、消费等各个环节仍旧存在着浪费和不合理利用现象。此外，由于人们对森林生态效益需求的增加，对森林资源进行保护的意识也逐渐增强，自20世纪90年代中后期开始限制对林木资源的砍伐，国内木材供给数量不断减少。从木材需求与供给两个方面综合考虑，木材供需缺口仍然存在，甚至呈现加大趋势，预计到2015年，国内木材供需缺口将达1.9亿m^3。按近10年中国木材消费平均年增长率3.71%计算，到2020年中国木材消费总量将达到6.78亿m^3，供需矛盾有增无减，林业资源问题的特征仍旧十分显著。

从农民的角度而言，进入21世纪，农民对林业经济价值的需求愈发增强。20世纪70年代末到90年代中后期，除个别年份外，农民人均纯收入增长率一直保持在10% ~33%之间。自20世纪90年代末开始农民增收速度逐渐减缓，下降到1% ~9%之间。在农民人均纯收入增速减缓的同时，城镇居民人均可支配收入与农民人均纯收入之间的差距逐渐拉大，增加农民收入对于缓解城乡收入差距和维持社会稳定发挥着重要作用。中国的贫困人口大多数集中于山区，对于山区的农民而言，林业收入是农民家庭收入的主要来源甚至是唯一来源，山区农民为了提高自身的经济收入，对林业经济价值的需求逐渐增加。另一方面，市场经济体制的建立和逐步完善改变了过去国家统一规划林业生产和统一调配资源的局面，农民享有更多自主权来进行林业生产经营，同时能够自由地在市场上进行林产品交易，这为满足农民对林业经济效益的需求提供了条件。

（二）对林业生态效益的需求不断增强

由于长期以来采取粗放型的经济增长方式，对资源的过度利用导致生态状况不断恶化，水土流失、土地荒漠化、土壤板结化、物种减少等生态问题日益凸显，洪水、泥石流、沙尘暴、雪灾、地震等自然灾害频繁发生。进入21世纪之后，中国经济呈现了平稳发展的特征，GDP总值从2000年的99214.6亿元增加到2008年的300670亿元，人均GDP也从2000年的7 858元增加到2008年的22 698元；城镇居民和农村村民的收入水平不断提高，城镇人均可支配收入由2000年的6280元增加到2007年的13 786元，农民人均纯收入也由2000年的2 253.4元增加到2007年的4 140元；人们的生活水平大大提高，城镇恩格尔系数由2000年的39.4%下降到2007年的36.3%，农村恩格尔系数也由2000年的49.1%下降到2007年的44.9%。经济发展水平的提高和人们生活质量的改善促使人们对改善生态状况的需求日益迫切，对林业生态价值的需求不断提高。尽管中国目前仍处于工业化中期后半段，与正处于林业生态问题阶段的西方发达国家相比，中国的经济实力、财政能力以及人们的生活水平还存在很大差距，但由于全球环境保护意识不断增强，发达国家对发展中国家乱砍滥伐森林的行为通过制定国际公约等形式予以制止。在全球范围内环境保护意识不断增强的国际形势下，中国对改善生态状况、提高林业生态价值的需求不断增强。中国自身实力的不断增强以及全球环境保护意识的提高促使对林业生态价值的需求不断提高。

二、以分类经营为特征的林权政策

对林业经济价值和生态价值需求的双重增加促使了以分类经营为特征的林权政策的制定。所谓分类经营是指在社会主义市场经济条件下，根据社会对林业的经济价值和生态价值两大需求把森林划分为公益林和商品林，分别按各自的特点和规律经营的一种新型林业经营模式。通常情况下把立地条件好、采伐和经营利用不会对生态平衡和生物多样性造成危害区域的森林和林木，划定为商品林；把生态区位重要或生态脆弱区域的森林和林木，划定为公益林。

（一）商品林的私有林权政策

商品林是以发挥林业经济功能为主的森林，主要用于满足人们对林业经济价值的需求，具有明显的私人物品特征。对商品林进行市场化经营有助于合理配置森林资源，调动农民营林、造林的积极性。进入 21 世纪，对商品林进行放权，制定私有林权政策是这一时期的一个主要特征。虽然此次实行林权私有的林权政策仍以保障木材供给为主要目的，但提高农民收入、保护生态环境也是此次实行林权私有政策的主要目标。

人们对林业生态价值需求的增加限制了对国内林木资源的砍伐，对天然林的保护限制了东北和西南国有林区供给木材的能力，在木材供给总量中，南方集体林区和山东、河北、江苏、河南四个平原省份提供木材数量之和所占的比例在 1997 年之前一直不足 50%，但该比例于 1998 年首次突破 50% 之后呈现逐年增加的趋势。在大面积天然林被保护的情况下，木材供给主要通过人工林来给予保障，如何调动农民造林、营林的积极性是保障木材供给的根本问题，集体所有并统一经营的林权模式能否起到这一效果是一个需要深入分析的问题。集体林权带有明显的共有产权特征，集体中每一个成员都是集体林权的主体，集体林权政策排除了集体之外的成员对集体内成员行使权利的干扰，但是集体内任何单个成员都无权利处置和分配集体林资源，因而达成一个最优行动方案的谈判成本比较高。而且在现行的《中华人民共和国森林法》中只是谈到“属于集体所有的宜林荒山荒地由集体经济组织组织造林”，而究竟何为集体经济组织并未明确表明。参照《中华人民共和国农业法》和《中华人民共和国土地管理法》的相关规定，集体主要是指乡(镇)村农民集体经济组织；村集体经济组织或村民委员会；村内农村集体经济组织或村民小组三个级别。这种对产权主体的规定往往造成产权主体不清、权责不明的后果，导致对林木资源的过度利用。特别是当农民对林木资源经济价值需求不断增加的情况下，对林木资源的破坏更会加剧，这一过程可以用下面的模型加以解释。

该模型的基本假定如下：木材市场是完备的，木材价格由木材供求关系决定；由于木材数量与林木资源数量之间存在着线性关系，不考虑林木加工成木材的成本和造成的损耗，可以用木材数量近似替代砍伐的林木数量；砍伐林木的成本主要为劳动力成本，砍伐每棵树的劳动力成本都是固定的。

N 表示某个集体组织中农户的数量；木材价格 P 和木材数量 Q 之间的关系为：$P=a-bQ$，其中 $a>0$，$b>0$；c 为砍伐每棵树的劳动力成本。从集体组织的角度而言，$TR=PQ=(a-bQ)\times Q=aQ-bQ^2$，则 $MR=a-2bQ$；$TC=cQ$，则 $MC=c$。根据 $MR=MC$ 这一实现利润最大化的原则，即 $a-2bQ=c$，求得对集体组织而言最佳的林木砍伐量为 $Q^*=(a-c)/2b$。令 Q_1 为某个农户砍伐林木的数量，其余农户砍伐林木数量之和为 Q_2，则 $Q=Q_1+Q_2$。从该农户自身的角度而言，$TR_1=PQ_1=aQ_1-bQ_1{}^2-bQ_1Q_2$，则 $MR_1=a-2bQ_1-bQ_2=a-bQ-bQ_1$；$TC_1=cQ_1$，则 $MC_1=c$。该农户也根据 $MR_1=MC_1$ 这一实现利润最大化原则决定自己的砍伐林木数量，$a-bQ-bQ_1=c$，若该农户砍伐林木数量占集体砍伐林木数量的比例为 k，$k<1$ 则 $Q_1=kQ$，则上式即为 $a-bQ-bkQ=c$，此时，集体组织砍伐林木的数量为 $Q^{**}=(a-c)/b(1+k)$，可知 $Q^{**}>Q^*$。由此可知，按照单个农户的利益最大化原则来决定林木砍伐数量势必会造成对集体林的过度砍伐利用。因而，对仍由集体组织统一经营的商品林进行放权，将林地使用权和林木所有权下放到农户家庭手中有助于合理利用森林资源。在这种情况下，中央于2003年开始在福建、江西、辽宁和浙江开始集体林权制度改革试点，将仍由集体统一经营的宜林地的林地使用权和林木所有权下放给农户。截至2007年6月，福建、江西和辽宁等省已基本完成了以确权发证为核心的林业主体改革任务。与此同时，云南、安徽、河北和山东四省的集体林权政策改革正在全面推开。随后其余省份的 80 多个县也已经开展试点工作。在此基础上，2008 年 6 月 8 日，中共中央、国务院制定出台了《关于全面推进集体林权政策改革的意见》，标志着新集体林权政策改革在全国的全面推广实施。

（二）公益林的公有林权政策

公益林是以提供森林生态和社会服务产品为主的森林，随着人们收入水平的提高和生态状况逐渐恶化，人们对林业生态价值需求的不断增加，对公益林的管护和经营逐渐给予更多关注。正如第三章所述，公益林具有明显的公共物品特征，私人在提供公共物品时往往会导致供给不足。公益林适宜采取公有林权政策，以克服私有林权制度安排下经济利益扩张给发挥林业生态功能带来的影响，因而在对公益林进行产权界定时大多采取了国有林权或集体林权的公有林权形式。据统计数据显示，国家级重点公益林有 59.52% 采取国有林权形式，34.06% 采取集体林权形式，仅有 6.42% 采取个人林权或其他私有林权形式。

在公有林权中由于国有林权所占的比重较大，为了使问题简化，仅以“政府”作为公有林权形式的林权主体；在私有林权中农户私有占有较大比重，故仅以“农户”作为私有林权形式的林权主体。在分析公益林的林权政策制定过程中，可以从林权主体之间的博弈进行分析，由于政府和农户可以同时决策是否供给公益林，而且双方只知道自己的支付函数，对于对方的支付函数处于未知状态，因而应选择不完全信息静态博弈模型进行分析。

模型的基本假设如下：

①模型的参与人集合为 $T=\{1, 2\}$，其中 1 表示政府，2 表示农户；

②由于公益林给政府和农户带来的效用不同，因而该博弈模型属于非对称博弈模型；

③每个参与者面临的 2 个纯战略决策均为“供给”和“不供给”；

④政府选择“供给”的概率为 z_1，选择“不供给”的概率为 $(1-z_1)$，农户选择“供给”的概率为 z_2，选择“不供给”的概率为 $(1-z_2)$。

政府在供给公益林时主要追求森林的生态效益。农户在供给公益林时往往会关注森林的经济效益和生态效益两个方面，并且随着自身收入水平的不断提高会对生态效益给予更多的关注。当政府和农户至少有一方供给公益林时，双方均可获得 I_e 单位的生态效益。农户在供给公益林时还会额外获得 (I_1+I_2) 单位的经济效益，其中 I_1 表示农户通过在市场上交易林产品获得的收益，这部分经济收益可能是在不影响森林发挥生态功能的前提下对森林进行间伐和抚育更新的收入，也可能是进行非法盗伐获得的收益。I_2 表示政府对林农支付的补贴。如果双方都选择不供给公益林，则双方获得的效用均为0。$C_s(C_s>0)$ 和 $C_p(C_p>0)$ 分别代表政府和农户供给公益林的成本，二者均非公共信息。农户通过市场交易获得的经济利益 I_1 也仅为农户的私人信息。政府与农户之间的博弈如图5-31所示。

		政府：供给（z_1）	政府：不供给（$1-z_1$）
农户	供给（z_2）	$I_1+I_2+I_e-C_p, I_e-C_s-I_2$	$I_1+I_e-C_p, I_e$
农户	不供给（$1-z_2$）	I_e, I_e-C_s	0,0

图5-31　政府与农户之间对于供给森林生态产品的博弈

农户选择“供给”的期望收益是 $(I_1+I_2+I_e-C_p)\times z_1+(I_1+I_e-C_p)\times(1-z_1)=I_1+I_e-C_p+I_2\times z_1$；选择“不供给”的期望收益为 $I_e\times z_1+0\times(1-z_1)=I_e\times z_1$。当政府供给公益林的概率 $z_1<(I_1+I_e-C_p)/(I_e-I_2)$ 时，农户才有可能选择供给公益林。政府选择“供给”的期望收益是 $(I_e-C_s-I_2)\times z_2+(I_e-C_s)\times(1-z_2)=I_e-C_s+I_2\times z_2$；选择“不供给”的期望收益为 $I_e\times z_2+0\times(1-z_2)=I_e\times z_2$。当农户选择供给公益林的概率 $z_2<(I_e-C_s)/(I_e+I_2)$ 时，政府才有可能选择供给公益林。由此可以看出，当 I_1 和 I_2 越大、C_p 越小时，农户供给公益林的概率就越大，即 z_2 与 I_1 和 I_2 正相关，与 C_p 负相关；当 I_2 和 C_s 越小时，政府供给公益林的概率就越大，即 z_1 与 I_2 和 C_s 负相关。

通过上述分析可知，采取公有林权政策能够集中资金建设公益林生产经营的基础设施、推广林业生产管护技术、统一进行防火防虫行动，在很大程度上能够发挥规模效益，促使 $I_2 > C_s$。将林权界定为公有林权，由国家或集体负责造林、护林和营林等林业生产经营活动，有助于供给数量充足的公益林。然而，公益林多分布于边远山区，或是处于大中型流域两侧地段，在具体实践中，由农户或其他组织经营公益林的现象普遍存在。由于山区农民的生活水平大多处于贫困线以下，据统计，全国 592 个贫困县中山区县就占了 496 个，在这些地区林业经济效益和生态效益的冲突还十分突出，通过上述博弈分析可知，提高对农户的补偿标准是保障林业发挥生态功能的主要措施。截至 2008 年年底，国家级公益林大部分实现了由国家财政承担的补偿，补偿标准为每亩每年 5 元；各省、市、县财政分别对各级公益林进行补偿，部分经济较发达省、市、县不同程度地提高了辖区内公益林的补偿标准，例如，浙江省的补偿标准为每亩每年 15 元。

三、分类经营的林权政策效果

由于生态状况不断恶化，早在 20 世纪 90 年代中国曾在试点地区试行林业分类经营。但是当时中国的经济水平、财政能力十分有限，而且对林业经济价值的需求十分突出，林业分类经营并未得到很好的落实，故于 21 世纪初再次推行林业分类经营。实行林业分类经营产生的政策效果主要体现在以下几个方面。

（一）造林面积波动增长

1998 年以后，中国造林面积呈现波动式增长特征。在 2003 年以前造林面积的增加主要是由于政府加大对公益林投资的力度。对六大林业重点工程的投资由 2001 年的 163.44 亿元增加到 2003 年的 351.35 亿元，其中对除了速生丰产林基地建设之外的 5 项具有生态功能的林业工程投资占对六大工程投资总额的比重由 98.49% 增加到 99.11%，投资额增加了 1.16 倍。2003～2005 年期间造林面积明显减少，由 2003 年的 911.89 亿 hm^2 减少到 2005 年的 363.77 亿 hm^2，在很大程度上是由于政府投资的增幅减缓。自 2006 年造林面积又开始明显增加，这主要是由于集体林权制度改革逐步深入，亿万农民获得了林权，造林积极性普遍提高，非公有经济造林比重不断增强。另外，国家加大对油茶等特色经济林、生物质能源林的扶持力度，形成了新的增长点。而且，国家对天保、三北、长江、沿海等林业生态工程建设的投资不断增加。这些因素使得2006年后中国造林面积不断增加，由2005年的363.77亿 hm^2 增加到2009年的588.49亿 hm^2，增加了61.78%。

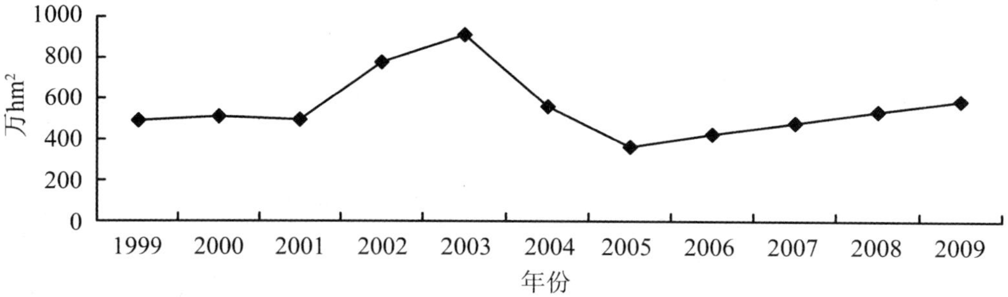

图5-32　1998～2009年中国造林面积变化趋势

不仅造林面积呈现出波动变化的特征，造林结构也发生了很大变化。由于生态状况不断恶化，人们的环保意识日益增强，对森林资源生态功能的需求逐渐增加，因而，国家对公益林的投资力度大大加强，造林面积中公益林的比重由1996年的28.18%持续增加到2006年的76.14%。然而，由于近些年来国际木材市场的压力，依靠进口木材来满足国内市场对木材的需求并不是一个长久之计。故而，在2006年以后造林面积中商品林的比重呈现出上升的趋势，由2006年的23.26%增加到2008年的30.57%，增加了31.43%，详见图5-33所示。

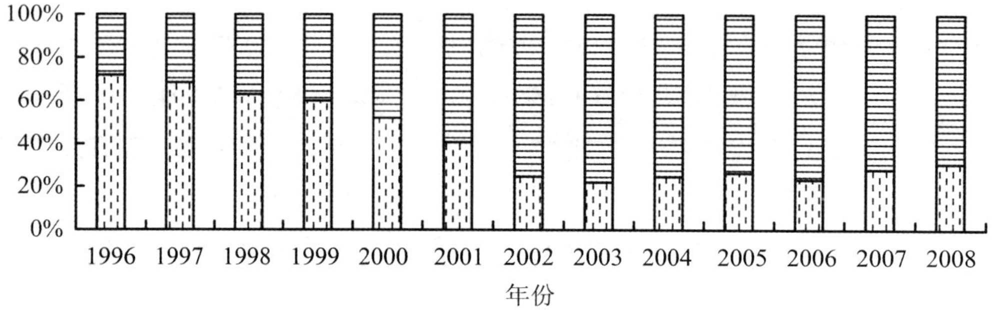

图5-33　1996～2008年中国造林结构变化趋势

(二)木材供给量不断增加

随着人们生活水平不断提高，对木材的需求大大增加，为了满足人们对木材日益增长的需求，一方面，在国内实行分类经营，砍伐人工林以提供木材供给，国家计划内木材产量逐年增加。如图 5-34 所示，木材产量由 1999 年的增加 5 236.8 万 m^3 到 2008 年的 8108.3 万 m^3，增长了 54.83%。另一方面，积极开拓国际市场，从国际市场进口木材，图 5-35 反映了 1999～2006 年中国进口原木的数量，由 1999 年的 318.55 万 m^3 增加到 2006 年的 3 215.24 万 m^3，增长了 9.09 倍。

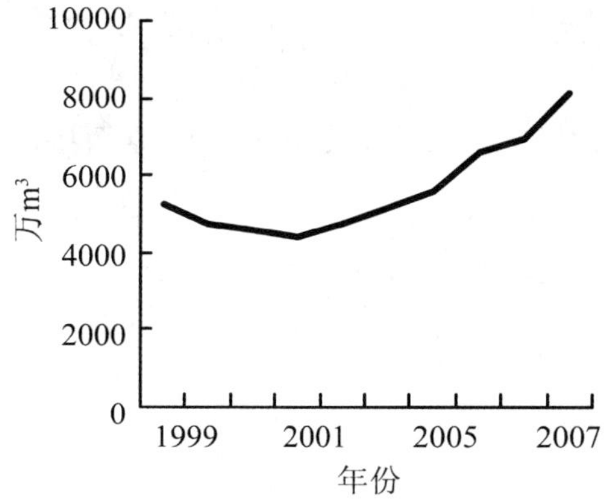

图 5-34　1999～2008 年中国木材产量的变化

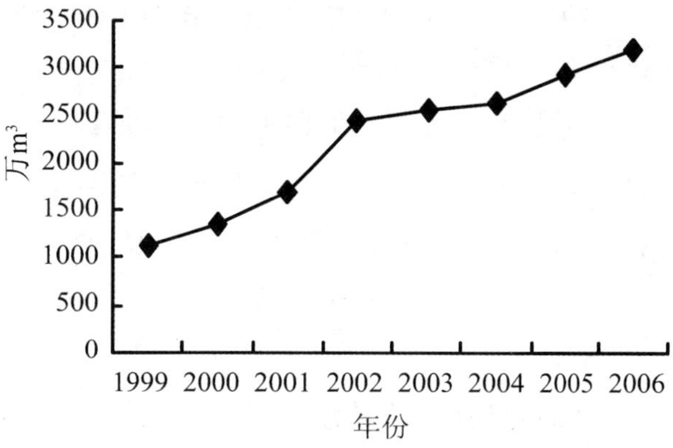

图 5-35　1999～2006 年中国进口原木数量

尽管进口木材在一定程度上缓解了对国内林木资源的砍伐，但以长远的眼光从整个世界角度来看，通过进口木材来满足国内市场对木材的需求以期达到减少国内林木资源砍伐的目的并不是一个长久之计。这主要是因为环保意识在全球范围内不断增强，无论是发达国家还是发展中国家对国内森林资源的保护日益凸显，例如与中国木材贸易较为密切的俄罗斯和马来西亚两国，先后推出了提高原木出口税率或是限制原木和木材出口数量的政策，大大增加了中国进口木材的成本。即便是相对落后的国家寄希望于出口林木资源换取外汇以支持本国经济发展，自身保护森林资源的愿望并未十分强烈，但是迫于世界范围环境保护的压力，原木出口的数量也大大受到限制。例如美国 2008 年 6 月再次通过雷斯法案，新法案增加了禁止进口非法获得的植物和林产品，并提高了进口木材的规格、增加了进口申报程序，这对于木材出口国而言无疑起到了限制作用。

(三)森林资源存量增加

尽管进入21世纪，造林面积呈现波动变化特征，国内木材产量不断增加，但是由于严格控制了木材砍伐率，确保木材砍伐量小于生长量。因而，进入21世纪之后，中国森林资源存量不断增加。这可以通过对第六次森林资源清查(1999~2003年)和第七次森林资源清查(2004~2008年)的结果进行比较来加以反映。据第七次森林资源清查统计数据显示，全国森林面积1.95亿hm^2。其中，天然林面积1.20亿hm^2，人工林保存面积0.62亿hm^2，森林覆盖率达到20.36%。森林蓄积137.21亿m^3，其中，天然林蓄积114.02亿m^3，人工林蓄积19.61亿m^3，活立木总蓄积149.13亿m^3。与第六次森林资源清查结果相比，森林面积净增加0.21亿hm^2。其中，天然林面积净增393.05万hm^2，人工林面积净增843.11万hm^2，全国森林覆盖率增加了2.15个百分点；森林蓄积净增加11.23亿m^3，其中，天然林蓄积净增6.76亿m^3，人工林蓄积净增4.47亿m^3，活立木总蓄积净增11.28亿m^3。

(四)林业产值持续增加

进入21世纪后，集体林权制度改革逐渐在全国范围内展开，随着林权逐步下放到农户手中，非公有制林业的比重不断增加。据第七次森林资源清查结果显示，有林地面积中个体经营的比例为32.08%，个体经营的人工林、未成林造林地分别占全国的59.21%和68.51%，作为经营主体的农户已经成为中国林业建设的骨干力量。林业经营者积极性的提高，政府为林业提供的各种优惠政策都大大推动了林业产业的发展，使得这一时期林业产值逐年增加。如图5-36所示，林业总产值从1999年的886.3亿元增加到2009年的2 379.06亿元，10年间增长了1.68倍。

(五)森林资源质量有所提高

与以往林业发展有所不同的是，进入21世纪之后，中国森林资源质量有所提高，森林的生态功能不断增强。由于实行了分类经营，对公益林实行公有林权，或是对公益林实行私有林权，但对经营公益林的私有林主给予经济补偿，此

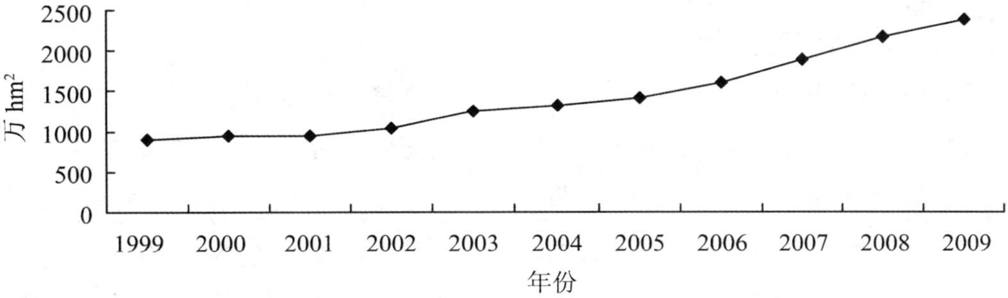

图 5-36　1999 ~ 2009 年中国林业产值变化趋势

种林权制度安排推动了森林资源质量的提高。与第六次森林资源清查的结果相比，第七次森林资源清查的结果显示：乔木林每公顷蓄积量增加了 1.15 m^3，年均生长量增加了 0.30 m^3，混交林比例上升了 9.17 个百分点。而且，有林地中公益林的比例上升了 15.64 个百分点，达到 52.41%。随着森林资源总量的增加、森林资源结构的改善和质量的提高，森林资源生态功能进一步得到增强。中国林科院依据第七次全国森林资源清查结果和森林生态定位监测结果评估对森林资源的生态效益进行了测算，结果显示，全国森林植被总碳储量达 78.11 亿 t，森林生态系统每年涵养水源量达 4 947.66 亿 m^3，年固土量 70.35 亿 t，年保肥量 3.64 亿 t，年吸收大气污染物量 0.32 亿 t，年滞尘量 50.01 亿 t。仅固碳释氧、涵养水源、保育土壤、净化大气环境、积累营养物质及生物多样性保护等 6 项生态服务功能年价值达 10.01 万亿元。

第四节　中国林权政策演进的路径依赖

在 1952 年之前，中国仍处于前工业化时期，当时生产力水平低下、物质比较匮乏、技术十分落后。为了维持基本生存，人们对毁林开荒、将林地转变为耕地的需求大大增加。政府一方面为了取得广大农民对执政党的拥护和支持，另一方面为了在经验、技术和财力十分有限的条件下节约林权制度变迁的成本，由政府主导的强制型林权制度变迁遵循了长期以来实行私有林权制度安排的路径，将地主私有林权转变为农户私有林权。

1953～1995年间，中国处于工业化初期，经济发展水平有所提高，对林木作为工业原料、利用其经济价值为工业发展提供资金和外汇积累的需求上升为主导地位。为了满足这一目的，这一时期林权制度发生了3次变迁，第一次变迁之后，1953～1980年间中国实行公有林权政策；20世纪80年代初至20世纪80年代中期实行了林地公有基础上的林权私有化；20世纪80年代中期至20世纪90年代末，形成了多种林权实现形式并存的局面。尽管在工业化初期，中国经历了3次林权制度变迁，但一直遵循着集体林权制度安排的路径。自1953年开始，中国开始了真正意义上的工业化建设，为了整合农村各家各户的资源，集中力量支持工业发展，实现"以农补工"，在尊重农户合作意愿的基础上进行了有需求的强制型林权制度变迁，将农户私有林权逐渐转变为集体林权。尽管之后实行的高度集体化的林权制度安排严重挫伤了农户及管理者的积极性，但是限于当时农户供给木材的意愿和能力以及实行私有林权制度安排的其他相关条件尚不具备。此外，仍有一部分政治力量极力维护"一大二公"的经济体制，因而，这一时期的林权制度安排一直被锁定在集体林权制度安排的路径依赖之中。

自20世纪末开始，中国进入工业化中期，经济增长方式由粗放型向集约型转变，经济发展水平大大提高，在对森林资源经济性需求不断增加的同时，对其生态功能和社会功能的需求日益上升。以"林业分工论"为理论指导推行分类经营成为这一时期的典型特征。森林资源用于不同用途时往往呈现出不同的物品属性，在林产品市场化程度不断提高、森林资源稀缺性日益增强、林业生产经营技术有所改善的条件下，根据林权客体物品属性的变化，制定合理的林权制度安排以满足对森林资源多种功能的需求，并且这一趋势将在工业化中期阶段得以延续。

随着工业化进程进一步推进，对森林资源生态功能的需求将逐渐上升到主导地位，这可以从目前西方发达国家对气候问题以及生物多样性等生态问题给予高度关注体现出来，林权制度安排将逐渐转变为以实现森林资源三大功能的相互协调，并逐渐突出对森林资源生态功能的需求。

第六章　林业环境产品的供给

正如本文前面反复论证的那样，当经济发展到一定水平，人们对林业活动的生态需求将上升为主要需求，林业活动也将以供给生态环境产品为主。因此，能否满足人们的需求，就将取决于环境产品的供给效率。在市场经济当中，私人物品的供给可以完全依赖价格机制调节到理想状态，但环境产品的供给显然具有很大的不同。在现实当中，政府供给显然是环境产品的主导供给模式，但这种模式在实践中的低效率又使人们期望和主张采用市场供给模式。因此，到底采用市场供给模式还是采用政府供给模式的争论一直进行着。

第一节　林业环境产品需求

一、概念的界定

当公众所需求的生态环境不再像阳光一样依靠天然供给，而需要通过人类的治理活动来改善其质量时，我们可以把后天人类通过林业活动治理过的生态环境称之为林业环境产品（文中所有林业环境产品一词，都是在这一意义上界定的）。依据公共物品等理论，从效用的分割性、消费的竞争性和受益的排他性等方面考察，林业环境产品属于公共物品，并由此可以回答这类林业环境产品以非市场方式提供的原因。但是，诸如环境治理的区域投入不均衡[①]、环境治理要由政府部门直接组织进行等问题，需要通过对林业环境产品的特征进行特定分析才能给予

① 环境治理的区域投入不均衡不是指由于区域生态环境质量不同而导致的资金投入数量的差异，而是指在现实当中存在的中心地区环境治理的单位资金投入（如单位面积上的投入）多于边际地区的现象。

比较充分的解释。

除林业环境产品一词外，为了便于分析，本文还提出了原环境这一概念。本文中的原环境是指相对于某一区域当前环境治理而言，以前这一区域的生态环境。原环境既可能是经过人类投入治理过的生态环境，也可能是没有经过人类投入治理过的生态环境。

二、林业环境产品需求愿望的确定

与私人物品相比，由于受公共物品特征的限制，林业环境产品的需求在多数情况下很难通过市场交换的手段来实现。当没有相应的机制提供林业环境产品时，公众对林业环境产品的需求只能停留在需求愿望的层面上。这时有两个因素对这一需求愿望产生较为强烈的影响。首先，林业环境产品的需求愿望的强弱决定于环境质量的变化。公众生存依托的原环境质量越高，其需求越表现为林业环境产品以外的其他物品或服务，而对林业环境产品的需求愿望则越弱。相反，当原环境的质量很低或质量不断降低时，林业环境产品给公众带来的效用就会不断增强，其需求愿望也会随之提高。现实中的这一现象可以看成是边际效用递减规律在林业环境产品上的具体表现。其次，公众的收入水平变化也对林业环境产品的需求愿望产生强烈影响。公众收入水平越低，越是首先满足基本生活需求，而对林业环境产品的需求愿望较弱。相反，在公众收入水平不断提高的情况下，剩余收入将导致公众对林业环境产品的需求愿望不断增强。

从总体上看，上述两个因素对林业环境产品需求愿望的影响非但不相互独立，而且还是相互关联的。这一关联关系可以用下图来表示。图中，纵轴代表原环境质量等级，用 R 表示。并假定等级越高，原环境的质量越差，那么，原环境质量由高到低的顺序为 $R_1 > R_2 \cdots\cdots > Rn$。横轴表示公众的收入水平，用 I 表示。Q 表示公众在不同质量等级与收入水平组合下对林业环境产品的各种需求愿望，并假定越远离原点，需求愿望越高。同时，在同一愿望曲线上各点所代表的需求愿望相同。当公众的收入水平与原环境的质量等级组合为 $A(I_1，R_1)$时，公众对林业环境产品的需求愿望为 Q_1。当这种组合变为 $B(I_1，R_2)$时，需求愿望则表现

为 Q_2。这表明在收入水平一定的情况下，原环境的质量越低，公众对林业环境产品的需求愿望越强。同理，与 A 点相比，当收入水平增加到 I_2，原环境质量等级变为 R_2 时，需求愿望将增加到 Q_3。这一图示表明，公众对林业环境产品的需求愿望同时受收入水平和原环境质量等级的影响，当收入水平和质量等级一定时，需求愿望也会固定在相应水平。

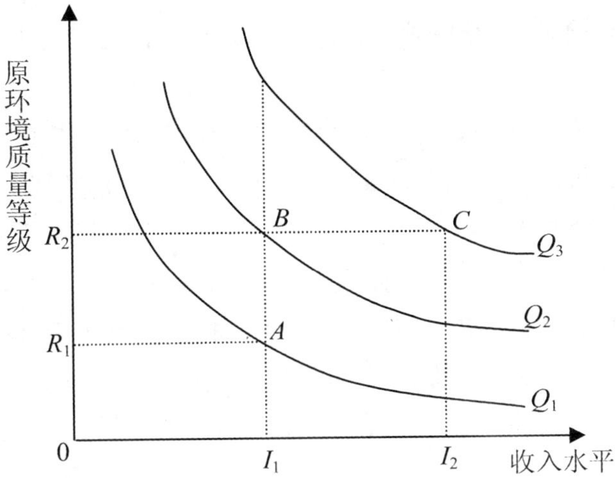

图 6-1　公众对环境需求愿望的无差异曲线

三、政府需求垄断的形成

在经济社会，面对公共物品或服务，免费搭车对任何人来说都是一种理性的选择。这样，即使在需求愿望很强时，公众也不会主动支付自己的收入来实现对林业环境产品的需求。既然林业环境产品不可或缺，免费搭车又不可避免，公众对林业环境产品的上述需求愿望就会通过政府对公众的强制性融资来实现。政府运用权力对公众进行融资的过程，可以被看成是公众通过纳税等方式委托政府购买林业环境产品的过程 。在这一过程中，公众和政府之间实质上形成了委托代理关系。与一般委托代理关系不同的是，公共管理者也是公众的一部分，他们同样也是林业环境产品的需求者，所以，在这一意义上，也可以将政府称之为林业环境产品需求者代表。这样，在购买林业环境产品这一事项中，政府就具有了需求者本身、需求者代表和需求者代理人的三重身份。下面，我们结合上述林业环境产品的需求愿望确定的论述，并利用公共选择理论，对政府在林业环境产品需求中所扮演的角色进行探讨。

作为需求者本身，政府对林业环境产品有着自身的需求偏好，而作为需求者代表，政府应该按照公众的需求偏好来选择林业环境产品。那么，只有在两种情况下，公众对林业环境产品的需求愿望才能通过政府的需求行为得到理想的实现。

第一情况：假定公众当中每一个人为单位环境品所承担的税收份额为t(t可能相同，也可能不同)时，他们按照$MB = MC = t$[①]的原则选择林业环境产品数量，并且每一个人所选择的数量都为Q_1。同时，公众当中的每一个人根据他们各自的(I，R)确定对林业环境产品的需求愿望，并且每一个人所确定的需求愿望都为Q_2。并且，政府根据自身的需求偏好所选择的林业环境产品的数量为Q_3。当$Q_1 = Q_2 = Q_3$时，政府自身需求的结果不但和公众当中每一个人在承担相应的税收份额后所确定的最佳林业环境产品数量相同，而且还刚好与每一个人对林业环境产品的需求愿望相符。这样，即使公众不参与选择，他们的需求愿望也会通过政府的自主需求行为得到最为理想的实现。

第二种情况：公众当中的每一个人依然按照$MB = MC = t$原则选择林业环境产品的数量，但结果并不相同，并且他们根据各自的(I，R)确定的林业环境产品的需求愿望也不相同。在这种情况下，如果公共选择的规则是以投票比例决定林业环境产品政策，那么，在每个投票者都呈现单峰偏好的情况下，中间投票者的最佳需求愿望将决定对林业环境产品的选择。政府按照这一选择所提出相关政策，虽不能保证符合每一个人的需求愿望，却可以做到与所有投票者最佳需求愿

① 在这里，MB为环境产品给公众当中每一个人所带来的边际效益；MC为公众当中每一个人为环境产品所承担的边际成本。

望的偏离程度最小①。

在上述两种情况下，政府在选择林业环境产品时，都没有偏离其需求者代表的职能。但是，现实中需求林业环境产品的公众个体数量非常之多，公众当中每个人的需求愿望以及他们按照 $MB = MC$ 原则对林业环境产品的选择不可能全部相同。至于和政府的需求偏好完全相符，即 $Q_1 = Q_2 = Q_3$ 更是在现实中很难出现。因此，第一种情况是不可能实现的。而第二种情况的出现需要同时具备三个条件，这三个条件分别是：公众具有投票的能力；公众具有投票的动机；林业环境产品的选择采用多数投票规则，而且投票者个人对林业环境产品的偏好是单峰的。但是，当我们对上述三个条件分别进行考察时就会发现，这三个条件都在不同程度上存在着某种缺陷或变异。

首先，公众存在投票能力上的缺陷。如前文所述，政府运用权力对公众进行融资的过程，可以被看成是公众通过纳税等方式委托政府购买林业环境产品的过程。在这种委托代理关系中，公众的投票过程，实质上是一种委托者形成决策的过程，所形成决策要由政府代理执行。而公众是否投票受到其投票能力的影响。当公众认为具有投票能力时，公众才有可能行使其投票权力，否则，就可能放弃投票。而影响公众投票能力的一个主要因素是公众对林业环境产品的相关信息的掌握程度。这些相关信息既包括林业环境产品的种类（如，在风沙治理中，林业环境产品可能是防护林，也可能是人工草地等）和区域配置，也包括林业环境产品的成本和效益。在现实中，受相关专业知识的限制，公众很难掌握种类和区域配置这类信息，至于生产成本和效益，由于原环境质量状况的复杂性和自然因素的干扰，其本身具有不确定性，这使公众获得林业环境产品成本和效益的难度高于其他物品。而且区域越大，原环境的状况就越复杂，自然因素干扰的可能性也越高，这样，上述专业知识限制和不确定性也会随着区域的扩大而增强。政府和公众同时面对林业环境产品在信息获取上的困难，但两者在解决这一困难上的能

---

① A. 唐斯（A. Downs，1957）在《民主的经济理论》一书中指出：如果在一个多数投票规则模型中，个人的偏好都是单峰的，则反映中间投票者意愿那种政策会最终获胜。这种简单多数规则所保证的是使所有投票者最偏好的结果和最终达成的政治均衡偏离程度最小。这被称为中间投票者定理（median voter rule）

力却存在很大差别。政府可以运用权力动员广泛的智力资源，从而在最大可能上获取林业环境产品的相关信息，而公众只能依靠自身的经验和知识进行判断。显然，公众在信息获取上的能力低于政府。而且，区域越大，政府和公众获取林业环境产品相关的信息的能力差距也会越大。当区域大到公众获取的信息已不能作为其投票依据时，公众就失去了投票选择的能力。这种能力上的缺陷，会使公众认可政府在获取林业环境产品相关信息上的优势，从而就可能依赖政府的选择而放弃自身投票选择的权力。

其次，公众存在投票动机上的缺陷。这种缺陷不但表现为上述投票能力的缺陷对投票动机的弱化，而且更多地来自下述两个方面：①投票的效益和成本。参加投票的效益，来自于投票者从行使公民权利中所获得的满足和利益；参加投票的成本，则是指为投票所花费的时间和精力。只有在参加投票有净效益的情况下，公众才会乐于参加投票。在林业环境产品涉及的区域很大时，投票者的人数很多。在这种情况下，由于每个人参加投票的成本为正数，而其又认为投票结果产生的影响很小，即投票者按对投票结果的影响力来衡量的效益接近于零，投票者选择弃权策略是合乎理性的(高培勇、崔军，2001)。②免费搭车。即使公众认为参加投票存在净效益，但由于林业环境产品属于公共物品，个人就会期望别人支付投票成本而使自己受益。如果公众中每个人都选择这种行为方式，投票选择林业环境产品的结果也不会出现。

再次，在公众的投票能力和投票动机存在缺陷的情况下，多数投票规则将发生异化。在多数投票规则中，投票的主体是公众。但由于公众在投票上的上述缺陷，多数投票规则将在政府内部实行，即公共管理者们根据各自的需求偏好，在多数投票规则下投票选择林业环境产品①。在这种情况下，投票者的主体由公众演变为公共管理者，在公众内部实行的多数投票规则也就随之异化为政府内部的多数投票的规则 。

---

① 需要说明的是，由于公共管理者的职位的不同，处于主要职位的公共管理者的投票结果可能对其他管理者的投票活动产生影响，而使投票者的投票结果与其真实的投票意愿分离。但在形式上，最终的投票结果依然是遵循多数投票规则而产生的。

上述三点表明，第二种情况，即在多数投票规则下由公众按照他们的需求愿望选择林业环境产品，在条件上并不具备。这样，林业环境产品的选择将按照政府的需求偏好进行。由此，林业环境产品的政府需求垄断就得以形成了。而且，由于公众投票能力和投票动机的缺陷程度随林业环境产品涉及区域的增大而提高，因此，林业环境产品涉及的区域越大，政府对林业环境产品的需求垄断程度就越高。

第二节　从需求垄断到林业环境产品的政府供给垄断

一、私人部门的供给障碍

作为需求垄断者，政府只有两种方式可以获得林业环境产品。第一种方式是由政府出资交由私人部门生产。第二种方式是由政府出资并直接组织林业环境产品的生产。

私人部门任何生产活动，都是本着利润最大化原则来进行的。生产林业环境产品也是如此。当私人部门想以投资林业环境产品来实现利润时，会面临三个困难。

首先，林业环境产品具有较强的不确定性。这种不确性在生产成本和产品质量上都有较强体现。①生产成本的不确定性是指，与普通私人物品相比，林业环境产品的生产成本在生产之前很难准确计算。私人物品的生产成本可以通过三个途径做到比较准确的计算。一是可以通过以前各期相同产品的生产成本来推算当前的生产成本，二是可以依据其他生产者相同产品的生产成本来推算自己的生产成本。三是对于以往市场中不存在新产品，生产者可以根据产品的设计及工艺要求，计算出各种生产要素的数量，然后再依据各种生产要素的市场价格来比较准确的估算生产成本。而林业环境产品的不同在于，相对于每一个生产项目，由于区域、自然条件、原环境状况等方面都可能存在较大差异，林业环境产品的生产成本很难像私人物品一样通过生产者自身前后各期的纵向参照以及不同生产者的横向参照来获得。即使在生产项目开始之前具有较为明确的技术方案，但在日后的生产过程中，也可能由于来自于自然界的不可控制的因素的干扰（如气候的变化以及各种自然灾害），而使生产成本具有不确定性。②产品质量的不确定性是指，与普通的私人物品相比，林业环境产品的质量在生产之前难以明确制定，而且生产成本与生产质量之间的对应关系不强。对于一般私人物品，其质量可以在寿命、结构、功能等方面制定较为明确的标准，而且还可以在消费者使用中得到确切的检验。并且私人物品在技术、管理等条件相同的情况下，单位生产成本和产品质量之间存在着较强的对应关系，即加大成本，产品质量也会随之提高。而确定林业环境产品质量标准的难点在于，在生产之前，无法准确预计干扰其质量的各种不可控的自然因素，更难以预计各种自然因素的干扰程度，这就使得林业环境产品质量在生产之前无法准确确定。在生产之后，还是由于自然因素的干扰，消费者无法准确判定林业环境产品带来的功效的大小（如，2003 年中国北京地区沙尘天气明显减少，这一现象既可能与北京周边地区环境治理有关，又可能与大的气候变化有关）。同样，不可控的自然因素的干扰还可能使生产成本的大小和林业环境产品质量之间的关系不如私人物品表现的那样明确。

林业环境产品在生产成本上的不确定性，导致生产者不知道生产林业环境产品获得多少利润，甚至能否获得利润都可能无法明确预计。而产品质量的不确定性将使交易双方在生产前都可能无法提出明确的林业环境产品的质量标准或各自提出的质量标准不一致，这不但使得交易前的谈判难度增大，而且还会增加日后交易的谈判难度。这使得林业环境产品的交易成本增大，生产者的获利风险性增强。由于上述因素，私人部门在与其他产品比较中，生产林业环境产品的动机就会减弱。

需要说明的是，上述林业环境产品的不确定性与环境治理的区域范围有关。区域范围越大，原环境的状况就会越复杂，自然因素甚至社会因素（如在防护林的营造过程中，经常会遭到放牧、滥伐等人为破坏）干扰的可能性越高，因此，林业环境产品的不确定性也就越大。这样，区域范围越大，私人部门生产林业环境产品的动机也就越弱。

其次，林业环境产品的受益对象具有不可替代性。对于一般产品，生产者可以根据交易状况对交易对象做出选择，即在和甲交易不成功的情况下还可以选择乙进行交易。但对于一般林业环境产品而言[①]，其受益对象只能是这一林业环境产品影响所及区域的公众整体。这种受益对象的不可替代性会限制对交易对象的选择，加大交易风险。显然，林业环境产品的这一特性也会弱化私人部门的生产动机。

再次，私人部门在林业环境产品的交易当中，讨价还价的能力较弱。在交易当中，交易双方的讨价还价能力取决于多种因素，其中交易双方的信息对称程度和他们各自群体所包含的个体数量将对讨价还价的能力产生重要影响。在其他因素不变的情况下，交易双方当中的一方对某一交易事项所掌握的信息多于另一方，则其讨价还价能力较强，反之则较弱。同样，交易双方当中某一方所在的群体当中的个体数量多于另一方，由于这一群体内部个体之间竞争因素的作用，其讨价还价能力较弱，反之则较强。对于林业环境产品，私人部门所掌握的信息不可能多于政府部门，而且，在政府对林业环境产品形成需求垄断的情况下，私人部门所面对的需求者只有一个（任何一级政府对所辖区域提出生态环境治理要求时，私人部门在这一区域提供林业环境产品时所面对的需求者就是该政府部门），这样，私人部门的讨价还价能力就会很弱。

二、政府供给垄断的形成

上述各因素不是相互独立的。政府对林业环境产品的需求垄断降低了私人部门的讨价还价能力，而林业环境产品本身的不确定性以及受益对象的不可替代性更会加重私人部门在讨价还价中的不利地位。在这三个因素共同作用下，私人部门生产林业环境产品的动机不强。当这一动机弱化到一定程度时，林业环境产品就只有由政府出资并直接组织生产，由此便形成了政府对林业环境产品供给的垄断。

---

① 这里所谓的一般环境产品，是指除旅游景区一类以外的环境产品。

需要说明的是，需求垄断本身并不能单独导致供给垄断的形成。例如，类似于公路、军备用品等公共物品同样存在着不同程度的政府需求垄断，但却可以由政府出资交由私人部门生产。这是因为，与林业环境产品相比，这类公共物品无论是生产成本还是最终的产品质量，都不会由于不可控因素的影响而存在高度的不确定性。即使存在，其程度也会很小。在成本、质量等存在比较明确标准的情况下，私人部门提出的交易条件就可能会被政府所接受，这样，这类公共物品的供给就可以由政府出资交由私人部门生产这种方式来实现。

三、林业环境产品政府双重垄断的后果分析

在政府对林业环境产品形成需求和供给双重垄断的情况下，会出现以下后果：

首先，由于处于双重垄断地位，政府可以根据自身的需求偏好对林业环境产品的供给做出决策。显然，与私人部门相比，这种决策省去了对需求者调研这一环节。因此，如果政府内部对林业环境产品的需求偏好是明确和一致的，就会比较迅速地做出林业环境产品的供给决策。

其次，在多元发展的社会中，社会利益是多元的，社会的价值也是多元的，而且利益和价值往往发生冲突。如短期利益和长期利益、弱势群体利益和强势群体利益、经济利益和政治利益以及效率和公平等。政府需要在多元的、甚至是冲突的利益和价值间作出平衡和抉择(张成福，2001)。这样，政府往往在权衡各种利益中形成对林业环境产品的需求偏好，而不是单纯地依据原环境的质量状况来确定对林业环境产品的需求量。因此，政府在利用其对林业环境产品的双重垄断优势来决定林业环境产品的区域配置和投入时，并不一定和这一区域的原环境质量状况相对应。并且往往会出现原环境质量较好区域的投入多于原环境质量较差区域的投入这种情况。

再次，在供给垄断情况下，政府缺乏提供林业环境产品的竞争动力。而在需求垄断情况下，由于对林业环境产品供给状况进行评价的是政府自身，因此，政府还同时缺乏监督压力。这将降低政府部门的工作效率 。同时我们看到，政府

部门提供林业环境产品时并不以利润最大化为目标。在没有利润约束的情况下，政府部门提供林业环境产品的成本往往会很高。

需要指出的是，上述分析并不是意在否定政府在提供林业环境产品中的作用。相反，本文对政府双重垄断的论述，恰恰可以证明政府直接提供林业环境产品这种形式的必然性。因此，分析的目的在于，在政府对林业环境产品处于双重垄断地位的情况下，政府内部管理的改进，可能是改善林业环境产品供给的关键因素。

第七章　低碳经济与林业发展

自20世纪80年代以来，全球气候变暖引起的一系列环境问题日益引起国际社会的广泛关注，并成为当前国际政治、经济、外交和国家安全领域的一个热点。究其原因，气候变化不仅对全球环境、生态等产生重大影响，而且还是一个涉及人类社会的生产、消费和生活方式以及生存空间等社会和经济发展的各个领域的重大问题。

科学研究的公认结论是：人类活动导致大气中温室气体含量增加是全球气候变暖的主要原因。因此，解决气候变暖问题的措施主要包括两个方面：一是减少温室气体的人为排放，二是从大气中清除温室气体。从事前者的任何过程、活动或机制被称为减少"源"，即减排，而从事后者的任何过程、活动或机制则被称为增加"汇"，即增汇。由于森林具有固碳功能，因此在解决气候变暖问题当中，人们对林业在增加森林碳汇方面的作用寄予了很高的期望。

正如人们对碳汇问题的理解，林业碳汇并不只是一个单纯的固碳过程，其更多是涉及为促使森林固碳而采取的一系列人类活动或机制。这种活动和机制依然是在资源的稀缺性和人类有限理性两个假设前提下被设计的，这一设计的主观动机或动力依然是如同企业活动一样的利益。因此，要想使林业在碳汇领域发挥其应有作用，必须在以下几个方面做出解释和说明：一是森林的固碳功能究竟如何？这涉及森林碳汇的价值，即实施碳汇的必要性；二是碳汇活动的特征和实施路径与形式，这是碳汇活动的具体和核心内容；三是碳汇活动实施的条件和对林业发展的影响，这一条件和影响可能涉及技术、产权制度、经营管理模式、宏观政治与经济形式等诸多方面，关系到碳汇活动的可行性。

第一节　森林碳汇功能的认识

一、森林的碳汇功能

总体而言，抑制全球变暖的对策可以分成两个方面：一是减少温室气体的排放源，即减少由使用化石燃料所造成的排放量。二是增加温室气体的吸收汇，如森林和海洋都是重要的吸收汇。

大气、海洋及森林等陆地生态系统通常被称为地球的三大碳库。在自然状态下，人类活动排放的二氧化碳等温室气体主要在海洋、陆地生态系统和大气中循环。作为陆地生态系统主体的森林在生长过程中，通过光合作用，可以吸收固定大气中的二氧化碳，将大气中的二氧化碳固定在森林植物体和森林土壤中，这就是森林的碳汇功能。2000 年 5 月由 IPCC 组织的世界百名科学家(其中包括一些世界著名科学家)，历时一年半，编写完成的《土地利用、土地利用变化和林业特别报告》指出：陆地生态系统在全球碳循环中具有重要作用，全球植被固碳总量约为 466G 吨碳，1 米深范围内的土壤含碳量为 2011G 吨碳。在各类植被类型中，森林面积虽仅占陆地面积的三分之一，但其储碳量却占植被总储碳量的五分之四，是一个巨大的碳储库，也因此被认为是最有效的生物固碳方式。报告分析指出：在 1980 – 1998 年期间，地球陆地生态系统碳吸收率和趋势虽然有相当程度的不确定性，但陆地生态系统仍然是一个“汇”。

二、低碳经济中林业的地位和作用

为了积极应对全球气候变暖危机，英国政府在 2003 年首次提出了低碳经济(Low Carbon Economy)概念。低碳经济倡导的是一种以低能耗、低污染、低排放为主要特征的经济发展模式，强调通过积极有效地利用现有的，或开发、应用新低碳技术，减少温室气体减排，缓解气候变暖，实现经济、社会全面可持续发展。

从发展低碳经济以实现减缓气候变暖的角度看，林业无疑具有十分重要的地位和作用，具体体现在增加碳吸收、保护碳储存和实行碳替代三个方面：

增加碳吸收是通过造林、再造林、退化生态系统恢复、建立农林复合系统、加强森林可持续管理等措施提高森林植被和土壤的碳贮量，即增加碳汇。

保护碳储存是通过包括减少毁林、改进采伐作业、提高木材利用率以及森林灾害控制等措施，保护现有森林生态系统中贮存的碳，减少其向大气中的排放。

实行碳替代是以耐用木质林产品替代能源密集型材料，以生物能源替代化石燃料，从而减少温室气体的排放。

三、森林碳汇功能的特点

森林的碳汇功能决定了林业在减缓气候变暖中的重要作用，这种作用已经得到广泛认可，但和其他减缓气候变暖措施相比，森林碳汇则具有其自身特点：

首先，森林的碳汇功能具有非持久性。这是指固定在森林里的碳，可能在火灾、病虫害、采伐等自然和人为因素干扰下，又被重新释放到大气中。因此，在实施森林碳汇项目是就需要寻找解决这一问题的办法，也是森林碳汇项目与减排项目重要区别之一。目前，在实施基于《京都议定书》清洁发展机制（CDM）的森林碳汇项目时，如何应对非永久性问题也成为各利益相关方关注的核心问题之一。在目前基于CDM机制下实施的造林碳汇项目实施过程中，规定由这样的造林项目产生的碳汇只能作为抵消排放的临时手段。但是，从希望获得碳排放权的一方看，他们是希望成本较低的森林碳汇可以和其他领域减排项目有同等效力，且不受任何限制，从而降低购买排放权的成本。而提供森林碳汇的一方也期望通过出售CDM下森林碳汇项目能够带来更大利益。为此，现在很多国家和国际组织主张应当采取风险补偿的方式，将一部分可用于出售的森林碳汇先保留下来，在出现森林火灾、病虫害等干扰而产生非永久性时，用预先留存的森林碳汇去抵消出现非永久性后而损失的碳汇，这样，可以出售的那部分碳汇，就应当具有和减排项目产生的排放权具有同等效力。

其次，森林碳汇项目存在较大的泄漏风险。泄漏是指由实施碳汇项目活动所导致的发生在项目边界之外增加的碳排放。最典型的碳泄漏方式就是由实施碳汇项目导致项目边界内的活动转移到项目边界外。如由于实施碳汇项目，使得原来在项目边界内的放牧或砍伐行为转移到项目边界以外。表面上看，泄漏是技术问题，但一旦涉及碳汇交易，就会由技术问题演变为利益问题。再加上这一问题界定的技术难度很高，这就为交易各方有可能偏离技术本身而进行讨价还价创造了条件，增加了谈判的难度。

再次，森林碳汇项目的实施必然会对当地的社会和经济发展以及生态环境产生影响。这些影响可能包括：生物多样性；森林、牧地等的数量和质量；水资源的质量和数量；食物、燃料和栖息地等的可获得性；就业、人体健康、贫困和公平性等。这将使碳汇项目不仅涉及人与人的关系，也涉及人与自然的关系；不仅要考虑代内公平，还要考虑代际公平；不仅要实现结果公平，也要保证过程公平。因此，森林碳汇项目会遇到在项目实施中进行利益分配或成本分担的公平问题，而对公平问题的不同界定，势必会影响碳汇交易各方的利益。

第二节　林业碳汇的经济属性与碳交易的实质

在现有的研究文献中，常常出现森林碳汇和林业碳汇两个概念，而且往往被作为同义词混合使用。据此进行的一系列探讨，如经济属性问题，也出现了相互替代现象。其实，详细研究我们会发现，森林碳汇和林业碳汇之间还是存在许多区别。

一、森林碳汇与林业碳汇的区别

森林碳汇是指森林生态系统通过光合作用，将排放到大气中的 CO_2 吸收并固定在森林植被和土壤中，从而减少大气中 CO_2 浓度的过程。只要森林生态系统存在，这一过程就会自然完成，因此是森林生态系统的一种自然属性。而林业碳汇是指通过实施增加碳吸收、保护碳储存和实行碳替代的一系列活动，如造林、再造林、森林管理、减少毁林、使用木质能源等，达到降低大气中 CO_2 浓度的过程、活动或机制。如果这一人为的过程、活动或机制的目的是进行交易并用于交易，那么林业碳汇就具有了商品属性。同时，由于林业碳汇是为吸收 CO_2 而进行的人类活动，并且要考虑相应的社会影响，因此也具有社会属性。

森林的碳汇功能随着气候谈判的进展而逐渐受到关注。在此基础上，造林、再造林碳汇项目被纳入到《京都议定书》中，并作为2008－2012 年第一承诺期间合格的清洁发展机制(CDM)项目，这种项目就是林业碳汇的一种形式。因此，森林碳汇是林业碳汇产生的基础。

二、森林碳汇与林业碳汇的经济属性

从经济学角度分析，森林碳汇具有稀缺性、公共物品性、外部性、公共产权等经济属性。

森林碳汇的稀缺性是指森林的碳汇功能相对于人类的碳汇需求是稀缺的。这一稀缺主要来自于以下两个方面：一是存量上的绝对稀缺。森林碳汇功能的大小主要取决于森林的数量和质量两个因素。而森林的数量则主要取决于林地的数量，森林质量则主要取决于立地条件、树种及其结构、经营管理水平等。在林地数量有限和立地条件、树种及其结构、经营管理水平的制约下，森林的数量和质量是有限的，这就必然制约了森林的碳汇存量和增量。此外，森林具有多种用途，随着社会对森林其他用途的需求不断增加，必然构成对森林碳汇供给的竞争，森林碳汇功能使用也就不可能避免地受到限制，进而加剧森林碳汇的短缺。二是由于工业迅速发展带来的相对稀缺。工业革命以来，钢铁、汽车制造、能源、石油化工以及交通运输等行业的迅猛发展，导致大气中 CO_2 浓度迅速升高，作为清除大气中 CO_2 的重要资源，森林碳汇的相对稀缺性则更为凸显。

森林碳汇除具有稀缺性外，还具有公共物品特征。需要说明的是，这里所说的森林是指不打算参与碳汇交易的森林。这类森林生态系统无论是人工的，还是自然形成的，只要其一旦形成，就会自然具有碳汇功能。在一定条件下，当森林碳汇导致气候改善时，任何社会成员(准确地说，应该是一定区域内的成员)都可以互不排斥、互不影响地享受气候改善带来的成果，享受森林碳汇所带来好处的消费者在数量上的任何变化，都不会对森林碳汇产权人的成本造成任何影响。

从产权的角度来看，森林碳汇似乎不属于任何现今人们所总结的产权类型，其自身具有的产权特征十分独特。现有的研究认为，按照拥有权利主体的不同，产权可以分为私人产权、公共产权和国有产权。划分这些产权的共同依据均来自于两个方面，即谁拥有产权的各项权力或某项权力，并决定该权力怎样使用。对于不打算参与交易的森林碳汇而言，公共物品特征决定森林碳汇的拥有者（私人、共同体或国家）并不关心其是否拥有和拥有哪种权力，当然也就不关心其权力如何使用。因为，不打算参与交易的森林碳汇不会因对其拥有而增加受益，也不会因不拥有而消失，作为主体，其只关心森林产权的拥有和行使就足够了。因此，森林碳汇很难划分到现有产权类型。

与森林碳汇相比，林业碳汇的经济属性存在明显的差异，这主要体现在以下几个方面：

一是林业碳汇虽然也具有稀缺性特征，但其产生的原因和外在表现却与森林碳汇具有明显区别。如前所述，林业碳汇的产生来自于对控制全球气候变暖的国际制度设计，如《京都议定书》所设定的清洁发展机制（CDM）。从这一机制的设计目的和执行过程来看，林业碳汇的稀缺性产生的原因应该是源自于全球温室气体排放空间的稀缺性而导致的 CO_2 排放权的稀缺。为了说清这一问题，我们假设 A 和 B 两个进行林业碳汇交易的主体（注：《京都议定书》下 CDM 项目的交易双方应当来自于发达国家和发展中国家，常常体现为发达国家和发展中国家的具体经济主体），按照合约，A 被赋予了在一定时间内允许排放 CO_2 的额度，或者说被规定了应完成的 CO_2 减排额度。这样，减排额度越大，允许排放的额度就越小，因此，减排额度的大小决定了排放权的稀缺程度。A 为了完成减排额度，从成本效益角度考虑，比如，可按照 CDM 机制，通过购买 B 创造的林业碳汇资源来完成其减排额度。由此可以看到，排放权的稀缺程度越高，A 需要购买的林业碳汇的数量就越大，林业碳汇的稀缺性就会越高。这一稀缺性虽然与由林地数量、立地条件、工业发展等原因产生的森林碳汇稀缺相联系，但就其直接动因而言，更加具有了市场经济中商品交易的属性。

二是从碳汇交易的角度来看，林业碳汇不再具有公共物品特征，与之相关，其"私人物品"特征已十分明显。按照清洁发展机制，林业碳汇交易中购买方的直接目的是完成合约所规定的减排额度，并进而获得其经济发展的碳排放权。对于某一具体的林业碳汇交易而言，（如上述 A 和 B 的假设）一旦 A 进行了购买，C 就不能购买，而且只有 A 会获得此项交易中的碳排放权。因此，参与交易的林业碳汇在消费上已具有了竞争性和排他性，具有了私人物品的特征。其实，一旦林业碳汇能够参与交易，其条件首先应该是具备"私人物品"特征，林业碳汇交易与林业碳汇的"私人物品"特征互为充分必要条件，上述说明只不过是一种反向证明罢了。

三是与森林碳汇产权类型模糊相比，因交易产生的林业碳汇产权却变得清晰起来。如果林业碳汇的卖方 B 为私人，则林业碳汇为私人产权；如果 B 为某一共同体，则林业碳汇为公共产权；如果 B 表现的主体形式为国家，则林业碳汇为国家产权。B 的产权形式可能会影响交易费用的大小，但一旦交易，其产权类型就应该是清晰的。

三、林业碳汇交易的经济实质

气候变化是全球十大环境问题之首，是涉及全人类生存环境和社会经济发展的重大问题。由于这一问题的"巨大"公共性，解决这一问题的难度之大，需要全人类共同努力才能完成。《联合国气候变化框架公约》的生效及其后继签署的《京都议定书》等一系列协定，标志着人类文明的巨大进步和总体理性的明显提高。

但是，由于人性的局限，人类的总体理性并没有完全战胜集体理性，更没有完全战胜个体理性。当讨论气候变化的原因时，人类普遍认为经济活动是其主要原因，当探讨如何防止气候变暖时，也普遍赞同要抑制某些经济活动。但是当讨论谁应该承担的责任时，各利益主体往往将保护自己的经济利益放在重要位置。因此，气候变暖虽然很大程度上源于人类的经济活动，而解决气候变暖往往也要通过经济手段。《京都议定书》中清洁发展机制（CDM）的产生即源于上述原因。由于直接减排意味着一个国家或利益主体需要投入大量资金减少工业、交通和运输部门的能源消耗，或花费高昂的费用进行技术更新和改造，提高能源利用效率，这无疑会直接影响一个国家或利益主体的经济发展。在减排额度的限制下，从成本效益的角度考虑，帮助发达国家或发达国家的某个利益主体完成其减排任务、而同时希望能够促进发展中国家可持续发展的 CDM 便被设计出来。因此，参与交易的林业碳汇活动更多表现为一种经济活动和经济机制，这种活动和机制依然是基于资源稀缺性和人类有限理性两个假设前提而设计和运行的。

上述讨论的意义在于，既然参与交易的林业碳汇活动更多地表现为一种经济活动和经济机制，那么从经济角度来研究实施林业碳汇的路径、方式、影响和条件将具有十分重要的意义。

第三节　林业碳汇市场化的内在机理与市场化障碍

截至目前，全球林业 CDM 项目一直处于较低的发展水平。根据联合国气候变化框架公约秘书处网站(http：//www. unfccc. int)，截至 2010 年 8 月，在联合国清洁发展机制理事会(EB)注册的清洁发展机制项目达到了 2379 个，其中造林再造林项目只有 15 个，占 0. 59%，而获得 EB 签发的核证减排量仍为零。

与上述林业 CDM 项目发展缓慢形成鲜明对照的是，林业 CDM 项目市场潜力却十分巨大。根据《马拉喀什协定》第 17 号决议，按照使用 CDM 造林再造林项目的碳汇总量不超过基准年排放量 1% 乘以 5 这一规定测算，全球 CDM 造林项目潜力约 320 万 ~530 万 hm^2；若按 10 ~15 美元/t 的市场价格计算，发达国家支付的林业 CDM 项目投资额每年将达到 3 亿 ~5 亿美元(靳丽莹、高岚，2010)。

为什么在森林碳汇功能已经得到充分公认，林业碳汇交易也成为《京都议定书》设定的 CDM 重要组成部分，且市场潜力巨大的情况下，林业 CDM 项目的市场化程度处于低水平状态？要想回答这一问题，首先要对林业碳汇市场的内在机理和市场化障碍两个问题做出合理解释。

一、碳汇交易的基本原理

正如在本章“林业碳汇经济属性”部分所讨论的那样，受到环境合理容量的限制，以 CO_2 为主的温室气体排放数量必然受到控制，由此导致碳的排放权和减排额度成为具有价格的稀缺资源。

按照《联合国气候变化框架公约》规定，发达国家与发展中国家在解决全球气候问题上应该坚持"共同但有区别的责任和各自能力"的原则。根据《京都议定书》，这种"有区别的责任"则体现在发达国家有量化的温室气体减排责任，而发展中国家目前还没有。因此，排放权或减排额度这一稀缺资源可转化为一种特殊商品，具备了国际间流动的可能性。与普通商品的国际贸易相同的是，碳汇交易依然遵循了比较利益原则：即发达国家的能源利用效率高，能源结构比较优化，新能源技术已被大量采用，进一步减排的难度较大，减排成本也比较高，而发展中国家能源效率低，减排空间大，减排成本比较低，因此导致了不同国家单位减排成本不同，国际碳汇交易因此产生。

由此可见，碳汇交易的基本原理是，按照比较利益原则，减排成本高的一方向减排成本低的一方进行购买支付以获得 CO_2 减排额，进而实现其减排目标。这一原理体现在林业碳汇交易上就是：减排成本高的一方，通过对另一方的造林再造林等林业碳汇项目产生的碳汇进行购买，使自己以较低成本实现减排目标。

二、碳汇交易的市场构成

任何市场的构成均由三部分组成，即供给方、需求方和价格。

从目前林业碳汇市场的运行情况来看，供给方大多体现为单一的减排成本较低的实体，但一旦各种市场条件成熟，供给方的构成可能会呈现出多元化的特征。例如国际金融组织、各种碳基金、银行和保险等金融机构，这些机构介入到碳交易市场后，均会成为二、三级市场的供给者。

林业碳汇市场的需求方则包括负有履约责任的企业、政府，以及承担社会责任的非政府组织和个人。此外，在二、三级市场中充当供给者的各种金融和基金组织，往往在一级市场中扮演的是购买者角色。

除上述直接从事碳交易的供给者和需求者外，由于林业碳汇交易的市场程序复杂，且在碳汇项目的估算、核查等方面具有很强的技术性，因此将衍生出各种咨询和技术开发转让等服务型商业机构。

林业碳汇市场的价格将取决于这一市场的结构类型以及供给与需求的数量。如果供给方的集中程度高于需求方的集中程度，则林业碳汇的议价优势倾向于供给方，相反，在需求方的集中程度高于供给方的情况下，议价优势将倾向于需求一方。就目前林业碳汇市场来看，由于购买碳汇的发达国家数量远远小于出售碳汇的发展中国家数量，且碳汇市场的供需比为5∶1（林而达，2003），议价优势必将明显倾向于需求一方，这一现象目前在一级市场上表现得十分明显。从目前其他碳交易市场的运行状况来看，如果金融机构介入林业碳汇市场，它将处于一级市场买卖双方的中间，林业碳汇交易的一级市场价格和二、三级市场价格很可能在相当程度上取决于金融机构在林业碳汇产品上的垄断程度和操作形式（金融机构可能开发出林业碳汇的保险产品、衍生产品及结构性产品，使林业碳汇不再是简单的商品）

三、林业碳汇的市场化保障

较之于其他碳汇市场，目前的林业碳汇市场主要基于《京都议定书》清洁发展机制、区域性立法和自愿交易规则形成的市场，但总体发育程度不高，主要源于以下市场化障碍：

第一，针对森林碳汇非永久性问题的解决措施制约购买方的积极性。以CDM造林再造林项目为例，国际社会通过谈判同意对此类项目产生的核证减排量（CER）签发长期和短期临时核证减排量（lCER和tCER），以解决非永久性问题。但长期和短期临时核证减排量到一定时期将失效并须通过实施工业、能源减排项目产生的CER来进行替代。尽管和工业、能源等领域实施的CDM项目相比，CDM造林再造林项目具有相当大的生态和社会效益，但却降低了购买方对CDM造林再造林项目产生的CER的兴趣，也注定了CDM造林再造林项目的CER价格低于工业、能源等领域的减排项目的CER价格。

第二，交易成本比较高。根据相关研究，从林业碳汇交易的实施程序角度，Stavins将林业碳汇交易成本划分为搜寻与信息成本、讨价还价与决策成本、检测和强制实施成本等3种；Dudek和Wienar将交易成本进一步划分为搜寻成本、谈判成本、批准成本、监测成本、强制实施成本以及保险成本等6种成本；OscarJ. Cacho等在Dudek和Wienar划分的基础上，又将其划分为搜寻成本、谈判成本、核实和认证成本、项目监测、强制实施和风险管理成本。除上述交易成本的种类识别研究外，进一步的研究表明，按照CDM项目的碳交易的实施程序，该市场发生的许多交易成本，如搜寻成本、项目文件设计成本、证实生效成本和监测成本等是固定的，一般不随项目模型的不同而改变(林德荣，2006)。但这些成本综合起来总体上比较高。

森林碳汇服务市场的交易成本，特别是固定交易成本的存在将改变森林碳汇服务市场的供给或需求曲线，从而影响碳汇信用的市场均衡价格和均衡数量，进而会降低林业碳汇交易的收益(林德荣，2006)，这预示着小规模的林业碳汇项目会因交易成本较高而失去吸引力。以全球首个注册的清洁发展机制再造林项目--广西珠江流域再造林项目为例，该项目从2003年年底开始准备，到2006年6月30日启动实施，中方项目实施主体及相关机构投入了大量的人财物和时间对项目点的林地、社区进行大量调研，聘请专家编写项目概念文件、项目碳融资文件、项目设计文件、项目方法学等，再加上项目土地租赁、造林、经营管护、监测投入，项目碳汇的交易成本相当高。

第三，相关政策设计不利于林业碳汇市场发展。国际气候变化政策较高的不确定性，相关市场制度和规则很不完善，市场交易各方要承担很大风险。这些风险可能来自于以下几个方面：一是林业碳汇市场主要是以项目投资获取碳信用的交易集合，而各种交易体系是否愿意将碳汇项目获取的碳信用纳入交易还是未知数；二是林业碳汇卖方必须对拟出售和已出售的碳信用做出各种承诺。目前来看，这种承诺的风险成本过高，不利于森林碳汇市场的发展。

第四，供给方的态度和能力可能对林业碳汇市场形成较强的限制。虽然发展中国家希望通过碳汇交易引入资金，但有的政府和个人可能会担心出售森林碳汇会限制其土地未来的用途，影响本国经济发展，再加上担心国内减排成本低的项目被别国利用，而使自己未来经济发展所必要的排放空间减少，这就会导致碳汇供给方的政府对森林碳汇市场交易持不鼓励和不支持态度。

第五，虽然研究和实践均表明森林碳汇项目的成本相对较低，但由于项目的实施周期过长，社会风险和自然风险很高，因此会加大买卖双方对项目实施的隐性成本的预期，从而进一步加大买卖双方对林业碳汇项目的观望态度，限制林业碳汇市场的发展。

第四节　林业在低碳经济中的政策取向

2009 年 12 月 7 日至 19 日，备受瞩目的《联合国气候变化框架公约》第 15 次缔约方会议在丹麦首都哥本哈根举行，119 个国家的首脑以及公约缔约国、国际组织、非政府组织代表共 5 万多人参加了本次会议。虽然参会各方没有就 2012 年后全球减排行动、资金技术支持等方面达成具体共识，但《哥本哈根协议》依然维护了《联合国气候变化框架公约》及《京都议定书》确立的"共同但有区别和各自能力的责任"原则，就发达国家实行强制量化减排和发展中国家采取自主减缓行动做出了原则安排。中国政府明确了自身减排目标：即 2020 年单位 GDP 二氧化碳排放比 2005 年降低 40% ~45%；非化石能源占一次能源消费 15%；2020 年森林面积比 2005 年增加 4 000 万 hm^2，森林蓄积量比 2005 年增加 13 亿 m^3。

一、实现"两个增加"目标的艰巨性

到 2020 年实现新增森林面积 4 000 万 hm^2，则需在 2010 ~ 2015 年期间每年度完成造林 585hm^2；到 2020 年实现增加森林蓄积 13 亿 m^3 目标，则需在 2010 ~ 2017 年间每年完成中幼林抚育 506 hm^2，低效林改造 150 万 ~ 200 万 hm^2。按照林木生长的自然规律，成林需要 3 年以上，抚育效果的显现至少需要 5 年以上时间。但根据第七次森林资源清查结果，中国现有宜林地 60% 分布在干旱、半干旱地区的内蒙古、陕西、甘肃、宁夏、青海、新疆等地，因此，成林成活率低，森林面积、蓄积增长缓慢。

此外，由于长期忽视森林经营，森林的经营基础巩固十分薄弱，现有的资金

和政策状况与需要完成的森林经营任务相比尚有较大差距。

二、对现有生态林业经营模式的反思

植树造林等林业活动是治理生态环境的主要手段。近几十年来，国内外学术界对此进行了大量研究，并取得了不少研究成果。但总体看来，政府干预和市场调节是目前理论界比较有代表性的观点。

（一）政府干预型理论

主流经济学家认为，生态环境治理存在外部效应和公共物品两大特征。外部效应存在两种表现，即外部正效应和外部负效应。外部正效应是指经济主体在市场上不支持费用而得到的收益，而外部负效应则指经济主体不支付代价而提高另一经济主体的支出。生态环境在治理过程中的主要表现为外部正效应，其治理的效益会自动地外溢到其他消费者或企业，而治理成本却很难在市场中得到补偿。与外部效应相联系的是公共物品。公共物品是只有外部效益的物品，每个个人对公共物品的消费取决于该公共物品向社会提供的总量。与私人物品不同，个人对公共物品的消费不影响其他消费者对同一公共物品的消费。此外，公共物品的供给具有不可分割性，在许多情况下，个人不管付钱与否都不能在公共物品的消费中被排除出去。生态环境在治理过程中向社会提供的正是公共物品。

按照上述理论，环境资源不能被市场所覆盖，从而失去了运用市场机制治理生态环境的可能性。因此，政府应在环境治理中发挥基础作用，即政府应当成为环境治理的策划者、实施者和监督者，这也是中国和世界上绝大多数国家目前普遍实行的一种做法。但是，政府要想在生态环境治理中发挥有效作用，必须具备以下条件：①作为计划制定和实施主体的政府，必须具备充分健全的信息系统，并保证信息的全面性和及时性。②作为社会整体利益和要求的体现，社会计划必须与每一个体之间的要求完全一致，即社会整体利益和个体利益以及个体利益之间不存在任何冲突，否则就无法以利益为动力来激发个体执行计划的积极性，也就不能从体制上保证计划不损害个体应有的合法利益。③完全计划管理方法要求政府有一支庞大且素质和效率极高的管理决策队伍，这样才能保证中央代替每一位生产者、消费者做出选择和决策的有效性。

上述条件在理论上是可以达到的，在实践中却难以实现。因而，必然导致宏观政策失效。其严重后果既造成自然资源配置上的低效率和极大浪费，又对生态环境产生破坏作用。比如中国对一些浪费资源、污染环境的 15 种小企业，基本上采取的是强制命令其关闭的管理方式，实际上是“一查就关，一不查就开”，没有从根本上解决问题。此外，在一些生态环境治理项目上，由于缺乏科学的论证和有效的监督，致使资金使用效率很低。

(二)市场主导型理论

针对政府在生态环境治理中的局限性，国外的一部分“自由市场环境主义者”主张否定政府的宏观调控作用，坚信市场理性，否认增长的极限和反对环境管制，无限夸大市场作用。他们认为能源危机是人为干预的结果，并非市场运行之必然；人口问题及环境污染问题，是由于资源无效率的应用。更为极端的市场理性观点认为，只要一种商品的价格体现了该商品的全部社会成本，就没有必要进行宏观干预。对于公共资源问题，持市场理性论的学者也承认存在市场失灵，但认为可通过明晰产权关系来解决，即通过生态私有化，使环境与生态资源融入经济体系，让自由市场来管理公共资源。

在实践中，完全的生态私有化尚未发现。这不是因为人们没有发现这一方法，而是因为其缺乏必要的私有化条件。按照效用价值论的观点，某种商品市场价格的高低完全取决于这种商品对消费者效用的大小。生态环境的改善对生活在其中的每一个公民都是具有巨大效用的，因此生态环境的治理者所得到的价格回报也应很高。在其他领域，明确产权关系就可以使商品的效用具有专用性，从而也就使效用决定价格成为可能。但在生态环境领域，明确产权却不能使生态效益获得专用性，生态效益一旦产生就会自动外溢出去，其效用无论多大，都很难在市场上得到补偿。这样，明确环境产权对改善环境的作用就可能很小。如明确林地和草场产权，只能使对林地和草场具有所有权或使用权的主体获得木材和牧草本身的收入，而林木和草地所产生的生态效益却不能得到补偿。而培育牧草，尤其是培育林木，具有初始投资大、经营周期长、风险高和投资回报率低等特点，这就使只能单纯获得林木和牧草本身收入的经营者因缺乏经营动力而放弃经营，从而，用明确环境产权来改善生态环境的目的在单纯的市场机制中也就无法实现了。

三、实现低碳经济的林业政策取向

上述分析使我们看到，单纯运用市场或政府干预机制，都很难使生态环境治理收到良好效果，必须寄托于一种新的机制，避开单纯的市场和政府干预两个盲区，而把政策有效和市场有效有机结合起来。在这一点上，发达资本主义国家几百年的市场经济经验和六七十年的宏观调控经验为我们提供了不少可供借鉴的方法。纵观发达国家生态环境治理方式，主要是依靠四种机制来驱动的。它们是：政府为捍卫公众环境利益而制定的环境法规以及有关政策，可称之为政策机制；政府对公共环境事业的投入，可称之为投入机制；环境企业成本—效益型驱动机制，称之为利益驱动机制；社会大众对更高生活质量追求而形成的消费需求机制，可称之为需求机制。

（一）政策机制和投入机制

尤其是投入机制，在环境治理初期，即以污染防治为主的阶段，起着关键性作用。在环境产业形成后，市场将发挥主导作用。首先是企业的成本—效益机制。企业对污染的控制性投入，并不是环境投入的最好选择。这种投入，在环境经济学上属于"抵御性支出"，它不会提高国内生产总值（GDP）与国民收入（NI）。因此，从成本—效益角度看，企业应选择新的更为积极的环境投入方式，这就是利益驱动机制，由此导致了洁净技术的发展，从而将污染问题解决于生产过程之中。

（二）需求机制代表了环境治理的方向与潮流

随着公众整体环境意识的提高，以及社会经济的不断发展，绿色消费将不仅是时尚，将由洁净技术时的"零污染排放"，升级为绿色产品时的"零资源废弃"；在经济上，它将直接从更新产品、增加价值、开拓新的市场需求等角度来提高环境治理的效率。绿色消费最终将使国民经济从制度、结构到增长方式经历一种绿色化过程。这时，环境与经济才能由相互制约的对立主体，变为相互和谐相互促进的统一体。

参考文献

阿尔钦.1994. 产权：一个经典注释.//陈昕. 财产权利与制度变迁——产权学派与新制度学派论文集. 上海：上海人民出版社：9～19.

艾连和.2005. 可持续发展战略下的森林分类经营思路与对策. 中国林副特产(3)：75～77.

巴泽尔.1997. 产权的经济分析. 费方域，段毅才，译. 上海：上海三联书店，上海人民出版社：107～109.

北京市科学技术委员会.1997. 可持续发展词语释义. 北京：学苑出版社.

曹光杰.1999. 中国生态环境问题分析. 临沂师专学报(3)：26～29.

曹新.2004. 可持续发展的理论与对策. 北京：中央党校出版社.

陈大夫.2001. 环境与资源经济学. 北京：经济科学出版社.

陈根长. 2007. 中国林业物权制度研究. 林业经济，2：12～15.

陈志刚，曲福田. 2003. 农地产权制度的演变与耕地绩效：对转型期中国的实证分析. 财经研究，29(6)：25～31.

程福祜.1993. 环境经济学. 北京：高等教育出版社.

迟德霞，王志爱.2005. 可持续林业及其经营理念. 水土保持科技情报(1)：3～4.

戴芳. 2006. 公益林供给主体分析. 林业经济问题，4(26)：370～373.

戴广翠，王前进，王焕良. 2002. 比较完备的林业生态体系的基本概念和特征. 林业经济，6：30～31.

董智勇.1992. 世界林业发展道路. 北京：中国林业出版社.

樊安群.2005. 中国经济转轨阶段论——兼论GDP的科学发展观. 北京：科学出版社.

甘泽广，等.1987. 环境经济学概论. 西安：西北工业大学出版社.

高鸿业.2000. 西方经济学. 北京：中国人民大学出版社.

高岚. 2005. 林业经济管理学. 北京：中国林业出版社：6，74.

关百均，等.1974. 世界林业概况. 北京：中国林业出版社.

关百均.1994. 世界林业发展概况. 北京：中国林业出版社.

郭菊兰，高尚仁．2000. 铁桥林场森林资源平衡率分析及预测．北京林业大学学报(3)：32～36.
郭克莎．2001. 结构优化与经济发展．广州：广东经济出版社．
国家林业局．2001，2002，2003，2005. 中国林业发展报告．北京：中国林业出版社．
国家林业局．2001. 中国林业统计年鉴(2000)．北京：中国林业出版社．
国家林业局．1999. 中国林业五十年：1949－1999. 北京：中国林业出版社．
国家林业局经济发展研究中心．2005. 重大林业工程监测报告．北京：中国林业出版社．
韩纪江，胡星．2003. 发展经济学．北京：中国农业大学出版社．
何炼成．2001. 中国发展经济学概论．北京：高等教育出版社．
贺东航，朱冬亮．2006. 中国集体林权改革存在的问题及思考．社会主义研究，5：79～81.
贺庆棠．1999. 森林环境学．北京：高等教育出版社．
侯元兆，吴水荣．2007. 私有化不是林权改革的方向．中国地质大学学报(社会科学版)，7：36～41.
回良玉．2006. 推进集体林权制度改革确保农民得实惠生态受保护．林业经济，10：3～6.
黄少安，孙圣民，宫明波．2005. 中国土地产权制度对农业经济增长的影响——对 1949－1978 年中国大陆农业生产效率的实证分析．中国社会科学，3：38～49.
胡春力．1997. 结构调整的原因和目标．北京：中国计划出版社．
黄景贵．2003. 发展经济学研究——制度变革与经济增长．北京：中国财政经济出版社．
黄清麟．2005. 浅谈德国“近自然森林经营”．世界林业研究(3)：74～78.
贾治邦．2006. 集体林权制度改革给我们的几点启示．林业经济，6：5～8.
江泽慧．1999. 中国现代林业．北京：中国林业出版社．
姜春云．2001. 中国农业实践概论．北京：中国农业出版社．
蒋敏元．2000. 林业经济管理．北京：中国林业出版社．
金钟浩，等．1996. 美国森林经营思想和法规的演变．世界林业研究(3)：57～63.
克莱夫·庞廷．2002. 绿色世界史——环境与伟大文明的衰落．王毅，译．上海：上海人民出版社.
柯水发，温亚利．2005. 中国林业产权制度变迁进程、动因及利益关系分析．绿色中国，10：29～32.
科斯，阿尔钦，诺斯，等．1997. 财产权利与制度变迁——产权学派与新制度学派译文集．上海：上海三联书店，上海人民出版社：38～46.

孔祥智，陈丹梅．2008. 林业合作经济组织研究——福建永安和邵武案例．林业经济，5：69 ~72.
蕾切尔·卡逊．1997. 寂静的春天．吕瑞兰，译．长春：吉林人民出版社．
李昌平．2007. 中国土地制度变迁与“三农”兴衰．炎黄春秋，6：40 ~46.
李荣玲．1999. 世界主要林业国家林业分类经营情况综述．林业资源管理(2)：19 ~25
李应春．2004. 我国竹林产权的界定及绩效分析．中国农村经济，11：60 ~65.
李玉栋．1997. 新西兰林业研究所的科技体制改革．世界林业研究(4)：64 ~69
林岗，张宇．2000. 产权分析的两种范式．中国社会科学，1：134 ~146.
林善炜．2003. 中国经济结构调整战略．北京：中国社会科学出版社．
林业部资源和林政管理司．1996. 当代中国森林资源概况(1949 ~1993)．北京：中国林业出版社．
林毅夫．2008. 制度、技术与我国农业发展．上海：上海三联书店，上海人民出版社：32 ~35.
林迎新．2001. 现代工业人工林发展创新研究．北京：中国林业出版社
刘璨，吕金芝，王礼权，等．2006. 集体林产权制度分析——安排、变迁与绩效．林业经济，11：8 ~13.
刘璨，吕金芝，王礼权，等．2006. 集体林产权制度分析——安排、变迁与绩效(续一)．林业经济，12：36 ~40.
刘璨，吕金芝，王礼权，等．2007. 集体林产权制度分析——安排、变迁与绩效(续二)．林业经济，1：53 ~57.
刘璨，吕金芝，王礼权，等．2007. 集体林产权制度分析——安排、变迁与绩效(续三)．林业经济，2：45 ~51.
刘宏明．2006. 试论林权概念的修正．林业经济，11：22 ~25.
刘江．2002. 中国资源利用战略研究．北京：中国农业出版社．
刘思华．1994. 当代中国的绿色道路——市场经济条件下生态经济协调发展．武汉：湖北人民出版社．
刘卫东．2002. 产权的性质和原因的研究．哈尔滨：东北林业大学．
罗斯托．1988. 从起飞进入维持增长的经济学．成都：四川人民出版社．
卢现祥．2003. 西方新制度经济学．北京：中国发展出版社：56 ~59.
马爱国．2003. 我国的林业政策过程——由单主体政策过程向多主体政策过程的转变．北京：中国林业出版社：9 ~16.

聂华．1995. 论林业经济的外部性．北京林业大学学报(2)：88 ~ 92.
聂振邦．2003. 世界主要国家粮食概况．北京：高等教育出版社．
钱易，唐孝炎．2000. 环境保护与可持续发展．北京：高等教育出版社．
邱俊齐．1998. 林业经济学．北京：中国林业出版社．
曲福田．2000. 可持续发展的理论与政策选择．北京：中国经济出版社．
沈文星，马天乐．江苏省林业产权制度改革林地流转政策研究．林业经济问题，2001，21：265 ~ 268.
沈月琴，徐秀英，吴伟光，等，2005. 浙江省林业专业合作组织发展对策研究．浙江林业科技，2：3 ~ 8.
沈照仁．1997. 生态林业理论与实践．北京：中国林业出版社．
施昆山，关百均，等．1997. 21 世纪世界林业发展战略和经营模式．世界林业研究(3)：2 ~ 9
施昆山．1998. 中国林业发展的回顾与展望．北京：中国环境科学出版社．
史颖．2004. 林业发展肩负“生态”使命．中国经济导报(10)：25.
联合国粮食及农业组织．2007. 世界森林状况：23 ~ 25.
速水佑次郎，神门善久．2003. 农业经济论．沈金虎，等，译．北京：中国农业出版社．
陶在朴．2003. 生态包袱与生态足迹——可持续发展的重量及面积观．北京：经济科学出版社．
田国强．1996. 内生产权所有制理论与经济体制的平稳转型．经济研究，11：10 ~ 19.
田明华，陈建成，邱俊齐．2002. 森林资源价值论初探．林业经济问题，22(5)：36 ~ 38
田明华，陈建成．2003. 中国森林资源管理变革趋向——市场化研究．北京：中国林业出版社．
王爱民．2005. 生态环境产品的政府双重垄断分析．社会科学(8)：6 ~ 10
王爱民．2005. 激励相容就、区域发展与政府规制．北京：中国文史出版社．
王爱民．2005. 退耕还林：林木收益的法律局限与预期收益分析．农业技术经济(6)：50 ~ 53.
王爱民．2005. 退耕还林的经济影响及现行政策的调整——以河北省为例．农业经济问题(11)：23 ~ 27.
王爱民．2001. 我国生态环境治理的政策选择．河北林业科技(4)：17 – 19.
王焘．1997. 园林经济管理．北京：中国林业出版社．
王官诚．2004. 消费心理学．北京：电子工业出版社．
王礼先．2000. 林业生态工程学．北京：中国农业出版社．
王天津．2002. 西部资源环境产业．大连：东北财经大学出版社．

王跃先．1987. 林业政策与法规．北京：中国林业出版社．
魏殿生．2003. 造林绿化与气候变化：碳汇问题研究．北京：中国林业出版社．
温铁军．2009. 我国集体林权制度三次改革解读．经济参考报(4)：08～12.
温铁军．2006. 农民社会保障与土地制度改革．学习月刊，10：20～22.
吴敬琏．2005. 比较．北京：中信出版社．
吴添祖．1997. 技术经济学概论．北京：高等教育出版社．
吴易风．2007. 产权理论：马克思和科斯的比较．中国社会科学，2：4～19.
西蒙·库兹涅茨．1985. 各国经济增长．北京：商务印书馆．
肖平，张敏新．1996. 外部性的经济内涵．林业经济(2)：58～62
徐国桢．1997. 森林生态系统经营——21 世纪森林经营的新趋势．世界林业研究(2)：16～21.
许涤新．1987. 生态经济学．杭州：浙江人民出版社．
徐国祯．2006. 社区林业——通向林业社会合作与和谐发展之路．林业经济，1：32～36.
徐秀英，马天乐，刘俊昌．2006. 南方集体林区林权改革之行政征用制度研究．林业经济问题，4：303～307.
姚昌恬．2002. WTO 与中国林业．北京：中国林业出版社．
姚顺波．2003. 产权残缺的非公有制林业．农业经济问题，6：28～33.
姚洋．2000. 中国农地制度：一个分析框架．中国社会科学，2：53～65.
姚洋．1998. 农地制度与农业绩效的实证研究．中国农村观察，6：1～10.
于同申．2001. 发展经济学——新世纪经济发展的理论与政策．北京：中国人民大学出版社．
张春霞，许金叶，许文兴，等．1998. 我国社会林业发展与制度变迁——中国社会林业发展道路研究．林业经济问题，1：11～17.
张建国，吴静和．2002. 现代林业论．北京：中国林业出版社．
张建国，余建辉．2002. 生态林业论．北京：中国林业出版社．
张建国．1986. 森林生态经济问题研究．北京：中国林业出版社．
张建国．1994. 中国林业经济学．哈尔滨：东北林业大学出版社．
张军．1994. 现代产权经济学．上海：上海人民出版社，上海三联书店：96～101.
张培刚．2001. 发展经济学教程．北京：经济科学出版社．
张培刚．1999. 农业及其工业化．武汉：武汉科技大学出版社：33～40.
张守攻．2001. 森林可持续经营导论．北京：中国林业出版社．

张维迎．2004. 博弈论与信息经济学．上海：上海三联书店，上海人民出版社：143 ~ 150.
张孝庆，等．1995. 中国生态林业发展研究综述．世界林业研究(6)：53 ~ 56.
张新光．2007. 建国以来集体林权制度变迁及政策绩效评价——以大别山区的河南省新县为例．甘肃联合大学学报(社会科学版)，11：1 ~ 9.
张振凯，段海峰．2005. 外部性理论和观景价值理论在矿山排岩收费政策中的应用．北京：中国矿业出版社．
赵爱云，卢琦．2000. 20 世纪全球森林政策与国际合作的回顾与展望．世界林业研究(1)：2 ~ 6.
赵冬缓．2000. 新发展经济学．北京：中国农业大学出版社．
郑德祥，陈平留．2005. 林业税费变化对林木资产评估价格的影响．西南林学院学报，25(1)：56 ~ 59.
郑风田，阮荣平，孔祥智．2009. 南方集体林区林权制度改革回顾与分析．我国人口 资源与环境，19(1)：25 ~ 36.
中国可持续发展林业战略研究项目组．2003. 中国可持续发展林业战略研究·森林问题卷．北京：中国林业出版社．
中国可持续发展林业战略研究项目组．2003. 中国可持续发展林业战略研究·战略卷．北京：中国林业出版社．
中国可持续发展林业战略研究项目组．2003. 中国可持续发展林业战略研究·总论．北京：中国林业出版社．
中华人民共和国林业部．1991. 全国林业统计资料(1990)．北京：中国林业出版社．
中华人民共和国林业部．1993. 中国林业在改革开放中前进．北京：中国林业出版社．
钟水映．2005. 人口、资源与环境经济学．北京：科学出版社．
周冯琦．2003. 中国产业结构调整的关键因素．上海：上海人民出版社．
周其仁．2002. 产权与制度变迁——我国改革的经验研究．北京：社会科学文献出版社：35 ~ 46.
周晓峰．1995. 中国森林与生态环境．北京：中国林业出版社．
周振华．1992. 产业结构优化论．上海：上海人民出版社．
朱冬亮．2007. 集体林权制度改革中的社会排斥机制分析．厦门大学学报(哲学社会科学版)，3：122 ~ 128.
朱冬亮，贺东航．2007. 集体林权制度改革中的林权升值因素分析：对福建林改的思考．东南学术，3：25 ~ 29.

朱冬亮，肖佳．2007. 集体林权制度改革：制度实施与成效反思——以福建省为例．中国农业大学学报(社会科学版)，3(24)：81 ~91.

朱·弗登博格，让·梯若尔．2002. 博弈论．北京：中国人民大学出版社：185 ~187.

朱俊凤．1991. 绿化神州．北京：中国林业出版社．

国家林业局．2003. 全国林业生态建设与治理模式．北京：中国林业出版社．

祝列克．2001. 森林可持续经营．北京：中国林业出版社．

朱巧玲．2007. 产权制度变迁的多层次分析．北京：人民出版社：146 ~147.

Angus Maddison. 2003. 世界经济千年史．武晓鹰，译．北京：北京大学出版社．

Arild Angelsen. 1999. Agricultural expansion and deforestation：modeling the impact of population，marker forces and property rights. Journal of Development Economics，58：185 ~218.

C A McAlpine，T A Spies P. 2007. Norman. Conserving forest biodiversity across multiple land ownerships：Lessons from the Northwest Forest Plan and the Southeast Queensland regional forests agreement（Australia）. Biological Conservation，4：580 ~592.

Brenda C McComb，Thomas A Spies，Keith A Olsen. 2007. Sustaining Biodiversity in the Oregon Coast Range：Potential effects of Forest Policies in a Multi－ownership Province，23：32 ~45.

Chadwick Dearing Oliver. 2003. Sustainable forestry：What is it？How do we achieve it？Journal of Forestry(4).

David B Kittredge. 2005. The cooperation of private forest owners on scales larger than one individual property：international examples and potential application in the United States. Forest Policy and Economics，9：767 ~688.

David Humphreys. 2001. Forest negotiations at the United Nations：explaining cooperation and discord Forest Policy and Economics. Forest Policy and Economics，3：125 ~135.

Doru Leonard Irimie，Hans Friedrich Essmann. 2008. Forest property rights in the frame of public policies and societal change. Forest Policy and Economics，5：25 ~36.

Eui－Gyeong Kim. 2006. Historical Change and Significance regarding the Management and Utilization of Forest Resources in Korea.

FAO. 1996. Forestry of Selected Countries in Africa.

FAO. 1989. Forestry Policies in Europe.

FAO. 1993. Forestry Policies of Selected Countries in Asia and the Pacific.

Ingrid Kissling-Näf, Kurt Bisang. 2001. Rethinking recent changes of forest regimes in Europe through property – rights theory and policy analysis. Forest Policy and Economic, 3: 99 ~ 111.

International Bank for Reconstraction and Development, The World Bank. 1992. World Development Report. Oxford University Press.

Jay Sulliva, Gregory S Amacher, Sara Chapman. 2005. Forest banking and forest landowners forgoing management rights for guaranteed financial returns. Forest Policy and Economic, 7: 381 ~ 392.

John A Gray. 2006. Forest Concession Policies and Revenue System Country Experience and Policy Change for Sustainable Tropical Forestry.

John M Hagan, Lloyd C Irland, Andrew A Whitman. 2005. Changing Timberland Ownership in the Northern Forest and Implications for Biodiversity.

Josemari AIZPURUA, Pedro GALILEA. 2000. Property rights on the forest resources.

Jouni Pykäläinen, Timo Pukkala, Jyrki Kangas. 2001. Alternative priority models for forest planning on the landscape level involving multiple ownership. Forest Policy and Economic, 2: 293 ~ 306.

L. Jylha, Unasylva. 2007. Forest Management Associations – value from cooperation for forest owners. Forest Policy and Economics, 8: 228 ~ 241.

Linda Fernandez. 2006. Natural resources, agriculture and property tights. Ecology Economics, 57: 359 ~ 373.

Mag. Eva Kvarda. 2004. Non – agricultural forest owners' in Austria – a new type of forest ownership. Forest Policy and Economic, 6: 459 ~ 467.

Mikko Kurttila, Timo Pikkala, Jyrki Kangas. 2001. Composing landscape level forest plans for forest areas under multiple private ownership. Boreal Environment Research, 6: 285 ~ 296.

Mustafa Fehmi TüRKER, Atakan ÖZTÜRK, Mehmet PAK. 2008. Ownership, scale size and economic analysis of the state forest enterprises constitute the frame of forestry sector.

Peter Ho. 2006. Credibility of institutions: Forestry, social conflict and titling in China. Land Use Policy, 23: 588 ~ 603.

Peter Glück. 2002. Property rights and multipurpose mountain forest management. Forest Policy and Economic, 4: 125 ~ 134.

Robert T. 2003. Brooks. Abundance, distribution, trends, and ownership patterns of early – successional forests in the northeastern United States. Forest Ecology and Management, 185: 65 ~ 74.

Rupa Basnet Parasai. 2008. Who Owns Carbon in Community Managed Forest.

Sinclair Tedder, Darcy Mitchell, Ann Hillye. 2002. Property rights in the sustainable management of non – timber forest products.

Stephen A Vosti, Evaldo Munoz Braz, Chantal Line Carpentier. 2003. Rights to Forest Products, Deforestation and Smallholder Income: Evidence from the Western Brazilian Amazon. World Development, 31: 1889 ~ 1901.

Su Mei Toh, Kevin T. 2007. Grace Case study: Sabah forest ownership. Malaysia, 27: 96 ~ 118.

Syed Mahmood Nasir. 2007. Trends in forest ownership, forest resources tenure and institutional arrangements. Pakistan(43): 96 ~ 110.

Thomas Sikor, Tran Ngoc Thanh. 2007. Exclusive verse inclusive devolution in forest management: Insights from forest land allocation in Vietnam's Central Highlands. Land Use Policy, 24: 644 ~ 653.

Tran Ngoc Thanh, Thomas Sikor. 2006. From legal acts to actual powers: Devolution and property rights in the Central Highlands of Vietnam. Forest Policy and Economic, 8: 397 ~ 408.

Vimal Kumar. 2007. Production, Appropriation and the Dynamic Evolution of Property Rights.

V L V Kameswari. 2006. Collective Management of Forest Resources in India: Lessons for policy formulation and stakeholders involvement.

Yaoqi Zhang, Shashi Kant. 2008. Forest Property Rights Evolution in Response to Forest Paradigms in Canada.

Yaoqi Zhang, Daowei Zhang, John Schelhas. 2006. Small – Scale Non – industrial Private Forest Ownership in the United States: Rationale and Implications for Forest Management.